D1683832

IRON ROAD WEST

An Illustrated History of British Columbia's Railways

IRON ROAD WEST

An Illustrated History of British Columbia's Railways

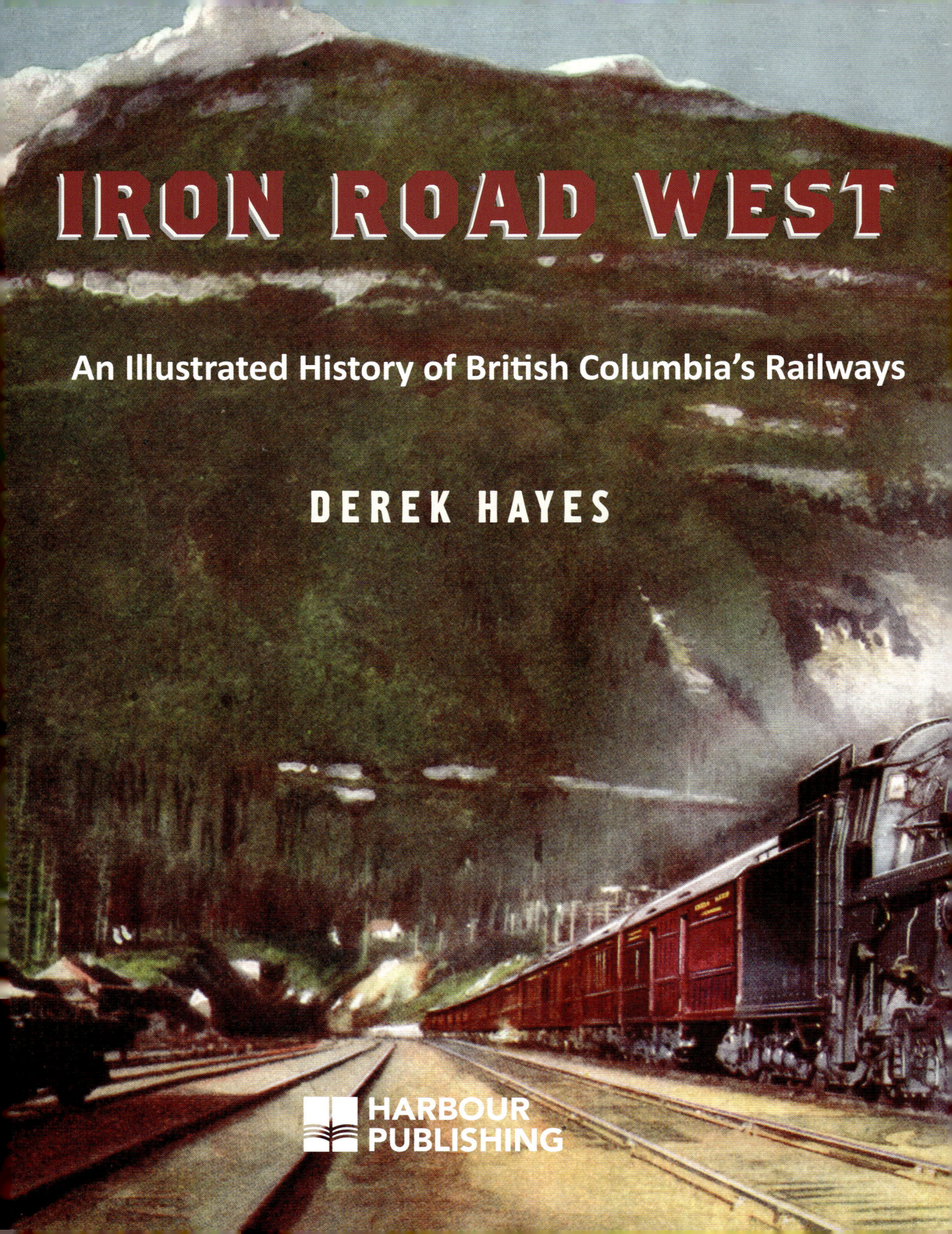

DEREK HAYES

HARBOUR PUBLISHING

Copyright © 2018 Derek Hayes

1 2 3 4 5 — 22 21 20 19 18

All rights reserved. No part of this publication may be reproduced, stored in a retrieval system or transmitted, in any form or by any means, without prior permission of the publisher or, in the case of photocopying or other reprographic copying, a licence from Access Copyright, www.accesscopyright.ca, 1-800-893-5777, info@accesscopyright.ca.

Harbour Publishing Ltd.
P.O. Box 219, Madeira Park, BC, V0N 2H0
www.harbourpublishing.com

All photographs by Derek Hayes except where otherwise noted.
Edited by Merrie-Ellen Wilcox, copy-edited by Patricia Wolfe, proofread by Arlene Prunkl and indexed by Ellen Hawman.
Design and layout by Derek Hayes.
Jacket design by Setareh Ashrafologhalai
Printed and bound in China.
Printed on acid-free paper.

Harbour Publishing Ltd. acknowledges the support of the Canada Council for the Arts, which last year invested $153 million to bring the arts to Canadians throughout the country. We also gratefully acknowledge financial support from the Government of Canada and from the Province of British Columbia through the BC Arts Council and the Book Publishing Tax Credit.

Library and Archives Canada Cataloguing in Publication

Hayes, Derek, 1947–, author
   Iron road west : an illustrated history of British Columbia's railways / Derek Hayes.

Includes bibliographical references and index.
ISBN 978-1-55017-838-8 (hardcover)

   1. Railroads--History--Maps. I. Title.
HE2809.B7H39 2018   385.09711   C2018-902147-0

Half-title page. A cyclist watches as the Kamloops Heritage Railway CNR steam locomotive No. 2141 pulls out of Kamloops station in August 2017. The locomotive was built for the Canadian Northern Railway in 1912.

Title page. A 1935 painting of CPR 2-10-4 Selkirk T1a locomotive No. 5903 pulling a long train with the Rockies in the background. See page 112.

Acknowledgements

Many people generously helped me in the preparation of this book, both in tracking down correct information and in supplying or giving permission to use photographs. Particular thanks go to Robert Hunter of the West Coast Railway Association (WCRA), and the family of the late Dave Wilkie for allowing me to reproduce a number of excellent photos from his extensive collection.

The following helped with images or information or both; they were much appreciated: Robert D. Turner; Barrie Sanford; Henry Ewert; John Sprung, Terry Nichol, Hugh Parkinson and Terry Lyster of the Fraser Valley Heritage Railway; Paul Clegg; Tim Repp; Bill Hooper; Greg Andrew, Westshore Terminals; Robert Hunter, WCRA Archives; Craig McDowall, WCRA; Rodney Holland, Brian Stokes, Paul Crozier Smith, and Timothy Horton; Jane Lemke, Burnaby Village Museum; Charles Campbell; Jessica Byman, Revelstoke Railway Museum; Cathy English, Revelstoke Museum; Kelly-Ann Turkington, BC Archives; Jim Foulkes; Daien Ide, North Vancouver Museum and Archives; Carol Miller, BC Forest Discovery Centre; Chris Bryan, TransLink; Brenda Land, CP; Kate Fenske and Jasdeep Devgan, CN; Benjamin Wilemon, BNSF; Hilary Strath, Rocky Mountaineer; Ryan Gallagher, Surrey Archives; Gina Tomanek, Alaina Wong and Samantha Lusher, Mattel; Alan Lill, Doug Davies, Shawn I. Smith and Leslie Kozma, members of the Canadian National Railways Historical Association.

Finally thanks to all those at Harbour Publishing, and to my editor, Merrie-Ellen Wilcox, copy-editor Patricia Wolfe, proofreader Arlene Prunkl, and indexer Ellen Hawman.

To contact the author:
www.derekhayes.ca
derek@derekhayes.ca

Other books by Derek Hayes:

Historical Atlas of British Columbia and the Pacific Northwest
First Crossing: Alexander Mackenzie, His Expedition across North America and the Opening of the Continent
Historical Atlas of the North Pacific Ocean
Historical Atlas of Canada: Canada's History Illustrated with Original Maps
Historical Atlas of the Arctic
America Discovered: A Historical Atlas of Exploration
Canada: An Illustrated History
Historical Atlas of Vancouver and the Lower Fraser Valley
Historical Atlas of Toronto
Historical Atlas of the United States
Historical Atlas of California
Historical Atlas of the American West
Historical Atlas of Washington and Oregon
Historical Atlas of the North American Railroad
British Columbia: A New Historical Atlas
Historical Atlas of Early Railways
(UK edition: *The First Railways*; US edition: *The First Railroads*)

Note: References in *italics* refer to names or images, or, in a map caption, to words actually present on a map.

Left.
One of the newest locomotives to run on British Columbia rails is this high-tech Charger SC-44, made by Siemens and delivered in late 2017 and early 2018. The train is the twice-daily Amtrak *Cascades* service from Vancouver to Seattle, and the scene is the waterfront at White Rock in July 2018. No. 1405 is one of a number of locomotives purchased by the Washington State Department of Transportation (WSDOT) for the *Cascades* service. One locomotive per train is used, with a cab car, or driving trailer, on the other end. Here, at the rear of the southbound service, the locomotive is pushing the train.

Right, top.
A 1910 Climax logging locomotive, on display at the BC Forest Discovery Centre in Duncan. See page 127.

Contents

The Railways of British Columbia   7
A Late Start   12
A Connection to Canada   14
Extensions, Branches and Improvements   36
Challenging a Monopoly   46
Accessing the Interior's Mineral Wealth   58
A Railway to Gold   68
Interurban and City   72
A Railway to the Orient   78
The Third Transcontinental   88
The Coast-to-Kootenay Idea   94
A Line to the North   102
The Golden Age of Steam   110
Logging and Mining Railways   122
British Columbia's Railway   134
The Evolving Modern Railway   146
A Legacy Preserved   180

Appendix 1 : List of British Columbia Railway Incorporations   220
Appendix 2 : Whyte Wheel Notation System   229
Sources   230
Further Reading   233
Index   234

Above.
Old meets new. On 24 August 2017 at CNR's 1915 station, Kamloops Heritage Railway CNR No. 2141 works up a head of steam, ready to transfer its train to the main station track once the Rocky Mountaineer, at left, has finished unloading its passengers for their overnight stay in the city. Both trains run on CN tracks. The Rocky Mountaineer is a luxury tourist train now considered one of the finest of such trains in the world. Kamloops Heritage Railway, whose locomotive is owned by the City of Kamloops, is one of only two standard-gauge, ex-main line steam heritage locomotives still operating in British Columbia; they both use original main-line tracks. Two other operating heritage lines use an ex-logging locomotive on standard-gauge track; two more use narrow-gauge track (see page 180). There are also two electric heritage lines, one of which is the Fraser Valley Heritage Railway (*right*).

The Railways of British Columbia

Railways were, and still are, vital to the development and economic growth of British Columbia. In railways, entrepreneurs found the answer to the need for timely movement of high volumes of the province's mineral wealth, something that would have been impossible using the rough roads and tracks of the nineteenth century, especially with horses or early motorized road transport vehicles. As a bonus, rails could usually be laid inexpensively on a narrow strip of land through the wild terrain that characterizes much of British Columbia.

People benefited just as much. Before the coming of the railway, a trip to another town might mean a trek of several days; the train reduced this to a matter of hours—slow, perhaps by today's standards, but lightning fast compared with what people were then used to.

At the time the first transcontinental was planned, some in the British press doubted the value of railways in the province. One (*Truth*, 1 September 1881) wrote that "British Columbia is a barren, cold, mountain country that is not worth keeping . . . fifty railroads would not galvanize it into prosperity." How wrong they were! Railways revolutionized the province, just as they did almost everywhere else in the world when they were built.

But British Columbia threw some difficulties in the railway builders' path, for it is a mountainous province, often with little space in which to build the necessarily linear and continuous track bed. The clearest example of this was when Canadian National was forced to the opposite bank of the Fraser Canyon because Canadian Pacific had already pre-empted the easiest side.

And there was another problem: the main desired flow of commerce, whether within the province or from the East, was from east to west, but the mountain ranges inconveniently mainly ran north to south, making tunnels or circuitous routes necessary and, of course, more expensive. In the early days competition was intense, particularly between the Canadian Pacific and its arch-enemy Great Northern, an American line owned by James Hill, who had once been on the CPR board of directors but had fallen out with his colleagues and left, vowing for revenge. Personal hatreds led men to make decisions that sometimes did not make economic sense. It all made for an exciting, frontier-like environment. For example, when the CPR completed its line into Sandon, then a new mining town in the Kootenays, late in 1895, men from the Great Northern–controlled Kaslo & Slocan Railway set upon the CPR men, destroying their new depot, derailing freight cars, and ripping up track!

But gradually the railways found that co-operation was better than confrontation and learned to live together for their mutual economic well-being. Today railways use each other's lines and equipment on a regular basis. In the Fraser Canyon, Canadian Pacific's mainly west-bank line is used for all northbound trains, while Canadian National's mainly east-bank line is used for those southbound, thus allowing both companies a more frequent schedule.

It is one thing to read about old railways and view historic photographs but even better if they can still actually be viewed. Thus this book includes an extensive section called "A Legacy Preserved," reviewing locations around the province where railway history can still be seen. These include operating steam and electric heritage railways, museums, static displays, and the unpreserved but still extant remnants of the railway landscape.

Right.
The Fraser Valley Heritage Railway, which runs on a portion of the old British Columbia Electric Railway (BCER) line to Chilliwack, opened in 1910 (see page 72). On 9 September 2017, in the presence of the lieutenant-governor and to a military salute by local cadets (and in pouring rain), newly restored BCER Car No. 1304 returns to Cloverdale station for the first time in over sixty years (see page 192).

British Columbia's Railways Today

Today there remain three major (class 1) railway companies operating in the province:

1. Canadian Pacific Railway (CPR) chartered in 1881, the first transcontinental and first to enter British Columbia (1884–87). It was known as CP Rail between 1968 and 1996. Canadian Pacific Ltd., created as a holding company in 1971, spun off Canadian Pacific Railway Ltd. in 2001. Also spun off at the same time were other remaining constituent businesses: CP Hotels (which became Fairmont Hotels and Resorts), Fording Coal, PanCanadian Petroleum, and CP Ships. Canadian Pacific Air Lines and Marathon Realty had been sold earlier.

2. Canadian National/Canadien National (CN): Canadian National Railways (CNR), created in 1918, to 1960, then Canadian National/Canadien National (CN). The government-owned railway was created by the dominion government between 1918 and 1923 from a group of bankrupt railways including the Grand Trunk Pacific (GTPR) and the Canadian Northern Railway (CNoR). Within BC, the latter railway was legally the Canadian Northern Pacific Railway (CNPR), though it was usually referred to—including, for marketing purposes, by the railway itself—as Canadian Northern. CN was privatized in 1995. In 2004 CN took over BC Rail, a 1984 renaming of the British Columbia Railway (BCR), itself a 1972 renaming of the Pacific Great Eastern Railway (PGE). CN still operates one passenger service in BC, the Kaoham Shuttle, to Lillooet from Seton Portage and D'Arcy.

3. BNSF Railway (BNSF): Successor to the Great Northern Railway. Amalgamations created Burlington Northern in 1970, then Burlington Northern & Santa Fe in 1996. The name was changed to BNSF Railway in 2005.

A proposal to the US Surface Transportation Board to merge CN and BNSF in 1999 to form North American Railways (NAR) was withdrawn in April 2000 following opposition from other railways. NAR would have formed an 80,500 km continental network.

There are also a few smaller or more specialist railways:

1. Southern Railway of British Columbia (SRY), branded as SRY Rail Link, a so-called short line. Its main line was originally the BC Electric Railway (BCER) interurban line to Chilliwack, taken over by BC Hydro in 1961 and known as the BC Hydro Railway. SRY is owned by URS, which also owns the Southern Railway of Vancouver Island (SVI), successor to the Esquimalt & Nanaimo Railway; the island line is currently disused and the track is owned by an inter-governmental body called the Island Corridor Foundation.

2. British Columbia Railway (BCR), which still exists—in much smaller form than before and since 2010 part of the provincial transportation ministry—owns most of the line connecting Roberts Bank Superport with the Canadian National main line, but it does not own any rolling stock or locomotives.

3. White Pass & Yukon Route (WP&YR), a now mainly tourist-oriented narrow-gauge railway, runs for about 60 km in British Columbia as part of its 109 km run from its main terminus at Skagway, Alaska, to Carcross, Yukon.

4. Kettle Falls International Railway has a short stretch of track in British Columbia, servicing industries in Grand Forks and part of the Columbia River Valley via two lines crossing the international boundary (see #1 under Others); it connects with BNSF at Chewela, WA.

The following own locomotives and rolling stock, but essentially no track:

1. Via Rail, which operates the two remaining regular passenger trains in the province, the *Canadian* (Toronto–Vancouver) and a service from Jasper to Prince Rupert via Prince George. Despite the lack of track, Via is classified as a class 1 railway.

2. Amtrak, the American passenger railway, which operates trains between Vancouver and Seattle on BNSF track. Also classified class 1.

3. The Great Canadian Railtour Company, which operates luxury tourist trains as Rocky Mountaineer on CP, CN and BNSF track.

4. The Royal Canadian Pacific, a luxury vintage passenger train based in Alberta, offers Rocky Mountain tours that use British Columbia rails from time to time. It is owned by Canadian Pacific and is based in Calgary.

5. The West Coast Express, a commuter line between Vancouver and Mission. It is operated under contract by Bombardier Transportation, part of the same company that built the rolling stock, and runs on CP track.

Others:

1. A number of companies move freight cars around on their properties (e.g.: Neptune Terminals, North Vancouver; Alcan, Kitimat; Viterra, Pacific Terminal, Port of Vancouver; Catalyst Paper, Powell River; Parrish & Heimbecker, Cloverdale); or have connecting tracks: Atco Wood Products has a 10 km line—named Nelson & Fort Sheppard Railway after its historical predecessor—from a Columbia Gardens interchange with the Kettle Falls International Railway to Fruitvale; Interfor's Grand Forks Railway, from a Kettle Falls International railway interchange at Grand Forks to Grand Forks Sawmill, 5.6 km).

2. Heritage tourist trains: the Kettle Valley Railway; the Kamloops Heritage Railway; the Cowichan Valley Railway at the BC Forest Discovery Centre in Duncan; the Fort Steele Railway; the Alberni Pacific Railway in Port Alberni; the Fraser Valley Heritage Railway, which runs interurban cars out of Cloverdale; the Nelson Electric Tramway Society, which runs two streetcars in Nelson; and the West Coast Railway Association's occasional trains run from their centre in Squamish. Underground mining trains now used for tourists include those of the Sullivan Mine in Kimberley and the Britannia Mine at Britannia Beach.

3. Vancouver's SkyTrain, an automated rail system with two differently operated sections with unconnected tracks, although passengers can interchange at Waterfront station. The sections are (1) the Expo and Millennium lines, and (2) the Canada Line.

4. There are also a number of miniature railways, such as the Burnaby Central Railway; one at the West Coast Railway Association in Squamish; one in Bear Creek Park in Surrey; the Cottonwood Railway at the Prince George Railway and Forestry Museum; the Fort George Railway in Fort George Park, Prince George; and one in Vancouver's Stanley Park.

Above. Amtrak *Cascades*, a twice-daily service between Vancouver and Seattle, is on the White Rock seafront on 30 August 2013 in this unusual infrared photo. The train is composed of a coach set manufactured by Talgo, a Spanish train supplier of high-speed trains. A power car immediately behind the locomotive is sloped to aesthetically transition from the higher locomotive to the lower coaches. The coaches tilt on bends. They were made at Talgo's plant in Wisconsin and were delivered to Amtrak in 2013.

Canadian Pacific No. 3716 pulls a tourist train on the Kettle Valley Heritage Railway in Summerland on the only part of the original Kettle Valley Railway that still exists as such. This locomotive was built in 1912 at the CPR works in Montreal as No. 3916. It was rebuilt in 1929 and renumbered as 3716. Still later it was converted from a coal burner to oil. This locomotive is one of the few surviving main-line steam locomotives still in operation in British Columbia (see page 184). Here it is pictured about to arrive at the Prairie Valley station on the heritage railway.

A Late Start

Left. The early steam locomotive Wellington No. 19, nicknamed *Victoria*, similar to the first British Columbia locomotives. It was built in 1889 by the Baldwin Locomotive Works in Philadelphia and was purchased by Dunsmuir, Diggle & Co., owners of a number of Nanaimo-area coal mines, to move coal from pithead to ship. During its career, which lasted until 1952, the engine moved coal in Nanaimo, Union Bay, Cumberland and South Wellington. It is the province's second-oldest preserved steam locomotive still in BC (see page 216).

Right, top left. This small part of a large map drawn in 1861 shows the location (the red line) of British Columbia's first railway at Seton Portage, between *Lake Anderson* and *Seton Lake*. In 1914 the Pacific Great Eastern Railway (see page 102) would be built along the shores of these two lakes and across Seton Portage. There still is a passenger service, in the form of the unique Kaoham Shuttle (see page 170). *Inset* is a photo of a later, similar portage railway (albeit with iron rails); this was at Canal Flats, connecting the Kootenay and Columbia Rivers.

Right, top right. The early Vancouver Island locomotive *Nanaimo*, a British-built engine of the Vancouver Coal Mining & Land Company, arrived in 1874, and probably looked very similar to the first locomotive, *Pioneer*. The diamond-shaped smokestack is a spark arrester, fitted to try to limit fires.

Right, bottom. A map of Nanaimo from about 1861. The red lines are railways. The bottom one is marked *Proposed shaft & Rail road*, and the other lines are marked *old Tram Road and Tram Road*. The latter would have been worked by mules pulling coal wagons, while the longer line is probably that on which *Pioneer* was first used.

Railways came late to British Columbia. By the time the first line we can call a railway appeared in the early 1860s, about 18,000 kilometres of railways covered Britain, where the concept was essentially developed, and there were a further 80,000 km or so world-wide, including 50,000 in the United States.

The British colony was enticed to join the Canadian Confederation, of course, by the promise of a railway connection with the East, but even that project took many years to come to fruition, bedevilled by politics, finances and the immensity of the physical challenge. As a result, the railway history of British Columbia is usually thought of as beginning with the completion of the Canadian Pacific main line from the summit of the Rocky Mountains through to Vancouver—the city itself a railway creation.

Railways in Europe began with horse-drawn or human-pushed conveyances on wooden rails as early as the sixteenth century, and the first railway built in British Columbia used wooden rails. This was the colony's first railway, at Seton Portage, carrying gold miners' baggage across the 2 km land gap between Anderson Lake and Seton Lake southwest of Lillooet. This route to the Interior had been found in 1846 by Hudson's Bay Company employee Alexander Caulfield Anderson as an alternative to the existing route to Fort Vancouver, on the Columbia River, which was lost to the Americans that year through an agreement on the forty-ninth-parallel international boundary.

Steam vessels were built on the lakes in about 1860, but the strip of land between the two lakes—the Seton Portage—was a problem. An entrepreneur named Carl Dozer saw an opportunity and purchased portage land and constructed a railway with wooden rails, which may also have had strips of iron on the upper face, following a by then hundred-year-old technique of building railways.

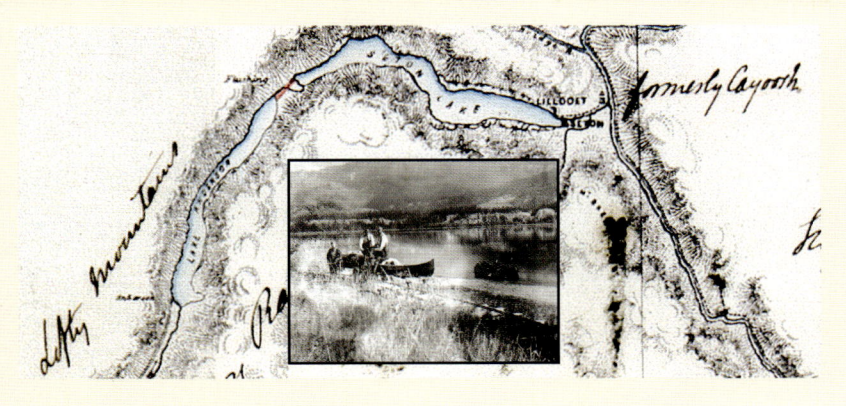

Operation is thought to have begun in 1861. The fare was "two bits" (25 cents) for baggage, and it was the same whether the miner also rode the rails or walked. Dozer's enterprise did not last long, as in 1864 the Royal Engineers completed the Cariboo Road through the Fraser Canyon. Nothing remains of Dozer's railway; wooden rails are not usually preserved, and it is likely the wood (and certainly the iron, if there was any) would have been quickly repurposed.

British Columbia's first steam locomotive arrived in September 1863. This was the *Pioneer*, purchased by the Vancouver Coal Mining & Land Company to haul coal from pits in Nanaimo to ships. In 1861 the company had bought the coal mines from the Hudson's Bay Company (which had been mining coal since 1853). The *Pioneer* might have been in Nanaimo earlier but for the fact that it was built in Britain and shipped around Cape Horn in a sailing ship, taking five months to make the journey. Considering that this was the first steam locomotive in the colony, one would think that it would have caused great excitement, but this does not seem to have been the case. The *British Colonist*, the paper of record at the time, mentions it only obliquely. In the 5 September 1863 issue, the paper's Nanaimo correspondent, writing on 31 August, noted that "the railway is fast approaching completion and will be ready in a few days for the conveyance of coal to the wharf." He also wrote that "the locomotive when in motion a short time ago, greatly excited the curiousity [sic] of the Indians." Thus the first operating date of September 1863 is known. A second, similar locomotive, *Euclataw*, also built in Britain, arrived three years later.

Robert Dunsmuir, then one of the Vancouver Coal Mining & Land Company employees, saw potential in the demand for coal from San Francisco—especially with the completion of the first transcontinental rail line in 1869—and from the Royal Navy coaling depot in Victoria. He started his own business, Dunsmuir, Diggle & Company, opening a coal mine at Wellington, just north of Nanaimo, where he had staked a claim in 1869. He built a narrow-gauge rail line to Departure Bay. His Wellington Colliery Railway at first was laid with wooden rails topped with iron strips and operated with mules, but in 1874 two steam locomotives converted from road traction engines were purchased. These were replaced by two purpose-built locomotives in 1878. They were named *Duke* and *Duchess*, and the latter is the oldest *surviving* locomotive that ran in the province. It is now on display at Carcross, Yukon (see page 199). Built at the Baldwin Locomotive Works in Philadelphia, these two locomotives were also the first North American–built locomotives to run in British Columbia.

Dunsmuir opened a number of other coal mines on Vancouver Island and built a network of rail lines to service them. But his big idea was a railway connecting Nanaimo with Victoria. When he was elected to the provincial legislature in 1882, he began planning that much larger venture, which would see life as the Esquimalt & Nanaimo Railway (see page 40).

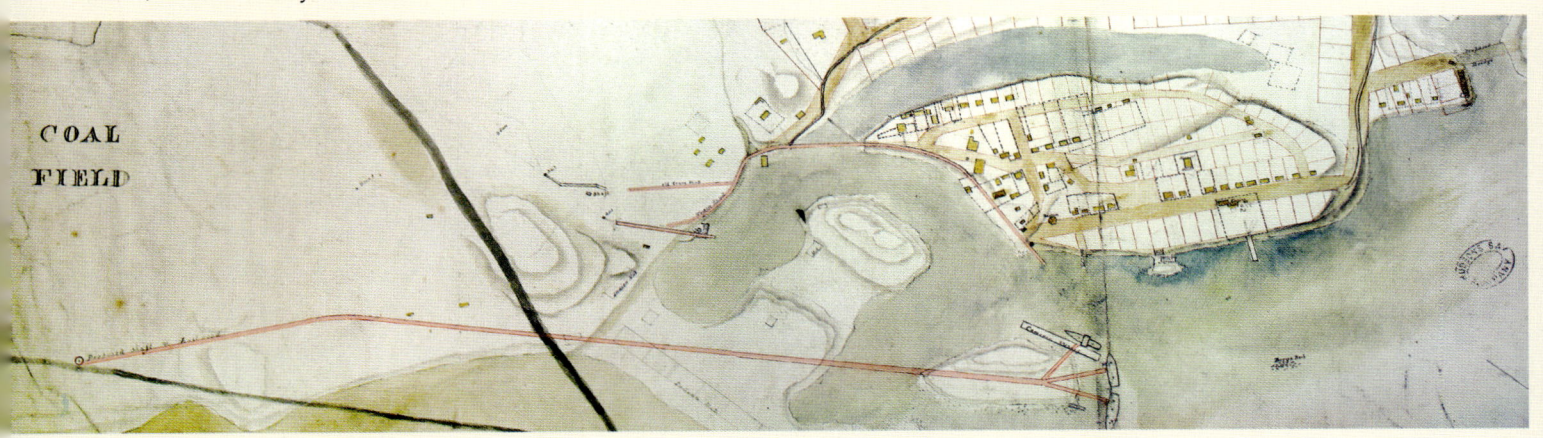

A Connection to Canada

The Canadian Pacific Railway's Engine No. 374 is the oldest preserved main-line locomotive to operate in British Columbia. It pulled the first train into the new city of Vancouver on 23 May 1887.

No railway has had as profound an effect on the history of a country as the Canadian Pacific Railway did on Canada. It literally was the reason that Canada exists in the shape and form it does today. Without it, British Columbia might well have ended up as just another state of the United States.

The idea of a transcontinental railway had been around for a long time. By 1868, a Victoria merchant, Alfred Waddington, repurposed a plan he had for a wagon road to one for a railway. But he could find no investors in Britain prepared to risk their money and no appetite in Ottawa for shelling out the vast sums of money that would be required.

That was about to change. A debate was soon raging as to whether the new United Colony of British Columbia (Vancouver Island and British Columbia, then separate colonies, had amalgamated in 1866) should join Canada or the United States. It was the promise of a transcontinental railway that tipped the scales. Article 11 of the 1871 Terms of Union required the Dominion government to begin building a railway link from the Pacific seaboard to the East within two years and to complete it within ten. Both goals were to prove optimistic.

A quick start was made with surveying, however. The Canadian Pacific Survey was authorized in 1871 and work began the following year. They were in the charge of Sandford Fleming, one-time chief engineer of the Intercolonial Railway in eastern Canada. He dispatched twenty-one surveyors across Canada and appointed Walter Moberly to work through the mountains of British Columbia to find the best route. Moberly surveyed four main routes. Two passes through the Rocky Mountains were surveyed: the Yellowhead Pass (today the route taken by Canadian National) and the Kicking Horse Pass (which would be used by Canadian Pacific).

A number of the surveyed routes ended at various fjords along the mountainous coast because the ultimate goal was thought to be Victoria, and a crossing to Vancouver Island could, it was thought, be made easier toward the north end of the island, or, alternatively, ships could be used to connect with the city. Vancouver, of course, did not exist at this time, and only one route ended at the Fraser Valley. The routes and sub-routes surveyed are shown on the map *below*.

A Canadian Pacific Railway was incorporated in 1873 but was a front for American investment and control. Then the Canadian prime minister who had overseen Confederation and the agreement to build the railway, John A. Macdonald, was found to have received improper campaign funds (the so-called Pacific Scandal) and was forced to resign. His successor, Alexander Mackenzie, feared enormous cost overruns and put the railway project on hold. This, of course, broke the Terms of Union and infuriated many in British Columbia, forcing a compromise settlement (the Carnarvon Terms) in which the dominion government agreed to build the railway, and a railway on Vancouver Island (the Esquimalt & Nanaimo), in exchange for a delay of completion until 1890.

But the dominion government did not really want to build the railway itself. In 1874 it tried to interest Canadian or British investors in the project by offering cash and land subsidies but to no avail. A start was made by the government just west of Winnipeg (where the line ended at that time), but there were many cost overruns, which would lead to the resignation of Fleming in 1880. In the meantime, British Columbia in 1878 elected a new premier, Anthony Walkem, whose government the following year prepared a memorial for presentation to Queen Victoria, giving May 1879 as the deadline for the start of construction, failing which British Columbia would secede.

But John A. Macdonald got himself re-elected in 1878 on a promise to complete the railway, and this time he would push the project through. In early 1880 the dominion government awarded contracts for two sections of the line, one west of Winnipeg and the other from Yale to Savona's

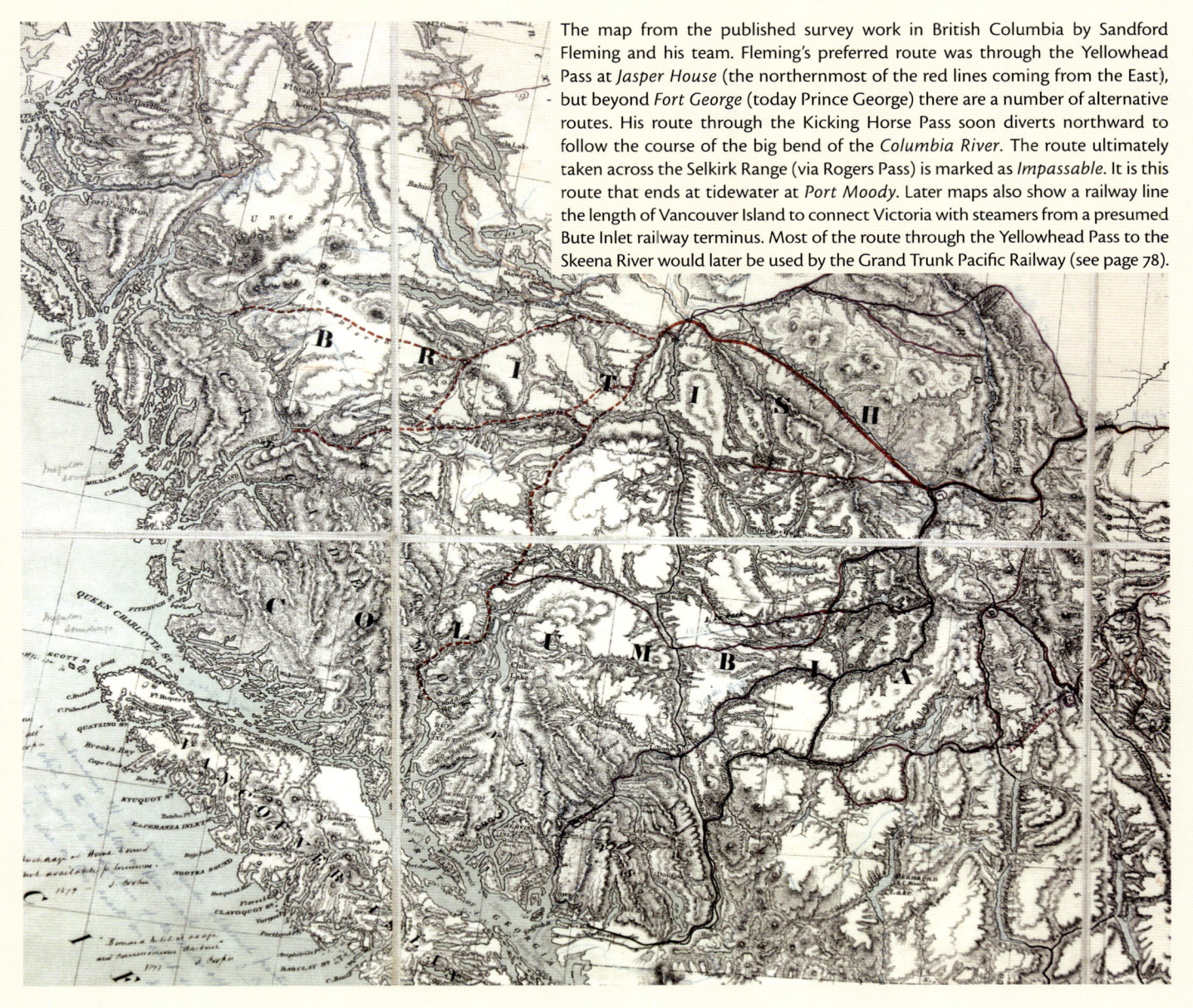

The map from the published survey work in British Columbia by Sandford Fleming and his team. Fleming's preferred route was through the Yellowhead Pass at *Jasper House* (the northernmost of the red lines coming from the East), but beyond *Fort George* (today Prince George) there are a number of alternative routes. His route through the Kicking Horse Pass soon diverts northward to follow the course of the big bend of the *Columbia River*. The route ultimately taken across the Selkirk Range (via Rogers Pass) is marked as *Impassable*. It is this route that ends at tidewater at *Port Moody*. Later maps also show a railway line the length of Vancouver Island to connect Victoria with steamers from a presumed Bute Inlet railway terminus. Most of the route through the Yellowhead Pass to the Skeena River would later be used by the Grand Trunk Pacific Railway (see page 78).

Ferry, on Kamloops Lake, the section that included all the difficult work in the Fraser Canyon. This latter section contract was awarded to an experienced American railway contractor, Andrew Onderdonk, in February 1880, and construction began in May that year.

New attempts were made by the dominion government to interest private investors in the project, and a group of entrepreneurs led by George Stephen, president of the Bank of Montreal, offered to build the line for $25 million and a land grant of 25 million acres (10 million hectares). The government accepted with alacrity, offering also to hand over the sections of line already built or under contract, which totalled 1,100 km. The contract was signed on 21 October 1880. The bill confirming the contract received royal assent on 15 February 1881, and the following day the Canadian Pacific Railway Company was incorporated.

Right.
The promise of a railway to the Pacific spawned many schemes for towns and land sales. This one, published in 1879, promotes the City of Emory, a short distance downstream from Yale, in the Fraser Canyon. At that time it was thought that the railway would merely run to the limit of navigation on the Fraser River, and that was indeed about where Emory was located. Many investors were no doubt upset when the decision was made to build to tidewater, although the route in the Lower Fraser Valley had been announced by the government in 1878. The poster promotes the government railway, here called the Canada Pacific Railway.

Below.
This map, published in 1883, shows the extent of the contracts let in 1880 and 1882 to Andrew Onderdonk as a dashed red line from *Pt. Moody* to *Savona's Ferry*, on *Kamloops L.*

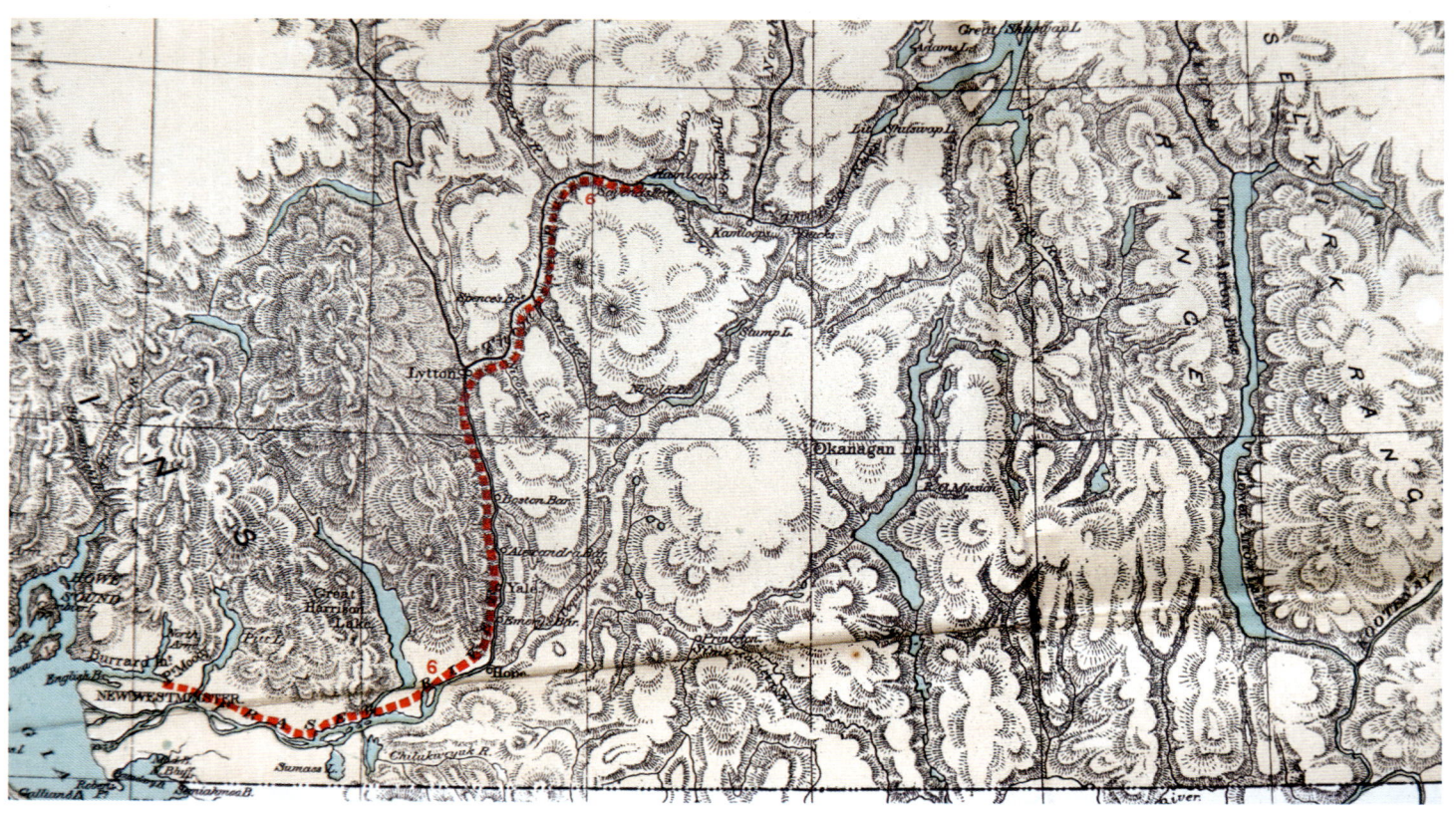

In British Columbia the dominion government defined a railway belt, a zone of land about 20 miles (32 km) on either side of the route from which the CPR could select its land grant. As required under the Terms of Union, in April 1884, once the route was established, the provincial government transferred land in this belt to the dominion government, thus making it available to grant.

Much of the initial success in the building of the CPR line lies with Onderdonk, whose work in the Fraser Canyon was nothing short of stunning. With the help of 10,000 men— including about 6,500 from China—he bored fifteen tunnels (one nearly 500 metres long) and built innumerable trestles and bridges. For supply, he used the Cariboo Road, constructed by the Royal Engineers soon after British Columbia became a colony. In so doing, however, he destroyed many sections of the road, supplanting it with railbed. He brought in five second-hand locomotives to transport rails and other materials, later adding four new ones. The rails were shipped to Port Moody and brought upriver on sternwheelers. Above Yale, Onderdonk had a smaller sternwheeler, the *Skuzzy*, constructed and hauled up the Fraser beyond Hells Gate by dozens of men.

Onderdonk obtained another contract in February 1882, which enabled him to begin building east from Port Moody and south from Yale. This section was completed in January 1884, with a last spike at Deroche, and Onderdonk ran the first through train from Port Moody to Yale—with two passengers riding in the locomotive cab—on 23 January 1884.

A steel bridge was built across the Fraser at Cisco Flat (now Siska). Fabricated in Britain and shipped in sections to Port Moody, it was erected on-site by the San Francisco Bridge Company and completed in June 1884. (It was moved in 1910 to Niagara Canyon, on the Esquimalt & Nanaimo Railway on Vancouver Island, when it was replaced by the present CP bridge; there are now two bridges at Siska, one CP and one CN.)

Right, top. Onderdonk's crews laying track in the Lower Fraser Valley, 1883.

Right, centre top. The first construction locomotive imported by Andrew Onderdonk and the first to work on the CPR main line in British Columbia. This was the *Yale*, built by the Union Iron Works in San Francisco in 1869. It originally worked on the Virginia & Truckee Railroad in Nevada, owned by one of Onderdonk's syndicate members. It was landed from a steamer at Emory, 3 km from Yale, in late 1880.

Right, centre bottom. Another of Onderdonk's construction locomotives, No. 2 *Emory*, better known by its nickname, *Old Curly*, a contemporary term for Satan. The locomotive had been used in the construction of the San Francisco seawall and was also brought to British Columbia in late 1880. This is the only locomotive of the construction period to have survived, being on display at the Burnaby Village Museum (see page 217).

Right, bottom. The 1884 steel cantilever bridge across the Fraser River at Cisco Flat with an empty ballast train on it, about 1886. Onderdonk's decision to cross the Fraser at this point compelled the Canadian Northern to cross to the other side when that railway was built here in 1914.

A CONNECTION TO CANADA

Left.
Onderdonk made some money as a side business by transporting passengers. Here he has a full load on one of the many trestle bridges in the Fraser Canyon. It is thought that the photo shows a picnic outing from Yale known to have taken place on 18 June 1884 on the occasion of the completion of the bridge at Cisco Flat. One of the ex–Virginia & Truckee locomotives is in charge. The photo illustrates well the immense difficulties involved in the construction of this pioneering line.

Left.
Many of Onderdonk's construction locomotives were acquired from the Virginia & Truckee because of his syndicate connections. This is one of the four new ones purchased from the Baldwin Locomotive Works in Philadelphia in 1884, No. 7 *Kamloops*. It is shown here on a marked railway crossing—with at least three tracks—directly in front of the Church of St. John the Divine in Yale. The church was completed in 1863 and still stands today. Onderdonk lettered all his larger locomotives with the Canadian Pacific Railway moniker as a courtesy; they did not belong to that railway. However, most were purchased by the CPR when construction ended.

Above.
Onderdonk's No. 2 *Emory* (*Old Curly*) in the Thompson River valley in 1885. Here it has a separate tender but has been preserved without one.

Below.
A superb photograph of No. 9 *Columbia*, another of Onderdonk's new locomotives purchased from Baldwin.

By the end of September 1884, trains were running through to Spences Bridge and work was well underway on the final stretch to Savona's Ferry. That month a tunnel being dug at Black Canyon, just south of Ashcroft, collapsed, necessitating the building of a temporary trestle around the bluff. Despite this setback, Onderdonk completed the line to Savona's Ferry by the end of 1884 and was soon given another contract, this time from the Canadian Pacific Railway rather than the government, to continue to build the line eastward to Eagle Pass.

Unsurprisingly, given the terrain over which he had to work, Onderdonk's government-contracted track was not laid to the standards the CPR required for its transcontinental line, and the company spent a lot of time and energy trying to get the dominion government to pay for improvements. In particular, many of the wooden trestles needed upgrading to masonry forms. The government eventually agreed to compensation, but it took several years of argument.

Onderdonk continued laying track eastward from Kamloops Lake in June 1885, after a longer-than-desired wait owing to the non-arrival of the rails. By 13 July he had reached Kamloops. That month, during a hot and dry summer, a fire completely destroyed the stockpile of an estimated 12–15,000 ties, so many more had to be cut from the surrounding forests. To cope, only every second tie was placed, on a 42-inch spacing instead of 21 inches. Some of the timber cut in haste for trestles was found to be substandard. Onderdonk also ran out of telegraph wire, delaying the advance of the accompanying telegraph line.

Despite all these difficulties, Onderdonk's men continued east until, on 28 September 1885, they ran out of rails 3 km west of the north fork of the Eagle River, on the west slope of Eagle Pass, in the Gold Range of the Monashee Mountains. On 30 September Onderdonk discharged his workforce.

This was the place that would soon be named Craigellachie when the rails from the east joined it, but at the end of September 1885 those rails were still 70 km away. The number of rails sent to Onderdonk had been based on what the two approaching armies of tracklayers were thought likely to achieve. In theory they were supposed to meet at the same time, but the terrain farther east was proving more difficult than anticipated.

Above.
No. 4 *Savona*, on a ballast train alongside Kamloops Lake east of Savona's Ferry, working on Onderdonk's CPR contract.

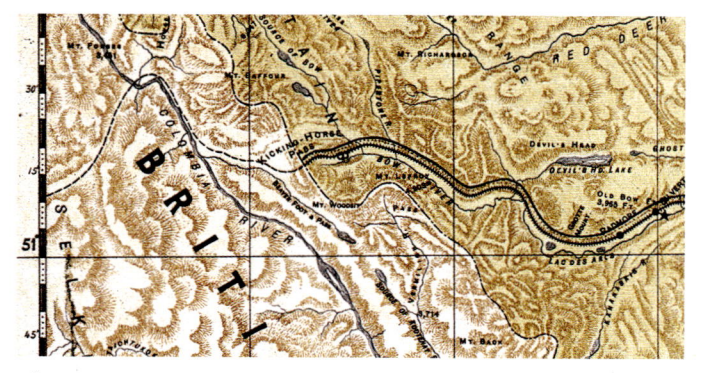

Above.
This map showing the telegraph (single black line) as well as the CPR track (cross-hatched) records the situation at the end of the 1883 season, with track poised to enter British Columbia. The dashed line shows the proposed route to the *Colombia River* (sic) and into the *Selkirk* Mountains.

Above.
The notice Andrew Onderdonk issued to his workers once he ran out of rails in Eagle Pass on 28 September 1885.

Canadian Pacific Railway track entered British Columbia from the east in May 1884, work having ground to a halt during the winter. The progress in the mountains was to prove quite different to that across the Prairies.

In charge of the construction crews was a capable CPR engineer, James Ross. A path at what was considered the maximum acceptable grade for a railway, 2.2 per cent, had been surveyed down the western slope in 1881 by an American railroad surveyor hired by the CPR, Major Albert Bowman Rogers. However, Ross soon realized that this route would involve extensive rock cutting and traverse unstable slopes, not to mention a 425-metre tunnel. The CPR's general manager (and, from 1884, vice-president), William Cornelius Van Horne, who was in overall charge of construction, refused to contemplate the delays that would be caused by following such a route because the company was fast running out of money and needed to generate revenue as quickly as possible. He came up with the famous temporary solution—albeit one not so temporary, since it lasted until 1909—the creation of the "Big Hill," a stretch of line at double the usually acceptable grade (see page 24).

Forewarned that much more powerful locomotives than usual would be required, the railway ordered the first of many powerful Consolidation locomotives from the Baldwin Locomotive Works. A service base was established at a flat area

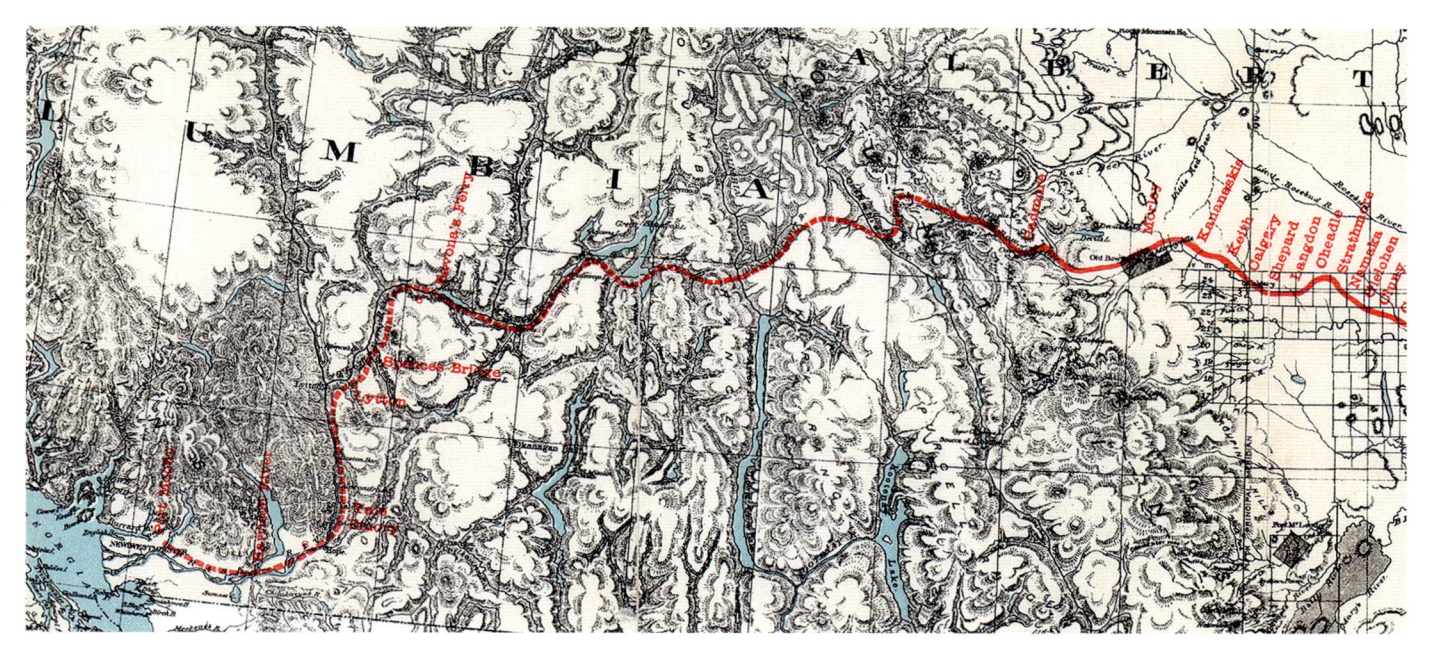

Above.
Following Major Rogers's location of a path through the Selkirks that year, this section of the 1882 *Railways of Canada* map published by the dominion government shows for the first time the CPR rail line in British Columbia more or less on the route it would actually follow.

named Field (after Cyrus Field, an American investor whom the railway was courting; he never did invest).

West of Field the track rose again to a low rise named Muskeg Summit and then wound down the canyon of the Kicking Horse River to the banks of the Columbia at a settlement named Golden City (now Golden). The narrow canyon required four tunnels and six large bridges, and unstable sections of gravel and mud gave the construction crews a lot of trouble. It was with a great deal of relief, therefore, that Ross telegraphed Van Horne on 5 November 1884: "Track on Columbia Thank God."

In the valley they could push on a little farther. At the end of the 1884 season, the tracks were at Beaver River (Beavermouth), 20 km northwest of Golden, poised to enter the Selkirk Mountains. This had required the building of a 120-metre-long wooden truss bridge across the Columbia at Donald. Only 120 km of track had been laid all year.

Major Rogers had found the pathway through the Selkirks in 1882, via a pass named after him, the 1,330-metre-high Rogers Pass. (He had gone up the Beaver River the previous year and had thought he saw a pass there, but he ran out of supplies and turned back before reaching it.)

In 1885 Ross had promised Van Horne he would connect with Onderdonk's track by September, but when he arrived back in the Selkirks he began to have misgivings because of the extent of snowslides and their accompanying windstorms. At one point he observed ten slides in six days. Clearly they would pose a considerable danger to trains, and once the railway began operation one of the first priorities would be to build snowsheds. The route also required the building of a number of high wooden trestle bridges, notably the 90-metre-high Stoney Creek Bridge (replaced by a steel structure in 1893), which was claimed to be the highest railway bridge in the world at the time. A short distance away was the Mountain Creek trestle, 60 metres high and 325 metres long. All these structures required a staggering amount of wood, all sourced from the forests nearby but requiring a vast amount of work to cut and shape. Rogers Pass was reached on 17 August 1885.

Even after surmounting Rogers Pass, it was a struggle to contain the line descending the valley of the Illecillewaet River to a 2.2 per cent grade. Ross and his engineers found the solution in a series of loops at Glacier Creek and the appropriately named Loop Creek. It was a superb bit of engineering. These loops would be replaced by the 8 km Connaught Tunnel in 1916; see page 43).

By the end of September the line was at the Columbia River (again, though farther downstream) and the town of Farwell, on land claimed by Arthur Farwell in January that year. The CPR largely avoided Farwell's land and created its own settlement—Revelstoke, named after Lord Revelstoke, head of Baring Brothers & Company, which had helped save the CPR from bankruptcy earlier that year. A bridge across the river here had been built ahead of the arrival of track. Now supplies could be brought upstream by steamer from the United States.

The going up Eagle Pass was much gentler than any of the previous work in British Columbia, and on 6 November 1885 Ross's crews reached the point on the western slope of the pass where Onderdonk had run out of rails.

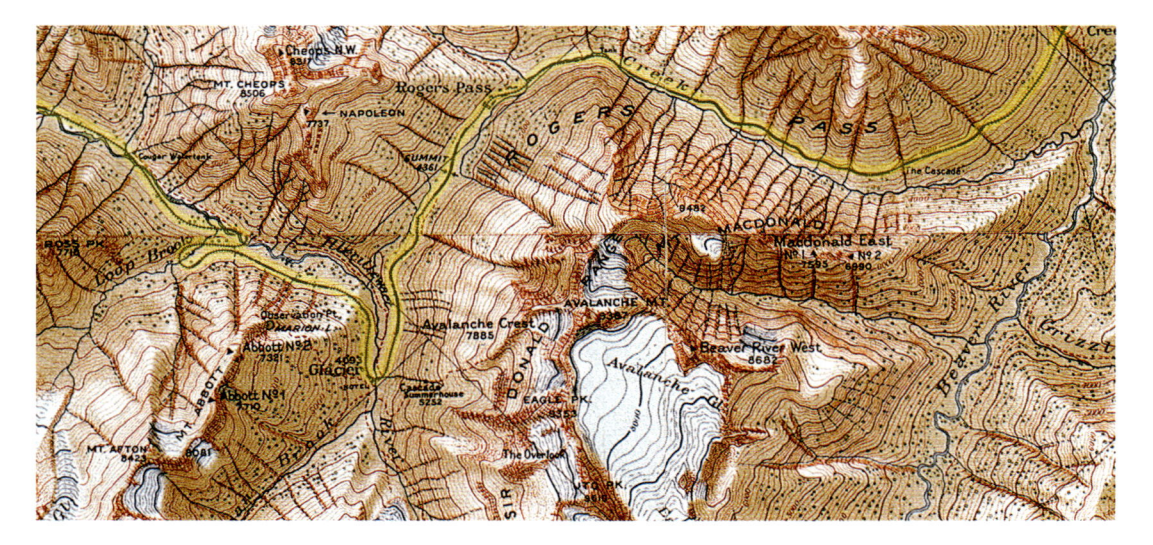

Left.
A map from 1902 shows the line of track (highlighted in yellow) in the Selkirk Mountains through *Rogers Pass*. Names such as *Avalanche Mt.* hint at the danger, partially addressed by the many snowsheds built in 1887. The *Illecillewaet River* is crossed four times on this map segment alone.

The governor general of Canada, Lord Lansdowne, had been in British Columbia, hoping to be able to officiate at the last-spike ceremony, but had had to return to Ottawa when the work took longer than expected. But company officials knew the tracks were nearly complete and had travelled west for the expected event.

The result, at about 9:20 a.m. on 7 November 1885, was the driving of the last spike by company director Donald Smith and the taking of arguably the most famous photograph in Canadian history.

Below.
The famous photograph. Donald Smith drives the last spike at Craigellachie. The honour should have fallen to company president George Stephen, but he was still in Britain, where he had been seeking investors for the venture. Behind Smith, to the left, stands a nonchalant William Cornelius Van Horne, with his hands in his pockets. Immediately behind Smith in the top hat and with a distinctive white beard is Sandford Fleming, original surveyor of the railway. Major Rogers is also in the photograph, partly obscured by others on the left; his Scottish cap sits on the rail tie. He had been holding things steady for Smith's blow, which missed the first time and bent the spike. Notably all the people in the photograph are Caucasian men; no one of Asian origin is visible, despite forming the vast majority of the workforce.

It was now late in the season and not much more could be done. A demonstration shipment was run—a shipment of forty drums of oil from the naval shipyard in Halifax to its counterpart in Victoria. The shipment had been held in Quebec pending completion of the line.

Several engineers were posted at stategic points in the Selkirks to record snowfall and avalanches so that location decisions could be made for the many snowsheds that would have to be built. A start was made the following spring and would take two years. Thirty-one sheds of varying length, totalling 8 km, were built at strategic locations throughout Rogers Pass and the Illecillewaet River valley, within a distance of less than 26 km. Some of the longer ones had "summer lines" built alongside them; Van Horne didn't want his tourist passengers to miss the wonderful scenery. They were used in the summer only. The railway spent $6.2 million on snow and grade improvements in 1886 alone.

Above.
On the way up the Beaver River valley to Rogers Pass, the 325-metre-long and 60-metre-high Mountain Creek trestle required over 2 million board feet of wood, making it one of the largest wooden structures in the world at the time. Note the forest laid bare by fire nearby.

A CONNECTION TO CANADA

The Big Hill

The Field Hill, or the Big Hill, as it soon became known, was the "temporary" 4.4 per cent grade on an 11.5 km stretch of line between Hector (Wapta Lake) and Field. The line here rapidly proved to be a major bottleneck for the railway. A complicated system was installed for controlling the line and offering a modicum of safety. Downhill, passenger trains were required to take a minimum of 47 minutes, with speed limited to 8 miles per hour (13 km/h). Train weights were strictly controlled.

Three safety switches were installed that acted as escape lanes do on modern highways, but switching the train to the escape track was controlled by a switchman to whom the engineer was to signal by means of whistle blasts. Four shorts meant the train was under control and should be given the main line, but if the switchman judged the speed still to be too high he would press a button in his railside shack that would then sound a gong at all other switches and at Field so that all available switches downhill were set to the runaway siding. Even when the train reached Field, the switch behind it was set away from the train, just in case some unexpected runaway came careering down the track behind it.

To regulate train movements in both directions an Electric Staff System was installed, and train movements regulated by block working. A block was a section of track with a passing place at each end. There were "absolute" and "permissive" block workings. The former allowed only a single train in the block and was applied to all westbound (downhill) traffic; the latter (for uphill traffic) allowed trains to follow each other at defined intervals. Special electrical-mechanical devices at the end of each block held and dispensed staffs—without which a train was not allowed in the block—and they were electrically connected so that a staff could only be taken from the dispenser by joint actions at both ends of the block.

Although there were a few terrible accidents with runaway trains, this system operated quite well over the 25 years of its operation. The steep grades of the Big Hill were replaced in 1909 with the opening of the Spiral Tunnels, which by lengthening the track distance cut the grades by half (see page 42).

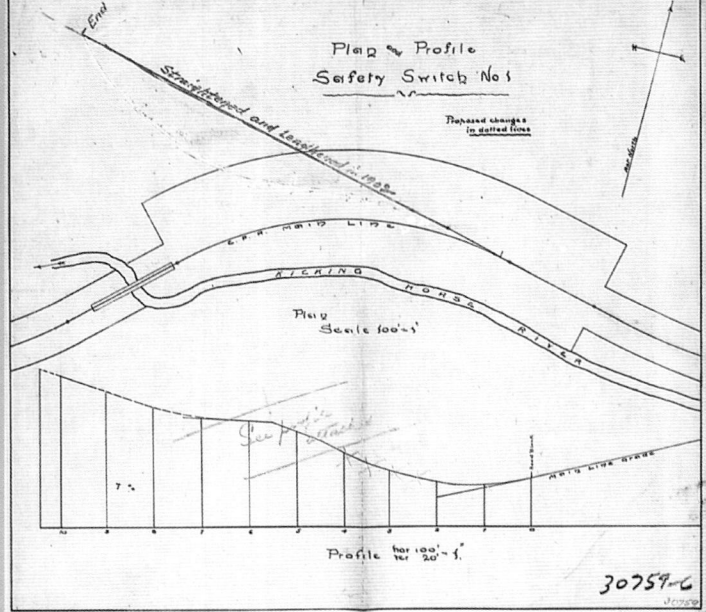

Left (two photographs and map).
Safety switch No. 1 in 1902 (*top*) and 1897 (*bottom*), and on a CPR sketch map dated between 1902 and 1909. The "escape" track appears to have been straightened in 1902, judging from the writing on the map. The track on the right is that to which a runaway train would be diverted; it slopes up again so as to hopefully slow the train before the end of track was reached. As the 1897 photo shows, a lot of power was required to haul trains up the 4.5 per cent slope, and trains often had to be cut in half for the uphill haul. This one has six cars but required three locomotives.

Above. One of the pusher engines stands on a safety track below the towering Mt. Stephen, probably in 1886, just prior to the beginning of scheduled services.

A CONNECTION TO CANADA   25

26   IRON ROAD WEST

Left.
Two excellent views of the same locomotive, a 2-8-0 Consolidation, No. 314, one of a number of powerful engines that had been purchased from Baldwin specifically for the Big Hill service. The top photo shows the Field Hotel in the background, advertising lunch and liquors. The bottom photo shows the locomotive, on the Field turntable, now with the characteristic spark arrester attached to its funnel. These were widely used in the West to try to avoid the forest fires locomotives could so easily start. No. 314 had a chequered history. In 1889, leading a 14-car coal train, it ran out of control on the Big Hill and derailed, killing several men. The safety switch procedure had not worked because a mistaken switchman thought he heard the engine whistle for the main line. No. 314 was rebuilt and put back into service, but in 1894 its boiler blew up 3 km east of Field while pushing an 8-car train up the hill. Its engineer and fireman were killed. Yet once again the engine was rebuilt and put back into service; no further incidents are recorded.

Above.
Building one of the many snowsheds in the Selkirks, 1886 or 1887.

Below.
Stoney Creek bridge, photographed soon after its completion. This was a truly massive structure to build out of wood, and it attracted tourists and photographers from around the world. It did not last long, however, being replaced by a steel structue in 1893.

A CONNECTION TO CANADA

Left.
This is a later photograph, taken in 1897, but it shows the engineering feats of the Illecillewaet Valley well. The *Atlantic Express*, headed by a Consolidation 2-8-0 and with a pusher locomotive at the rear, is crossing the river on a long trestle bridge. It has just exited two long snowsheds (originally built as three) behind it. Note the snow diversion structures covering the gap between the snowsheds. Note also the scarred mountainside, the result of fires during the construction period still evident more than ten years later.

Left.
Rogers Pass in the summer of 1885. A train headed by engine No. 132, with a spark arrester, is leaving, laden with supplies for the railhead.

Late in April 1886, the line began to be reopened using snowplows and manual labour. Snowslides and mudslides had to be cleared and track repaired where necessary. Harry Abbott had been appointed general superintendent of the Pacific Division, west of Donald, and he put two hundred Chinese labourers to work clearing and repairing—without any mechanical help, since the line farther east had to be cleared before locomotive reinforcements could be sent in.

But the line was cleared, and the first scheduled train for the Pacific left Montreal on 28 June and connected with a train from Toronto; there would be daily departures thereafter, except on Sundays. Service from Port Moody eastward would only start with the return of this first train, scheduled for 6 July. To much acclaim, the first train arrived at the Port Moody terminus at noon on 4 July, having taken five days and nineteen hours to travel from Montreal. However, engine No. 371, which arrived with the train, had only taken over charge at North Bend.

By this time the residents and land speculators of Port Moody were not as keen on the railway as they had been, for Van Horne had decided that the terminus of the railway would be farther along Burrard Inlet, at a place where the company could control much more of the land. At the time of the first train's arrival, the route to the new city, which Van Horne named Vancouver, had been located and surveyed, but construction had not yet started.

Below.
Photographer T.S. Gore captured the arrival of the first scheduled passenger train at the Pacific seaboard of British Columbia on 4 July 1886. Another photographer can be seen recording the event.

Above.
A poster-timetable advertising the new train service from Port Moody to the East. Note the time to Montreal: 137 hours (5 days, 17 hours).

The extent of the problem with forest fires was soon driven home. The second train to leave Port Moody for the East was partially destroyed by a fire in Beaver Canyon. With a forest fire raging all around the train, a pile of wood beside the track fell over and soon much of the train was alight. The passenger cars in those days were made of wood. The engine escaped with one sleeper car. Crews at Donald spent several days clearing areas around trestles and other wooden structures to save them from fire. Van Horne must have wondered about the long-term viability of a railway in British Columbia, beset as it was with fires in the summer, snow in the winter—and overwhelming grades all year round!

Van Horne had met with British Columbia premier William Smithe in February 1885 and managed to secure a land grant of some 6,245 acres (2,527 hectares) in exchange for the western extension plus the building of a hotel and an opera house. Another 213 acres (86 ha) were privately donated to the company. The province hoped thereby to create a new major city and, not coincidentally, make a lot of money from the sale of land. Construction of the western extension was delayed when Port Moody landowners filed suit to stop the railway crossing their land, but they were overruled. The track into Vancouver was completed in mid-May 1887, and the first scheduled transcontinental train, decorated for the event and to celebrate the Golden Jubilee of Queen Victoria, pulled into Vancouver on 23 May. It was pulled (but again only on the last leg of its journey) by No. 374, now the only locomotive from that era that has been preserved (see page 216).

Above. Much was made in Britain of this new line of communication for the Empire. This patriotic cartoon commemorating the completion of the transcontinental railway appeared in the British magazine *Punch* in October 1887.

Far left and left.
On 23 May 1887 Vancouver was officially linked with the rest of Canada when the famous passenger train pulled by CPR Engine No. 374 arrived. It was very decorated, in the overdone style of the times, both for the event and for Queen Victoria's Golden Jubilee. The partially hand-coloured photo at *far left* reveals some of the words painted on the locomotive, but the caption reading "First CPR Locomotive to Reach Vancouver" is incorrect, as the freight cars on the wharf behind the scene in the photo at *left* attest. Clearly they did not arrive by themselves! The train hauled by No. 374 was just the first scheduled passenger train to arrive from the East.

Below.
This 1886 map of lots in the new City of Vancouver shows the main CPR line into the city along the waterfront, where distances and directions to points on the North Shore are marked. The line continued westward to the entrance to Stanley Park. Also shown is the line connecting the main line with the new yards and roundhouse on False Creek through an already subdivided part of the city. This involved crossing *Hastings Street* and other streets and would remain an issue for the city until a tunnel was built connecting the yards with the main line in 1931 (the tunnel is now used for part of the SkyTrain system). The line is shown at a reduced scale on the inset map; the yard buildings are not yet included. This line continued out to Kitsilano as the English Bay branch—technically actually the main line—which ended at today's Vine Street. For many years the railway harboured plans to build massive docks on English Bay in this location, and this notion had formed part of Van Horne's agreement with BC premier William Smithe in 1885.

A CONNECTION TO CANADA

Above.
A wedge-type snowplow of the type initially used to clear the line in 1886. Behind it is an unidentified 4-4-0 locomotive and the conductor's van, no doubt a warm place of refuge now and again for the crew. The large flaps on the plow's side push the snow from the wedge away from the track.

Above.
This is likely a photo of first tests of a rotary-type snowplow carried out in 1888. The ability of the plow to throw snow well clear of the track is a definite advantage. The plow is clearing the summer track outside one of the snowsheds.

Right.
Snow has always been a problem for Canadian Pacific in the mountains. This is a wedge-type snowplow from 1926, of much the same design as the 1880s one, on display at the Revelstoke Railway Museum. Note the adjustable front scoop (the black part), and the retracted flaps.

32   IRON ROAD WEST

T.R.H. The Duke and Duchess of Cornwall and York en route to Vancouver. Sept. 1901

Above.
The first royal visit to British Columbia was in September 1901, when the Duke and Duchess of Cornwall and York (later King George V and Queen Mary) travelled by train to Vancouver and Victoria. The two-locomotive-headed train pauses at Field, likely to remove an assisting (with braking) locomotive at the rear. Note the several baggage cars behind the engines to ensure that a minimum of smoke would reach the royal couple.

Right.
The royal train, returning east and now with five engines, leaving Field on 4 October 1901. This was two more locomotives than usual.

A CONNECTION TO CANADA 33

Above.
CPR pusher locomotive No. 1603, an M4a 2-8-0, was photographed at Field in 1905, the year after it was built, along with other pusher engines. Clearly its crews were proud of it and were pleased to have their photos taken with it.

Left.
The Last Spike monument at Craigellachie. The plaque reads (not wholly accurately): "Here was driven the Last Spike completing Canadian Pacific Railway from Ocean to Ocean November 7 1885." Craigellachie was never a settlement of any sort but always was shown on CPR route maps as a station.

Below.
A modern CP train passes the monument in July 2018.

Hands Up!

The first train robbery in British Columbia appears to have been the holdup of a CPR train at Silverdale, just west of Mission. The holdup occurred on 10 September 1904, and is thought to have involved Canada's most famous train robber, Bill Miner, though the robber's identity has never been conclusively proven. Born Ezra Allen Miner, and also known as the Grey Fox, Miner is reputed to have invented the phrase "Hands Up!" Miner was captured after another CPR train robbery, in May 1906, at Monte Creek, about 10 km east of Kamloops. He escaped from the New Westminster Penitentiary the following year and fled to the United States, leaving only an enduring legend behind—and a story used by re-enactors to thrill heritage railway passengers and tourists today.

Rails Not Rubber

Rails preceded roads in many parts of British Columbia, particularly in the mountains. Thus it is perhaps not surprising that the first automobile to cross the Rocky Mountains travelled by rail. A Boston resident, Charles J. Glidden, was a pioneer motor car owner with a sense of adventure. He set out with his wife one day in July 1904 and drove to Minneapolis, Minnesota, where suitable roads ran out. Here his car went into a railway workshop, and flanged wheels were substituted for the conventional ones, so he could then drive on railway tracks. Luckily the axle width on his car more or less matched the 4 feet 8½ inches of the standard railway gauge. From Minneapolis he drove to Moose Jaw, Saskatchewan, on the Soo Line. Here he was designated as a special train by Canadian Pacific and had to make room for a conductor, as required on all trains. He then drove west on the Canadian Pacific tracks to Calgary and across the Rockies to Vancouver, thus becoming the first car to reach Vancouver by driving across the mountains.

Below.
Charles Glidden's "train" arrives at Vancouver's CPR station from the East on 18 September 1904. Clearly his arrival was expected, given the crowds watching. Glidden's wife sits next to him and the railway conductor sits behind. Of course, Glidden did not have to touch the steering wheel for the entire trip from Minneapolis. But one wonders if he had rigged up some sort of primitive cruise control—such as a brick on the accelerator pedal. Then he could have relaxed and enjoyed the view, at least until his next stop! In the background is the massive chateau-style second CPR station, at the foot of Granville Street. It was completed in 1899 and replaced with a larger one—the present building—in 1914.

Extensions, Branches and Improvements

Even before the completion of the transcontinental line, extensions to it were being planned. The first were to New Westminster, which was fuming at being overlooked as the railway's terminus, and to Okanagan Lake, where it could connect with lake steamers. And on Vancouver Island, plans were afoot for a railway running the length of the island, much of it along the route intended for the transcontinental when the plan was for it to terminate at Victoria.

Fraser Valley Branches

The merchants of New Westminster were as displeased as those in Port Moody to discover that the transcontinental railway was not going to terminate in their city. In November 1885 the New Westminster city council passed a Railway Bonus By-Law, which offered the CPR money if it would build a branch line to its city. After a lot of arguing, the railway agreed, and the line was completed in August 1886. A little community grew up at Westminster Junction, the place where the branch left the main line. By July 1891 it was large enough to become a municipality in its own right. It was named Coquitlam.

In 1911 the CPR decided to move its freight yards from Vancouver to Westminster Junction, and 200 hectares were appropriated for it. The move set off a flurry of real estate speculation. Speculators were convinced the yards would form the nucleus of a vast industrial city and resolved to petition to create a breakaway municipality to foster growth in that direction. A real estate company, the Coquitlam Terminal and Townsite Company, held a competition to name the proposed city. The winning name was Port Coquitlam. The emphasis on the word "port" was favoured because it was thought railway-served port facilities would be sure to follow the opening of the Panama Canal, then under construction. The new city was born on 7 March 1913, just in time for a real estate bust the following year, caused by the onset of the First World War.

At about the same time as, or shortly after, the railway was extended from Port Moody to Vancouver in 1887, a branch was built with a trestle across False Creek as far west as today's Trafalgar Street in Kitsilano, not coincidentally the western limit of the railway's land grant. The reasons for this branch remain unclear. It may have been intended as a possible extension of the main line to English Bay, where docks could be created so that ships would not have to pass through the First Narrows, or it may have been intended as a location for yards, as the 1886 map (*left, bottom*) suggests. The line ended up being used as a streetcar route to Kitsilano.

A group of businessmen had founded the Vancouver & Lulu Island Railway in 1891 to construct a line from False Creek to the north arm of the Fraser River, through rich farmland to Steveston, where many salmon canneries were located.

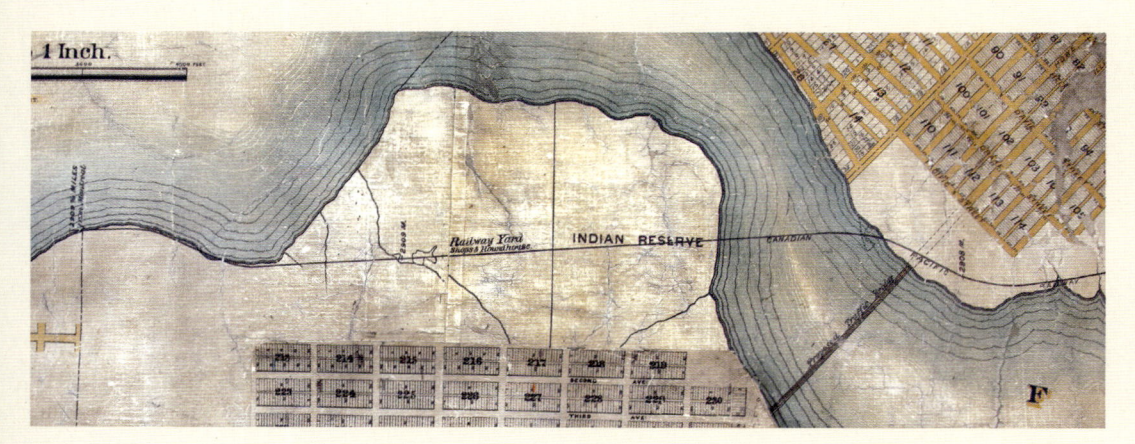

Left, top.
The CPR branch line to New Westminster, completed in 1886, is shown on ths 1905 map. The "Y" was the location of Westminster Junction.

Left.
The branch to English Bay across False Creek, with *Railway Yard* marked in Kitsilano. At the western end of the line is a label, *2909 7/12 Miles from Montreal*, which suggests it might have been intended as the main line.

36 IRON ROAD WEST

Above.
About 1895, a train comes off the CPR main line at Mission on its way to Sumas.

The line was not completed until 1902, by which time it had been acquired by Canadian Pacific, which ran a service quickly dubbed the "Sockeye Limited." In 1905 the line was leased to the British Columbia Electric Railway, which added overhead wires to begin an electric interurban service (see page 72).

Canadian Pacific had had its eye on Seattle for some time because that city was not served directly by a transcontinental line. (The Northern Pacific Railway, completed in 1883, terminated in Tacoma.) The Seattle, Lake Shore & Eastern Railway was building north with the aim of connecting with the Canadian Pacific transcontinental line, as was the Bellingham Bay & British Columbia Railway, a smaller-scale affair, which was being built from New Whatcom (now Bellingham), hoping to divert some traffic to a new American port on Bellingham Bay. Canadian Pacific built a branch line from Mission to Sumas, connecting with both American lines in 1891.

Above. The branch to English Bay continued the line from the False Creek yards, which cut across downtown streets, disrupting traffic every time a train went through. Here is the scene in June 1932, a few weeks before the line here was closed in favour of the Dunsmuir Tunnel (see page 114).

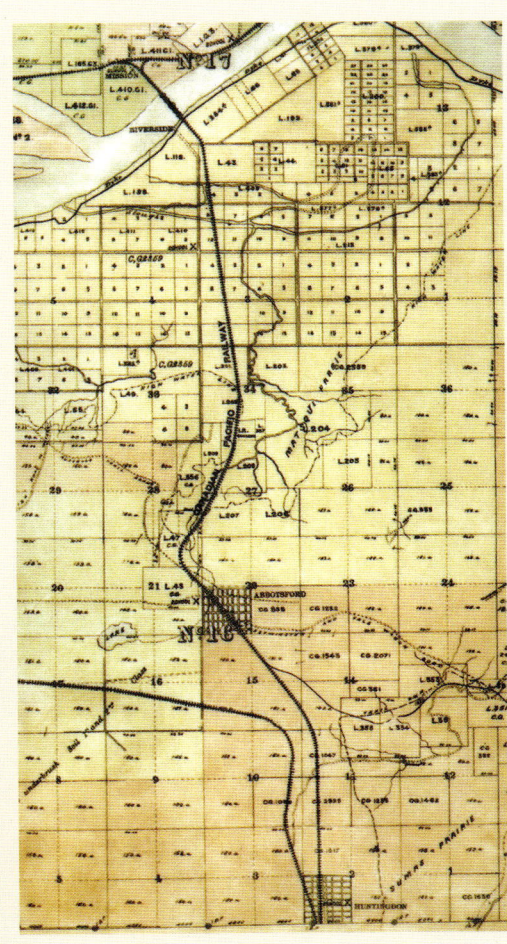

Above.
The CPR branch line from Mission to the US border at Sumas is shown on another 1905 map. The other line shown is the Vancouver, Victoria & Eastern, then only planned (see page 55). Note the platted sections of *Abbotsford* and *Huntingdon*.

EXTENSIONS, BRANCHES & IMPROVEMENTS 37

In 1893, with an eye on the looming mineral wealth of the eastern Interior, Canadian Pacific laid a 27 km line south along the banks of the not easily navigable Columbia River from Revelstoke toward Arrow Lake, reaching Wigwam. Three years later the line was extended to Arrowhead. From here steamers could go south to Nakusp in the rich Slocan mining district. (For further discussion of southern Interior mining railways, see page 58.)

The Shuswap & Okanagan Railway

Lake steamers were to play a major role in opening up the valleys of the Interior. This was particularly so in the Okanagan, where the attraction was not so much mineral wealth as agricultural produce.

Steam navigation had begun on Okanagan Lake in 1886. The Canadian Pacific main line at Sicamous was only 60 km away from the head of Okanagan Lake, and a branch line would then be able to connect with lake steamers and open up a considerable region. And the railway was keen to generate traffic along its route to improve the economics of the main line.

A charter for the branch, the Shuswap & Okanagan Railway, had been granted in 1886 to a group of local businessmen led by Forbes Vernon, who owned land in the North Okanagan and also was one of the investors in the Okanagan Land & Development Company, which was set up to sell land to the expected influx of settlers. The initial survey had been carried out for the provincial government, but subsidies from the dominion government were forthcoming and an agreement was reached whereby the Shuswap & Okanagan was to build the line and on completion lease it to the CPR, which was to operate it. The railway was completed to Okanagan Lake in 1892.

The CPR decided to build and operate its own fleet of lake steamers, and the first was the *Aberdeen*, named after the governor general of Canada, who was also a prominent local landowner. It was the beginning of an integrated transport network that opened up the region for fruit farming. The first harvest, a crop of apples, matured in 1896 and was purchased by the railway for its dining cars and hotels.

Above.
A train at the Arrowhead station waiting to leave for Revelstoke, about 1915. The locomotive, CPR No. 7340, was built in 1894.

Left.
Photographer G.H.E. Hudson has left his car beside the tracks while he takes this very interesting and revealing photo of freight cars laden with Okanagan Valley canned fruit. Since the cars are all festooned with banners proclaiming their destination in Edmonton, it seems likely that Hudson was commissioned to take the photo for advertising purposes. The place is Kelowna and the date 1909, but no locomotives are to be seen because this rail line was completely disconnected. Fruit was loaded into the cars, which were then assembled at dockside by horses, seen on the right, before being hauled onto a lake steamer or barge with rails on its deck. When the steamer reached Okanagan Landing, a locomotive would pull the partially assembled train (it looks to be in sets of four cars) off the ship. Note the freight car at front right; it is a refrigerated car because it has ice doors on top (and the word *refrigerator* on the side). One assumes the canned goods currently being carried did not require refrigeration.

Above.
A Canadian Pacific train from Sicamous, on the main line, to Okanagan Landing is shown at the first station at Vernon about 1900. A larger station built of stone would be constructed in 1912.

Right.
A prospectus for potential investors published in 1888 contained this map showing the railway's route from the *Canadian Pacific* main line at *Sicamous*.

Right, centre.
The lake sternwheel steamer *Sicamous* was the only one of the CPR ships to be preserved. Now fitted out as a museum, she sits in a permanent berth at Penticton, at the south end of the lake.

Below.
A busy scene at Okanagan Landing, near the head of the lake. Steamboats *Okanagan* (at centre) and *Sicamous* (at right) are framed by a CPR locomotive at left. The photo was taken in 1914.

EXTENSIONS, BRANCHES & IMPROVEMENTS

The Esquimalt & Nanaimo Railway

Vancouver Island's Esquimalt & Nanaimo Railway (E&N) was part of the route originally planned for the transcontinental, but Victoria was not as practical to reach from the mainland and lost out to Vancouver. The delay in building the transcontinental led to the Carnarvon Terms in 1874, which guaranteed that a federally subsidized railway would be built on Vancouver Island. Esquimalt was named as the intended terminus the following year. The railway was built by a separate company, the E&N, but it became part of the Canadian Pacific network via a lease in 1905, although it was always a detached branch that would be a relatively sleepy relative of the main line.

After an aborted attempt to get the railway built by an American company led by ex–Central Pacific engineer Lewis Clement (who had built the western part of the first US transcontinental), John A. Macdonald, then both prime minister of Canada and member of Parliament for Victoria, persuaded coal baron Robert Dunsmuir that his interests would be well served by connecting his coal mines and the Victoria market with a railway. Dunsmuir interested some of his friends in investing in the line—including three of the so-called Big Four of the Central Pacific, Leland Stanford, Charles Crocker and Collis Huntington—and they took up a half share in the line. Part of the enticement was a massive land grant amounting to about 10 per cent of Vancouver Island.

Surveys began in 1884, and two contracts were awarded for construction: the first was for 80 km south of Nanaimo and the second for the remaining 30 km north from Esquimalt. Chinese workers were brought in for some of the construction; a total of about nine hundred workers toiled on the line.

While the northern section was relatively easy, the southern part, with its climb over the Malahat, was more difficult, involving a number of spectacular trestles. Some quite long trestles were also required nearer Esquimalt. The

Above.
The southern section required a number of large trestles, including this one over Goldstream, near the southern end of Saanich Inlet. Engine No. 2 poses.

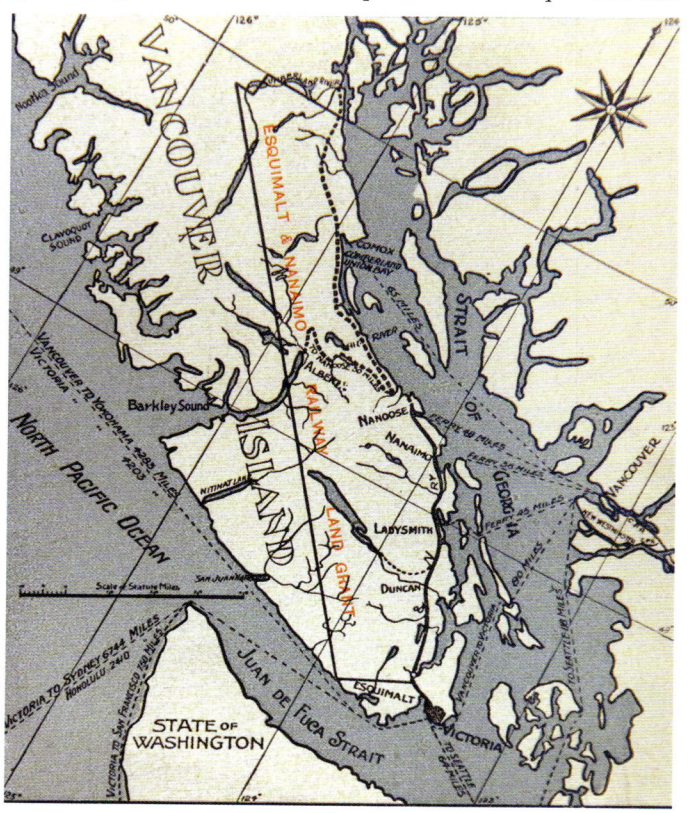

Above.
This map is from a 1914 E&N land sales booklet but shows the situation as of about 1905. The track extends from *Victoria* to just north of *Nanaimo* (to the Wellington coal mines) and as projected track to Campbell River and Lake Cowichan (both not marked) and Port *Alberni*. In fact, the line never extended beyond 13 km north of Courtenay. Also shown is the massive land grant, a small part of which, at the north end, was added in 1905 to compensate Canadian Pacific for already alienated lands within the main grant.

last spike was driven by Macdonald at Cliffside, on the eastern side of Shawnigan Lake, on 13 August 1886, thus preceding the completion of the transcontinental into Vancouver.

Pleased with the rapid progress of construction, Dunsmuir extended the line toward Victoria, and it was complete to Russell's, on Lime Bay, by 24 September. The following year Dunsmuir extended the line north to his coal mines at Wellington.

The citizens of Victoria wanted the line to end in the business district of Victoria, and city council petitioned Dunsmuir to extend the line a further 1,200 metres east, which would necessitate a 250-metre-long rock cut and the construction of a swing bridge across the harbour. Dunsmuir complied, and the line was completed into Victoria. The first train arrived at the new station on 29 March 1888.

In 1905, Canadian Pacific purchased the assets and land grant (except for coal and fire clay rights) of the railway and leased the company. Thus the Equimalt & Nanaimo retained its name. The track was extended north to Parksville in 1909 and to Lake Cowichan and Port Alberni in 1911. The latter line had grades right up to the maximum, 2.2 per cent, normally allowed. By the summer of 1914 the track had been extended north to Courtenay. The intention was to reach Campbell River and then Hardy Bay, now Port Hardy, but the First World War intervened and construction was halted 13 km north of Courtenay, never to resume.

Above.
Engine No. 10 is about to leave the coal mines at Extension on a branch built in 1899 to connect new mines with the railway at a place called Fiddick's Junction. The train is bound for wharves at Oyster Bay, which was soon to become Ladysmith. Robert Dunsmuir's son James, who took over his father's business when he died in 1899, kept this engine in 1905 when the E&N was sold to the CPR. The Wellington Colliery later built its own, and more direct, line to Ladysmith.

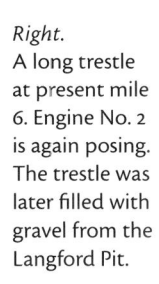

Above.
The first train into the new downtown Victoria station east of the harbour arrives on 29 March 1888.

Right.
A long trestle at present mile 6. Engine No. 2 is again posing. The trestle was later filled with gravel from the Langford Pit.

EXTENSIONS, BRANCHES & IMPROVEMENTS 41

Easing the Mountain Grades

Canadian Pacific's "Big Hill" solution to the grade between Field and the summit of the Rockies was always intended to be temporary. But finding a better way took a lot longer than at first supposed. The incentive for improvement was competition. The company could see the other transcontinentals on the horizon—and probably regretted leaving the Yellowhead Pass, with its gentler grades, unused.

The Big Hill, with its 4.4 per cent grades, was the first obstacle to be tackled. Possible solutions were analyzed: other passes were surveyed in 1902 and 1905 and were rejected as being just as bad. Double tracking was considered, as was using electric locomotives (and damming the Kicking Horse River to provide the electricity). Looping the track into the Yoho Valley was rejected because of the similar steep and unstable mountainsides.

Chief engineer John E. Schwitzer came up with the solution: reduce the grade by lengthening the path by creating two circular tunnels. Called the Spiral Tunnels, they had arcs of 232 and 234 degrees but, importantly, because they essentially doubled back on themselves, they did not lessen the opportunities for viewing the scenery, something that the railway had realized was a valuable way to attract tourists. One of the engineers who worked on the location of the Spiral Tunnels was Andrew McCulloch, now better known for building the difficult Kettle Valley Railway (see page 184).

The idea was ingenious, but it was not new. Schwitzer knew about a similar solution applied to the building of the Gotthard Tunnel in Switzerland. Completed in 1882, that tunnel was actually a series of twelve tunnels, a number of which were of the spiral type. Indeed, the map of the loop tunnels near Wassen looks almost identical to their Canadian counterparts.

Tunnelling began in January 1908, continued through the winter, and was complete by August the following year. Considerable work was also required to realign about 5 km of approach track on either side and rebuild some snowsheds. The tunnels rapidly became a tourist attraction in their own right and were promoted by the railway as one of the engineering wonders

WHITE DOTTED LINES REPRESENT THE ROUTE TAKEN BY TRAIN THROUGH SPIRAL TUNNELS.

of the world. Promotional material such as the three-dimensional map *below, left,* served to explain and to encourage visits.

The remaining significant bottleneck was over Rogers Pass in the Selkirk Mountains. Here a more conventional solution was arrived at in the form of a straight tunnel that allowed the line to bypass Rogers Pass and emerge in the Beaver Valley, where the grade was again gentler down to Revelstoke.

Work began in the summer of 1913, and the tunnel was completed in July 1916. Originally intended to be named the Selkirk Tunnel, it was changed to the Connaught Tunnel when it was officially opened by the governor general of Canada, the Duke of Connaught. When it was completed, the tunnel was the longest in North America. It was augmented in 1988 by the longer-still Mount Macdonald Tunnel (see page 163), which allowed the railway to dispense with helper locomotives, and this tunnel is now usually used by trains going west, while the Connaught continues to be used by trains going east.

Left. This bird's-eye map from the 1930s explains the Spiral Tunnels better than any words could do. It was an illustration in a railway menu. Part of the old grade became a road, shown on the map, and today part of the Trans-Canada Highway follows its path.

Above. This 1940s view shows the Lower Spiral Tunnel with a train about to enter. The exit portal is beneath the train.

Left, centre. A contemporary railway cartoon depicts CPR engineer John Schwitzer in his spiral tunnel.

Left, bottom. A work train and steam shovel excavate the approaches to the Spiral Tunnels in 1908.

Above. This promotional postcard was likely published at the time the Connaught Tunnel opened in 1916.

Right. Building the Connaught Tunnel. A new, quicker method of boring this tunnel was adopted. A small tunnel was bored on one side of the main tunnel and galleries were then driven out to the line of the main tunnel.

EXTENSIONS, BRANCHES & IMPROVEMENTS 43

On a bright summer day in 1969 a CPR freight train with multiple locomotives headed by No. 5504 and No. 5550 emerge from the Lower Spiral Tunnel. The train is now long enough to loop back on itself without any shenanigans, such as carefully positioning two trains, which the railway used to do for publicity purposes. Since the lower tunnel is 891 metres in length, this train must be at least 1 km long. Note the date on the tunnel portal.

Challenging a Monopoly

Vancouver grew rapidly, creating a city that was the preferred destination for other railways. In particular, James J. Hill of the Great Northern Railway (GN) was looking for a way to challenge the Canadian Pacific Railway, with which he had vowed to get even since the company chose the north side of Lake Superior for its transcontinental route rather than the southern, American side, where it would have tied in with his own railway, the St. Paul & Pacific. But any attempt to breach the CPR's monopoly was hindered by its large land grant, which covered any approach directly from the south, leaving only the east as a way onto the peninsula on which Vancouver is built.

Hill's Great Northern was not completed to Seattle until 1893, but even before that he was making plans for feeder lines. One of these was to be south from Vancouver using railway charters for companies that he would control.

The New Westminster Southern Railway was originally chartered in 1883 to build from the international boundary through to Burrard Inlet, but that charter had been cancelled when challenged by the CPR. Chartered again on 7 April 1887, the company was then content with a line from the boundary to a point opposite New Westminster, where a ferry could take passengers into that city and would soon be able to continue into Vancouver on the Canadian Pacific line.

In 1891, the line was completed from Blaine to Liverpool, where the river narrowed slightly, and then to Brownsville and South Westminster, where a new ferry docked. After a dispute with a landowner, the track between South Westminster and Brownsville was ripped up in 1893 and the ferry then had to call at Brownsville to pick up train passengers. (The track was relaid in 1901.) At Blaine, the railway connected with another Hill line, the Fairhaven & Southern. The latter connected with Fairhaven (Bellingham) and then Seattle, using other Hill lines, by the end of 1891. Both of the coastal railways had been chartered by a group that at various times included Nelson Bennett, an American railway builder, and John Hendry, the pre-eminent local businessman and owner of the Royal City Planing Mills. Hill had acquired the charters in 1889.

When the New Westminster Southern began operating, Canadian Pacific cancelled its service between Vancouver and New Westminster, leaving passengers to struggle from the ferry to the interurban terminus to continue into Vancouver.

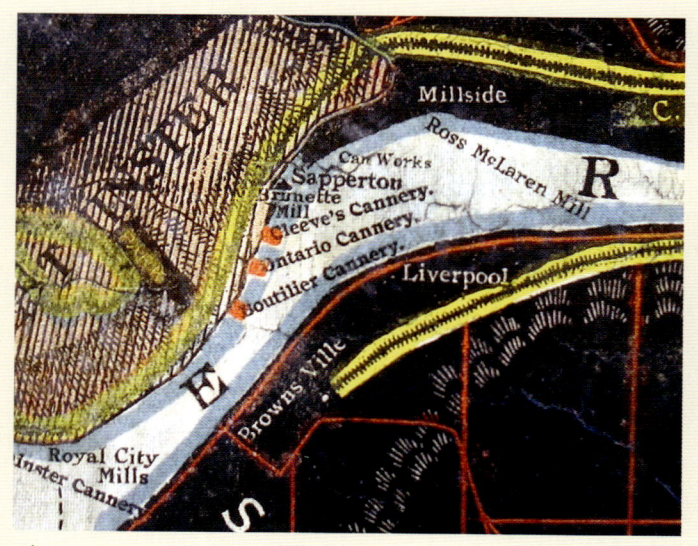

Above.
This 1899 map shows the New Westminster Southern Railway ending at *Browns Ville*, opposite New Westminster, after the track was taken up between there and South Westminster. *Liverpool*, the advertised first terminus, is also shown.

Above, top. An ad for Liverpool that appeared in the New Westminster newspaper on 13 June 1890. Anywhere a railway terminus was planned, real estate speculators could be found.

Above. Two locomotives bound for service on the New Westminster Southern Railway, No. 202 and No. 199, were both class 33 (later called B-20), 4-4-0 engines originally manufactured in 1882–83 for the St. Paul, Minnesota & Manitoba Railway.

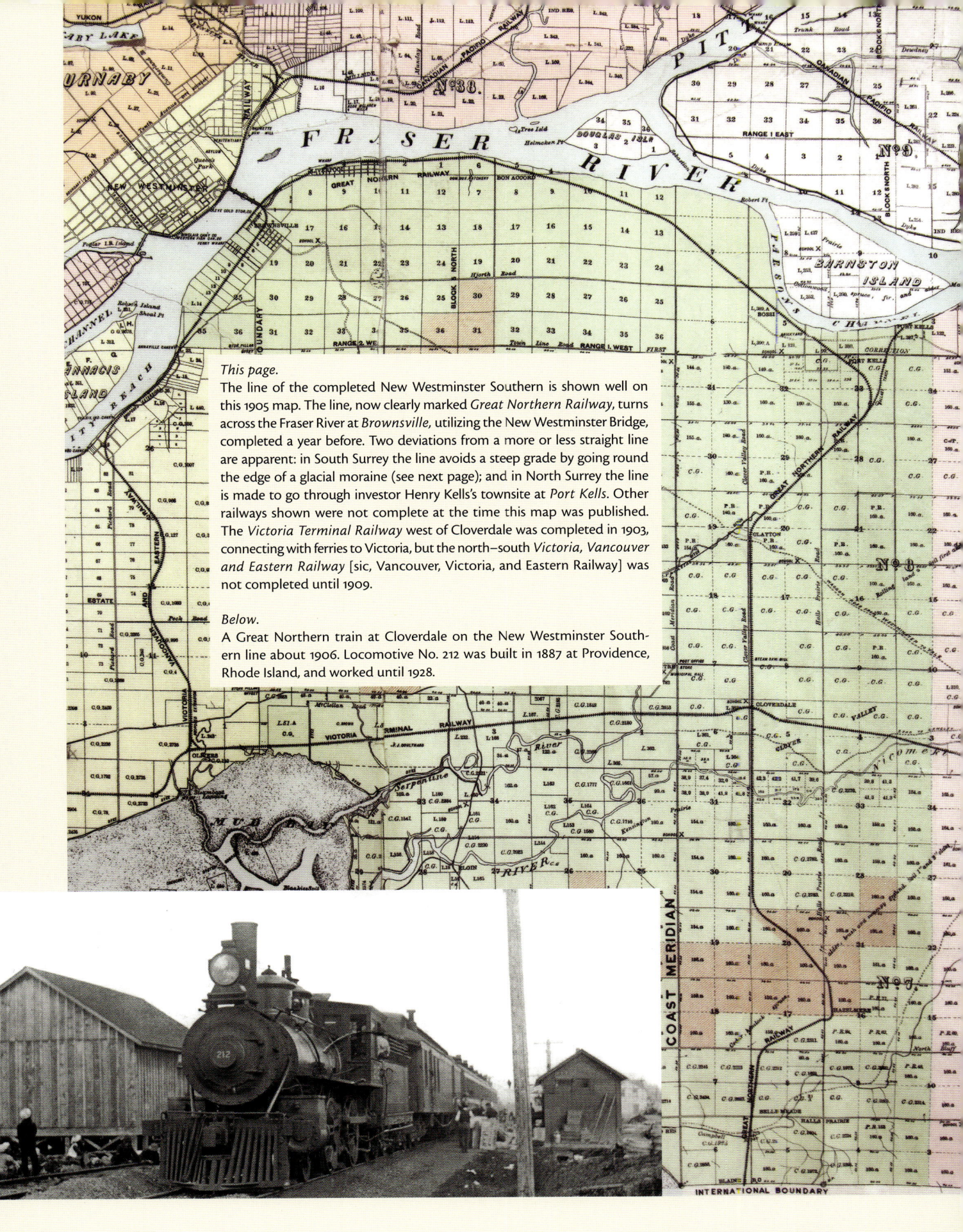

This page.
The line of the completed New Westminster Southern is shown well on this 1905 map. The line, now clearly marked *Great Northern Railway,* turns across the Fraser River at *Brownsville,* utilizing the New Westminster Bridge, completed a year before. Two deviations from a more or less straight line are apparent: in South Surrey the line avoids a steep grade by going round the edge of a glacial moraine (see next page); and in North Surrey the line is made to go through investor Henry Kells's townsite at *Port Kells.* Other railways shown were not complete at the time this map was published. The *Victoria Terminal Railway* west of Cloverdale was completed in 1903, connecting with ferries to Victoria, but the north–south *Victoria, Vancouver and Eastern Railway* [sic, Vancouver, Victoria, and Eastern Railway] was not completed until 1909.

Below.
A Great Northern train at Cloverdale on the New Westminster Southern line about 1906. Locomotive No. 212 was built in 1887 at Providence, Rhode Island, and worked until 1928.

CHALLENGING A MONOPOLY

Tracing the Path of an Old Railway (1)

The routes of railways that have long since disappeared can be found on contemporary maps, but they are often hard to relate to the present landscape because a great deal has often changed. You are only going to see where the railway ran if you know exactly where to look.

Helpful in this regard are modern computerized municipal engineering and planning maps, used to record the precise location of infrastructure ranging from street lights to storm drains. These maps also show legal land parcels, so that it is possible to determine ownership. Railways surveyed and bought, or were granted, the linear strips of land they needed for their railbeds, and these are often still visible on the municipal maps, despite ownership having changed hands.

As an example, the southern part of the route of the New Westminster Southern Railway, opened in 1891 and completely closed in 1929, has been traced in this manner using a computerized map from the City of Surrey. The map, together with the present-day view on the ground of critical points, is shown here. This line has now almost totally disappeared, and may be compared with another line, the Vancouver, Victoria & Eastern, on page 56, which left more evidence of its route, at least in places. It is fun to stand at a rural roadside realizing that many years ago steam trains rushed through the very spot you are standing on!

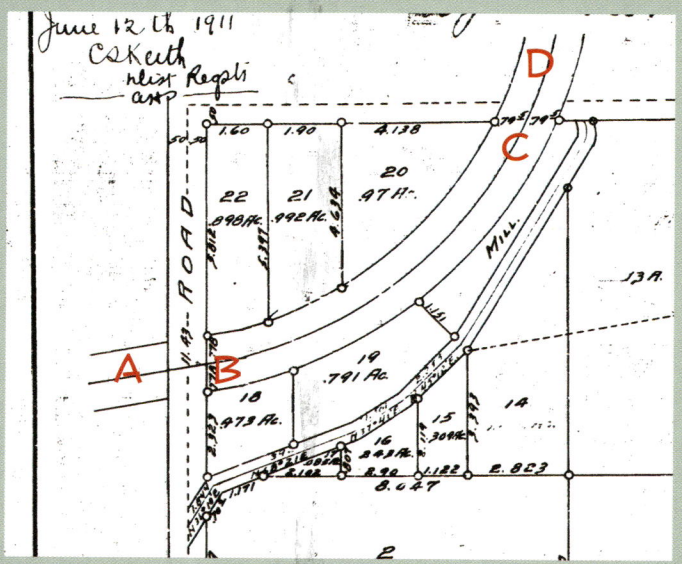

Left, centre. Part of a 1911 survey, done when the railway was still active, included for comparison. This shows the portion of the trackbed from *AB* to *CD* on the City of Surrey map, *above, top*, and enlarged, *above, centre*, and also on the larger 1918 map at *right*.

Left, bottom. This bump in 184 Street just north of 24 Avenue had always intrigued the author and inspired the research that led to these maps. It is the old crossing of the road by the railway at *E* to *F* on the map *above, top*.

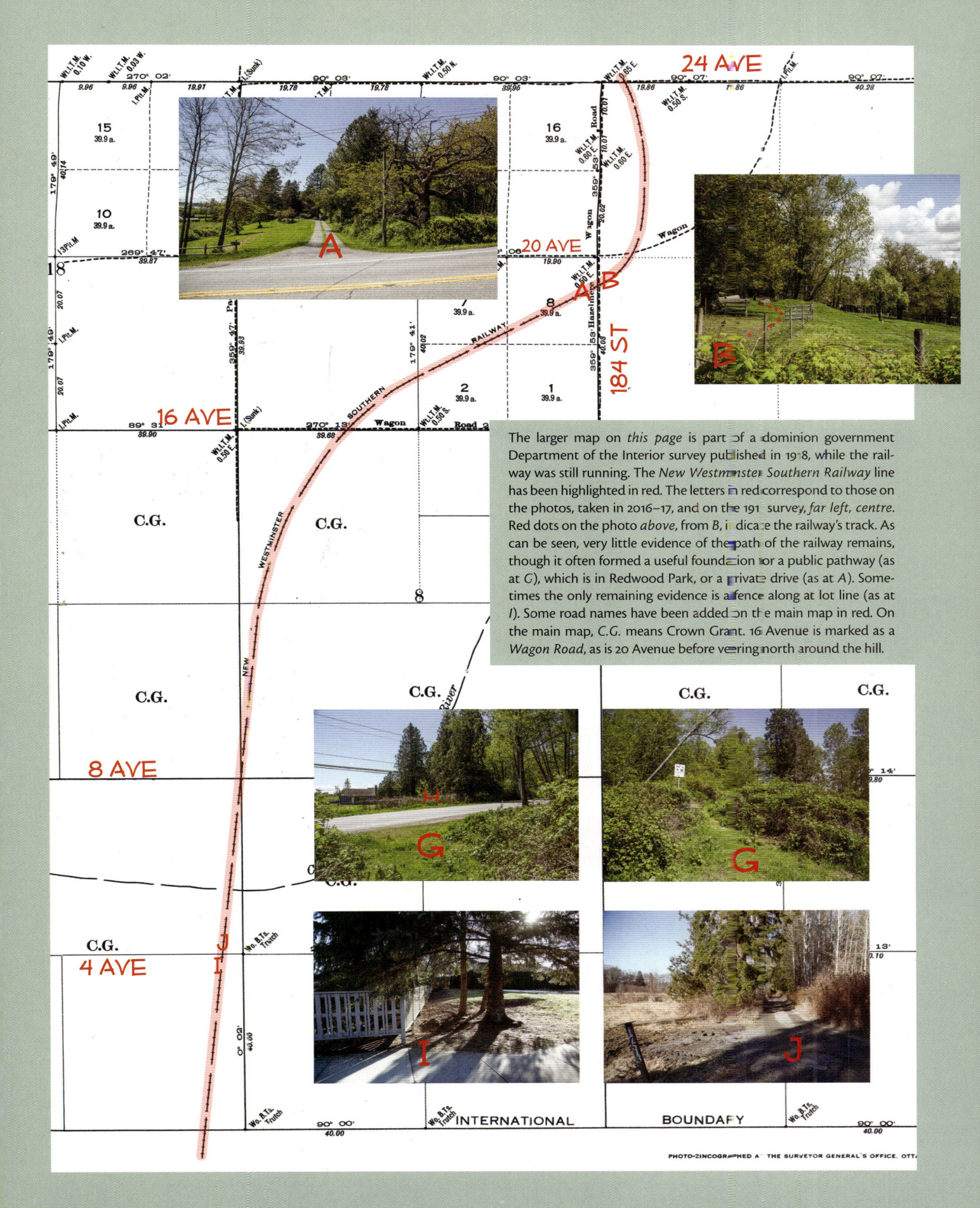

The larger map on *this page* is part of a dominion government Department of the Interior survey published in 1918, while the railway was still running. The *New Westminster Southern Railway* line has been highlighted in red. The letters in red correspond to those on the photos, taken in 2016–17, and on the 1915 survey, *far left, centre*. Red dots on the photo *above*, from B, indicate the railway's track. As can be seen, very little evidence of the path of the railway remains, though it often formed a useful foundation for a public pathway (as at *G*), which is in Redwood Park, or a private drive (as at *A*). Sometimes the only remaining evidence is a fence along at lot line (as at *I*). Some road names have been added on the main map in red. On the main map, *C.G.* means Crown Grant. 16 Avenue is marked as a *Wagon Road*, as is 20 Avenue before veering north around the hill.

CHALLENGING A MONOPOLY 49

Hill and his Great Northern would also challenge the Canadian Pacific monopoly in Victoria. In 1892 a group of investors had formed the Victoria & Sidney Railway and, after gaining tax concessions and mortgage guarantees from the provincial government, had completed a line from Victoria to Sidney, at the tip of the Saanich Peninsula, in 1894.

The line had been intended at first simply to provide a local service for farmers in this rich agricultural area so they could easily ship their produce to Victoria, but it soon became apparent

Below.
The steam ferry *Victoria* at the Port Guichon ferry terminal with a Vancouver Terminal Railway train alongside. The Great Northern used the Vancouver Victoria & Eastern name for much of its work.

Below, centre. A map showing the location of the Port Guichon terminal.

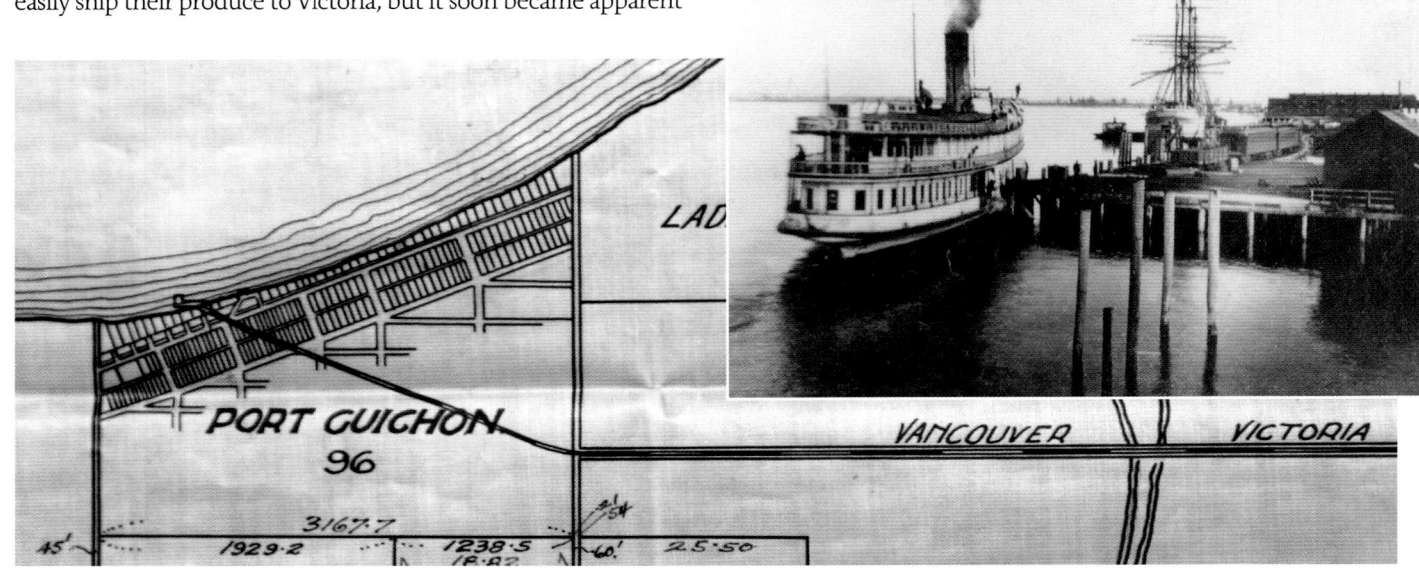

Below.
A Victoria & Sidney train about to leave Victoria from a depot built in 1900 near city hall after the line was extended a short distance south into downtown Victoria. This locomotive (V&S No. 1) was later sold to Bloedel, Stewart & Welch and ended its life as a logging engine (the first BS&W No. 5).

50   IRON ROAD WEST

that the line could be used as part of a connection to Vancouver. In 1900 the Victoria Terminal Railway & Ferry Company was created. This included the island railway, a ferry and a mainland line from New Westminster to a place just west of Ladner to be called Port Guichon. While the mainland line, then officially the Liverpool & Canoe Pass Railway, was under construction, the company was taken over by the Great Northern and the route of the line modified to connect with the New Westminster Southern at Cloverdale. The line was completed in April 1903 and the railways and ferries began operating together.

This was one scheme of Hill's that did not really work out. Intense competition from Canadian Pacific steamers, coupled with inadequate service and an indirect route, led to marginal profits. The Victoria line later faced competition from an electric interurban that began operating in 1913, and the V&S was abandoned in 1919. The mainland Victoria Terminal Railway line was abandoned by 1938. Much of the railbed of the latter line is now used by the British Columbia Railway line to Roberts Bank (see page 158).

The Great Northern's task of accessing downtown Vancouver became a lot easier in 1904, when the New Westminster Bridge was opened. The bridge did not even cost the railway any money, for it had been financed by provincial and federal subsidies and built by the province. Originally a road as well as a rail bridge, it was to prove valuable to other railways in future; the interurban would use it, as would the Canadian Northern Railway.

Another railway that Hill was involved with had begun building a line from New Westminster into Vancouver; it would be a critical link for the Great Northern. It was called the Vancouver, Westminster & Yukon Railway (VW&Y). Hill's associate John Hendry had chartered the line as a railway to the goldfields of the Klondike. Some maps of the day show the railway's hoped-for route, crossing the Second Narrows,

Above.
The centre fixed span of the New Westminster Bridge is floated into position on 11 November 1903.

Below.
An official photo of the first train to cross the New Westminster Bridge, on 23 July 1904. The train has a Victoria & Sidney Railway engine, and one of the coaches is of the Vancouver, Westminster & Yukon Railway. Dignitaries from Victoria had taken the train from Victoria via the ferry to Port Guichon. The train has taken the branch to the northwest, toward Sapperton; there is also a line to the right. Five years later a locomotive would plunge into the river because of a split switch at this point. Note the white-railed road part of the bridge at right, above the railway, curving off in the other direction.

following the North Shore, and then going north along Howe Sound. The route out of New Westminster had involved crossing the CPR track in Sapperton, and this was legally challenged after VW&Y crews had inserted a diamond crossing in the early morning darkness of 27 August 1903. But the VW&Y prevailed, and the first train between Vancouver and New Westminster ran on 31 December 1903, though regular passenger service did not begin until the following August. Regular passenger service between Vancouver and Seattle also began in 1904, possible because the New Westminster Bridge had opened in July.

The route into Vancouver was not ideal, but it was better than nothing. It followed the Brunette River, the north side of Burnaby Lake, and Still Creek, and parts were very boggy and difficult to grade. Once when a sinkhole appeared, halting all trains, a crew had to dump hundreds of carloads of gravel into it.

Canadian Pacific, doing all it could to hinder what it saw as an encroachment on its territory, had in 1905 extended its line from the south side of the Kitsilano trestle eastward along the south shore of False Creek and then leased it to the British Columbia Electric Railway (BCER)—on the express condition that it do no business with the VW&Y!

GN officially took over the VW&Y (except for the authority to build to the Yukon) in 1908.

There was the problem of where to put a permanent station. Later that would be solved by filling in part of False Creek, but for now a trestle was built across the water into a station on Pender Street, right next to the Canadian Pacific right-of-way from its main line to the False Creek yards (see maps *below* and *right*). This station opened in 1909.

Also that year a branch was laid to the Burrard Inlet waterfront at the old Hastings Mill site, which Hendry had acquired by a combination of twisting arms in Ottawa to obtain Crown grants and buying up much of the rest of the waterfront to the east. The CPR and BCER both unsuccessfully tried to require the VW&Y to use overpasses on its branch to the waterfront. And the title to the Hastings Mill terminal site was also claimed by CPR. All these things just delayed the VW&Y, but did not stop it. Hendry, indeed, was not a man to

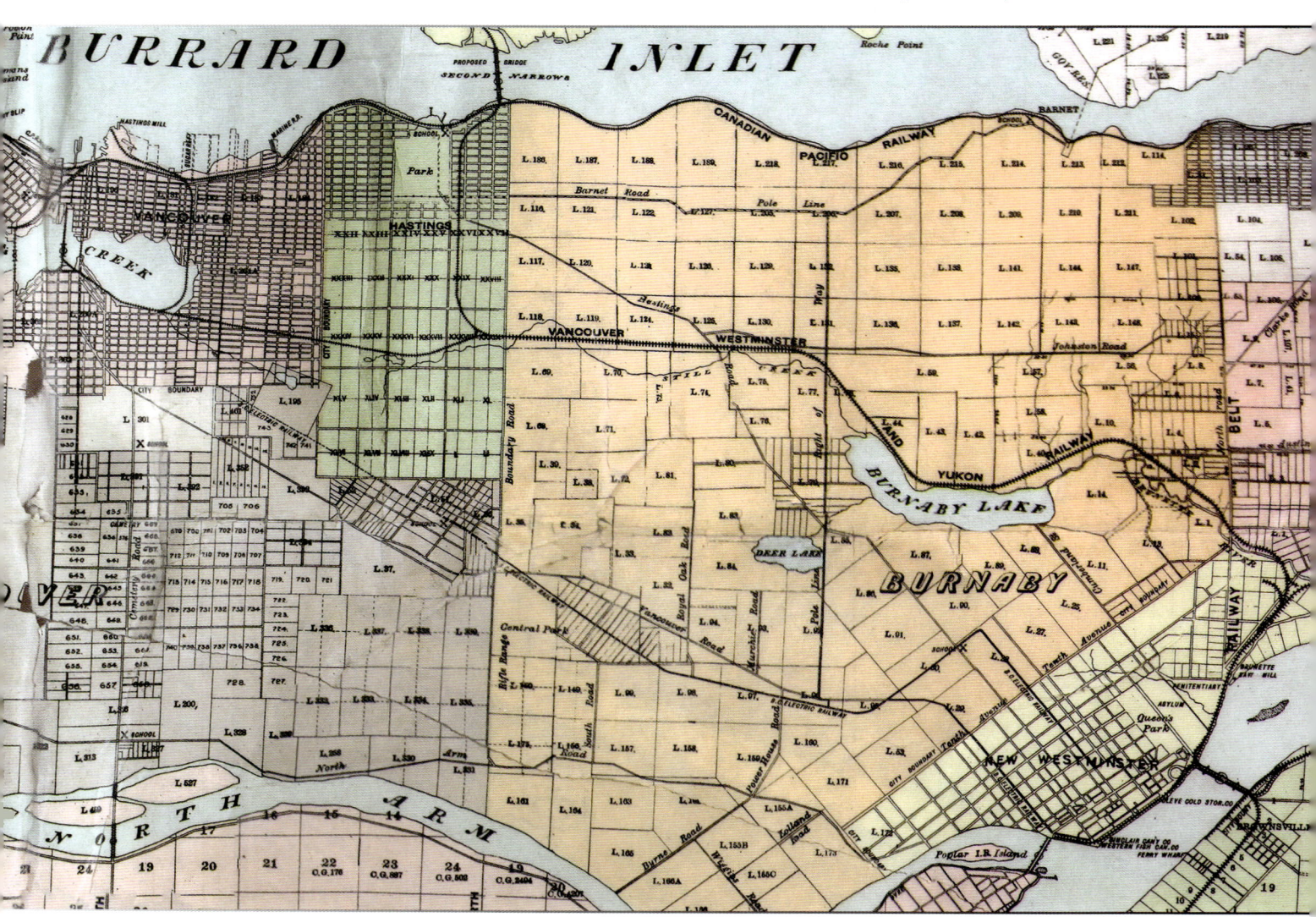

Above.
The Grandview Cut being excavated in 1913. The excavated material was used to help reclaim False Creek. Despite the cut, the grade was still steep, at 1.1 per cent.

Left. This map was published in 1905. It shows the route of the *Vancouver, Westminster and Yukon Railway* from the New Westminster Bridge across the Fraser to Sapperton, where the CPR line was crossed, and then west, past a branch—or was it the main line?—across a *proposed bridge* over the *Second Narrows* (which would not be built until much later), into Vancouver along the south side of *False Creek* (which still extended east almost to today's Clark Drive), before crossing False Creek on a trestle and swing bridge into a terminal on Pender Street, right beside CPR's branch to False Creek. The line to *Burrard Inlet* at *Hastings Mill* seemingly is built over the waters of eastern False Creek, but in reality these were but mud flats relatively easily crossed on a trestle. The CPR runs along the shore of False Creek.

Right. Details of the VW&Y/Great Northern station on *Pender E.* Street, between *Carrall* Street and Columbia Street, is shown on this 1913 fire insurance plan. The station was a corrugated iron structure with wood plank platforms. False Creek is immediately to the south. *Great Northern Railway Tracks* are at right, while the *Canadian Pacific Railway* branch to its False Creek yards is at left. The southern half of the station site is today occupied by the Dr. Sun Yat Sen Classical Chinese garden.

be circumvented in business dealings. In the end the VW&Y—and through it Hill and the Great Northern—gained access to downtown Vancouver and to Burrard Inlet.

The final approach into Vancouver involved more grades, which were eliminated between 1910 and 1913 by a large cutting, the Grandview Cut, today used by SkyTrain as well as the railway.

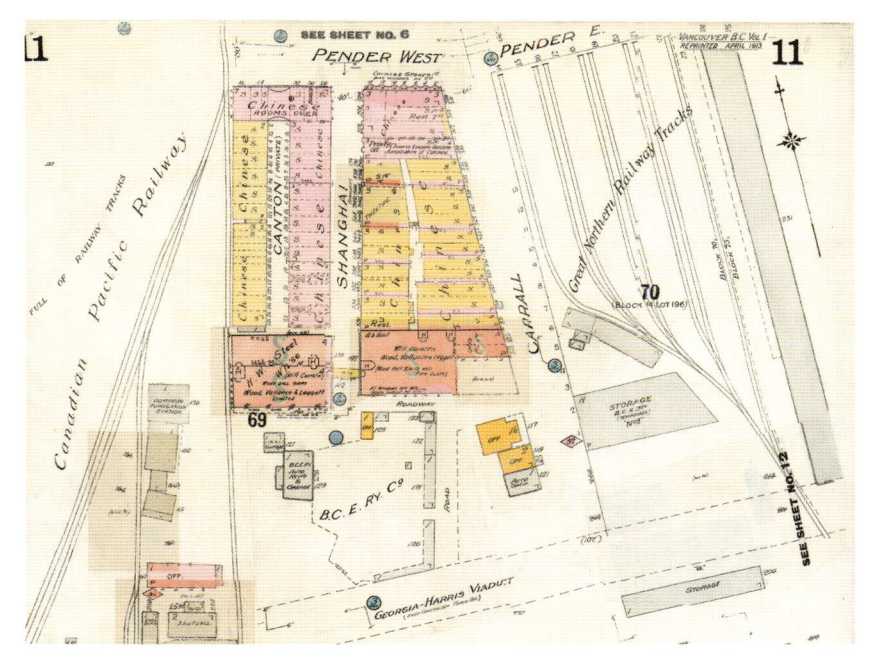

Hill used a company originally incorporated in 1897 with the intention of building from the coast into the southern Interior. He used it for much of the railway construction in the Fraser Valley in the early 1900s. This was the Vancouver, Victoria & Eastern Railway (VV&E). In 1907–09 this charter was used to build east from Cloverdale, connecting the Victoria Terminal

CHALLENGING A MONOPOLY 53

Above. This photo is believed to show the last southbound train on the New Westminster Southern at Cloverdale after the rerouting of the line through White Rock and Crescent Beach in 1909. The NWS line was not used as a through route after that.

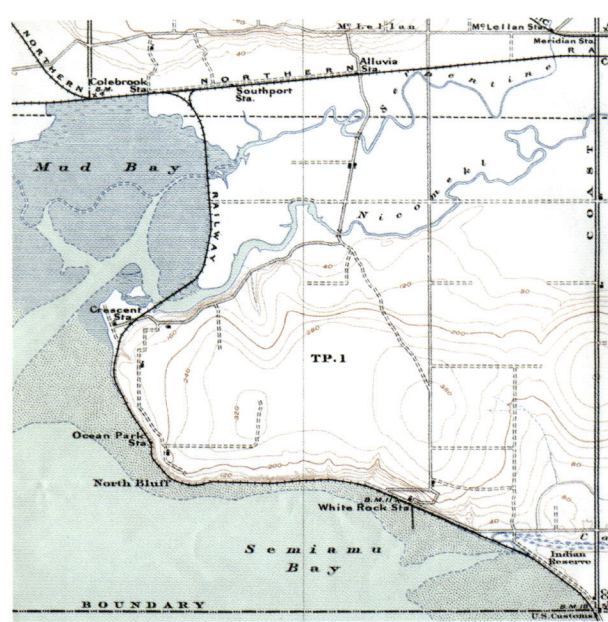

Above. The new route of the Great Northern around the perimeter of the Semiahmoo Peninsula. There are stations at *White Rock*, *Ocean Park* and *Crescent* Beach. The new route had easier grades than the old, but more maintenance was required because of frequent landslips.

Railway (since 1908 absorbed into the VV&E) to Huntingdon–Sumas and the international boundary. The route, completed in early 1909, was quite circuitous in its western half because of the hilly topography caused by glacial moraines, particularly around Murrayville.

In 1912–14 the VV&E charter was used to connect with the Canadian Northern Pacific farther up the valley at a place near Chilliwack named Cannor (a name derived from Canadian Northern Railway; see page 88 and overleaf). The line was never very successful; it did not extend to the Interior and had too many bends to compete with other Fraser Valley main lines. In 1919 Kilgard to Cannor was abandoned; from 1929 to 1942 the part of the line from Kilgard to Abbotsford was used by the Kilgard Brick Company.

Much the same fate awaited the New Westminster Southern line, which only lasted until 1919, but here the reasons for decline were different. The line was replaced by a new one that avoided the glacial moraines of South Surrey by hugging the coast around the Semiahmoo Peninsula and

Above. The arrival of the train from Vancouver at White Rock, probably in the summer of 1915. Compare this photo with a modern one on page 215.

54   IRON ROAD WEST

the edge of the high ground of North Delta to access the New Westminster Bridge from the west.

The new line was also built using the VV&E charter, and was opened for general use on 15 March 1909. The route made access to White Rock and Crescent Beach much easier for Vancouver residents, and the two areas soon became favourite seaside resorts. The Great Northern began running commuter trains from Vancouver during the summer months. Although the new route was flatter, it required more maintenance because of landslips onto the track from the cliffs between White Rock and Crescent Beach. The line still suffers from landslips today.

The following year the Great Northern (through the VV&E) asked the City of Vancouver for a semicircular piece of land around False Creek, 61 acres (25 ha) in all, which it promised to reclaim from the mud flats and build a grand terminus and marshalling yards. In June 1910 a public vote gave the railway what it wanted, and infilling and building began. Fill from the Grandview Cut, excavated in 1910–13, was used for the reclamation work. The city retained the central part of the mud flats, then intended for a proposed dock area, but it would not be long before another railway, the Canadian Northern Pacific, would acquire that area for its own grand terminus (see page 91 and map, *page 93*) and, east of Main Street, False Creek would disappear.

Below.
There is a wealth of detail shown on this 1911 map, which shows the Great Northern's plans for a new passenger station, freight depot and yards on reclaimed land on the mud flats of the perimeter of eastern False Creek, as well as the then-existing station arrangements west of Main Street. The Grandview Cut, the railway's entrance into the city, begins in the bottom right corner of this map, where an *Engine House* (roundhouse) was to be built. The main passenger and freight terminals are on the north side of the creek, and additional yards are on the south side. The Canadian Pacific branch into False Creek crosses at top left, next to *C.P.R. Freight Sheds*. Next to it, on the water, is *B.C. Elect. Ry* sheds, sold by CPR to BCER to prevent them from falling into Hendry's hands. Also shown is the 1909 VV&E station on *Pender Street* and the *Swing Bridge* that accessed it. The 1909 line to Burrard Inlet parallels *Raymur* Street at top right.

Inset.
A view of the still very new-looking Great Northern passenger terminal (nearest to the camera on the right) and freight sheds in July 1917, from the area to the south that was being infilled for the Canadian Northern Pacific (see map on *page 93*). The pipes in the foreground are presumably going to be used for drainage.

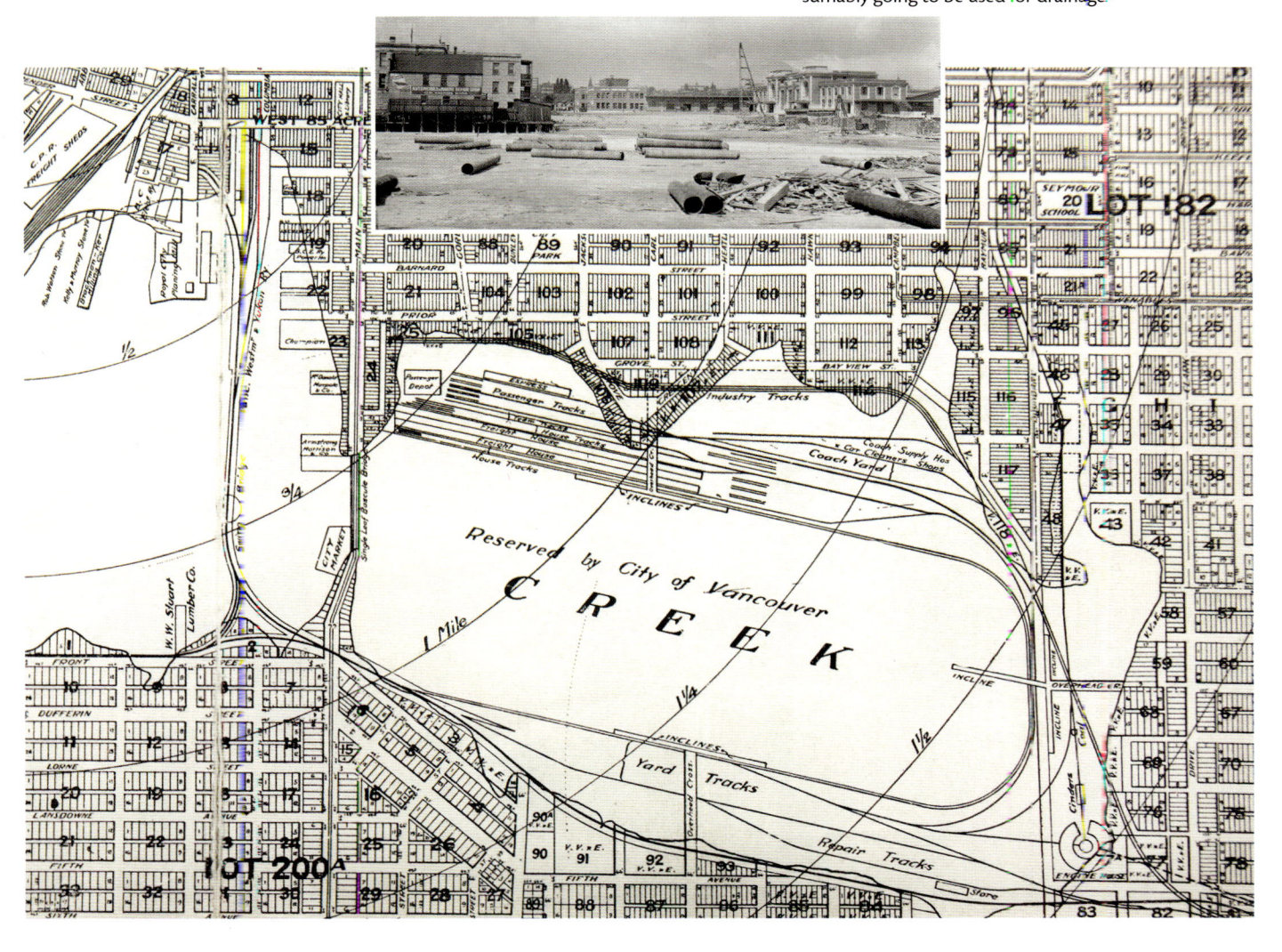

Tracing the Path of an Old Railway (2)

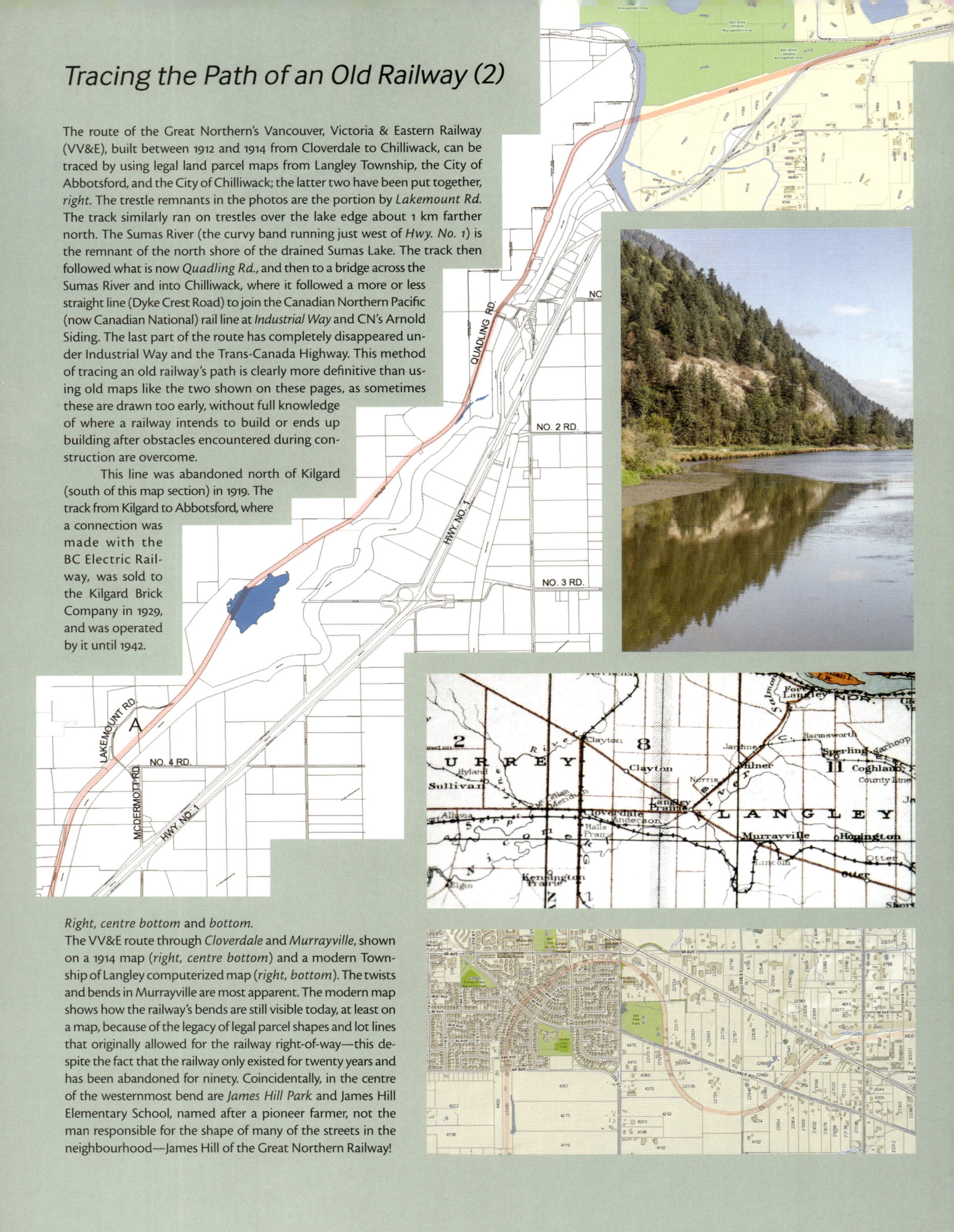

The route of the Great Northern's Vancouver, Victoria & Eastern Railway (VV&E), built between 1912 and 1914 from Cloverdale to Chilliwack, can be traced by using legal land parcel maps from Langley Township, the City of Abbotsford, and the City of Chilliwack; the latter two have been put together, *right*. The trestle remnants in the photos are the portion by *Lakemount Rd*. The track similarly ran on trestles over the lake edge about 1 km farther north. The Sumas River (the curvy band running just west of *Hwy. No. 1*) is the remnant of the north shore of the drained Sumas Lake. The track then followed what is now *Quadling Rd.*, and then to a bridge across the Sumas River and into Chilliwack, where it followed a more or less straight line (Dyke Crest Road) to join the Canadian Northern Pacific (now Canadian National) rail line at *Industrial Way* and CN's Arnold Siding. The last part of the route has completely disappeared under Industrial Way and the Trans-Canada Highway. This method of tracing an old railway's path is clearly more definitive than using old maps like the two shown on these pages, as sometimes these are drawn too early, without full knowledge of where a railway intends to build or ends up building after obstacles encountered during construction are overcome.

This line was abandoned north of Kilgard (south of this map section) in 1919. The track from Kilgard to Abbotsford, where a connection was made with the BC Electric Railway, was sold to the Kilgard Brick Company in 1929, and was operated by it until 1942.

Right, centre bottom and *bottom*.
The VV&E route through *Cloverdale* and *Murrayville*, shown on a 1914 map (*right, centre bottom*) and a modern Township of Langley computerized map (*right, bottom*). The twists and bends in Murrayville are most apparent. The modern map shows how the railway's bends are still visible today, at least on a map, because of the legacy of legal parcel shapes and lot lines that originally allowed for the railway right-of-way—this despite the fact that the railway only existed for twenty years and has been abandoned for ninety. Coincidentally, in the centre of the westernmost bend are *James Hill Park* and James Hill Elementary School, named after a pioneer farmer, not the man responsible for the shape of many of the streets in the neighbourhood—James Hill of the Great Northern Railway!

Above.
Modern evidence of the VV&E route can be dramatically and positively seen on the banks of the Sumas River, which is a remnant of the north side of Sumas Lake, in the form of this trestle, the location of which can be seen on the map at *left,* marked A. The railway here was built in 1912–14 (and was abandoned in 1919), so these piles—or their remnants—have lasted over a hundred years. Another view of the scene, *left,* shows how the railway was built along the very edge of Sumas Mountain, the steep slope of which dominates the view.

Below.
The entire route of the VV&E east from *Cloverdale,* where it connected with the Victoria Terminal Railway, is shown on this undated map. The map also shows the connection with the Canadian Northern east of *Chilliwack.* The correct connection, at Cannor, just east of the Sumas River, is determined from the legal map on these pages, and the correct path shown here by the red overlay line. The map may well have been drawn before this part of the railway was completed, hence the inaccuracies. The western half of the line is correctly shown.

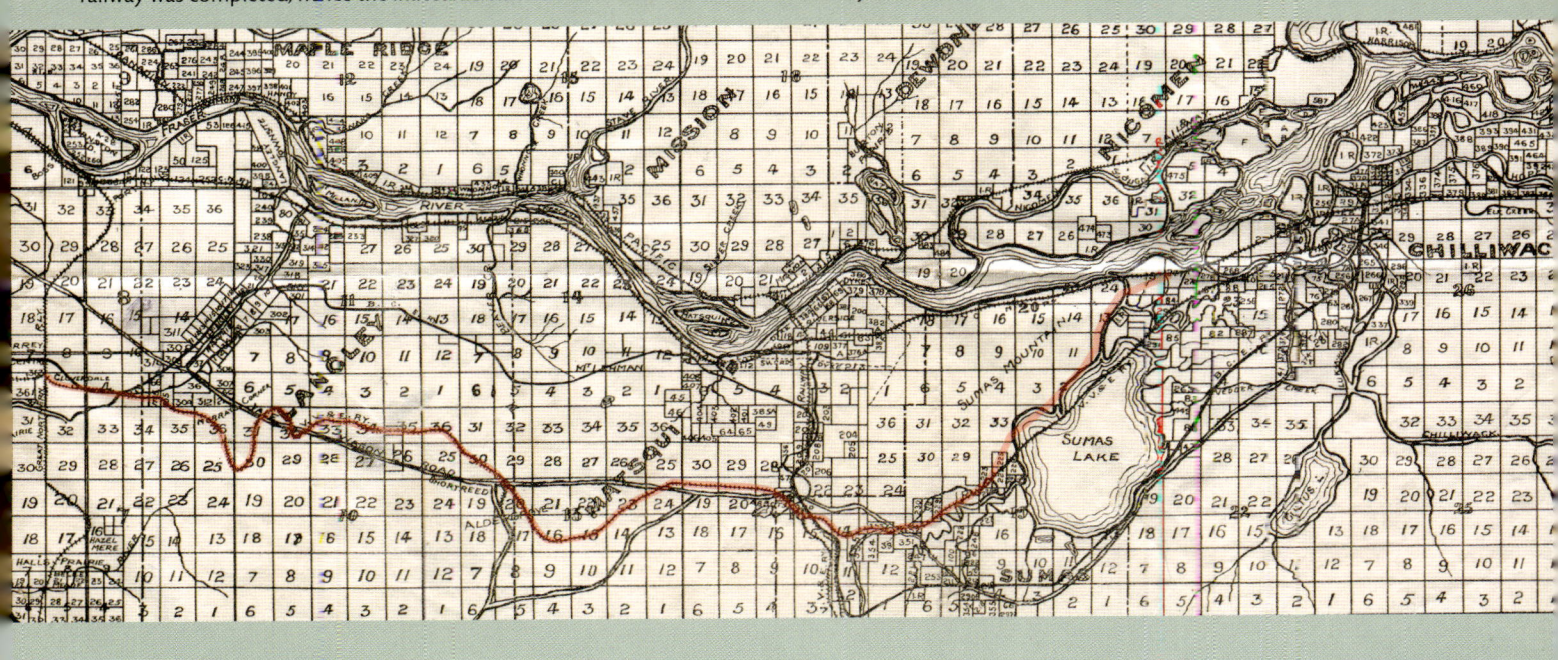

CHALLENGING A MONOPOLY 57

Accessing the Interior's Mineral Wealth

The mountains of the southern Interior of British Columbia had long been known to contain minerals, but the difficulty of access had limited their exploitation. The mountain ranges run naturally north to south and this inhibits transportation links westward toward the coast. Indeed, this was what had made life difficult for the Canadian Pacific's transcontinental.

The orientation of the mountain ranges and valleys also tended to make it easier to transport minerals southward, where a connection could be made with American railroads, notably the Northern Pacific, completed in 1883, and the Great Northern, completed in 1893.

Even before that, minerals were being packed south to smelters in the United States. By 1887, silver ore from newly staked mines—including the large Silver King mine—above the Kootenay River at a settlement soon to be known as Nelson, was being taken south on packhorses.

Cornelius Van Horne of the Canadian Pacific wanted in on the action, and in 1891 the railway built the Columbia & Kootenay Railway from the southern end of Lower Arrow Lake at Robson to Nelson. This section of the Kootenay River was unnavigable owing to rapids and falls. Now Canadian Pacific could connect Nelson to its main line via steamers on the Arrow Lakes and its branch from Revelstoke. By 1895 an aerial tramway had been built to bring the ore down the mountain from Silver King to the rail line.

Canadian Pacific did not have the field to itself for long. In 1894 American railroad entrepreneur Daniel C. Corbin built the Nelson & Fort Sheppard Railway from Northport, Washington, to Nelson. This line had received a Canadian charter in 1891 for the section north of Fort Sheppard, on the US–Canada boundary.

Intense competition was the order of the day farther north in the area popularly known as the "Silvery Slocan." Here Canadian Pacific was up against the Kaslo & Slocan Railway, rumoured to be bankrolled by James J. Hill of the Great Northern, an avowed foe of the CPR since he had quit that railway's board over a dispute about whether the transcontinental should run north or south of Lake Superior.

Far left.
An early train on the Columbia & Kootenay Railway on the river crossing at Taghum.

Left.
This 1893 map shows Canadian Pacific's *Columbia & Kootenay Railway* (between Robson and Nelson), and Daniel Corbin's *Nelson and Fort Shepherd Railway* between Fort Shepherd [sic] and Nelson. At the boundary the line connected with his American line, the Spokane Falls & Northern. When Corbin reached Nelson he found the rights to the waterfront taken up by Canadian Pacific and so had to be content with a station higher up.

Below.
A train pauses on a trestle near Fruitvale on the Nelson & Fort Shepherd Railway, the line with which Daniel Corbin hoped to channel the wealth of the Kootenays through the United States.

The Kaslo & Slocan Railway was chartered in 1892 and began laying narrow-gauge track westward from Kaslo, on Kootenay Lake. Canadian Pacific began building a line from Nakusp, on the Upper Arrow Lake, to New Denver, on Slocan Lake, and then to Three Forks, in the heart of the mining district. That line was completed in 1894, the Kaslo & Slocan line a year later. But then the Kaslo & Slocan extended its line farther, reaching Sandon in October 1895 and Cody in November. Space was tight. Sandon, in particular, was built over the river bed in a narrow valley—its main street was a wooden walkway with the river beneath it—that left little room for things like railways. Canadian Pacific, not to be outdone, also managed to find a path into Sandon and by December the two railways were at war with one another. The men of the Kaslo & Slocan descended on the newly built facilities of their rival, ripping up track, derailing freight cars, and even demolishing the new depot by pulling it over with a wire lasso tied to a locomotive!

Although Canadian Pacific admitted defeat for a while, it was soon planning a further extension to tap into it's rival's

ACCESSING THE INTERIOR'S MINERAL WEALTH   59

PAYNE BLUFF, K. & S. RY., NEAR SANDON, B.C.
R. H. TRUEMAN & CO., PHOTO., VANCOUVER, B.C.

Left.
This photograph is much-reproduced for obvious reasons. It shows very well the extreme terrain through which the Kaslo & Slocan was built. This view is at Payne's Bluff, where "sensitive" passengers were advised to look the other way. The photo, and the one opposite, were taken about 1897 by Vancouver photographer R.H. Trueman, who was responsible for recording many views of British Columbia at this time.

Right.
Another Trueman photo shows a Kaslo & Slocan train. The on-photo caption says it was taken in Carpenter Creek Canyon, but it is thought to have been taken in the Kaslo River Canyon, 25 km west of Kaslo. Notice how in those days photographers were able to get trains stopped and posed along with all their crew. Try that now!

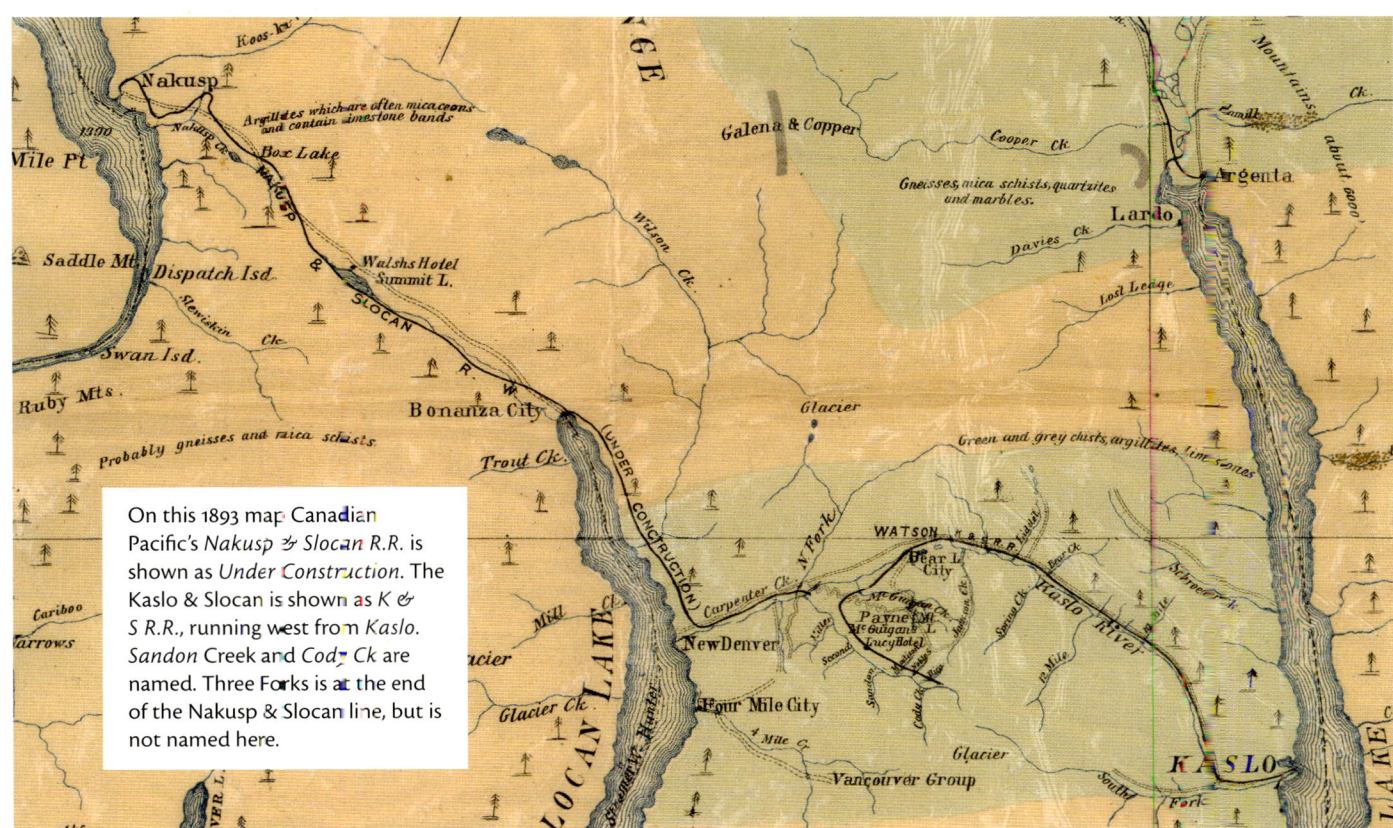

On this 1893 map Canadian Pacific's *Nakusp & Slocan R.R.* is shown as *Under Construction*. The Kaslo & Slocan is shown as *K & S R.R.*, running west from *Kaslo*. *Sandon* Creek and *Cody Ck* are named. Three Forks is at the end of the Nakusp & Slocan line, but is not named here.

business. In the end, nature decided the battle. Landslides took out long sections of the Kaslo & Slocan line, and in 1910, after a forest fire had also wiped out its stations, the company halted operations. In 1912 Canadian Pacific took over the Kaslo & Slocan, standardizing the gauge, connecting the two lines, and operating a line from Nakusp to Kaslo that lasted until 1955, when torrential rains washed out many sections of track and also destroyed Sandon, whose inhabitants came to regret their town being built over a riverbed. Sandon is today one of the most interesting of the Slocan ghost towns.

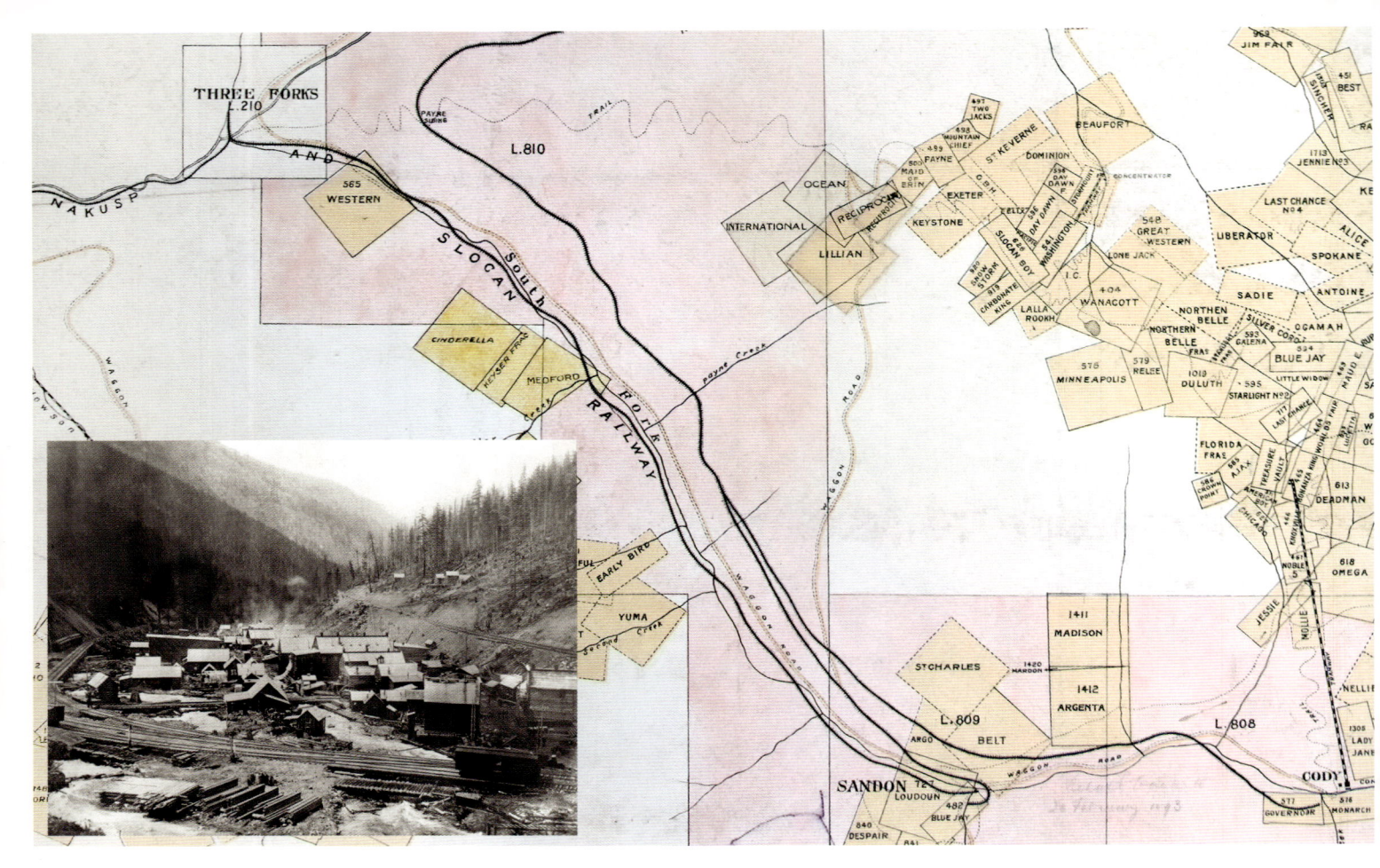

Above.
Three Forks, Sandon, Cody and the lines of the *Nakusp and Slocan Railway* and Kaslo & Slocan Railway (the latter is not named on this map segment but is the track on the north side of *South Fork*) are shown on this map published in 1897. Dozens of mining claims are scattered about the mountainsides. *Payne Siding* is marked, close to Payne Bluff, location of the photograph on the previous page. Inset is a view of Sandon in 1896, before the river, seen flowing down the main street, was boarded over. The Nakusp & Slocan Railway line is in the foreground and that of the Kaslo & Slocan runs along the higher ground to the right.

One of the richest discoveries ever in British Columbia was the Le Roi mine in Rossland, which held gold, silver and other metals. This mine and others staked around it created the town of Rossland. After passing through several hands, the mine was purchased by F. Augustus Heinze, the owner of a smelter at Butte, Montana, who built a smelter on the Columbia River down the valley from Rossland and a railway to connect with the mine. The railway, constructed during 1896 and at first named the Trail Creek Tramway, was narrow gauge and involved very steep grades and switchbacks. During construction, Heinze came to realize that there was money to be made in railways and their accompanying land grants and changed the name of his railway to the Columbia & Western, with an announced intention of building all the way to Penticton. He did this via a connecting line from Trail to Robson. In 1898 the railway—and its land grants—were sold to Canadian Pacific. The line was converted to standard gauge and was extended to Midway by the end of the century. It was incorporated into Canadian Pacific's evolving southern main line and the Kettle Valley Railway (see page 94).

Columbia & Western land grants, which Canadian Pacific would inherit and add to those of the Columbia & Kootenay and British Columbia Southern, amounted to 1.35 million acres (546,000 ha). The Columbia & Kootenay received a grant of 188,593 acres (76,323 ha).

Heinze's railway was not without competition. The Rossland mines were proving so valuable that American railway builder Daniel Corbin decided to connect them with his Spokane Falls & Northern line just across the border. Since he already had the line to Nelson (the Nelson & Fort Sheppard), it was just a matter of building a relatively short spur from Northport, Washington. This was his Red Mountain Railway, built, like the Columbia & Western, during 1896. Although the line was only about 25 km long, the terrain was difficult and Corbin had much the same difficulty accessing Rossland from the south and west as Heinze had had from the east. Corbin harassed Heinze when he could, suing him at one point for incursions onto his Nelson & Fort Sheppard land grant.

Above.
A Red Mountain Railway passenger train, the railway by then admittedly part of the Great Northern, runs downhill across a trestle at Little Sheep Crossing just west of Rossland. This is a later photo, dating from about 1920.

Below.
A map published in 1897 shows the hairpin bends and switchbacked route of the Columbia & Western Railway, here still named the *Trail Creek Tramway*. Note the additional switchbacks approaching *Trail*, where the bench of the Columbia River had to be negotiated. The also difficult path of the Red Mountain Railway (not named on this map segment) is at left. The region is littered with mineral claims and the platted square of *Rossland* township is shown.

Above.
About 1910, a Columbia & Western (Canadian Pacific) ore train on the tail track at Tiger, at the bottom of the switchback on Rossland Hill. Trains were required to stop here to cool their brakes and wheels and the photographer clearly took advantage of that stop. Note the wooden ore cars.

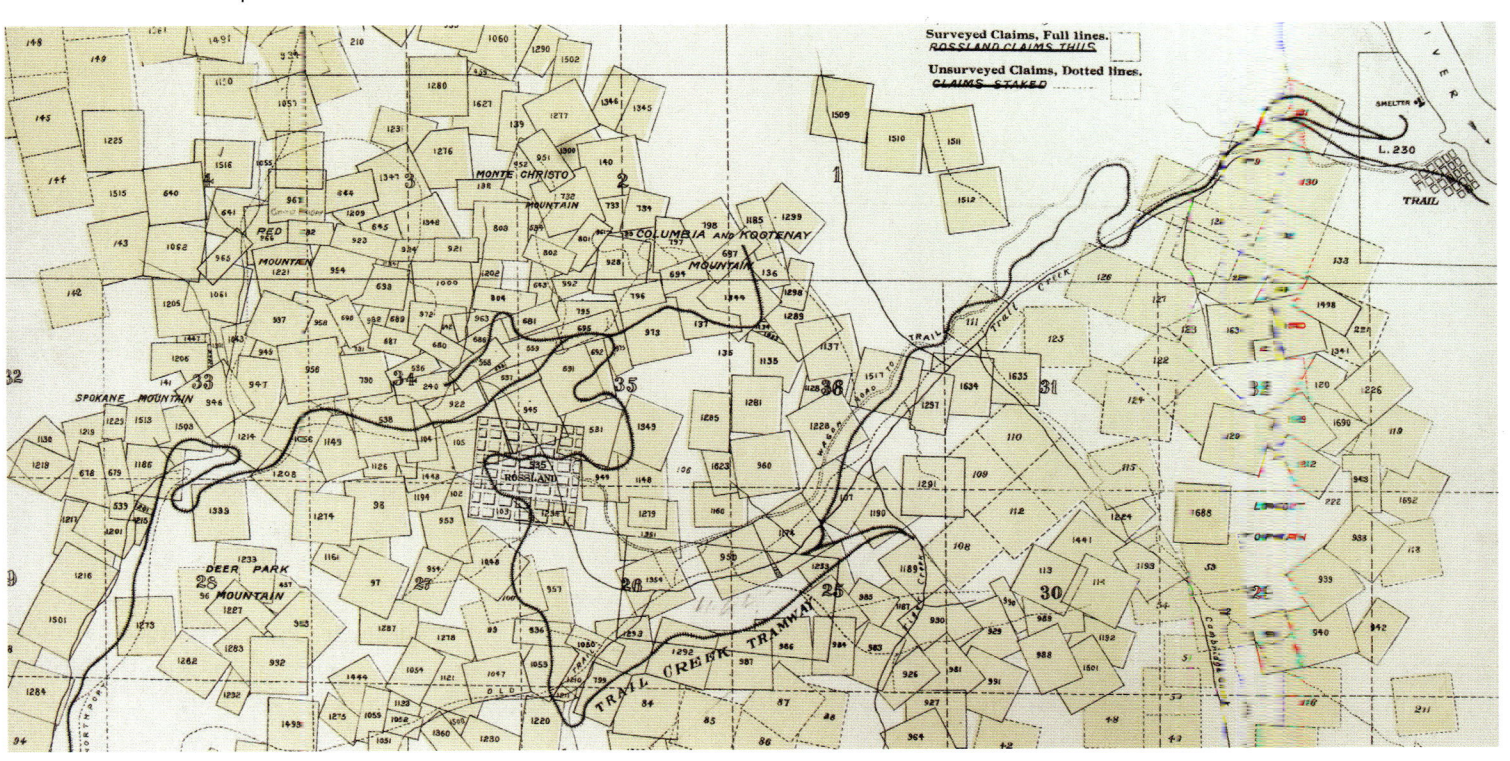

ACCESSING THE INTERIOR'S MINERAL WEALTH 63

Above.
A Columbia & Western (Canadian Pacific) ore train posing before leaving Rossland for Trail about 1910. The buildings above the train are the Centre Star Mine.

Above.
A Red Mountain Railway (Great Northern) passenger train sits at Rossland station, about 1920, ready to depart for Northport and Spokane.

The dominion government did not like to see American incursions into Canada any more than Canadian Pacific did, and with an agreement signed in September 1897 the railway gained subsidies and other concessions in return for building a southern line and agreeing to the "Crow Rate," whereby farmers' grain would be shipped east at reduced rates. Canadian Pacific acquired the charter of the British Columbia Southern Railway, which ran from the Alberta boundary in the rich coal-mining area of the Crowsnest Pass all the way to the southern end of Kootenay Lake, where it could tie in to lake steamers to Nelson. The Crow's Nest & Kootenay Lake Railway had been incorporated in 1888 and awarded large land grants, but had not begun construction, partly because of a lack of investor interest following a recession in 1893. The British Columbia Southern was created in 1894, and it was this company the Canadian Pacific purchased in 1897.

Canadian Pacific thus gained a federal subsidy of $11,000 per mile and a provincial grant of 20,000 acres per mile (5,029 ha per km). The railway was completed the following year. A short branch to Kimberley was opened in 1899.

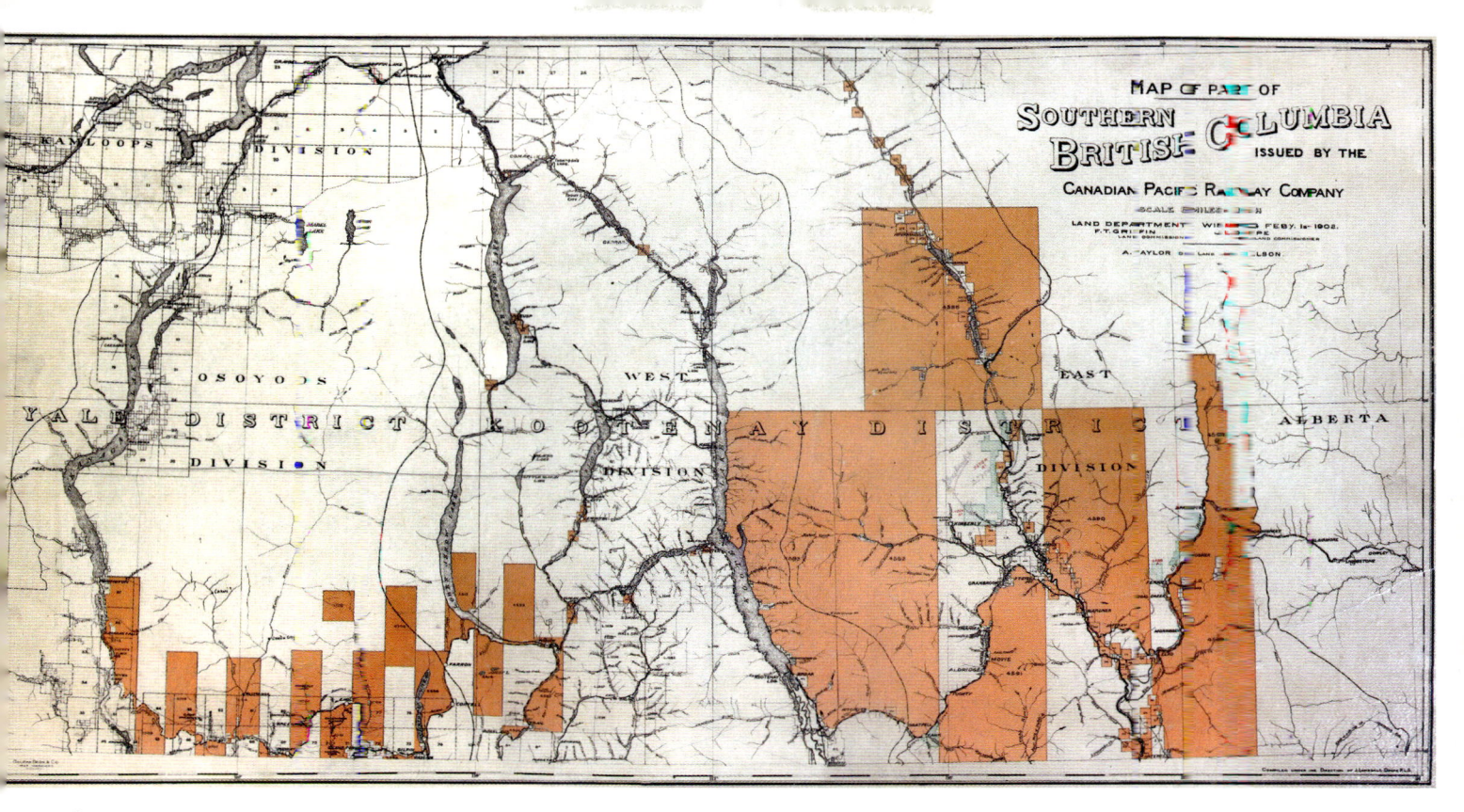

Above.
In 1902 the CPR's lands department produced this map summarizing (in orange) all the land grants the company had been awarded or inherited in southern British Columbia. Roughly speaking, the land tracts on the west part of the map are those of the Columbia & Western, and those in the central part the Columbia & Kootenay; the large eastern tract came with the Crow's Nest & Kootenay Lake and British Columbia Southern. The map is a generalization that does not show many details, but it covers a huge area. The line of the railway west of Midway was eventually incorporated into the Kettle Valley Railway and did not follow the path shown on this map (it was routed up the valley of the Kettle River).

Below right.
The Boundary and Phoenix-area railways, shown on a map dating from 1914. The Columbia & Western (Canadian Pacific) line enters *Grand Forks* from the east, then runs north, past a branch to *Granby*, where there was a copper smelter. At the peak of the "arc," is *Eholt*, a busy junction from where the branch to *Phoenix* leaves the main line. The Canadian Pacific line then continues west to *Greenwood* and *Midway*, where it joined the Kettle Valley Railway (see page 94). The Great Northern line entered Canada at Laurier, a little east of this map, and ran along the boundary until, south of *Grand Forks*, it shot north to *Weston*. From there it reached *Phoenix* by a very circuitous route, even crossing the Canadian Pacific line (just south of *Denoro*), completely encircling the town before reaching it.

Another emerging mining area at this time was along the Boundary, and in particular at a place named Phoenix. The location, northeast of Greenwood and south of Eholt (both are on the map *right*), is difficult to find now because it has completely vanished, having been finished off by open-pit mining in the 1960s and 1970s. But at the turn of the twentieth century the region was a hub of mining activity, principally for copper.

Canadian Pacific completed a tortuous branch into Phoenix in May 1900, and the Great Northern–controlled Vancouver, Victoria & Eastern (VV&E) followed suit four years later. Like Rossland, both lines had difficult access because of the topography, though the Great Northern had lower grades resulting from a circuitous path, as the map at *right* shows.

ACCESSING THE INTERIOR'S MINERAL WEALTH   65

Above. Charles McKinnon Campbell, the Phoenix mine superintendent, took this photograph of the first ore train ready to leave in 1900. Note the wooden ore cars, and the scene of total devastation in the foreground.

Below. Sharp curves, steep grades and heavy loads sometimes led to derailments. Here, in another excellent photo by Charles McKinnon Campbell, an accident is being cleared up.

Copper ore was shipped from Phoenix via the Canadian Pacific line to a smelter that was built at Granby. By 1903 open-pit mining was being carried out because the deposits were near the surface; this was one of the first uses of this method of mining in the province. The mine closed in 1919, following the First World War, but in 1959 lived up to its name and opened again; this time mining erased all vestiges of the town.

A 230 km line between Golden and Fort Steele was chartered as the Kootenay Central Railway in 1901, though nothing was done until Canadian Pacific leased the line in 1910 and began construction. It was completed in 1914. A sleepy branch line for most of its life, it was principally built to shut out any possible competition. However, the Kootenay Central line gained critical importance in the late 1960s when it was upgraded to allow coal unit trains to run from the Elk Valley coal mines to the coast via the Canadian Pacific main line (see page 156).

Above.
Colvalli, a station at the southern end of the Kootenay Central Railway, probably sometime in the 1920s.

66   IRON ROAD WEST

Above.
Another Charles McKinnon Campbell photo. An ore train, pulled by a Shay locomotive well able to negotiate the tight curves of the branch line, is ready to leave Phoenix for the Granby smelter.

Right.
The busy Canadian Pacific junction at Eholt. At least four locomotives are in the photo. The branch to Phoenix is off to the left.

Below.
The same place today. The busy junction has been reduced to a mere pile of rubble.

ACCESSING THE INTERIOR'S MINERAL WEALTH 67

A Railway to Gold

Any consideration of railways in British Columbia has to include the White Pass & Yukon Railway (WP&YR), later the White Pass & Yukon Route, because it runs through the extreme northwestern tip of the province, despite the fact that it originates at Skagway, in Alaska, and terminates at Whitehorse, in Yukon Territory.

When gold was discovered in the Klondike area of the Yukon in 1897, it was excruciatingly difficult to get there. It required either a steep climb followed by a long overland trek or a hazardous sea voyage to the mouth of the Yukon River followed by a riverboat voyage up the river to Dawson City, the whole expedition taking about six weeks; even this could only be done in the summer months.

Clearly there was a demand for a railway, but the difficulties involved in building it meant that by the time it was finished the gold rush was essentially over. But built it was. The White Pass & Yukon Railway Company, financed by British investors, bought out the interests of another company that had begun construction, and two others. Three charters were required, one for the United States, one for British Columbia, and another for the Yukon. In British Columbia the company was officially the British Columbia Yukon Railway Company.

There were no reliable maps of the region at the time, so several surveying parties were sent out to find a route to Lake Bennett. Even the location of the US–Canada border was undefined and disputed. From five surveys, the route over the White Pass was selected as being the path of least resistance.

Construction began in April 1898 with the laying of track down the main street of Skagway. The construction work was carried out by Michael James Heney, an Irish contractor who earned his reputation building the WP&YR. The track was 3-foot narrow gauge, which allowed much tighter curves than would have been possible using standard gauge. But it also allowed for more hair-raising trackbed along the sides of sheer cliffs, as can be seen in the photo on this page. Heney had major issues just keeping his workforce intact, as men were easily tempted by the prospect of gold just over the mountains. Even cargo space on ships coming north was at a premium.

In February 1899 the track reached the summit of the White Pass after a tortuous climb out of the port of Skagway, and Lake Bennett was reached by July that year. Here gold seekers could transfer to steamboats that had been hastily built at lakeside. That got them a good part of the way to the goldfields, though they were still on their own for a long distance.

Left.
A White Pass & Yukon Railway train on some of the first railbed, here on a shelf straight out from bare rock and supported on spindly-looking legs.

Right.
An attractive map of the *White Pass & Yukon Route*. The short Atlin Southern line from *Taku City* (see page 71) is also shown, highlighted in red. The map was a promotional one and was part of a set published in 1919.

Right, inset, top right.
A White Pass & Yukon train at Bennett, BC, about 1905. By this time the town had been bypassed and the buildings were derelict.

Right, inset, top left.
One of the first locomotives of the WP&YR, No. 52, built in 1881 and acquired by the WP&YR in 1898, on display at Skagway along with a large rotary snowplow.

Right, inset, bottom.
The first locomotive of the White Pass & Yukon Railway. It arrived in July 1898 (and is here photographed at that time in Skagway). Originally built in 1881, it had been purchased from the Utah & Northern Railway, and worked on the WP&YR until 1940, a remarkably long working life.

A RAILWAY TO GOLD   69

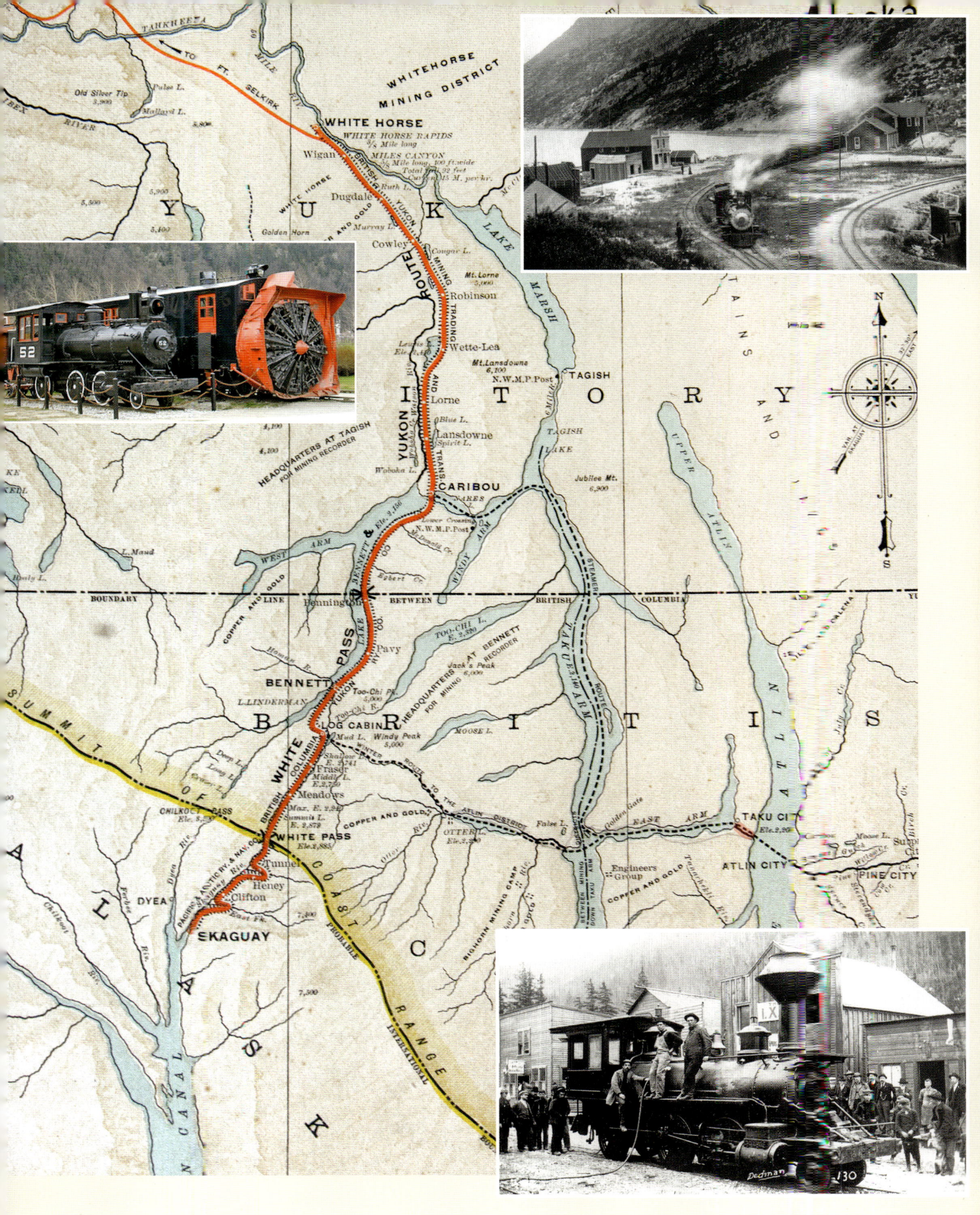

Left.
The railway at first made its way to the summit of White Pass using a series of switchbacks. This is one near the summit. It was used until a steel bridge was completed in 1901.

Below.
A scene at Bennett, on the lake of the same name, in 1899. Steamers *Clifford Sifton* (named after Canada's minister of the interior, responsible for encouraging western settlement) and *Gleaner* are docked and a WP&YR train is in the foreground. For a brief period in 1899, while the railway was complete to Bennett and until it was completed through to Carcoss, freight and passengers were transshipped here.

Track reached the 2,885-foot (880-metre) summit of White Pass 32 km from Skagway, in February 1899, Bennett in July, and a year later, with crews working north from both Bennett and Carcross, Whitehorse was reached and the line completed on 29 July 1900. The entire 177 km line had been built in 27 months, a remarkable achievement given the extreme topography. However, many improvements were still required, such as bridge building and switchback removal.

Although it had originally been intended that the line would terminate farther north at Fort Selkirk, this objective was abandoned, largely because of the decline of the gold rush. The railway proved useful, however, though it was always marginally economical. During the Second World War it was taken over by the US military to help with the building of the Alaska Highway. In the 1950s it pioneered the use of containers on trains and ships (see page 152). It is now a heritage railway (see page 198).

After the WP&YR was finished, another (as it turned out, much more minor) gold rush occurred in an area just east of Atlin, called Pine City. To allow miners to get to this new region more easily, a group of provincial investors financed the Atlin Short Line & Navigation Company and built a 4 km line across a neck of land, connecting steamboats from Caribou, on the WP&YR, with steamboats across Atlin Lake to Atlin. The line opened, using horse-powered traction, in June 1899. A year later, the WP&YR took over the company and shipped in *Duchess*, a locomotive built in 1878 and previously working in the coal-mining area of Nanaimo (see page 13). Steam-hauled service began in July 1900. The train, dubbed the Taku Tram, ran for twenty years, and the locomotive still exists, on display in Carcross, Yukon (see photo *page 199*).

Right, top.
The first train to White Pass Summit, February 1899, clearly posed for the photographer.

Right, centre top.
Taku Tram locomotive *Duchess* at the northern terminus of the Atlin Southern Railway about 1909.

Right, centre bottom.
Duchess pulling an unusually large load, which looks like a portable building of some kind.

Right, bottom.
The Taku Tram as it normally ran, a one-coach train with ex-Nanaimo locomotive *Duchess*.

Interurban and City

On the muddy, uneven, horse-dung-strewn streets of early Vancouver, a smooth and clean alternative was sure to find favour. The electric streetcar era was already underway when Vancouver was created in 1886. Victoria and Vancouver built streetcar systems in 1890, with New Westminster following a year later.

The Vancouver Electric Railway & Light Company began laying track in 1889, and streetcars began running on 27 June 1891. The company soon extended its network, lured by the promise of profits from land. Canadian Pacific gave the company 68 lots in Fairview to bring tracks to that area.

Victoria began running streetcars in February 1890. The National Electric Tramway & Lighting Company began operating an 8 km system, extending the lines to Esquimalt in October that year.

New Westminster began work on streetcar systems in 1891. One company built within the city and another laid track between Vancouver and New Westminster. The two amalgamated in 1891 as the Westminster & Vancouver Tramway Company, and service between Vancouver and New Westminster began on 8 October 1891. Initial promise did not hold, however, and with the onset of a recession that lasted from 1892 to 1897, all the companies failed. In 1897 a new company, the British Columbia Electric Railway Company (BCER), either purchased the assets or took over all the others.

In the Interior, Nelson was the only city to acquire streetcars. Here the Nelson Electric Tramway Company, financed by the British Electric Traction Company, began service in 1899. Service lasted until 1949.

BCER found that its streetcars had the ability to stimulate urban growth like nothing else; lay down a track and development seemed sure to follow. This was particularly the case in the years before the First World War in 1914, and lines extended into Vancouver, Point Grey (incorporated 1908), South Vancouver (1891) and Burnaby (1892). The line from Vancouver to New Westminster was in fact one of the final impetuses for the creation of the latter municipality.

In 1905 BCER added a line to Steveston, leasing existing tracks from Canadian Pacific, and in 1907 BCER added 8 km of lines in North Vancouver, despite the fact that it was not at the time connected to Vancouver. A line ran down Lonsdale Avenue to meet the ferry to Vancouver. On the streetcar one could then penetrate the tree stump–covered wilds of the Lynn Valley, where, of course, real estate agents were hard at work trying to sell lots. Another line from Vancouver to New Westminster, the Burnaby Lake line (part of which, south of Burnaby Lake, ran where Highway 1 is today) opened in 1911 and lasted until 1953.

The Vancouver to New Westminster lines operated essentially as long streetcar routes. BCER developed into more of a railway in 1910, when on 3 October that year the company opened a line all the way up the Fraser Valley to Chilliwack, using the

Above.
Interurban car No. 1207 was built in 1905 and worked on the line to Steveston. It worked for some years in preservation along the south side of False Creek before being relocated to the Fraser Valley Heritage Railway, in Cloverdale, in 2016.

Below, left.
Streetcars on the Vancouver to New Westminster line, in a photo taken in 1892 near today's Central Park in Burnaby. The line was essentially built through the wilderness and would encourage settlement all along it and particularly near where stations had been established.

Below, right.
A streetcar in Esquimalt. The photo was taken about 1893.

Right.
A Vancouver streetcar in a photo taken about 1900. Note the "cowcatcher" at front, designed to catch anyone who fell in front of the streetcar and scoop them up.

Below.
A streetcar on the Kitsilano line on 4th Avenue at Waterloo Street in 1909, the year the line opened. The streetcar drove urban growth. Soon houses and businesses would appear along the line, taking advantage of the mobility the streetcar endowed. Clearly BCER was confident growth would soon follow, as the company laid down two tracks. The photo was taken by James Quiney, a real estate agent, whose sign is prominent at right. Note also the arc streetlight.

Right.
Jitneys seem to be crowding out the streetcars in this view of Hastings Street from a postcard from about 1914. Jitneys were private automobiles that plied streetcar routes, typically just ahead of streetcars, and picked up passengers waiting for the streetcar. They carried route signs similar to those on the streetcars. With no overhead they could be more profitable than a railway. They became a serious threat to streetcar operation and were legislated out of existence in 1918. Despite this, they demonstrated to the public the availability and flexibility of cars.

INTERURBAN AND CITY   73

Above, top.
No. 1304 in service on the Fraser Valley line about 1948. The 1911-built car had been converted to a luxury carriage in 1912 for the use of the Duke of Connaught, the governor general, who was touring British Columbia, and became known as the Connaught car. The photo *above, inset*, shows a scene during the governor general's tour. The original livery was green and cream. No. 1304 was reconverted for regular use after the duke left, but in 1945 was gutted by fire. Rebuilt once again, it spent five more years in service on the valley line. No. 1304 appears to have been the last interurban to run in service in the Fraser Valley, deadheading back to New Westminster on 1 October 1950 at 2:15 in the morning. One of a few survivors, it has recently been restored by the Fraser Valley Heritage Railway and once more sports gleaming red paintwork (see *pages 76* and *192*).

Below.
An attractive perspective view of the BCER network, published in 1913 and intended for tourists. The central feature is the 103 km Fraser Valley line.

New Westminster Bridge, conveniently built by the province in 1904 and open to all. Like the Burnaby Lake line, the Fraser Valley line was built using the charter of the Vancouver, Fraser Valley & Southern Railway, incorporated in June 1906. The bridge and this interurban line opened up the valley to settlement and allowed farmers to sell fresh produce and milk in Vancouver daily. Here trains consisted of multiple cars; often there was a driving car, one or two more passenger cars and a baggage car for all the local freight. The 103 km line brought not only mobility but also electricity to the valley.

The service lasted for forty years, but by 1950 BCER had determined to replace it with buses, placating many of the municipalities with $40,000 or $50,000 to spend on road maintenance for roads that were to become bus routes. It was, as we know with hindsight, a ridiculously short-sighted decision. Service was temporarily reactivated in March 1951—using diesel locomotives—when buses could not get through deep snow, yet the obvious warning was not heeded. The line remains, used by the Southern Railway of British Columbia after many years as the BC Hydro Railway (see page 178).

Passenger service to Steveston lasted another eight years, with the last train running on the night of 27–28 February 1958. By that time streetcars had been gone for three years, so this represented the passing of an era. That track also remains but is used only very occasionally. And much of the route between Vancouver and New Westminster is now used by the elevated tracks of SkyTrain (see page 176).

BIRD'S-EYE VIEW OF COUNTRY COVERED BY B. C. ELECTRIC RAILWAY SYSTEM

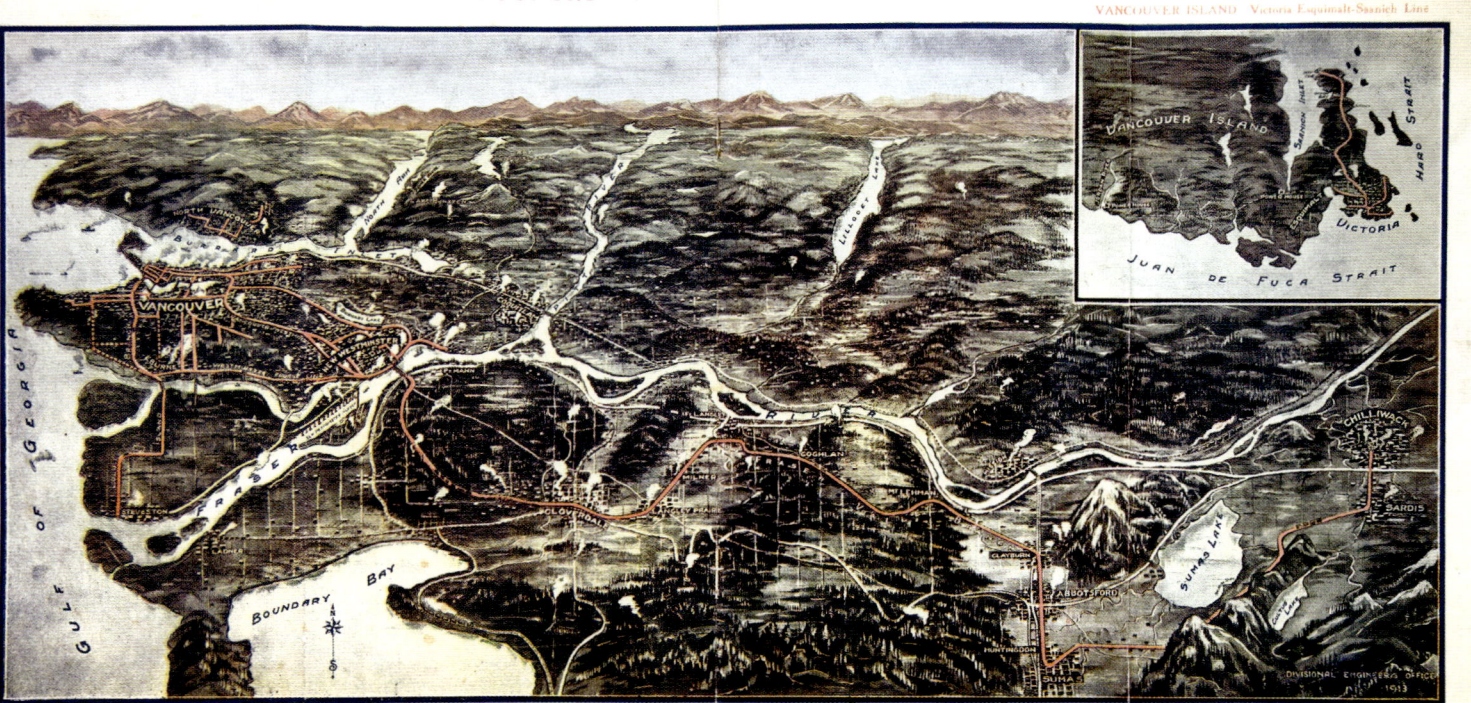

MAINLAND LINES—Vancouver, South Vancouver, Point Grey, North Vancouver, New Westminster. Vancouver and Chilliwack. Vancouver and New Westminster (3 lines). Vancouver and Steveston.

Above.
On the night before 3 October 1910, the opening day for the BCER line to Chilliwack, a storm knocked a power pole down across the line, cutting off the electricity. This forced BCER to tow the first train, with the lieutenant-governor and BC premier Richard McBride on board, the last few miles into Chilliwack with a steam locomotive. This rather grainy photograph taken by a spectator recorded the scene; one suspects that the company was not so keen to have the situation recorded. The photo makes an intriguing comparison with the photo, *overleaf*, of another steam locomotive pulling electric streetcars, taken forty years later.

Below.
In this classic interurban view, No. 1700 heads a train of four cars as it arrives at Sullivan station, at 64 Ave. and 152 St. in Surrey, in 1923. One of the strengths of this kind of transportation over buses and the like is the ability to multiply the carrying capacity instantly by simply adding more cars to the train.

Above.
BCER Interurban No. 1402 was heading for Vancouver in this photo likely taken in 1950 as the service was about to be axed.

INTERURBAN AND CITY 75

Above.
A BCER electric freight locomotive with a unique octagonal cab that must have been excellent for visibility. It was built by the company shops in New Westminster in 1907. The photo was taken three years later, likely on the new line to Chilliwack; the ballasting and ties of the trackbed look as though they have just been laid.

Above. Decorated with appropriate period bunting, a restored interurban car No. 1304 arrives at the Fraser Valley Heritage Railway's Cloverdale station on 9 September 2017.

Above.
Streetcars form the predominant traffic on the Connaught (Cambie) Bridge over False Creek in August 1916. This was the second bridge in this location, built in 1911. The bridge lasted longer than the streetcars; it was replaced by the present Cambie Bridge in 1985.

Right. The BCER Fraser Valley interurban line (left to right) crosses the CP line from Mission to Huntingdon and Sumas with a rare diamond crossing. The hut, now at the Fraser Valley Heritage Railway, contained manual interlocking controls, set and then reset by BCER crew from the front and rear of the train, respectively.

76 IRON ROAD WEST

Above.
Daily collection of milk from Fraser Valley farms for transport into Vancouver was an important function of the interurbans. Here two BCER freight cars pose with a collection of milk churns probably sometime in the 1920s. The milk train ran until 1939.

Below.
A sad photo indeed. In this 1950 scene Canadian Pacific No. 3460 drags a line of streetcars through the Drake Street yards to their doom. They will all likely be stripped of metal parts and then burned, though a few "lucky" ones may be sold to be used as cabins for recreational use. Or perhaps that is sadder still?

A Railway to the Orient

First Through Train Prince Rupert BC...

Above.
The first GTPR through train—suitably decorated with a Union Jack on the locomotive tender—arrived in Prince Rupert on 9 April 1914. The last spike had been driven two days earlier, 46 km west of Vanderhoof.

One of the routes to the Pacific surveyed by Sandford Fleming for the government's Canadian Pacific Railway in the 1870s was a northerly route via the Yellowhead Pass to the Skeena River valley (see map, *page 15*). The advantages of this route were that the grades over the Yellowhead were much gentler than Canadian Pacific's, even after the construction of the Spiral Tunnels in 1909. The CPR grades of 2.2 per cent would compare with Grand Trunk Pacific Railway (GTPR) grades, using the Yellowhead route, of 0.4 per cent eastbound and 0.5 per cent westbound. GTPR grades would in fact be considerably lower than any of the transcontinentals at the time, including the Great Northern.

The other advantage of this route over all transcontinentals was that the Pacific terminus was nearer to Asian markets by about 600 km, a significant saving for ships in time and coal. The disadvantage, of course, was that any northern terminus would be starting from scratch, with no existing business to tap, although the potential for lucrative land sales was higher.

An earlier northern transcontinental scheme had foundered. This was the Trans-Canada Railway, proposed by Quebec interests in 1895 and intended to develop the northern part of the province; the plan extended track west to Port Simpson on the British Columbia coast by 1902 and was then also intended to develop the northern part of the Prairies, the latter a goal of the prime minister, Wilfrid Laurier.

This project was sidelined by an equally grand scheme of the Grand Trunk Railway (GTR), an eastern railway controlled in London. The company's president, Charles Melville Hays, thought that the railway would pay for itself and be a long-term profitable venture, by virtue of land sales from hoped-for land grants and subsidies, and as a fast land bridge between eastern Canada and even Britain and Asia. The GTR was not interested in the eastern part of the line, however, and because this was critical to Laurier, whose main support came from Quebec, he agreed that the dominion government would build that portion, between Winnipeg and Moncton, as the National Transcontinental Railway, connecting at Winnipeg with the GTPR. The dominion government agreed to loan the money for the western section to the GTR. The Grand Trunk Pacific was incorporated as a subsidiary of the GTR in 1903, and construction began from the east in 1905 and from the west in 1908.

Port Simpson, near the Alaska–British Columbia boundary, was the original choice for a Pacific terminus, but after the Klondike gold rush of 1897–98 tensions had been rising between Canada and the United States and Laurier wanted a terminus farther away from the boundary for strategic reasons. As it happened, the boundary dispute was settled in 1903, but by then Hays had found a better location for his terminus—Kaien Island, about 30 km south of Port Simpson. He had the harbour there checked out by a harbour engineer who gave it a glowing report. An island offered the possibility of ridding the railway

78 IRON ROAD WEST

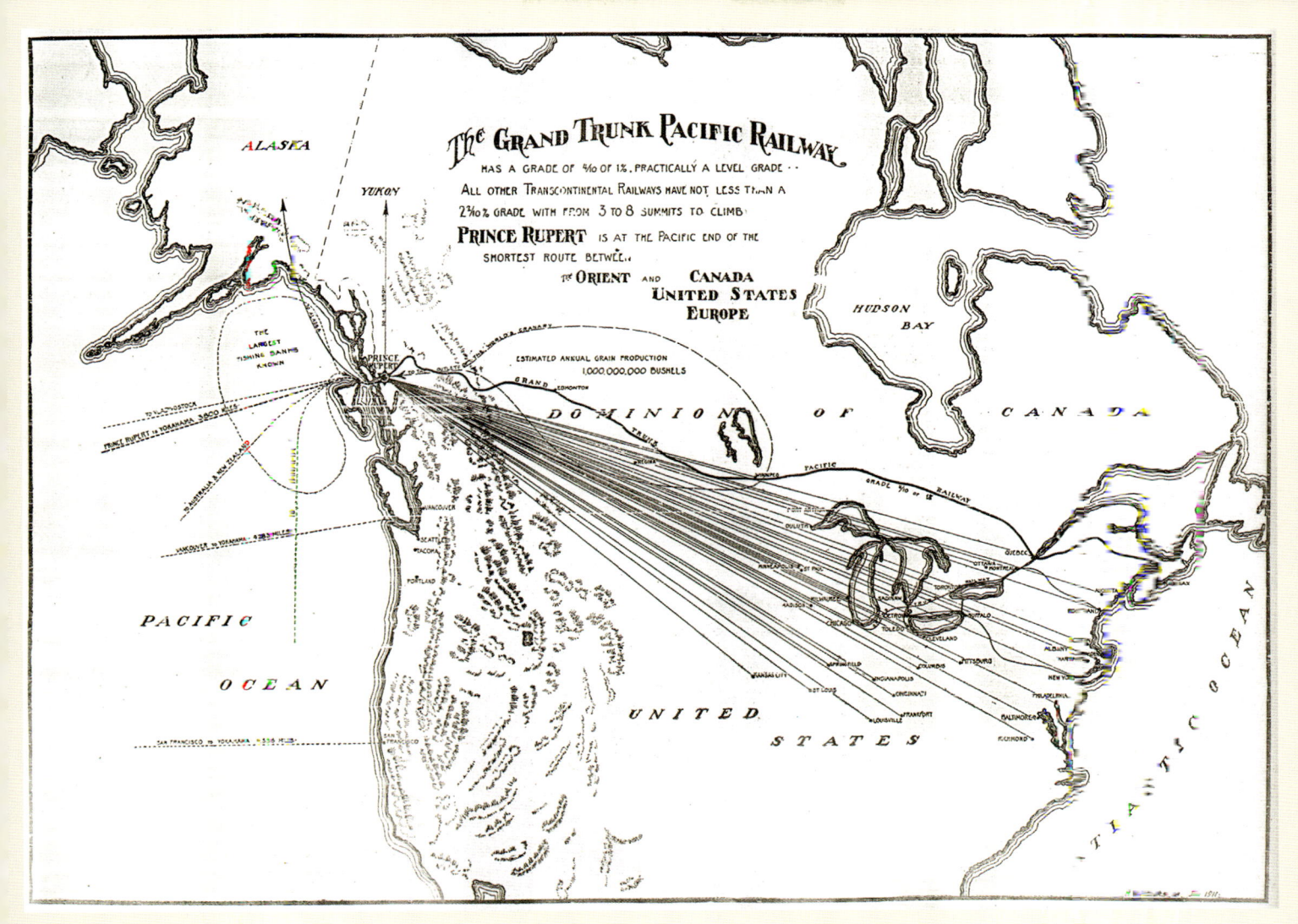

Above.
This promotional map appeared in the *Prince Rupert Journal* on 4 July 1911 and shows the city's location as the epicentre of much of North America. Prince Rupert is shown between *The Largest Fishing Banks Known* and a prairie with *Estimated Annual Grain Production 1,000,000,000 Bushels*. The shipping distance to Yokohama, Japan, is given, with equivalent, but longer distances from Vancouver and San Francisco for comparison. The fact that shipping distance to Japan from the eastern US cities shown would be less if routed though the Union Pacific and San Francisco is, of course, not mentioned. The GTPR had an advantage for shippers in Canada, but not so much for Americans. The map also highlights the high standard of construction of the line, the low grades being a deliberate feature of the GTPR to make it more economical to run than its main competitor, Canadian Pacific. These standards created high construction costs that the railway was never able to recoup.

Right.
By the time the Grand Trunk Pacific was built, mechanization had come a long way from the pick-and-shovel era, though the latter were still extensively used. This is a Pioneer tracklaying machine in operation on the GTPR in 1912. Popularly known as a "praying mantis," it swung rails into position using a system of arms and pulleys and was capable of laying 5 km of track per day.

A RAILWAY TO THE ORIENT

Above.

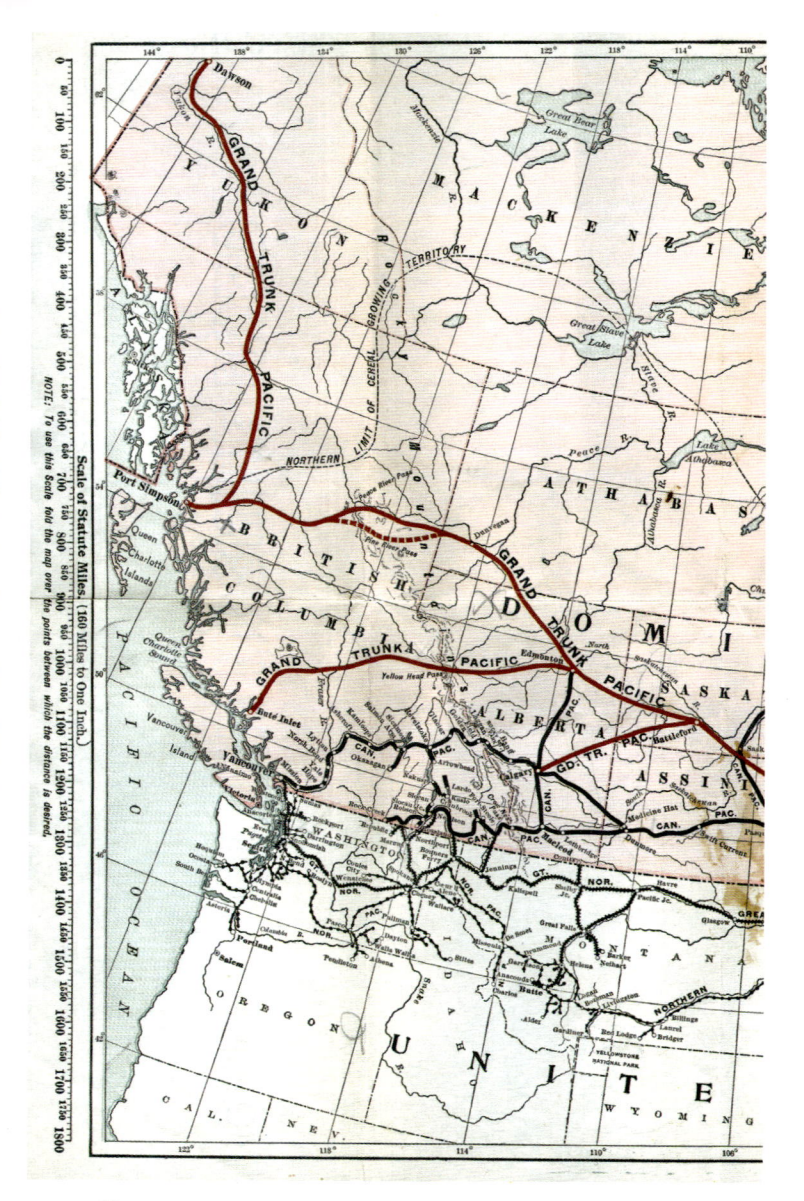

The Grand Trunk Pacific's view of western Canada shown on a 1903 map, complete with all the competing railways of the period. This shows not only the line to the originally planned terminus of Port Simpson, but also another to Bute Inlet along another of the routes surveyed by Sandford Fleming for the government's Canadian Pacific. Also shown is a branch north to Dawson, the notion being that this could serve the gold rush area of the Klondike; indeed, there were several charters that likely could have been acquired to build this line. However, the gold rush had been and gone before the GTPR began construction.

of a problem it usually faced—that of land speculators trying to figure out ahead of time where the railway would run and where it would put stations or divisional points. (By 1914, 520,000 hectares of land contiguous to the railway location was held by real estate speculators.) If the railway could control most of the island, the land speculators would be shut out.

The process by which this was achieved is convoluted and complex and later (1906) led to an investigation by the legislative assembly into its propriety. Acting through a contractor, in 1904 the GTPR acquired a Crown grant for 10,000 acres (4,046 ha) for a payment of only $10,000. Some of the waterfront and townsite was reserved for the province. Another 3,200 acres (1,295 ha) of Crown grant land was obtained by the contractor and split with the GTPR.

Two years later the railway obtained more land from an Indian reserve, which covered more of Kaien Island and most of Digby Island (site of the container transshipment port today). The purchase involved more negotiations with the dominion and provincial governments, the latter necessary because Indian reserve land that was taken out of reserve reverted to the province. After initially refusing to agree to the purchase, the province was persuaded by the promise of one-quarter of the land and $2.50 per acre. The agreement was passed by the legislature in March 1908. The total size of the GTPR's land holdings at the Pacific terminus was larger than that acquired in Vancouver by Canadian Pacific in 1886.

The GTPR had also agreed to begin construction from the Pacific end, working eastward, and a start was made in May 1908, three years after work had begun from the other end. Foley, Welch & Stewart were contracted to build the railway. Progress along the Skeena River valley was slow because there was no room for a railway at the river's edge; ledges had to be blasted to provide a path. Sternwheelers delivering wood and other supplies had in many places to be winched up the river against a strong current. West of Hazelton the river runs between cliffs, and a narrow ledge for the railway required more extensive blasting. In the first 350 km from Prince Rupert there were 211 tunnels.

In the meantime, work progressed on clearing a townsite at Prince Rupert and constructing wharves where large coastal steamers could dock. Determined to outdo the Canadian Pacific in Vancouver, the GTPR hired a town planning company from Boston, Brett & Hall, to produce a model plan for the city laid out on the most modern principles. One of the owners of the firm was George D. Hall, who just happened to be Charles Hays's son-in-law. Nevertheless, the plan was a superb design based on the emerging "City Beautiful" movement, with circles and crescents and vistas, and was sensitive to the topography of the site. Prince Rupert benefits from this today. By early 1909 the townsite had been cleared and 2,400 lots staked. Sales began in Vancouver and Victoria in May, and by the end of the year the population had swelled to 3,000.

Progress on the railway, however, was slow. Labour shortages compounded the problems posed by the difficult topography. Not until July 1910 was a bridge completed to connect Kaien Island to the mainland. By June 1911 the first hundred miles (161 km) east from Prince Rupert had been completed, as far as Copper City (shown on the map, *pages 84–85*). The contracts were let in 100-mile sections, and this was the

Above.
The first GTPR locomotives to arrive in Prince Rupert came in 1910, not by rail but by sea, on a barge. Here two of them are being unloaded onto a temporary track connecting to the rails on the barge. The connection does not look very secure, but clearly the job was done.

Below.
The docks of the Grand Trunk Pacific Steamship Company, a railway subsidiary, at Prince Rupert in 1911. The company also built docks in Vancouver and Seattle. Plans to expand the coastal service into a trans-Pacific one never materialized. The docks at Seattle burned down in 1914.

Right.
One of the company's steamships, the SS *Prince George*, in Prince Rupert harbour in 1911.

Above.
The first hundred miles of track east from Prince Rupert were opened by the GTP with an inaugural train on 14 June 1911. This photograph shows a remarkably flat and straight stretch of track, no doubt chosen for its promotional value. The writing on the photo states that it is at Mile 33 (53 km) from Prince Rupert, but at that distance (about 1 km past the Khyex River) the track is tight on the bank of the Skeena River.

Above.
Another view of the inaugural train on 14 June 1911, this one of the rear of the train, stated to be at Mile 45 (72 km) from Prince Rupert.

first section. A special train was run to celebrate (photo, *above* and *left*). By the end of 1912 the track was near Hazelton, 285 km from the coast.

Faster progress had been made on the flatter land east of the Rocky Mountains, however. Track was laid across the Yellowhead Pass into British Columbia in November 1911. Tête Jaune Cache was reached by the end of 1912, and soon it became possible to supply the railhead from steamboats on the Upper Fraser River. There were four large bridges over the Fraser and twenty-eight smaller ones. Here the main construction issue was not rock blasting but creating a stable bed over what was called "gumbo," a gluey clay.

On 27 January 1914 rails were laid over a temporary bridge over the Fraser (so temporary that it was destroyed the next day by an ice jam) at what was then called Fort George, the original Hudson's Bay Company name that had been

82 IRON ROAD WEST

used by a land developer, George Hammond, for a large subdivision he had laid out just to the west of an Indian reserve next to the river. Of course, the GTPR wanted land sales in the new city for itself and outmanoeuvred Hammond by persuading the dominion government to sell the entire reserve to the railway. The $125,000 purchase took place in November 1911, and British Columbia's reversionary interest was gained by selling the province 200 acres (81 ha) of it for $59,296. The GTPR had been using the name Prince George for this townsite to differentiate it from Hammond's project, and this is what it became; the city was incorporated on 6 March 1915.

By June 1914 a steel bridge over the Fraser was complete and the first train crossed it on 12 June 1914 (photo, *overleaf*).

Rails from east and west finally met at a place often referred to as Finmoore, though no such place exists. It was near Fort Fraser, about 585 km east of Prince Rupert and 135 km west of Prince George. The last spike was driven, without a great deal of ceremony, on 7 April 1914. The National Transcontinen-

Below.
Construction near Prince George in 1913.

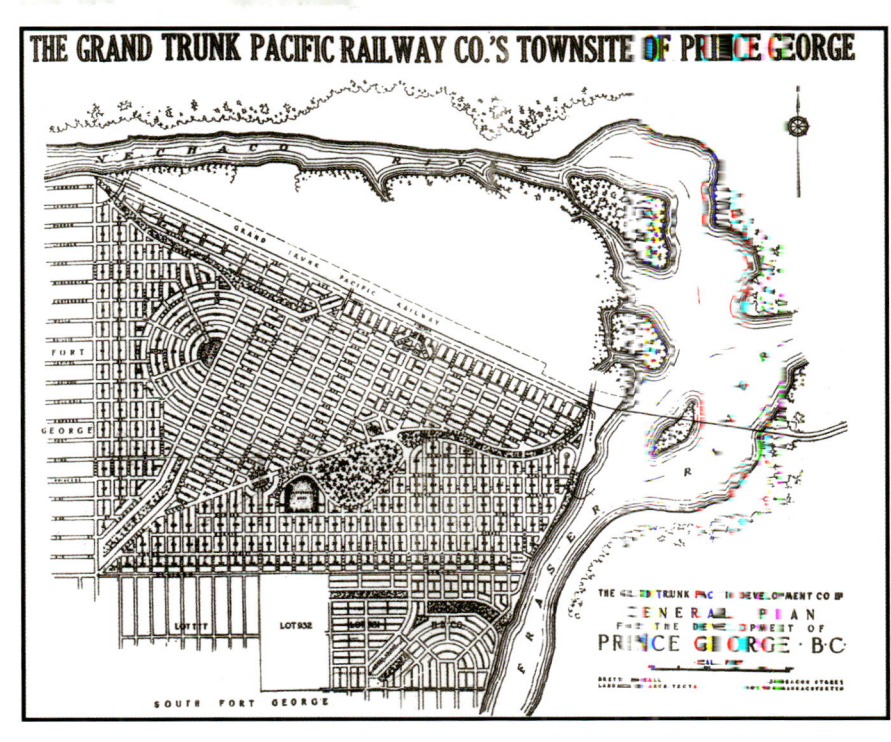

Above. The Grand Trunk Pacific engaged Brett & Hall, the same firm as had designed the Prince Rupert townsite, to lay out a grand plan for the major city Prince George was intended to become. This was the site on the Indian reserve purchased from the dominion government. The rail line crosses the *Fraser River* at right (site of the steel bridge) and the station and yards are along the northeast side of the subdivided area. Scattered in the subdivision, but not shown on this map, were the 25 per cent of lots to be given to the provincial government under an 1896 law on townsite development. It is thought that the crescents on the left were deliberately placed to prevent easy access to rival developer George Hammond's *Fort George*, at left.

Above.
The Fraser River rail bridge was built by the Grand Trunk Pacific Railway and completed in June 1914. It cost the railway $1.6 million and was considered a great engineering accomplishment. Here the first train to cross the bridge is seen entering Prince George on 12 June 1914. Pilings from the temporary wooden bridge, used until the steel one could be completed, can be seen in the foreground. The steel bridge is 810 m long, with a lift section in the middle that was hardly ever used as such; the bridge was declared a fixed span rather than a lift span in 1952.

Above.
This undated view of the railway station at Pacific, a divisional point 42 km east of Terrace (and named after the railway), emphasizes the "newly hacked from the forest" look. Pacific was 193 km east of Prince Rupert and was known first as Nicholl and is shown as such on the map, *right*. A roundhouse was built here in 1915.

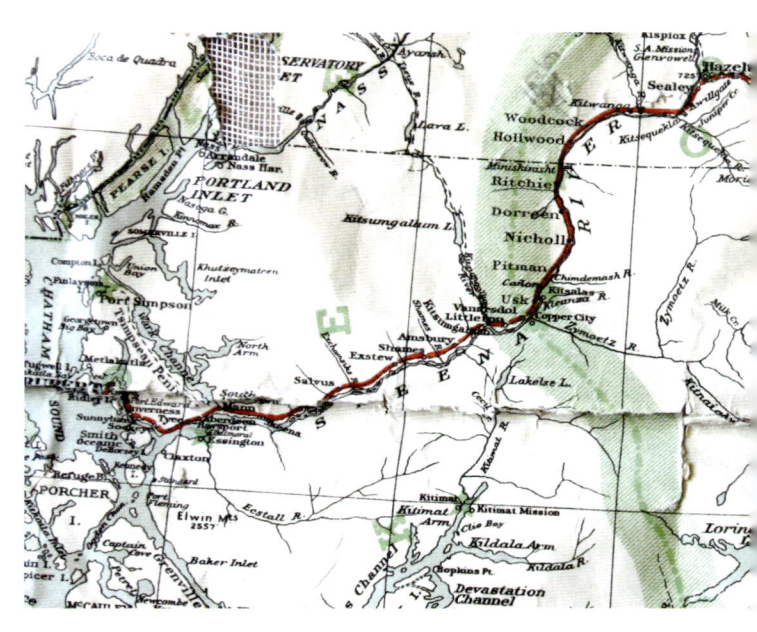

84　IRON ROAD WEST

Right.
A GTPR train headed by a sparkling No. 614 readies to leave Prince Rupert for Winnipeg in 1915. Compare with the photo on *page 78*.

tal line from Moncton to Winnipeg had been completed a few months before (except for the Quebec Bridge, which was being rebuilt after its first collapse), and so another true transcontinental railway came into existence. It was not until the following year, however, that a multitude of track deficiencies were rectified well enough to begin regular service.

Charles Hays was not there to see it, however. Returning from a consultation with Grand Trunk directors in London in 1912, he had the misfortune to embark on the *Titanic* for his return to Canada, and perished in that disaster along with hundreds of others.

The railway that had taken so long to plan and build did not last very long as a separate entity. The First World War began seven months after the last spike had been driven, and the revenue the railway had been counting on failed to materialize. British investment faded away, along with the projected traffic. The original agreement of the Grand Trunk Railway with the dominion government included the operation of the National Transcontinental in concert with the Grand Trunk Pacific. However, the cost of constructing that railway had proved to be so high that the GTP balked at the rental cost, which was to have been 3 per cent of the cost of construction.

The poor financial condition of the GTPR only got worse, and in 1915 the new president of the Grand Trunk, Alfred Smithers, asked the dominion government to take over the GTPR. In 1916 its rails through the Yellowhead Pass, which ran alongside those of the Canadian Northern, were ripped up, intended for shipment to France for use on railways to the front (though there is no evidence they were actually shipped) GTPR was given running rights on the adjacent Canadian Northern tracks. The latter were later moved onto the better-built ex-GTPR railbed.

By 1917 the GTPR owed $225 million. On 7 March 1919 the GTPR defaulted on loans due to be repaid to the dominion government and was nationalized. It was integrated into the government-owned Canadian National Railways in 1920.

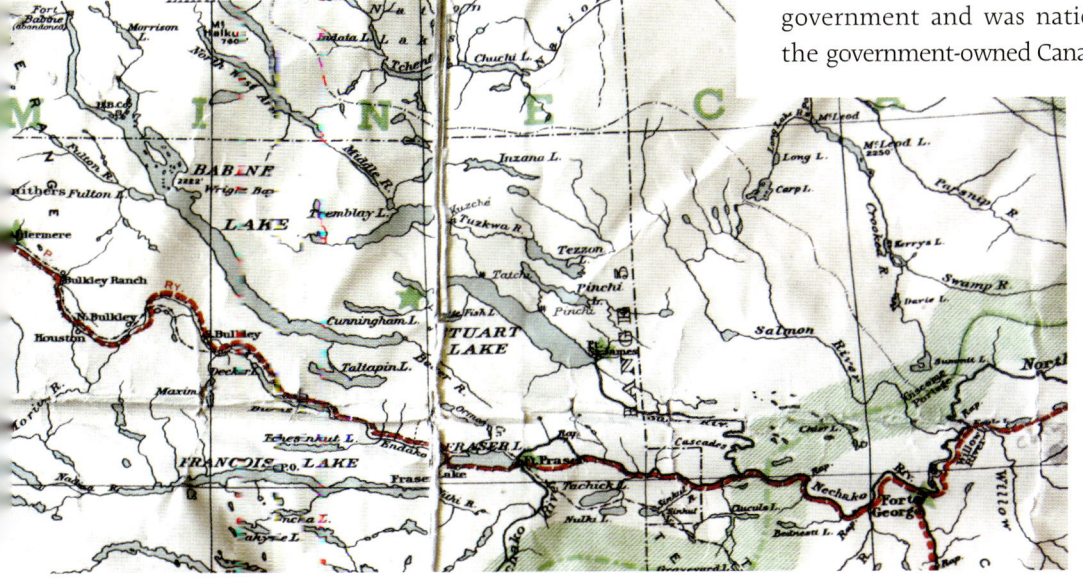

Left. This 1913 provincial lands department map with the GTPR route west of *Fort George* overprinted on it in red actually has name that date from about 1911. Fort George became Prince George, and Littleton became Terrace. The divisional point of Pacific, which now no longer exists, is shown on the map as Vedoll. Copper City, just east of Littleton Terrace, is on the map; this was the eastern limit of the first 100-mile contract, the completion of which is being celebrated by the trains shown on *page 87*. Note the railway south from Fort George. This is the Pacific Great Eastern Railway, a child of the GTPR (see page 102).

Promoting Railways

In the period from when the Canadian Pacific Railway arrived in British Columbia in 1886 to the beginning of the First World War in 1914, railways were seen as the essential engine of economic development, without which no city or town could survive. This was not far from the truth, for the province had few roads—and even fewer decent ones—and automobiles and trucks were either non-existent or highly unreliable; railways were the only way to move ore to smelter, trees to sawmill, and produce to the city.

And then there were the real estate promoters, who used the promise of a coming railway to sell land otherwise for the time being essentially worthless—and, of course, make a lot of money in the process.

In the period from 1882 to 1913 some 212 railways were provincially chartered, plus a few that were federally chartered, Canadian Pacific and the Grand Trunk Pacific being the most significant. A list of BC railway charters is included in Appendix 1, page 220.

From 1903 to 1915 British Columbia's premier was Richard McBride, who was a firm believer in railways as a means to encourage the economy, not to mention to make him more popular and re-electable. In a speech to the legislature on 20 February 1912, McBride pointed to 2,922 miles (4,675 km) of railways in the province that were "built or under contract," as compared with only 650 miles (1,040 km) of track existing in 1904. His "railway policy" amounted to aiding railway construction any way he could, which, he hoped, would add another 845 miles (1,352 km) of track very soon. Included in the latter figure was the whole of the planned Pacific Great Eastern (see page 102), "with an estimated length of 450 miles" (720 km). McBride found himself on the wrong side of popular opinion with the coming of the war, which ended the railway boom and lost many people a lot of money. McBride resigned as premier in 1915.

More roads, better roads and the advance of automobile technology, plus the availability of surplus vehicles after the war, meant that the railway boom had gone forever. In 1927 the provincial government passed the Defunct Railway Companies Dissolution Act, which revoked the charters of 133 companies that had never laid any track.

Above.
This is what every settlement that wished to call itself a town or city wanted: a railway link to the rest of the world. Port Alberni's moment came in December 1911, when the first train was a moment to savour and photograph for posterity. The city was incorporated in 1912 as a result of the railway's arrival.

Right.
In this 1908 newspaper cartoon BC premier Richard McBride contemplates building railways while Charles Melville Hayes (Hays) of the Grand Trunk Pacific and Thomas Shaughnessy of the Canadian Pacific peer over the Rocky Mountains. "Not much likelihood of those chaps building railways this side of the mountains," McBride says. "We should build our own."

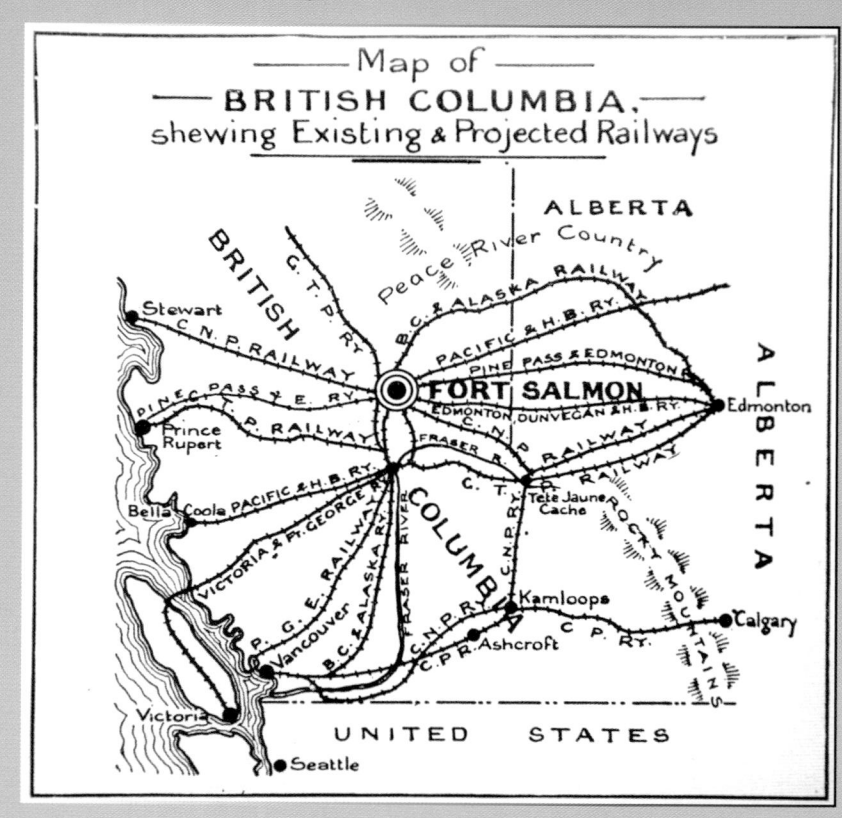

Left and *right, top.*
These two maps, one (*left*) published in December 1912, and the other (*right, top*) in May 1913, attempted to show all the railways built, under construction, or planned—many, in fact, no more than faint possibilities. The railways depicted just happened to focus on the publisher's real estate venture, one at *Fort Salmon*, a stillborn townsite just north of Prince George, and the other at *Fort George*, George Hammond's rival townsite immediately west and adjacent to the Grand Trunk Pacific's Prince George townsite (see map, *page 83*). Most of these railways can be found in the list of railway charters (Appendix 1, page 220).

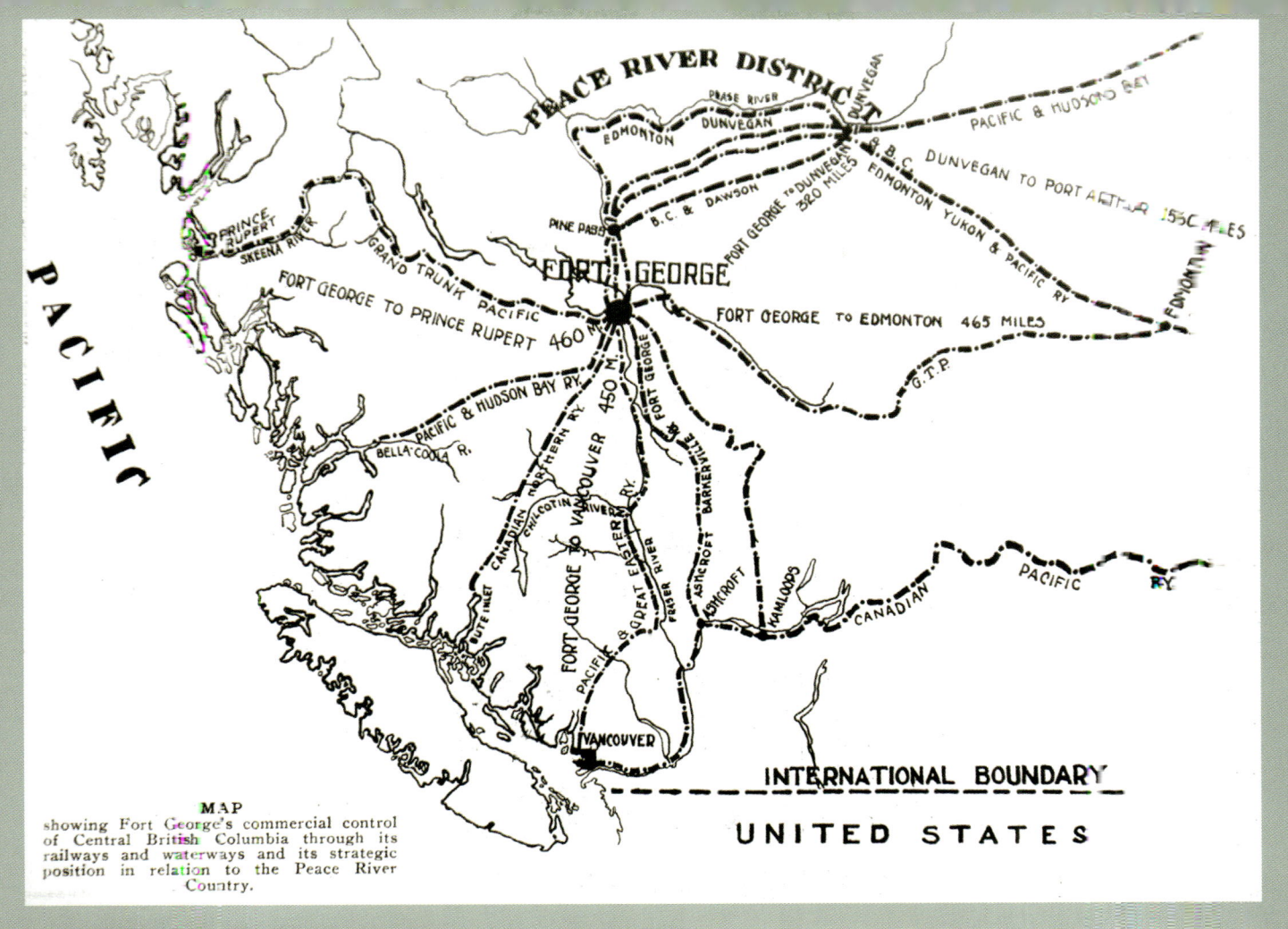

MAP showing Fort George's commercial control of Central British Columbia through its railways and waterways and its strategic position in relation to the Peace River Country.

Above.
Canadian Pacific No. 1140 is on switching duties on the Vancouver waterfront in this photo believed to date from 1911.

The Third Transcontinental

Above. No. 1520 was built in 1906 for the Canadian Northern Railway as No. 1223 and was principally used for main-line freight. It became a Canadian National locomotive when CNoR was absorbed into the nationalized company. The engine still belongs to CN but is on long-term loan to the Prince George Railway and Forestry Museum, where it is on display.

In British Columbia, the Grand Trunk Pacific Railway provided one part of the future Canadian National Railways. The Canadian Northern Railway provided the other, as both railways got into financial trouble after the beginning of the First World War, soon after both companies' transcontinental systems were completed.

The Canadian Northern (CNoR) was officially the Canadian Northern Pacific Railway in British Columbia largely because the provincial government had guaranteed its bonds and wanted it under its control; it was built under a 1910 provincial charter. Nevertheless, the railway was always marketed under the Canadian Northern name in order to synchronize marketing with the system in the rest of Canada.

Canadian Northern was created by two remarkable railway builders, William Mackenzie and Donald Mann. They began as railway contractors, and purchased and built short lines in Manitoba, on the Prairies and across the border in the United States, connecting them to make a network. In 1899, Mackenzie and Mann consolidated all their railway holdings into the Canadian Northern.

Right. A 1914 map of the Canadian Northern (Pacific) Railway in British Columbia. From Kamloops south the line paralleled the Canadian Pacific line, but always on the other side of the river.

By 1905 CNoR lines had reached Edmonton. In the East, track had reached Ottawa and Montreal in 1908 and a direct Toronto to Montreal line was completed in 1910. With a now extensive network covering the entire centre of Canada, continued expansion westward seemed a natural thing to do.

Mackenzie and Mann were very good at sniffing out subsidies for their lines. As early as 1898 they had signed an agreement with the dominion government, which was interested in creating Canadian routes to Klondike gold, to build a railway from Telegraph Creek, in the extreme northeast corner of British Columbia, to Teslin Lake, just over the Yukon border. Mackenzie and Mann were interested largely because the government promised a land grant of 25,000 acres per mile (6,293 ha per km) and other subsidies, and the Canadian Yukon Railway Company had been chartered for this project. Public outcry at what was seen as Ottawa's giving away of BC land led to the project's cancellation. Mackenzie and Mann were awarded over $300,000 in compensation.

The BC premier at this time, James Dunsmuir, then offered Mackenzie and Mann the charter of the Canadian Western Central Railway, which allowed for a line from the Yellowhead Pass to Bute Inlet, a route originally surveyed by Sandford Fleming in the 1880s (see page 14). In exchange for building this line plus a train-ferry connection to Vancouver Island and a line south to Victoria, the BC government offered a land grant of 20,000 acres per mile (5,034 ha per km) and a subsidy of between $4,000 and $4,800 per mile ($2,536 to $2,983 per km). This too fell by the wayside, this time because of public distaste for land grants moulded by an upstart politician intent on taking Dunsmuir's place—Richard McBride. However, once McBride was in power (he was BC premier for twelve years), he turned out to be a great believer in railways as an instrument of development and after an election in 1907 asked Mackenzie and Mann to resubmit proposals for a line to the coast. In September 1908 they did so, but now had dropped the route to Bute Inlet in favour of one to Vancouver.

In January 1909 McBride announced that negotiations were underway to bring a third transcontinental railway to a Pacific terminal, though a contract was not signed until 19 October, a day after he had called an election. The election ridded the premier, as he had hoped, of ministers opposed to his railway policy; he won 30 of 34 seats in the provincial legislature.

Below.
An eastbound CNoR freight pauses at Langley (Fort Langley) station in 1917. Compare this photo with a modern one in the same location on *page 215*.

Legislation was introduced on 1 March 1910 enabling the Canadian Northern Pacific Railway Company to build 600 miles (965 km) of line, of which one-sixth would be on Vancouver Island. The province was to guarantee construction bonds up to $35,000 per mile ($21,700 per km) and the railway would be exempt from provincial taxation until 1924. McBride, who had not in the past been happy about the Grand Trunk Pacific and its dominion government land grants, specified that the railway must remain under provincial jurisdiction—hence the separate company for BC only.

A location survey had been completed in the summer of 1909. The railway was directed to a Vancouver terminus using another route first surveyed by Sandford Fleming in the 1880s, down the valley of the North Thompson River to Kamloops; indeed this had been Fleming's recommended route. From there the railway would have to follow the same route as the CPR. This created high construction costs because the most desirable side of the river was occupied already by the CPR.

While Mackenzie and Mann had every intention of creating a Vancouver terminus, for the time being they created one on the south side of the Fraser River not quite opposite New Westminster, at a place they named Port Mann, after Donald, of course. Running rights over the New Westminster Southern (Great Northern) line west from Port Kells were negotiated (and purchased in 1916). In June 1910 a contract was awarded for the section from Port Mann to Hope to the Northern Construction Company, a subsidiary of Foley, Welch & Stewart, in which Mackenzie and Mann held an interest. In July the following year contracts were awarded for the sections from Hope to Kamloops and Kamloops to the Yellowhead Pass.

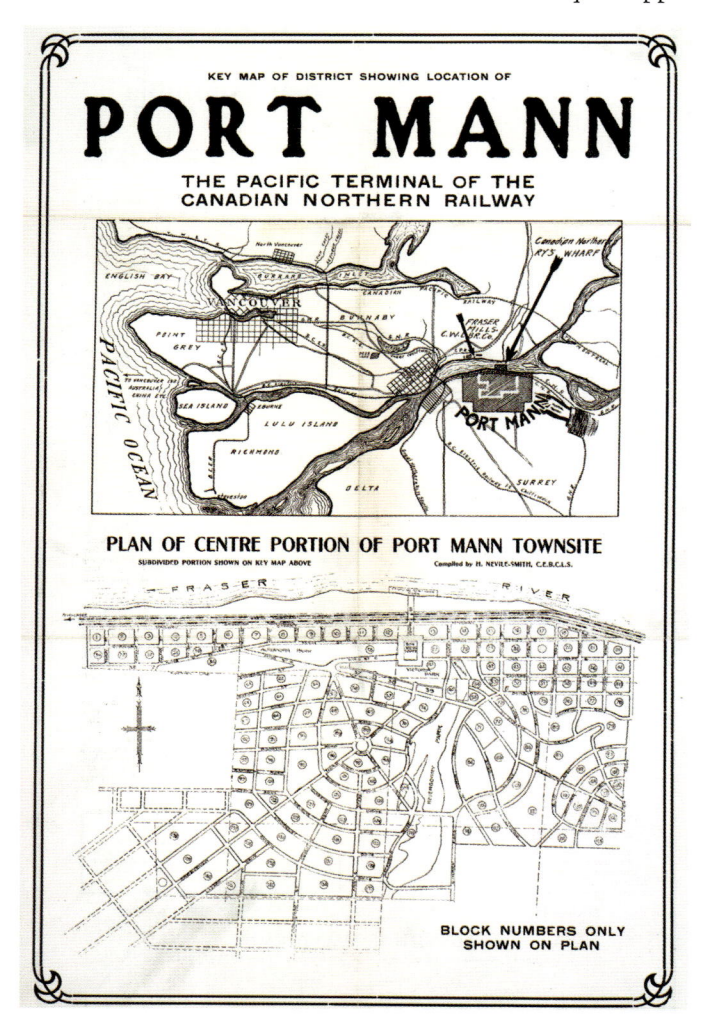

By October 1910 a townsite was laid out at Port Mann on land purchased by Mackenzie and Mann in 1908, and real estate speculators had a field day trying to sell lots based on an elaborate plan, the remnants of which survive in today's street layout.

The work in the Fraser Canyon was as difficult as it had been for Andrew Onderdonk's crews in the 1880s. Over 3 km of tunnels were required, and the river had to be crossed wherever the CPR had done this because most of the time there was not enough room on one side of the river for both lines. Crossings were made at Cisco (see photo, *page 17*), at Lytton, and twice more before Ashcroft. An 864-metre tunnel was required at Battle Bluffs, on Kamloops Lake. Even in the North Thompson valley there were 40 km of difficult gorge.

At Hells Gate in the Fraser Canyon so much rock was dumped into the river that the salmon run was interrupted for years and later required the provincial government to fund

Left and *below*.
Two promotional real estate advertisements for the Port Mann townsite, both dating from the height of real estate mania in Vancouver in early 1912. One is factual, the other humorous. Both emphasize Port Mann as the Pacific terminus of the Canadian Northern, but by this time plans were well underway to extend the track into downtown Vancouver, thus more or less by-passing Port Mann, though this would remain the location of railway yards.

expensive remediation work. Canadian Pacific complained to the Board of Railway Commissioners about 27 km of the CNoR trackbed through the Fraser and Thompson gorges, which ended up adding to costs.

The result was predictable. The line cost much more to build than had been estimated and required the CNoR to get deeper and deeper in debt. And it was debt that would finally sink Mackenzie and Mann.

In the meantime, track was being laid west of Edmonton toward the Yellowhead Pass, essentially duplicating the newly laid track of the Grand Trunk Pacific. By the end of 1913 track had been laid to Lucerne, 8 km west of the Alberta–BC boundary, but since it took longer to complete a number of trestles and bridges on the line, it did not become operational until 4 October 1915. Despite many insufficiencies the British Columbia line was declared complete in January 1915, and on 23 January a last spike was driven at Basque, 16 km south of Ashcroft. However, regular freight service to Vancouver did not begin until April 1916.

After the route to Bute Inlet had been abandoned, the corresponding terminal on Vancouver Island was moved from Union Bay, 209 km north of Victoria, to Patricia Bay, on Saanich Inlet only 27 km from Victoria. But this would not work unless the CNoR had a terminus in Vancouver, and

Above. No. 2141, a 2-8-0 Consolidation class locomotive seen here in action on the Kamloops Heritage Railway in 2017, was built in 1912 for the Canadian Northern Railway and spent many years hauling freight on (by then) Canadian National tracks on Vancouver Island. It was sold to the City of Kamloops in 1961 and restored to running condition in 1995–2001, with further restoration in 2013–15.

365 metres of waterfront on the north bank of the Fraser some 13 km downstream from Port Mann were purchased in July 1912 with the stated purpose of providing mainland terminals. This led to a branch to Steveston, which opened in 1917. The next year a long trestle on this line burned down, and a new line was built, this time from the north end of the New Westminster Bridge, which crossed onto Lulu Island 5 km farther downstream; this is the line still in use today.

Mackenzie and Mann's real intentions still required a terminus in Vancouver, and when in 1911 the VW&E (Great Northern) purchased a U-shaped piece of eastern False Creek for its terminal and yards, the pair saw their opportunity in the middle piece not claimed by the VW&E (see map page 55). In February 1913 an agreement was reached with the City of Vancouver whereby the CNoR would reclaim this middle 66 hectares of mud flat. The railway agreed to return 12 hectares to the city, make Vancouver its headquarters, build a large hotel within five years, and establish a trans-Pacific steamship service within eight. Mackenzie and Mann also agreed to build

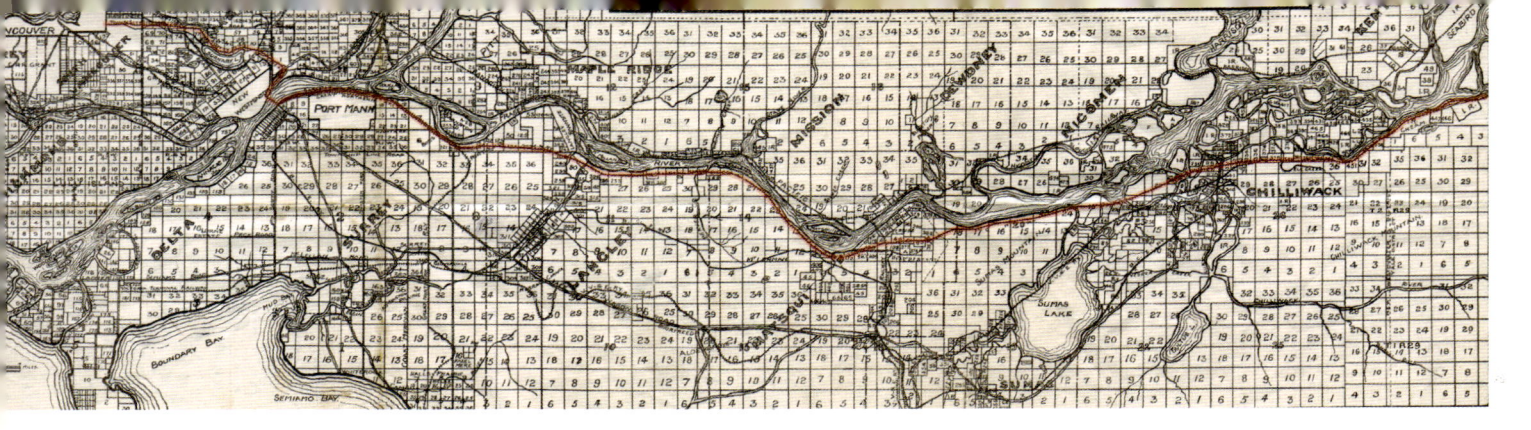

Above. The route (highlighted in red) of the Canadian Northern Pacific line in the Fraser Valley, first to Port Mann and its large townsite, and then across the New Westminster Bridge and, using the tracks of the Vancouver, Westminster & Yukon Railway, into Vancouver.

a double-track, electric locomotive–operated, 13 km tunnel from the Fraser to False Creek to access the new land. This last item was not as far-fetched as it might seem, because the CNoR at the time had under construction the 5 km Mount Royal Tunnel in Montreal to access its terminal in that city (and in 1914 ordered six electric locomotives to operate it; the tunnel opened in 1918). CNoR posted a $1.5 million surety bond and agreed to begin work within ninety days. On the strength of all this the BC legislature passed a bill guaranteeing $10 million, about half the estimated construction costs.

Gathering financial clouds delayed the start of reclamation, and nothing was done for two years until an ultimatum from the Vancouver city council induced Mackenzie to travel hurriedly to Vancouver; he arrived on 28 August 1915 on what proved to be the first through CNoR train from the East. Only then did reclamation begin. It was essentially completed two years later, and a magnificent terminus building was completed in 1919; this still stands today as Pacific Central Station.

The tunnel became unnecessary in November 1915 when the CNoR negotiated an agreement with the Great Northern to use its line from New Westminster into Vancouver, though Mackenzie still maintained to the press that this was only a temporary arrangement.

On Vancouver Island the CNoR proposed two branch lines: the one from Patricia Bay to Victoria, and another from Victoria to Muchalet Inlet, an arm of Nootka Sound, on the west coast of the island. In fact this latter line was only ever built as far as Kissinger, 18 km from Youbou, on Cowichan Lake. Wartime requirements for Sitka spruce for aircraft manufacture led the federal government to pay for a substantial length of the line to be laid, but once the war ended construction slowed. A branch to Cowichan Bay was also built, allowing lumber to be loaded there. Kissinger was not reached until 1928—but the Youbou–Kissinger part was abandoned only three years later. The line to Youbou remained open until 1979 (see map, *page 154*). The line had a passenger railcar service that began in 1922 as far as Sooke, using a converted bus nicknamed the "Galloping Goose." This service was extended to Youbou in 1925 but was not a success; it was withdrawn in 1931.

The Saanich Peninsula line opened in February 1918 but only lasted until 1925; the line was ripped up in 1935. A ferry, the SS *Canora* (the name derived from Canadian Northern Railway), served Patricia Bay, and then Victoria directly, until 1968.

Mackenzie and Mann had planned a branch from Kamloops into the Okanagan, but financing issues led to delays and with the start of the First World War the project was suspended. In 1920, after Mackenzie and Mann had left the scene, the dominion government authorized construction, but now with the use of running rights on CPR tracks to avoid duplication. Rights were obtained for 18 km east from Kamloops to Campbell Creek; from there a line to Armstrong was built, where again rights for 24 km to Vernon were obtained from the CPR on the Shuswap & Okanagan line (see page 38). Another line was built from Vernon to Lumby. The whole line was opened in September and October 1925 and proved viable; it is in operation today, although from 1999 to 2013 the route was leased to the short line Kelowna Pacific Railway.

The First World War cut off investment from Britain, and it became illegal to export capital. Mackenzie and Mann had worn out their welcome with both the dominion government—where a new, less railway-friendly prime minister, Robert Borden, had taken over in 1911—and in British Columbia, where Richard McBride resigned in 1915, in much political trouble for his railway promotions. The CNoR now could only obtain short-term financing at relatively high rates of interest from American investors. The dominion government grew impatient with having to meet interest payments on CNoR debt it had guaranteed. On 14 July 1917 Borden told Mackenzie the government was going to take over the railway. CNoR passed into public ownership on 6 September 1918, and operated under the name Canadian National Railways from 20 December; it was formally absorbed by CNR in 1923.

During the first decade of the 1900s, Mackenzie and Mann still believed they could build railways to northern goldfields. After all, the Canadian Northern had been created from numerous short lines the pair had built. Mann owned properties at Bear Creek, in northwest BC, that he thought contained silver, lead and copper. In 1910 Mackenzie and Mann (independently from the CNoR) purchased the charter of the Portland Canal Short Line Railway, renamed it the Canadian Northeastern Railway and began construction of a line from Stewart, at the head of the Portland Canal and the boundary between BC and Alaska, to Bear Creek, which they thought might eventually be able to link up with the Grand Trunk Pacific. Some 21 km of track was laid by the end of 1911, but no mineral finds were confirmed and work was halted. The line was never completed and the track laid never used.

Above. The historical marker on Highway 1 at Basque, to the south of Ashcroft, where the last spike of the Canadian Northern Pacific was driven on 23 January 1915. Just visible, a CN train is passing eastbound and a northbound CP train is on the far bank of the Thompson River.

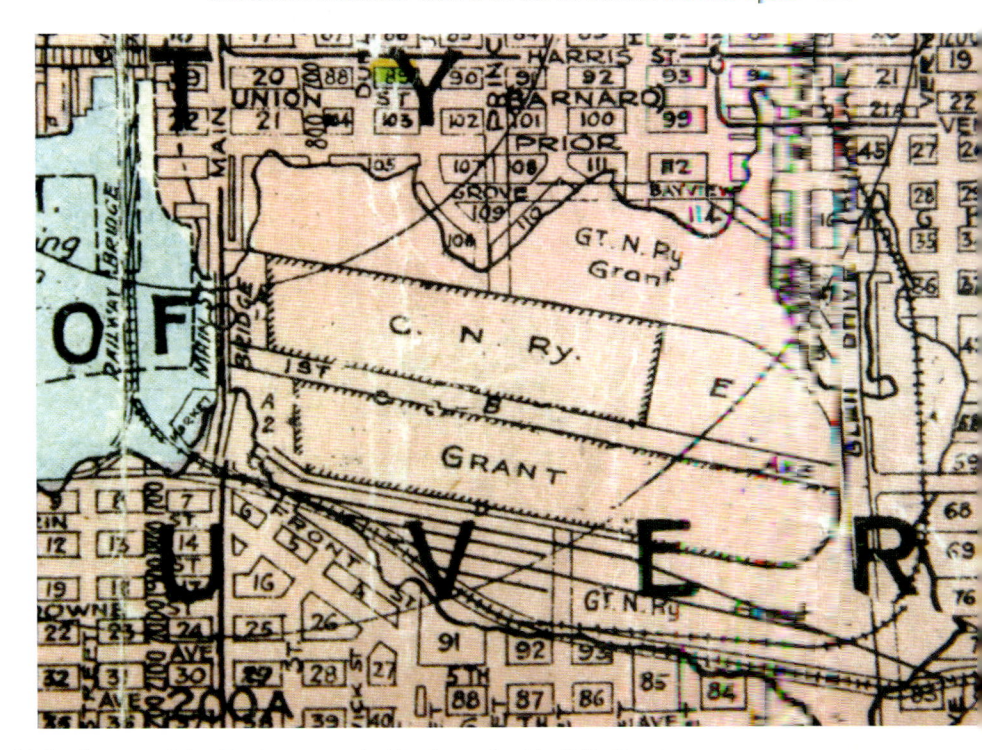

Above. This 1914 map shows the *C.N. Ry. Grant* in the middle of eastern False Creek, surrounded by the earlier *Gt. N. Ry Grant*.
Below. A panorama of the reclamation work in eastern False Creek taken on 10 March 1917. Main Street, with the bascule bridge, on the right and the new Great Northern "Union" station is on the left; it would be opened on 1 June that year. At centre, work has begun on the Canadian Northern station, which would be completed in November 1919. Until then CNoR also used the GN station. For most of 1918 Northern Pacific trains, running to Vancouver from Seattle via Sumas, Cloverdale, and Colebrook, also used the GN station.

The Coast-to-Kootenay Idea

The American invasion of the southern Interior of British Columbia following the discovery of rich metal ores in the region in the 1890s riled the businessmen of Vancouver from the beginning. The Canadian Pacific Railway had engineered a number of lines to try to divert this traffic to its more northerly main line, but the desire for a more direct connection with the coast remained.

By 1900 CPR's Columbia & Western Railway reached as far west as it would go, to Midway. A year later James Hill's Great Northern Railway acquired the charter for the Vancouver, Victoria & Eastern Railway (VV&E) from the Canadian Northern Railway. This charter was for a line from the Kootenays to the coast, and was one Hill would use for several other lines that could conceivably be considered part of such a link, such as the Cloverdale to Huntingdon (Sumas) line and the rerouting of the New Westminster Southern around the Semiahmoo Peninsula (see page 54). At the time Hill was serious about his coast-to-Kootenay link, intending to connect with Spokane, in Washington, and Canadian Pacific certainly took it seriously too.

Canadian Pacific completed one possible leg of a route to the coast in 1907, using a hastily purchased charter, that of the Nicola, Kamloops & Similkameen Coal & Railway Company. This was for the line from Merritt to the CPR main line at Spences Bridge. Although there had been several proposals for a railway on this route before, it was not until 1905 that the impetus to build it arrived—in the form of a strike by miners at the Vancouver Island coal mines. The railway needed coal to run its trains and excellent coal had been found in the Nicola Valley, so the 65 km, relatively easily built link was really a no-brainer. For the first three years the station at Merritt was a boxcar.

Canadian Pacific looked on with dismay in April 1907 as Hill announced that the Great Northern had plans to build extensively in western Canada. His plans included lines into the Crowsnest Pass and then to Calgary, Edmonton and Peace River, as well as a line from the Kootenays to the coast. That same month Hill's son Louis took over the reins of the Great Northern, promising that the railway's system in Canada would soon equal that in the United States. Using the VV&E charter, within a week of Louis's assumption of office, track was laid into British Columbia, crossing the border at Chopaka, where the Similkameen crosses the forty-ninth parallel, and headed for Keremeos, which it reached on 10 July 1907. Construction slowed because of labour and material supply problems and the washing out of a new bridge (which when rebuilt was promptly damaged by fire caused by a train crew's careless disposal of firebox ashes). And the economy slowed between 1907 and 1908, leading to the cancellation of the grander plan to reach into Alberta. But when business conditions improved in 1909, the Great Northern was poised to complete the line in southern British Columbia.

Princeton was reached late in 1909, although the first passenger train did not arrive until 23 December, because of a switchmen's strike. In January of that year the VV&E line from Cloverdale to Huntingdon had been completed (see page 53), and so now only a relatively short distance separated the two parts of the Great Northern's ambition to reach the coast—but what a distance that was going to prove to be.

Below.
A Great Northern Railway map published in 1915 shows the intended route across southern British Columbia, including the Hope Mountains section (depicted with a dashed line) that would never be built. The map was an advertisement for irrigated land shown in red, and no doubt the direct route was still shown in the hopes of a few more sales.

Right.
A system map of the Kettle Valley Railway dated 1914 and issued as part of a brochure for the railway—this despite the fact that through trains were not yet running. The unfinished sections east of Princeton and those in the Coquihalla Valley are shown as carefully disguised dashed lines! But the map does show the railway's route and, more generously than the GNR one, does at least have its rival's line depicted with a thin line, labelled *GNRY*.

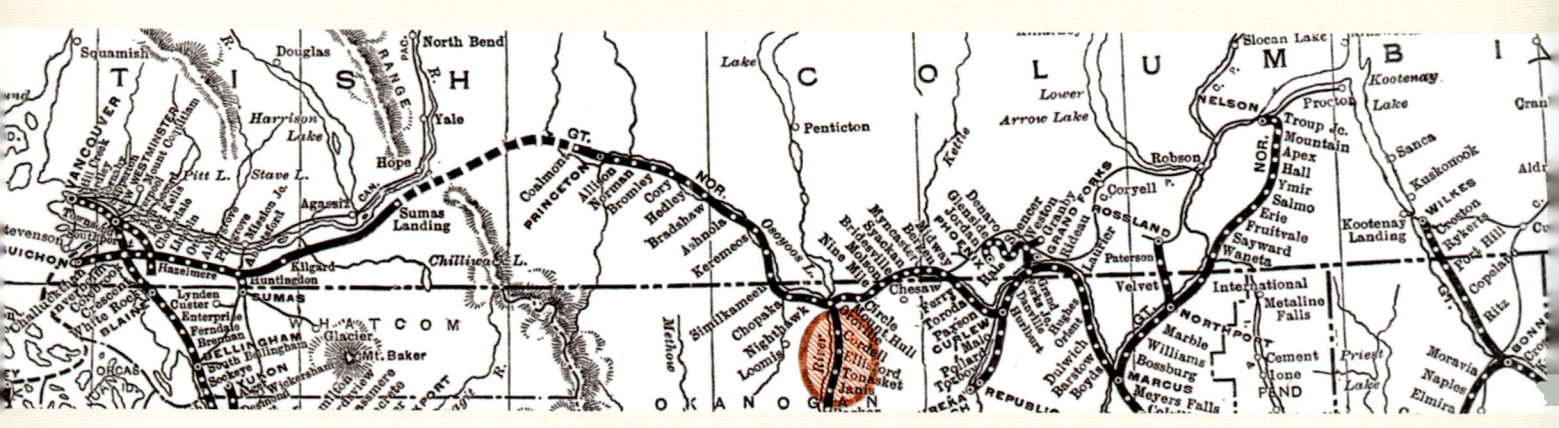

Above.
Canadian Pacific No. 3716 pulls a tourist train on the original line of the Kettle Valley Railway just a short distance west of Summerland. This Kettle Valley Heritage Railway is the only part of the original Kettle Valley Railway that still exists as such. This locomotive was built in 1912 at the CPR works in Montreal as No. 3916. It was rebuilt in 1929 and renumbered as 3716. Still later it was converted from a coal burner to oil. The engine is similar to those that worked on the Kettle Valley Railway, but it is not known if this specific one ever worked the route. It is one of the few surviving operating main-line steam locomotives in British Columbia (see page 184), and it is pictured about to arrive at the Prairie Valley station of the heritage railway.

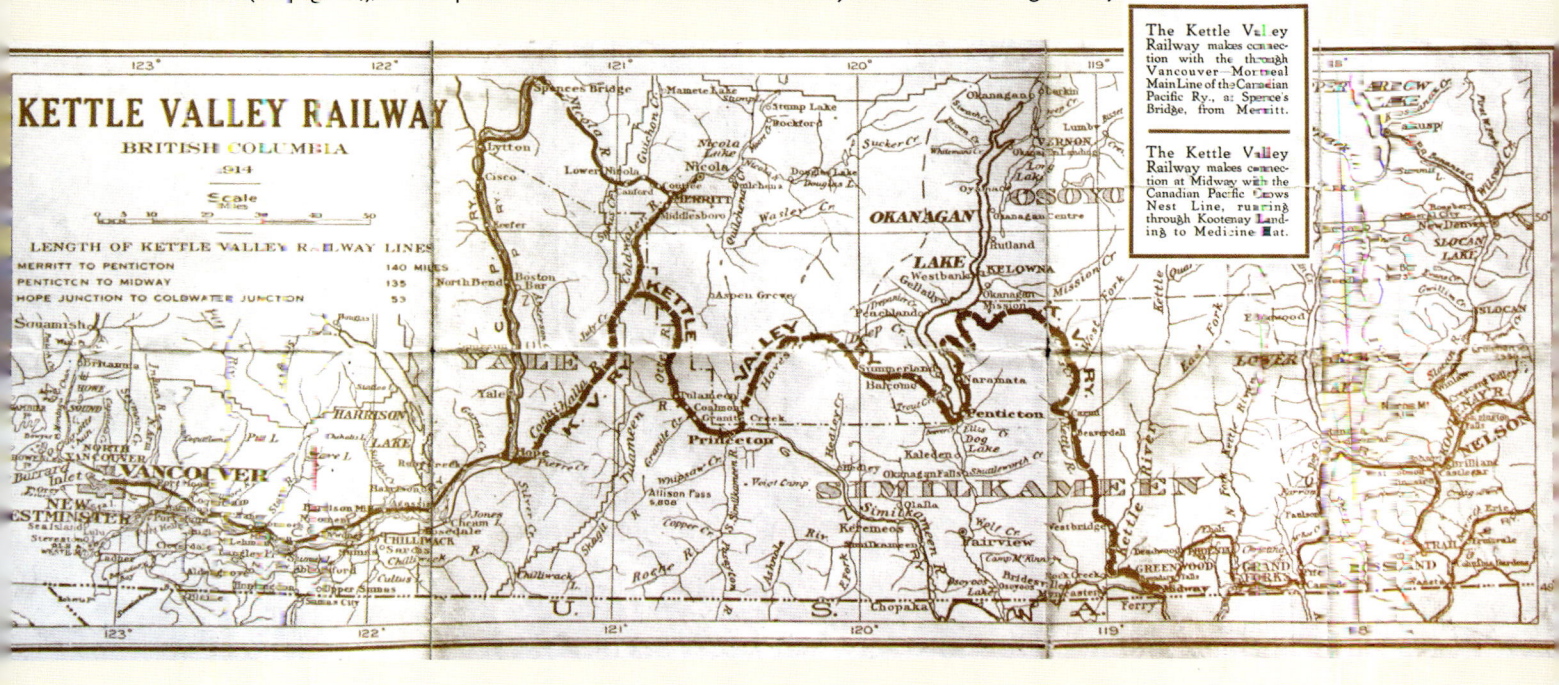

THE COAST-TO-KOOTENAY IDEA 95

Left.
One of several bridges still standing from Canadian Pacific's Nicola Branch between Merritt and the main line at Spences Bridge. The bridge crosses the Nicola River.

Left, centre.
The first Great Northern train arrives via the VV&E line at Keremeos on 5 October 1907.

Left, bottom.
Due to poor economic conditions and labour issues it took Great Northern over two years to extend the line the 67 km west along the Similkameen River valley to Princeton. Here the first passenger train arrives at Hedley with few people there to welcome it; they did not know a switchmen's strike was over.

On 2 September 1909 James Hill announced that he had rejected a survey across the difficult Hope Mountains, which would have required a 2.5 per cent grade for almost 50 km on a circuitous route, in favour of a 13 km tunnel that would have been the longest in North America at that time.

It was in this environment, then, that Canadian Pacific president Thomas Shaughnessy made a decision to go ahead with CPR's own line from Midway to Merritt, where it could complete a path to the coast, despite predictions of poor traffic potential. To carry out these plans the CPR gained effective control of the Kettle River Valley Railway (KRVR), which had been granted a charter in 1901 to boost the accessibility to Grand Forks and had successfully battled Hill to gain access to the mines at Republic, Washington.

Scrappy from the beginning, in 1902 the company had famously positioned a locomotive across a diamond crossing that had been built by VV&E crews overnight across its tracks in Grand Forks, thus preventing the American line from entering the town. However, by 1910 the KRVR, hampered by lack of money, had only reached a point 29 km north of Grand Forks. The CPR takeover of the KRVR, which the smaller railway had been trying to achieve for some time, was accompanied by a name change, to the more simple Kettle Valley Railway (KVR), and the dispatch of a talented railway engineer, Andrew McCulloch, to oversee construction of a line from Midway to Merritt. McCulloch had worked on the location of the CPR's Spiral Tunnels and was then a division engineer of construction for lines in eastern Canada.

Penticton, at the southern end of Okanagan Lake, was selected as the headquarters of the railway, and a lakeshore station was built to enable easy transfer to and from the steamboats already plying the lake. The KVR was built through some of the most difficult railway terrain in the province, and fully taxed McCulloch's engineering skills; someone less talented would quite possibly have failed. Many trestles and bridges were required, especially east of Penticton. The intended route was surveyed, utilizing some previous surveys done for the Columbia & Western. The final route (which was altered as construction progressed, most notably to go through Princeton and Coalmont, site of new coal mines, instead of via a route farther north) was northward in the Kettle River valley from Rock Creek in the Similkameen River valley, then down into Penticton, a difficult descent down the steep lake bench; then up again to Summerland (one of the CPR requirements was that the line serve the rich agricultural area around Summerland) and by an arc sweeping into Princeton, with yet more difficult valley sides to be negotiated with multiple loops to keep the grade manageable. The latter had been devised by McCullough, no doubt drawing on his experience with the Spiral Tunnels. Then up once more north to Otter Summit—which would be renamed Brookmere—where it would connect with a line from Merritt, a section that was completed south in the Coldwater River valley in November 1911. From Otter Summit the most difficult section of all continued westward down the Coquihalla River valley to Hope, where it would join the CPR main line for the run into Vancouver.

Finances were buoyed in 1909 and 1912, provincial election years, with promises from ardent railway supporter and BC premier Richard McBride (see page 86). In 1909 he promised a subsidy of $5,000 per mile ($3,107 per km) for the line between

Below.
An undated photo of a Great Northern train at Princeton station.

Above.
The first locomotive in Penticton, brought in on the lake in October 1912 to begin construction of the KVR line.

Merritt and Penticton and in 1912 a subsidy of $12,000 per mile ($7,458 per km) for the Coquihalla Pass section. McBride also offered $200,000 for a bridge over the Fraser River at Hope.

The line from Merritt to Brookmere, a relatively easy route, was completed in November 1911. Construction began at Midway in October 1910 and tracklaying in January 1911. Progress was slow. Labour was hard to come by because of a general boom in the economy and the fact that many railways were being built at this time (not least the Canadian Northern Pacific and Grand Trunk Pacific in British Columbia). Early in 1912 the dominion government rescinded all legislation restricting the entry of foreign labour into Canada, which, although opposed vehemently by labour groups who feared an "Oriental invasion," was very successful in relieving the labour problem.

The KVR line was built east from Penticton to join that coming from Midway beginning in October 1912, using

Above. McCulloch's loops at Jura, northeast of Princeton, used to reduce the grade descending into the town, are still visible on a satellite photo today and are now part of the Great Trail (the renamed Trans Canada Trail), as is much of the KVR trackbed. This is from Google Maps. The labelled, thicker white lines are roads.

locomotives brought in on lake steamers, as were most supplies. The last spike on the Midway–Penticton section was driven on 2 October 1914 and the first train from Midway arrived at Penticton four days later.

The section from Penticton west to Princeton also involved some steep grades, particularly with the descent into the Similkameen Valley at Princeton, where McCullough used his wide loops to maintain a 2.2 per cent grade. The 24 km descent into Princeton became the longest stretch of unbroken 2.2 per cent grade in Canada. The first contract was awarded in October 1911, but track did not reach Princeton until 21 April 1915.

In the meantime, Hill and his VV&E had made some progress, building east of Abbotsford in the Fraser Valley and

Above.
Canadian Pacific wanted the KVR line to serve the Summerland area, which required a steep climb up the western lake bench and the bridging of the Trout Creek Canyon. Here the trestles on either side of a bridge, yet to be placed, are shown under construction in 1913. Falsework for this bridge was washed out during construction in May 1913. It was completed in October that year. This is the location of the eastern end of the modern Kettle Valley Heritage Railway (see photo, *page 185*).

reaching the Sumas River, when it was announced on 22 May 1911 that Hill had signed a deal with the Canadian Northern Pacific Railway (see page 54) to share the line from a place they named Cannor, near Chilliwack, to Hope. It would be owned by Canadian Northern, with Great Northern–VV&E running rights.

The grand plan for a long tunnel up the Tulameen Valley and under the Hope Mountains was officially abandoned in November 1910, because Hill recognized that it would take too long to construct and thus would allow the KVR to beat him to the coast. Thus the alternative route north to Otter Summit and southwest down the Coquihalla would now be required. But surveys had shown that there was only room for one line in the Coquihalla—both railways had surveyed more or less the same path in many locations—so it would be critical for both railways to be the first to build a line.

The VV&E completed its line from Princeton to Coalmont on 10 November 1911. The KVR awarded a contract for 14 miles (23 km) from the proposed junction with the Merritt line at Brodie, just west of Otter Summit, in August 1912, and it was followed the next month by the VV&E awarding a contract for the line from Coalmont north toward Otter Summit. Then something unexpected happened: L.C. Gilman, the VV&E's assistant to the president—Hill was strangely nowhere to be found—publicly offered a truce. He offered to allow the KVR to build the Coquihalla line with no competition from the VV&E if the KVR would lease trackage rights over the line to his railway at a reasonable price. After two meetings between Gilman and KVR president James Warren, in November 1912 and April 1913, peace was declared. The agreement was formalized in a document signed on 1 July 1914. The KVR was given running rights over the Coalmont to Brookmere section in return for VV&E rights over the Coquihalla section.

Deteriorating economic conditions probably had a lot to do with it, but there is also no doubt that Hill's son Louis,

Left.
Kettle Valley Railway construction crews approach Princeton on 21 April 1915. The bridge across the Tulameen River was called the Bridge of Dreams because it was the last river they had to cross before linking to the coast, albeit via the Nicola Valley line and the CPR main line south of Spences Bridge. In the background is the VV&E bridge across the Similkameen River and the line in to Princeton with which the KVR would link under the agreement to use each other's tracks signed in July 1914.

Above.
The first Kettle Valley Railway scheduled train from Merritt to Penticton at the lakeshore station on 31 May 1915. A train from Midway would arrive later in the day. The lakeshore station was located at the southern end of Okanagan Lake, adjacent to the steamer dock, allowing easy transfer from one to the other. Trains had to back up to this station from the railway yards farther south.

who was now in charge of the Great Northern, was much less enthusiastic about the whole coast-to-Kootenay concept, given the physical barriers—and hence financial costs—involved, than his father had been. James Hill was essentially out of the picture by this time; he died in 1916.

VV&E track reached Otter Summit—now Brookmere—and was joined with the KVR track from Merritt on 25 October 1914.

Work on the section into Princeton from Osprey Lake was still to be completed, with its big loops at Jura; this was finished in April 1915. On 31 May the first passenger trains operated between Merritt and Midway and the connection with the coast was made, albeit still via the CPR main line from Spences Bridge.

The last and most difficult section through the Coquihalla Valley remained. At least McCulloch's contractors would have no competition for the best path, but nonetheless they faced some daunting physical obstacles. Work had begun with the awarding of a contract in August 1913.

One of the most well-known obstacles to be overcome was in the narrow canyon of the Coquihalla River just a short distance from Hope. Here a series of four tunnels were used by McCulloch, all in a straight line and crossing the river twice between them. These were the Quintette Tunnels, so called because an open side on part of one made it look like there were five separate tunnels, but also called the Othello Tunnels because of their proximity to Othello station—McCulloch, a

THE COAST-TO-KOOTENAY IDEA 99

Shakespeare fan, named all the stations in the Coquihalla after characters in Shakespeare plays.

A bridge over the Fraser River at Hope was completed in March 1915 to connect the KVR with the CPR main line on the north side of the river. This was a dual road and rail bridge. The rails may have long gone, but the road remains—it is the Trans-Canada Highway bridge just to the north of the town.

In December 1915, with work fast approaching completion, a very heavy snowfall halted work on the line despite the use of snowplows, one rotary and one wedge, brought in by Canadian Pacific. At one point the rotary snowplow, pushed by two KVR locomotives, became stuck in the deep snow for three days before the crew could be rescued, despite use of the other plow. There were reports of water in engine tenders freezing. Snow 20 metres deep was recorded in parts of the Coquihalla Pass that winter. Work was halted for three months.

When work resumed, there was a lot of cleaning up to do; landslides and broken snowsheds obstructed the track. Winter snow would be an ongoing problem for the railway. On 31 July 1916 the line was opened, and passenger train service began the same day between Nelson and Vancouver.

On 27 September a special GN train with Louis Hill on board made the journey from Vancouver via the KVR to Princeton, and the following day continued to Spokane. This was the only GN train ever to operate over the whole GN line between the two cities.

Recognizing that the KVR would require considerable skill just to keep it running, CPR president Thomas Shaughnessy asked Andrew McCulloch to stay on as the railway superintendent, a position he accepted.

The Brookmere to Spences Bridge line officially became a branch of the Kettle Valley Railway. Two other branches were built. A 19 km line from Princeton south to Copper Mountain was completed in October 1920, though it required twenty-four

Below.
The Othello Tunnels today are a provincial park, but even that is closed during the winter. They are an attraction partly because of the way they align in a straight line. These two views are looking north and south from almost the same position; the bridge is the same bridge in both photos. Beneath roars the raging Coquihalla in its confined canyon. To begin these tunnels men had to lay charges, then quickly run up a ladder to get out of the way of the blast. Improvements in the tunnels to make them safer were carried out by Canadian Pacific when the route was used as an alternate main line to the coast.

trestles and much blasting of rock from the mountainside to form a ledge on which the rail line could run. The other branch was longer, from Penticton to Osoyoos, via Oliver. The Oliver area was the focus of an irrigation scheme after the First World War, instigated by BC premier John Oliver to provide homes and an occupation for returning soldiers—and not incidentally, help to populate the province. The Kettle Valley Railway was extended to Haynes, just south of Oliver, in 1923 and was extended to Osoyoos in 1944.

Despite the Kettle Valley Railway's eventual demise, it remains as a world-class feat of railway construction. It was used for many years as an alternative main line to the coast by Canadian Pacific (see *page 148*), a line it was glad to have when the main line was blocked for some reason. Even after closure it remained useful; much of the modern Highway 5 through the Coquihalla Pass used the railbed of the Kettle Valley.

Below. The Kettle Valley Railway had many trestles and bridges, including quite a few spectacular ones. This is one of those, over the west fork of Canyon Creek in the Carmi Subdivision. A train—probably the service from Penticton to Nelson—is posed for the photo about 1916 or 1917.

Above. Not until 1949 was there a road connection between Hope and Princeton. Before that, the Kettle Valley Railway offered a ferry service. Cars were driven onto flatbed trucks for the ride. In 1927 the charge to transport a car was based on weight: 77¢ per 100 lbs (45 kg) but with a minimum of 5,000 lbs (2,268 kg)—$38.50. Here a train is being prepared at Hope. Until the completion of a road around the "Big Bend" of the Columbia River in 1940, Canadian Pacific offered a similar service between Golden and Revelstoke.

Below. Princeton station with a GNR train arriving from Spokane, about 1930.

Above. Residents of Merritt were abuzz with railway euphoria when this cartoon was published in the local newspaper, the *Nicola Valley Advocate*, on 13 January 1911. The VV&E and KVR and CPR might legitimately be said to be coming, but the Canadian Northern and even the Grand Trunk Pacific?

THE COAST-TO-KOOTENAY IDEA 101

A Line to the North

Although railways were proposed to connect Vancouver with the Yukon and the goldfields, none ever got beyond the Lower Mainland. Unless there was a clearly remunerative objective, the costs of creating a railway path through difficult terrain were prohibitive. This applied particularly to the first section up Howe Sound. A railway to the Peace River region had also been proposed, and the original intentions of the Grand Trunk Pacific Railway (GTPR) included a line connecting Prince George with Vancouver, shown on the map *below*. Indeed, in 1910 the GTPR surveyed most of a line from Prince George to Vancouver, though using a route down the shore of Harrison Lake.

In 1907 a group of Vancouver businessmen chartered the Howe Sound, Pemberton Valley & Northern Railway (HSPV&N) to build a line north from Squamish as far as Anderson Lake to tap the resources of the region and develop agricultural land around Pemberton. A charter previously granted to the Vancouver, Westminster & Yukon Railway was ignored, the HSPV&N claiming that it had lapsed. It had not, but it appears that John Hendry, its main sponsor, was more interested in selling to James Hill's Great Northern, which in turn was more interested in building east. In 1910 the HSPV&N changed its name to simply Howe Sound & Northern (HS&N) and applied to extend the railway from Anderson Lake to Lillooet. It also applied for a charter for another company, to be called the British Columbia Central Railway, to continue north to Prince George after connecting with the HS&N at Lillooet.

The GTPR in the meantime sent its solicitor, D'Arcy Tate, to see BC premier Richard McBride to ask for a government guarantee of its bonds, in return for which the GTPR—but in reality its contractor, Foley, Welch & Stewart—would build a line from Vancouver to Prince George, connecting there with the GTPR main line. Financing was also forthcoming from a British investor—the (British) Great Eastern Railway. As a result the new railway was called the Pacific Great Eastern—the PGE.

McBride's Conservative railway-friendly government granted the PGE a charter in February 1912. The railway was to be under the control of the BC government and not dependent on the GTPR or any other railway. It would also purchase the HS&N, and so benefited from the survey work done to date for that railway. Thus, from its inception, the PGE was a very politically controlled business, something that continued right up to its ultimate privatization in 2004 (see page 145).

The evaporation of British financing and the disappearance of potential customers because of the First World War was to cripple the PGE and destroy the contractor, Foley, Welch & Stewart, until then one of the most successful railway contractors in North America. In 1915 the railway ran out of money. In late 1915 McBride resigned and a year later his Conservatives lost power to the Liberals. In 1918 "Honest John" Oliver became premier, and he was distinctly less enamoured of railways than McBride had been. By then work on the PGE had ground to a halt. The company was in desperate financial straits, and was taken

Far left.
Part of a 1906 map showing the intentions of the Grand Trunk Pacific (see page 78) on the West Coast. In addition to the main line to *Prince Rupert,* there is a line north to *Dawson* and one south to *Vancouver,* even continued onto *Vancouver Island.* The line south from *Ft. George* approximates that over which the PGE would be built.

Left.
Part of a 1914 map that still shows the line of the John Hendry–chartered Vancouver, Westminster & Yukon as the *Pro.* (proposed) *Yukon Ry.*

Right.
Pacific Great Eastern No. 2, the only surviving steam locomotive from that railway, is now preserved and on display at the West Coast Railway Heritage Park in Squamish. No. 2 was the first locomotive of the PGE and was built for the railway's predecessor line, the Howe Sound, Pemberton Valley & Northern Railway. It was built by the Baldwin Locomotive Works in Philadelphia in 1910. It is a saddle tank, so called because the water tank saddles the boiler and firebox. No. 2 spent from 1920 to 1965 as a logging locomotive with the Comox Logging & Railway Company on Vancouver Island, which helped preserve it until it was considered historical and worth

saving. In 1965 the locomotive was donated to the Town of Squamish and was displayed in a local park until 1994, when the heritage park was established. The photo below shows the same locomotive in its logging days.

over by the government. Construction north from Squamish had by that time only reached Chasm, a few kilometres north of Clinton.

The southern part of the line west and north of North Vancouver had reached only to Whytecliff, a town platted a few years earlier at today's Horseshoe Bay. It had soon become clear that any line along the eastern shore of Howe Sound was going to be an engineering challenge and thus very expensive, and so the line was "temporarily" halted at Whytecliff. Construction of the southern portion had begun in 1912 and by the end of 1913 had reached Dunderave, in the newly created municipality of West Vancouver. Service was inaugurated on 1 January 1914, principally using gas-electric railcars. By August that year the line had been completed to Whytecliff, and regular passenger service began on 21 August.

Two steam locomotives were used on the North Shore Subdivision. No. 2, the first, had arrived on the North Shore on a transfer barge on 12 November 1913 and was used to help build the line westward. The other, No. 3, was a yard engine built for the PGE in 1914. In 1928 most PGE equipment was transferred to Squamish, but No. 3 remained on the North Shore to be used by the Vancouver Harbour Commissioners Terminal Railway.

The gas-electric railcars No. 101—and a replacement after this car was destroyed by fire in 1914, No. 102—and No. 103 were built by Hall-Scott, a California railcar manufacturer, and No. 104 and No. 105 by General Electric. In addition, there were a number of trailer cars to increase capacity. Regular service was provided by the railcars, but the steam locomotives were often used for special workings, as was the case when the accident recorded in the photos on these pages occurred in September 1916. Judging by all the accidents recorded, the line seems to have been rather casually run. But it provided a valuable service, and the initial development of West Vancouver owed a great deal to the PGE.

When the company ran out of money in 1918, the service halted for a while but was restored when the government took over. The line was closed in 1922, but public pressure led the government to reinstate the service. This proved to be only a temporary reprieve. In 1925 the opening of the first Second Narrows Bridge increased competition from automobiles, and in 1928 the government reached an agreement with the Municipality of West Vancouver to close the line in exchange for $150,000 to pay for the paving of Marine Drive to Horseshoe Bay. Significantly, in light of future events (see page 136), the right-of-way was disused but never formally abandoned.

Above.
On the southern section of the Pacific Great Eastern, service was maintained mainly with gas railcars such as this one, No. 104, shown at Whytecliff, with a boxcar in tow, in July 1925. It seems it was warm at the time, for all the windows on the railcar are open. The railcars took 40 minutes to reach here from North Vancouver's ferry terminal. The line was closed three years later.

Above.

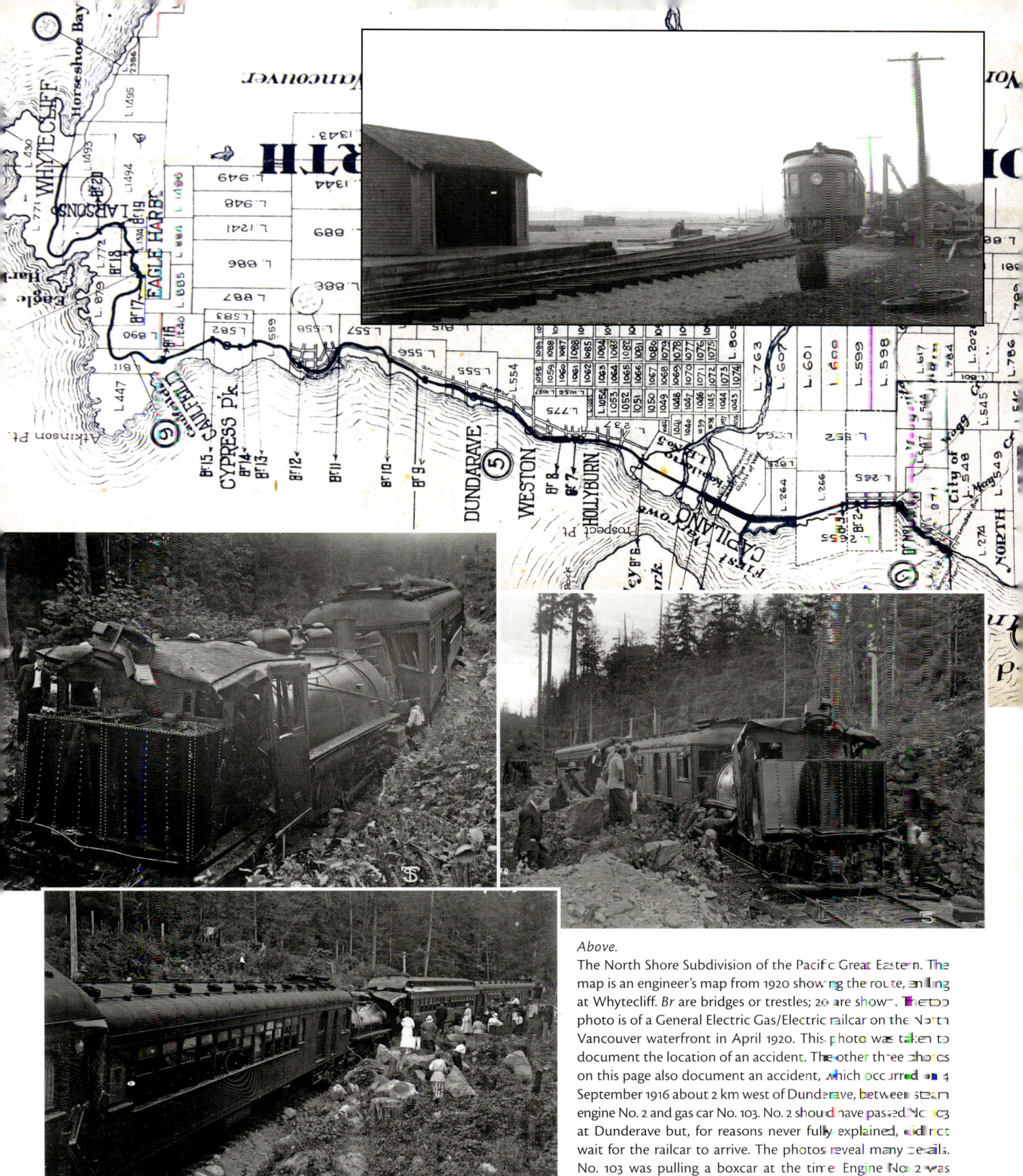

The North Shore Subdivision of the Pacific Great Eastern. The map is an engineer's map from 1920 showing the route, ending at Whytecliff. *Br* are bridges or trestles; 2s are shown. The top photo is of a General Electric Gas/Electric railcar on the North Vancouver waterfront in April 1920. This photo was taken to document the location of an accident. The other three photos on this page also document an accident, which occurred on 4 September 1916 about 2 km west of Dundarave, between steam engine No. 2 and gas car No. 103. No. 2 should have passed No. 103 at Dundarave but, for reasons never fully explained, did not wait for the railcar to arrive. The photos reveal many details. No. 103 was pulling a boxcar at the time. Engine No. 2 was repaired and went back into service and is now preserved (see previous page), but gas car No. 103 was too severely damaged and was scrapped. The glass plate photo at *left* shows more.

A LINE TO THE NORTH   05

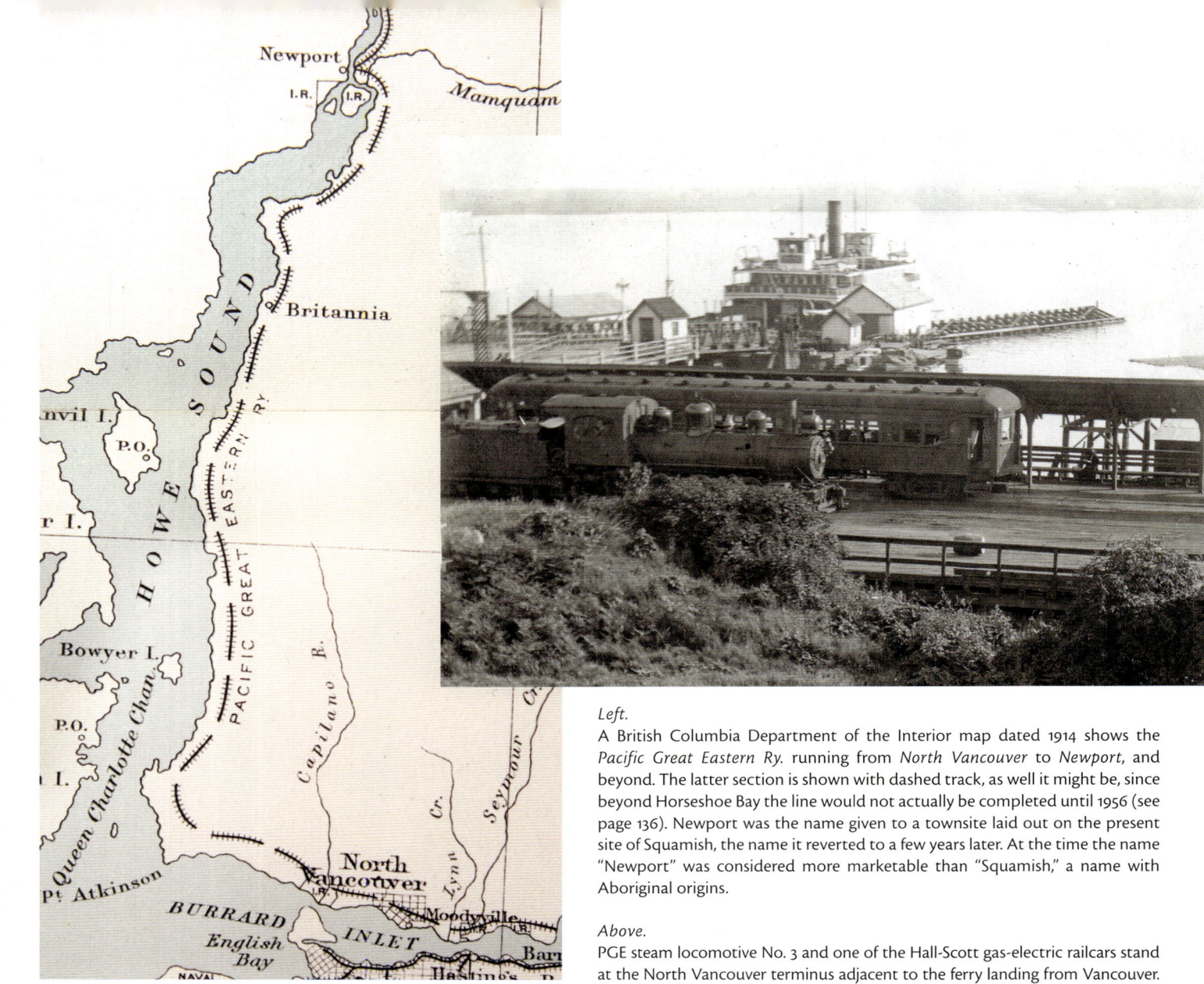

Left.
A British Columbia Department of the Interior map dated 1914 shows the *Pacific Great Eastern Ry.* running from *North Vancouver* to *Newport*, and beyond. The latter section is shown with dashed track, as well it might be, since beyond Horseshoe Bay the line would not actually be completed until 1956 (see page 136). Newport was the name given to a townsite laid out on the present site of Squamish, the name it reverted to a few years later. At the time the name "Newport" was considered more marketable than "Squamish," a name with Aboriginal origins.

Above.
PGE steam locomotive No. 3 and one of the Hall-Scott gas-electric railcars stand at the North Vancouver terminus adjacent to the ferry landing from Vancouver. Behind the trains is North Vancouver Ferry No. 3. From 1914 to 1928 this site, at the foot of Lonsdale Avenue, was a transportation hub, with streetcars leaving for other parts of North Vancouver as well. The photo was taken in 1919.

Left.
PGE No. 2, the railway's first locomotive—and also the only one from that railway to survive—stands behind a crowd gathered to welcome it to the North Shore on 12 November 1913. It had been shipped by barge from Squamish, where it had worked since 1910 for the Howe Sound, Pemberton Valley & Northern Railway (which became the Howe Sound & Northern Railway in 1912). Note the locomotive does not yet have a tender.

Above. In this excellent photo, Pacific Great Eastern steam locomotive No. 3, with two trailer coaches in tow, is shown just beyond Altamont Station—at Bridge 10 (B*r* 1C) on the map, *page 105*—heading for Whytecliff on 15 July 1923. No. 3 was built for the PGE in 1914.

Construction resumed on the northern section in 1918, after the government takeover. Williams Lake was reached in September 1919, and Quesnel in July 1921. By the end of 1922 the track had reached the Cottonwood River, where a long and expensive bridge was required. Construction continued north of the river, and the line was partially constructed to Red Rock Creek, only 30 km from Prince George. At this point the government commissioned a report from John G. Sullivan, a former Canadian Pacific consulting engineer, to determine what should be done. Sullivan produced a scathing report in which he stated his doubt that the railway would ever be able to pay its way. As a result the government halted construction and, following Sullivan's recommendations, ripped up the track north of Quesnel, making that city the railway's northern terminus. The Cottonwood bridge was cancelled, despite the fact that the steel for it had already been ordered. Sullivan also recommended the abandonment of the southern part of the line—which was why it was closed in 1922—and the cancelling of plans to connect the two rail lines along Howe Sound. The latter was covered, albeit not very efficiently, by a railway barge and steamer service.

The railway was long derided for going "from nowhere to nowhere," and with its apparently easy-going operating style acquired monikers such as "Please Go Easy," "Past God's Endurance," and "Prince George—Eventually." Eventually would come—but not until 1952, with the revitalization of plans for northern development, covered in a later section of this book (see page 134).

Below.
A PGE train at Alta Lake in 1925. The lake can be seen in the right background. Rainbow Lodge, a favourite stopping place for passengers and crews alike, is behind the locomotive. This location is now Whistler.

Right.
The area shown on a 1920 PGE engineer's map with the *Mons Y* clearly marked. A wye was a triangle of track on which a locomotive, or even an entire train, could be turned to face in the opposite direction.

The photos on this page were taken by passengers on PGE trains. At *left* is a trestle at the Canyon of the Cheakamus River, a tributary of the Squamish River, which flows into the head of Howe Sound. It gives a good idea of some of the engineering challenges the railway faced. *Centre left* is a open-air tourist train leaving the wharf at Squamish, where it will have just met an incoming steamer from which the people disembarked. Part of the 1920 engineer's map *below* shows the *Gov't Wharf*—the government, of course, owned the railway after 1918. These two photos, and the Alta Lake one opposite, were taken on the same outing, on Sunday, 14 June 1925.

Below. This photo was taken on an outing of the BC Mountaineering Club and shows some of its members—presumably up for something more daring than riding in a coach—being pushed through a new tunnel by a PGE locomotive.

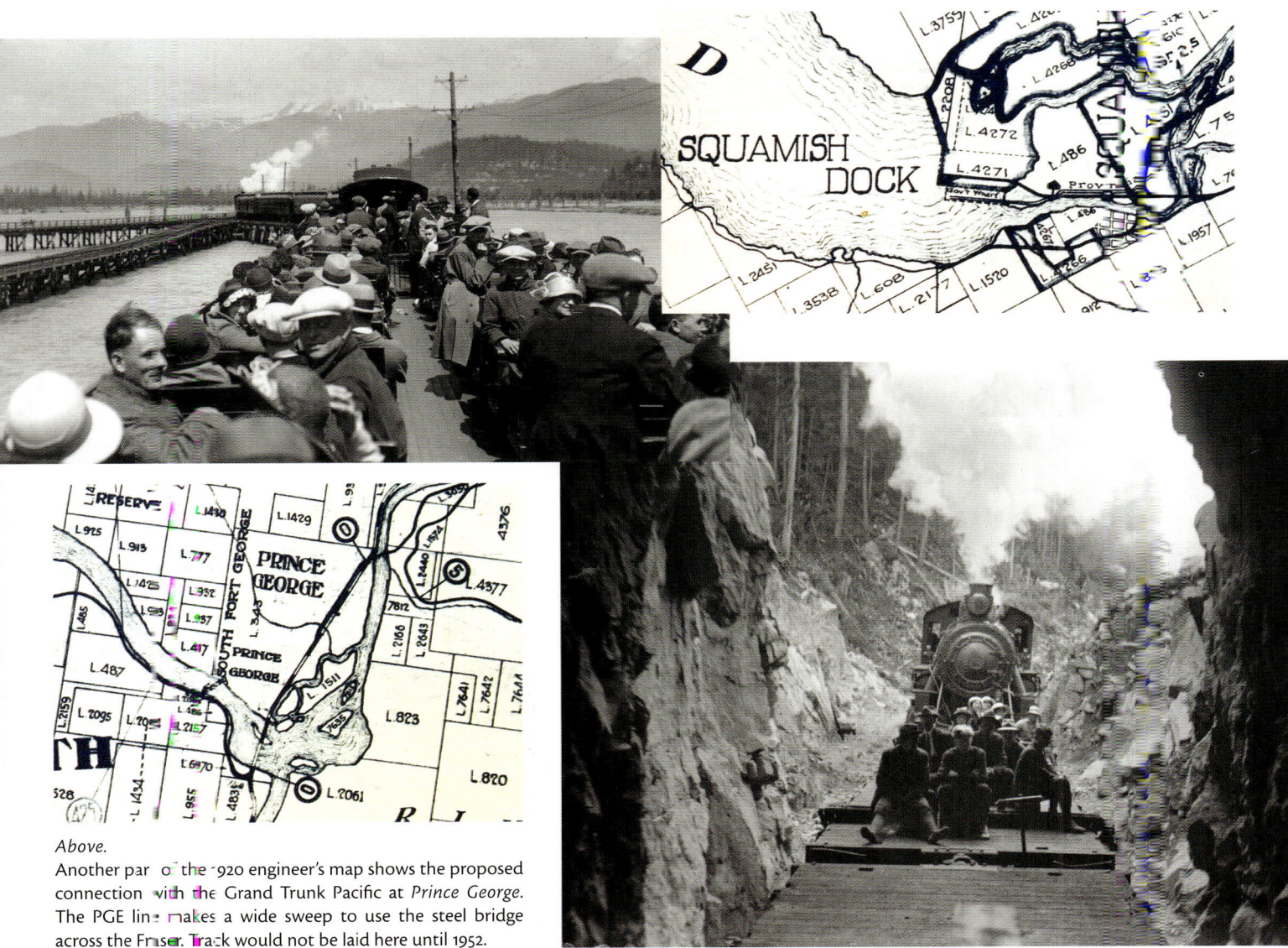

Above.
Another part of the 1920 engineer's map shows the proposed connection with the Grand Trunk Pacific at *Prince George*. The PGE line makes a wide sweep to use the steel bridge across the Fraser. Track would not be laid here until 1952.

A LINE TO THE NORTH 109

The Golden Age of Steam

If there ever was a golden age for the steam locomotive, it was between the First and Second World Wars, when steam locomotives reached a pinnacle of power and speed before succumbing to diesels. But a golden age for steam did not mean a golden age generally—the Great Depression of 1929–35 saw to that.

Indeed, the golden age in terms of locomotive development was more marked elsewhere in the world; relatively little cutting-edge technology found its way to British Columbia. In eastern Canada, Canadian National Railways introduced streamlined locomotives, and in the United States, famous—and fast—trains like the Milwaukee Road's art deco–styled *Hiawatha* were unveiled, capable of sustained running at 100 mph (160 km/hr). And in Europe, Germany's diesel railcars and Britain's steam East Coast expresses battled for supremacy at speeds in excess of 120 mph (193 km/hr), with Britain's A4 Pacific *Mallard* taking the world steam speed record in 1938 at 126 mph (203 km/hr), a record that still stands today.

Such speeds were impossible over much of British Columbia's mountainous terrain. The emphasis was more on power and the ability to haul long passenger trains over the steep grades of the Rockies. So the province's steam locomotives retained more traditional looks, though they grew immensely powerful. The iconic (and now preserved) Royal Hudson (photo, *left*) was one of a class of locomotives specially designed for the trans-mountain service. They were considered semi-streamlined in that attention had been paid to their shape and its relationship to the ease with which air flowed over it. In this they were sleeker-looking than a previous class of powerful locomotives designed for the same service, the Selkirks, introduced in 1929 (see illustration and photo, *overleaf*). Both types were Canadian Pacific locomotives, for that railway had the steepest inclines to conquer.

Left.
On 9 February 2010, British Columbia's most well-known steam locomotive, 2860 Royal Hudson, creates a steam world for itself while waiting on the international boundary at the Peace Arch for ceremonies related to the Winter Olympics. On the previous day the locomotive had visited White Rock with a special train (see photo, *page 187*). While not a "golden age" photograph, the locomotive is from that period. The royal moniker was bestowed on the class after 2850 hauled King George VI across Canada in 1939—one engine, 25 crew changes, and 5,189 km—without failure.

Below.
The Great Northern's *International Limited* leaves the Vancouver station sometime in the 1930s at what seems like high speed but is more likely the slow shutter speed of the amateur photographer taking the shot. The back of the train, with less motion relative to the photographer, is noticeably sharper. The CNR station is visible in the background.

THE GOLDEN AGE OF STEAM

Below. Echoing the classic pose in the painting above, massive Selkirk CPR 5902 hauls the *Dominion*—since 1933 the railway's flagship Toronto-to-Vancouver train—near Yoho on 4 August 1938. A single Selkirk could haul 2,895 tonnes on a flat grade. It made a stunning—and very Canadian—sight!

Above.
Glorifying the railway, steam, express trains, and the Rockies all in one, this evocative painting appeared in a popular British railway magazine in March 1935. It shows CPR 2-10-4 Selkirk T1a locomotive No. 5903 pulling a long train, with the Rockies—or perhaps it is the Selkirks—in the background. The location is probably loosely based on Field. Selkirks, named after the mountains they were built to cross, were proudly advertised as the largest and most powerful non-articulated locomotives in the British Empire. (The "non-articulated" qualifier had to be added because there were more powerful engines in South Africa, the huge Beyer-Garratts, but they were not as fast as the Selkirks.) Some 20 Selkirks were built by CPR in Montreal in 1929, 10 more, slightly modified and classified T1b by CPR, were built in 1938, and another 6, classified T1c, in 1949. The latter were the last standard-gauge steam locomotives built in Canada (for a Canadian railway). The last Selkirks were taken out of service in 1959.

Canadian National Railways had fast trains too, of course. Like the Pacific Great Eastern, the railway was now in government hands, but there was a lot of debt to be paid off. CNR was doing quite well, in fact, and solvency seemed not far off when the Depression struck, decimating the economy and railway traffic with it.

Both CPR and CNR operated special fast trains carrying silk, arriving in Vancouver from the Orient and destined for New York markets. The silk was unloaded at dockside straight into the wood-lined steel boxcars of a waiting train, and these trains were given top priority, sidelining everything else, including express passenger trains. The reason for the haste was that silk was a very expensive commodity—a single train could be carrying $2 million worth and sometimes much more—and the insurance was prohibitive. Thus every minute that could be cut from the journey saved a lot of money. In addition, silk was being carried on American railways from Seattle, so there was an element of competition; of course, this also applied to the two Canadian railways. When CNR first got into the business in 1925—using oil-fired locomotives—the railway made a lot of having beaten the CPR's time to the East by two hours. Transporting silk fast made the railways a lot of money.

Right, top.
A CPR silk train about to leave Vancouver in the 1930s. The man in the hat in front of the locomotive has variously been described as a CPR official anxious to see the train on its way and a CPR policeman making sure no unauthorized persons are aboard; the latter description seems the most likely.

Above. A CNR silk train headed by J class Pacific No. 5083 leaving Vancouver in the 1930s.

Santa Fe 2-10-2 CP No. 5809 leads Selkirk No. 5909 and a long passenger train up the grade near Field in August 1938, making an impressive show of power.

THE GOLDEN AGE OF STEAM

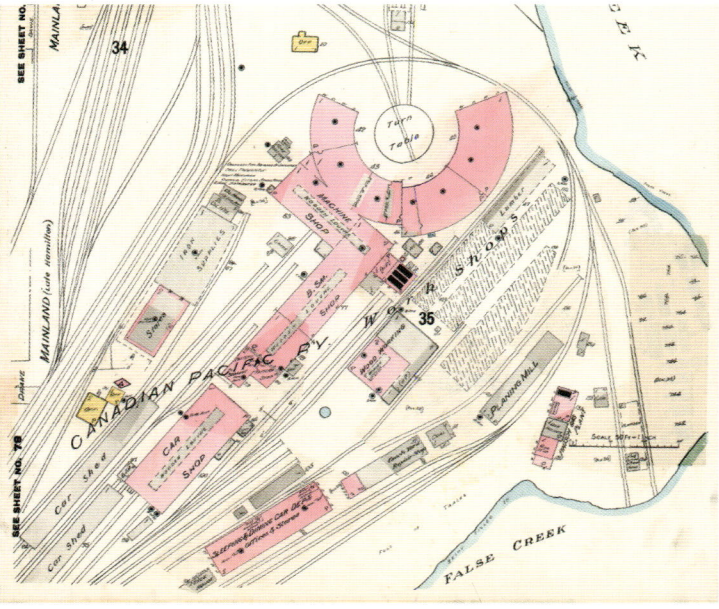

After the First World War the federal government reinstated the Crow's Nest Pass Agreement (the Crow Rate; see page 64), suspended during the war. This governed freight rates for Prairie grain. The result was that it became cheaper to haul grain to the nearest port, which for much of the Prairies meant Vancouver. The federal government completed a grain elevator in Vancouver in 1916, but it was not until 1921 that the first shipment of Prairie grain left Vancouver on a ship bound—via the Panama Canal—for Britain. This was the beginning of a major source of traffic for the railways. An elevator built in Prince Rupert was not used, however, because CNR had a shorter route via Vancouver.

With the coming of the Depression after 1929 most businesses stopped unnecessary expenditures, but the CPR continued with some planned improvements. One of these was the construction of the 1,396 metre Dunsmuir Tunnel in downtown Vancouver, enabling the abandonment of the surface tracks across a number of Vancouver streets (photo and map, *above*).

Above.
In June 1932, a Canadian Pacific train crosses Hastings Street in Vancouver on its way to the railway yards in False Creek, disrupting all traffic, including streetcars. The map (*left, top*), originally drawn in 1917 but updated to 1943, shows the railway's route diagonally through the city lots.

Left, centre.
The north-end, Vancouver Harbour portal of the Dunsmuir Tunnel, opened in July 1932. The tunnel was built to provide an alternate route from CPR's main line to the False Creek yards. Today most of the tunnel is utilized by SkyTrain (see page 176), but the narrow but high tunnel means the westbound and eastbound tracks are stacked on top of each other.

Left, bottom.
This is a detail of Canadian Pacific's False Creek yards, drawn in 1913 but with some updating. Prominent is the *Turn Table* surrounded by the roundhouse, the location today of preserved locomotive No. 374 (see page 216). The map is from an atlas produced for fire insurance purposes.

Above. The first Second Narrows Bridge, opened in 1925, was a combined road and rail bridge with a rising centre span. Here traffic is held up for a train coming off the bridge into Vancouver. The track is that of the connecting Vancouver Harbour Commissioners Terminal Railway (a locomotive from this line is pictured on *page 235*), which could be used by any railway company on payment of a fee, in much the same way as the line to Roberts Bank works today (see page 158). The CPR main line is in the foreground.

In January 1929 a bridge near the Connaught Tunnel collapsed while being rebuilt, forcing the CPR to divert its main-line traffic to its southern line. This led to backups at the gaps in the line at Kootenay Lake, where service was provided by rail barge, and as a result the railway bridged the 54 km gap with new track connecting Kootenay Landing with Nelson, a line that opened on 1 January 1931. A branch line south of Penticton likewise had a 13 km stretch of track built to eliminate a barge service on Skaha Lake.

Construction of Canadian National's Hotel Vancouver (the third with that name) had begun in 1928 but soon ground to a halt, leaving it a skeletal structure for most of the 1930s. It was finally completed in 1939 under a joint operating agreement between CNR and CPR.

The first Second Narrows Bridge was completed in 1925 and carried the Vancouver Harbour Commissioners Terminal Railway, built in 1925–27 to connect the PGE at the foot of Lonsdale (via a 1929 tunnel) with the south side of the harbour and the CPR and CNR lines. The bridge was damaged in September 1930 by a barge full of logs (it became wedged under a span and was lifted by a rising tide) and similarly lay unrepaired and unused for several years, though it was finally repaired and reopened in 1934.

Many people found themselves on hard times during the Depression and many men hitched rides on trains to travel from one place to another looking for work. The railways, as part of their less humane side, employed security men known universally as "bulls" to protect their property, but this job seemed to attract the worst kind of men, and in an age when it was not considered a crime, they were fond of billy-clubbing a sleeping transient—popularly known as a hobo—for no other reason than being in the wrong place at the wrong time.

One brighter event during the 1930s came as Britain prepared for the coming of the Second World War in 1939. King George VI and Queen Elizabeth, rallying the Empire to its cause, embarked on an immensely popular cross-Canada tour that, of course, was undertaken by train. CPR and CNR shared the

THE GOLDEN AGE OF STEAM

Above. Canadian National's *Continental Limited* makes a fine scene storming up the grade in a snowy Grandview Cut in 1933, at the height of the Depression. The locomotive is a J class 4-6-2 Pacific, No. 5117.

responsibilities: CPR undertook the westbound journey and CNR the return east. CPR had just built a new class of locomotives, the 4-6-4 Hudsons, intended for express passenger traffic. The railway was not immune to the trends in locomotive design in Europe and the United States, so the new locomotives had a semi-streamlined design. They would soon be used for the run from Vancouver to Revelstoke, where the Selkirks would take over. Specially painted and with royal crests installed, Hudson No. 2850 pulled the royal train the entire distance across Canada, going through twenty-five crew changes to do it. It seems the king was very impressed, as he gave his consent for the locomotive class to be called the Royal Hudsons. Although the CNR locomotives—which included the new semi-streamlined 6400 class—were similarly painted in royal blue and silver, they received no such honours.

Less than three months after the end of the tour Britain, and Canada, were at war with Germany. Demand for natural resources increased dramatically and the railways were called upon to move large volumes of heavy freight. That they were able to do so despite the general running down of the system in the previous decade was a lesson that would prove useful in the years after the war.

SPEED!

To EUROPE via CANADA

THE Scenic attractions and service of CANADIAN NATIONAL RAILWAYS are World famous in every respect.

This route Across CANADA should be considered on your next leave.

Bookings made on all Steamship Lines. Full particulars, of reduced through fares furnished also illustrated booklets.

CANADIAN NATIONAL
THE LARGEST RAILWAY IN AMERICA

HONG KONG OFFICE · GROUND FLOOR · GLOUCESTER BUILDING

Left, bottom. After the completion of Canadian Pacific's transcontinental, the route across Canada was promoted for quite some time as the "All-Red Route," a passage to the Orient from Britain, primarily to Hong Kong, then a British colony, that did not involve going through "foreign" ports. Both CPR and CNR promoted their services as fast coast-to-coast routes. This is an ad for the CNR service, published in the early 1930s.

Above. Several locomotives of the Royal Hudson class have been preserved, including No. 2850, which pulled the royal train across Canada in 1939. This is British Columbia's own No. 2860, universally known simply as "the Royal Hudson" (see page 187), shown at White Rock in 2010. There is no finer representative of the "Golden Age of Steam."

Below.
Canadian National N class No. 2423, built in 1913, is stopped at New Westminster station just prior to heading onto the New Westminster Bridge. It will pull the train to Port Mann, where a faster locomotive will take over. This slow but powerful engine was used because of the 1.1 per cent grade in the Grandview Cut, the steepest grade of the entire line west of Winnipeg.

THE GOLDEN AGE OF STEAM 117

Above. The Grandview Cut. This photo was taken in 1939 and shows a Great Northern freight train leaving Vancouver. The cut was excavated in 1910–1913 and material excavated was used to help reclaim False Creek. Compare with a modern photo on *page 167*.

Left. During the 1930s Canadian National advertised what it called "The Triangle Tour"—from Jasper to Vancouver, then by steamship to Prince Rupert and back to Jasper. This was the cover of the brochure.

Below. CNR N class No. 2753 with a freight train at Port Mann in June 1944. The engineer poses with his oil can.

118 IRON ROAD WEST

Right.
CPR No. 479 with a passenger train leaving Nanaimo on the Esquimalt & Nanaimo Railway in 1940.

Below.
About 1948, CPR No. 2701, a 4-6-2 G4 Pacific class locomotive built in 1925, heads the eastbound *Dominion*, then the railway's main transcontinental service. It is passing Clanwilliam Lake, near the summit of Eagle Pass.

Below, inset.
A British cigarette card issued in 1937 showing the *Dominion* in the Rockies. The train was famous the world over.

THE GOLDEN AGE OF STEAM   119

Above.
A pair of massive CPR steam locomotives at Revelstoke about 1948: No. 5466 (nearest the camera), and No. 5920. Mount Mackenzie is in the background. The photo is a combination of the original black and white image from a negative in the Revelstoke Museum and Archives and a colourized version displayed at the Revelstoke Railway Museum that lost a lot of its detail when it was printed. The cold air has enhanced the look of the steam, resulting in an evocative image. No. 5466 is a 2-8-2 Mikado built in 1948 at the Montreal Locomotive Works for CPR. Its sister engine, No. 5468, is preserved at the Revelstoke Railway Museum (see pages 199–201). No. 5920 is a Selkirk T1b class 2-10-4 built in 1938 and has smooth lines influenced by the design of the Royal Hudsons, also built at this time. It was also built at the Montreal Locomotive Works. These powerful engines were used to haul trains over the steep grades of the Rocky Mountains between Revelstoke and Calgary. The undated photo was taken in the period between 1948 and 1954, as no steam locomotives were based at Revelstoke after 1954. The "golden age" of steam in British Columbia was drawing to a close. Both CP and CN ran their last regular steam trains in 1960. The change to diesels allowed the railways to eliminate many divisional points, where previously steam locomotives had to be resupplied with water and coal.

Left.
In this classic view photographed about 1947, U class Mountain type 4-8-2 CNR No. 6044, built in 1929, coasts through an S-curve east of Redpass Junction (where the lines to Kamloops and Prince George diverge) with the westbound transcontinental train. Mount Robson forms a dramatic backdrop. A more Canadian scene cannot be imagined!

The Armoured Train

British Columbia's coast was considered vulnerable to Japanese invasion during the Second World War, and the Skeena Valley was thought to be a likely target. Prince Rupert was connected to the rest of Canada by a rail line, the Canadian National ex–Grand Trunk Pacific Railway line to Prince George and beyond, but there was no road west of Terrace. Prince Rupert itself was defended with seven coastal gun batteries. But for defence of the 150 km between Terrace and Prince Rupert, the only answer lay with the railway.

In early 1942 the Canadian military establishment dreamed up the idea of an armoured train, a concept first used during the American Civil War in 1861–65 and then in Europe during the Franco-Prussian War in 1870–71 but never before—or since—used in Canada. The train was assembled in the CNR workshops in Winnipeg. It had five modified open freight cars complete with Bofors and Bren guns and searchlights, plus two boxcars modified to hold soldiers; all the rolling stock and the locomotive, which was in the middle of the train, were armour-plated. The train was manned by about 150 soldiers and was hauled by a steam locomotive, CNR class H-10 4-6-0 No. 1426. Such a source of motive power was not the best choice, clearly, since it would produce plumes of steam visible to the enemy from a long way off, and would have to be kept fired up in case it was required urgently.

When the armoured train first began its patrols along the banks of the Skeena River it was found that the railbed was not very even, causing the searchlights to jitter about and make the guns hard to aim. The guns were sent to Vancouver to be adjusted. For security reasons, the train did not run to any particular schedule and, as a result, caused at least one accident to railway personnel when the train showed up unexpectedly.

There were plans to replace the steam locomotive with a new diesel electric one and one, CNR No. 9000 (originally built in 1929), was armour plated in readiness. But the Japanese withdrawal from the Aleutian Islands and their reoccupation by the US Army in the summer of 1943 lessened the likelihood of invasion of the West Coast and the armoured train was taken out of service in October 1943. The unit was disbanded in July the following year, which was also the year in which a road to Prince Rupert was completed, lessening the need for such a train in any case.

There are relatively few photos of the armoured train, probably because it operated in a remote area, security was very tight, and photographing military installations had been banned.

Right.
A Bren gunner sits atop the train in a distinctly unprotected position. The locomotive CNR No. 1426, with its armour plating, can be seen in the distance.

Above. CNR No. 1426, seen before being fitted with armour plate.

Right. The gun cars. A searchlight can be seen on the far car.

Below. The end of the train with gun and cowcatcher. These were fitted at both front and back.

Above. The armoured train sits on a siding in Terrace after having been taken out of service in October 1943.

THE GOLDEN AGE OF STEAM 121

Logging and Mining Railways

Logging Railways

Early logging amounted to no more than felling a tree and rolling it into the nearest water. But as the forest immediately adjacent to water was removed, it became necessary to transport logs overland. The first means of doing this was the skid road, a series of laterally laid logs arranged to provide a surface with less friction than the ground alone. Power to pull the logs was provided first by teams of oxen, as in the photo at right, and later by similar teams of horses, a perfectly suitable solution for short distances.

Steam power began to be used in sawmills around 1860, but these engines were not suitable in the woods because they had large flywheels. Around 1875 steam donkeys began to be used. These were simply stationary engines that powered winches to haul logs to a landing or central point. They still required a "line horse" to drag the main line out into the forest.

The first use of a railway for logging in British Columbia appears to have been by Rogers Logging, hauling logs a short distance from what is now central westside Vancouver to Jerry's Cove, on English Bay—now Jericho Beach—along a route that is today Valley Drive. About 1871 Jeremiah Rogers bought two second-hand British-made steam tractors that had been pulling freight on the Cariboo Highway to the goldfields and replaced their wheels with steel double-flanged ones to run on a track made of wood poles.

A little later the British Columbia Mills and Trading Company used a steam railway—with steel rails—in South Surrey. In 1888 the locomotive No. 2 *Emory* (*Old Curly*), then finished with its construction duties building and improving the Canadian Pacific Railway, was sold to the Royal City Planing Mills in New Westminster, and set to work in South Surrey. A well-known photograph of it in that location is shown *overleaf*. With the completion of the New Westminster Southern Railway in 1891 (see page 46), a line was built to connect to it. Then logs could be carried directly from the South Surrey forests to a log dump on the Fraser River at Port Kells.

Logging in the United States was more advanced than in Canada at the time, and it is perhaps not surprising that specialized logging locomotives were developed there. The key difference between locomotives designed for logging and their main-line brethren is that they had sets of wheels on trucks that were some distance apart so that they could negotiate very tight curves and also cope with greater differences in elevation between the back and the front, common on temporary, irregular, roughly built logging tracks. They also were constructed to provide greater torque, through small wheels and gearing or a similar arrangement, to allow for climbing steep grades. Their weight was spread out as much as possible to distribute it over minimally built track. And all the specially built types were quite slow, though this was no disadvantage for their type of work. "Normal" steam locomotives (with a steel rod and arm connection to the cylinders) were, of course,

Above, top.
Before railways, brute animal or human force was used to remove logs from the forest. These oxen are pulling a string of logs over a road with embedded logs to provide a skid road. Early ties, but no rails! The method was slow but reliable. This photo is dated 1889 and the location is South Surrey, at the Royal City Mills camp.

Above.
A primitive early railway using a home-built locomotive that was little more than a boiler on wheels. Dated about 1910, the photo shows the logging operation of A.G. Lambert and partner at Taghum and Sproule Creek, a few kilometres west of Nelson. The railway was apparently fondly known as the P.P. & J. Railway—Push, Pull & Jerk.

Left.
A 1915-built Climax logging locomotive at the Forestry Discovery Centre in Duncan. This engine belonged to Hillcrest Lumber and worked in the Cowichan Valley. Climax locomotives have cylinders mounted on both sides at an angle—the one on the right side can be seen here—which power not the wheels directly but drive shafts running down the centre underneath the engine, and are therefore not visible in the photo; the shaft is connected to all the axles via skewed, or offset, bevel gears.

LOGGING AND MINING RAILWAYS

Above.
This is one of the most well-known photos of railways of any sort in British Columbia. Taken in 1894, it shows the ex–Andrew Onderdonk–CPR locomotive No. 2 *Emory*, better known as *Old Curly*, sold in 1888 to the Royal City Planing Mills in South Surrey and used in the forests around Hazelmere. Logging in the area started in 1887 using a logging ditch dug from the Nicomekl River connected to an oxen- or horse-powered railway that ran about 5 km east, connecting with a number of skid roads. When the New Westminster Southern Railway (NWS) was opened in 1891 (see page 46), the ditch was replaced by a railway line extension farther east to connect to the main line at Hazelmere station. One of the skid roads connecting with the logging railway can be seen on the right in this photo, as can a log-loading ramp. Also visible, in the foreground, is a water trough and piles of hay to feed and water the oxen or horses that hauled the logs along the skid road to the railway. The connection to the NWS line allowed logs to be taken directly north to a log dump on the Fraser River at Port Kells (*left*), though a larger, ex–Great Northern locomotive was later acquired for this purpose (photo, *overleaf*). No. 2 is one of the very few surviving locomotives from this era and is on display at Burnaby Village Museum (see photo, *page 217*).

124 IRON ROAD WEST

used, often purchased second-hand from main-line railways, but they could only be used on relatively good track.

Three main types of logging locomotive were developed, and all were used in British Columbia. The most popular was the Lima Shay, built in Lima, Ohio. The Lima Shay has cylinders mounted vertically on the right side of the engine that transfer power to the wheel sets at back and front using drive shafts running along the side. Because this places more weight on the right side, the boiler is located off-centre to the left to balance the weight distribution.

The second most popular was the Climax locomotive, which had cylinders mounted on both sides at an angle that powered drive shafts running down the centre underneath the engine and connected to all the axles via skewed bevel gears (see photo, overleaf).

The third type was the Heisler, which featured a V-type engine coupled to centre drive shafts that were coupled to only one axle of each truck, avoiding the need for the bevel gears of the Climax. They were promoted as having the best balance of any design. A number of BC-worked Shay and Climax locomotives survive in preservation, but unfortunately no Heislers do.

As can be seen from most of the old photos, the majority of logging locomotives operated with a large spark arrester on the chimney. Steam locomotives have a tendency to eject red-hot embers in their exhaust, and starting a fire in a forest was always a real danger. Logging companies in later years were required to maintain firefighting equipment, so most had large rail-borne water tanks that could be moved to the source of a fire quickly.

The majority of logging railways in British Columbia were "standard gauge" (4 feet 8½ inches or 1.435 metres), perhaps surprisingly, since narrow-gauge railways can usually be built more cheaply and navigate tighter curves. This may be because of the availability and higher power of standard-gauge

Above, top.
This is the beautifully restored Lima Shay No. 2 "two-spot" of the Alberni Pacific Railway. Alberni Pacific was a lumber company in the Alberni Valley; now the line that bears its name is a heritage railway based in Port Alberni. The right side displays the three vertically mounted cylinders and the drive train along the side of the locomotive that they power shown close up, *above*. There are lots of exposed moving parts to a Shay, which made it fun to watch but a workplace safety nightmare.

locomotives, preferred compatibility with main lines, or because the wider track provided greater stability.

It was only natural that good stands of timber close to the cities or close to navigable waterways would be logged first, but as these became exhausted, logging moved deeper into the province's forests and the problem of how to efficiently get the logs to market became more acute; railways provided a convenient solution.

Logging in the Interior for the most part had to await the development of main-line railways to connect to.

LOGGING AND MINING RAILWAYS 125

Above.
This ex–Great Northern 4-4-0 was purchased by Royal City Planing Mills to transport logs from South Surrey to the Port Kells log dump, replacing the veteran No. 2 *Emory*. Here the locomotive poses in 1899, with everyone involved getting in on the photo. Damage to the photo has been partially repaired.

Above.
This 1910 Climax logging locomotive is preserved at the BC Forest Discovery Centre in Duncan. Note how the wheel sets are far apart to allow the locomotive to navigate tight curves.

Left, bottom.
A CPR train laden with logs destined to become railway ties near Canal Flats about 1930. This was part of the CPR's Yahk tie operation. Note the immense spark arrester on the locomotive.

Below.
The crew of a well-laden Shay locomotive belonging to Anderson Logging of Union Bay poses for a photograph about 1900. The engine also has a huge spark arrester on its chimney.

Settlements based on mining, such as Nelson, were growing and required wood to build their cities. And railways needed wood. The CPR operated its own facility at Yahk in the East Kootenays to supply it with ties. By 1908 about 28 per cent of the province's approximately 243 km of logging trackage was in the Interior, while 15 per cent was on the mainland coast and in the Fraser Valley; more than half was on Vancouver Island, the result of easier access to larger trees.

In the southeast corner of the province, extensive multiple forest fires led to a decline of logging and its accompanying railways, and by the end of the 1920s most large operations had ceased. The focus shifted to the coast.

By the end of 1918 there were 530 km of logging railway tracks in the province, according to provincial Department of Railways statistics, and 64 logging locomotives. By 1924, which is close to the peak of railway logging activity in the province, the department reported 1,125 km of logging tracks and 126 steam locomotives, plus 12 gas locomotives, the harbinger of steam's eventual demise, though these early ones were

LOGGING AND MINING RAILWAYS   127

Above.
This unusual photograph was taken by W.J. Moore, a professional photographer, using a panorama camera that rolled film past the lens as the camera was panned. It shows an Abernethy-Lougheed Logging Company train of logs, with a Climax locomotive in charge, backing down to a log dump at Port Haney, on the Fraser River, in 1921.

essentially trucks on rail wheels and were only able to pull a very limited load. These latter statistics do not include another 40 km of track belonging to the CPR's tie operation at Yahk, and three more locomotives.

Some logging railways were quite extensive. The Comox Logging & Railway Company, a subsidiary of Canadian Western Lumber at Fraser Mills, began operations in the Comox Valley in 1909 and within ten years had a veritable web of lines that stretched 30 km between Oyster River and Royston, across Comox Harbour from Comox. Many switchbacks were used to access the steepest areas. Comox Logging & Railway became the largest logging company in the British Empire and one of the largest in the world. The railway operation lasted until 1946 in the Comox area, and operations near Ladysmith, the company's focus after that, ended only in 1984. (The company was purchased by Crown Zellerbach in 1954 and Fletcher Challenge in the early 1980s.)

In the Lower Mainland, the mountain slopes of what is now Golden Ears Provincial Park were logged with a large railway network by the Abernethy-Lougheed Logging Company (photo, *above*) until 1929, when a massive forest fire destroyed most of the trees, causing the operation to close two years later.

Logging railways were everywhere there were commercially valuable trees. In the Powell River area alone some fifteen separate logging railways were known to have operated, though not all at the same time. The first had been an 8-mile line built around 1890 by BC Mills, Timber & Trading Company, operator of the Hastings Mill in Vancouver, as it moved up the coast in search of new fields to log.

One interesting innovation, used only as the very steepest locations were logged, came in the early 1920s. This was the incline, where logs on skeleton cars were lowered down a steeply inclined track by special braking winch devices installed

Above.
Part of the 760-metre-long Green Point Logging incline on the east side of Harrison Lake, sometime in the 1930s. Note the scene of total devastation on either side of the track.

Left. One of the largest rail logging operations was that of Comox Logging & Railway on Vancouver Island. The large scale allowed for this five-track engine shed, shown surrounded by workers' housing.

Above, centre. A long Hillcrest Lumber logging train with Climax locomotive No. 10 on the company's Sahtlam logging division, above the Chemainus River on Vancouver Island, in 1935.

Right. A Shay locomotive and train of logs on the wonderfully named Theodosia, Powell Lake & Eastern Railway, near Powell River on the Sunshine Coast in 1926. The offset boiler is clearly visible in this view.

Above.
About 1925, a Heisler locomotive and logging train of Eagle Lake Spruce Mills poses at Giscome, about 40 km northeast of Prince George.

Below.
This huge locomotive, Canadian Forest Products No. 111, built in 1929, is believed to be the largest logging steam locomotive ever to have worked in British Columbia. It ran on the Canadian Forest Products main line on northern Vancouver Island, and worked longer trains assembled from shorter trains hauled by smaller locomotives from branch lines. This early colour photograph was taken by railfan Elwood White at Woss in 1956. Diesels arrived two years later and No. 111 was scrapped in 1961.

at the top of the slope. Stationary steam engines or horses were used to return the empty cars to the top of the slope. If the topography allowed, inclines could be quite long. One near Sechelt was 2 km long, with grades as steep as 45 per cent. These logging inclines were an adaptation of the inclined plane, a feature of many of the earliest railways of the 1820s and 1830s, before mobile steam engines became widely used.

On the main-line railways, steam power succumbed to diesels by the late 1950s, but only two logging railways changed over: Comox Logging & Railway at its Ladysmith operation, and Canadian Forest Products (Canfor) in the Nimpkish Valley at the north end of Vancouver Island. The main reason was simply that railway logging as a whole was in decline, with logging roads and logging trucks taking over. Diesels were more reliable than steam locomotives, required less maintenance and were less likely to start fires, but could only compete with trucks on longer-haul routes.

British Columbia's last logging line was the Englewood Railway of Western Forest Products (purchased from Canfor in

Above.
In 2011, two Englewood Railway EMD SW 1200 diesel locomotives, Nos. 302 and 304, lead a train of empty skeleton railcars across the steel bridge over the Kokish River, which flows into Beaver Cove on northern Vancouver Island. It is an impressive scene on what was the last operating logging railway in North America.

2006), a 90 km line on the north end of Vancouver Island, from Vernon Lake through the headquarters at Woss, to Beaver Cove. It was the last operating logging railway in North America when it shut down in November 2017 after a six-month "temporary" shutdown for investigations following the deaths of three employees resulting from a runaway train.

The line was built by the Nimpkish Timber Company in 1917 as a 16 km connection from Beaver Cove to Nimpkish Lake, where logs were collected after being floated from other parts of the lake. Later the company built an unconnected section from the other end of the lake, deeper into the forests of Vancouver Island. In 1957, after an agreement with a new iron-ore mining company to share the line and the cost of building it, the two sections were connected by a line along the east side of Nimpkish Lake. It opened in 1960. Mining ceased only three years later and the line reverted to a logging-only line

At closure, the railway had four EMD SW 1200 diesel switcher-type locomotives, three of which were normally working, with the fourth in reserve. These are powerful but not particularly fast, and were part of more than a thousand built by General Motors Electro-Motive Division (EMD) between 1954 and 1966.

Right.
Logging railways typically used gas speeders to move men and equipment. This is a preserved one (in yellow) on the Alberni Pacific Railway in Port Alberni. This was the typical shape of a speeder, although they came in all shapes and sizes, some powerful enough to move a few logging cars, others intended only for the transportation of men to logging sites. The driver/engineer sat in the top cab.

LOGGING AND MINING RAILWAYS

Mining Railways

As with logs, transporting heavy metal ores was also a job well suited to railways. And as with logging, the first railways used animals to pull the trains, in this case usually horses, but sometimes mules.

Underground, there was a very considerable benefit to the use of a guiding rail in narrow tunnels, in that some speed could be achieved without the possibility of rubbing against the tunnel sides. But underground conditions were dangerous enough without adding the open fires of steam engines, so locomotives developed for underground use were either electric or used compressed air to power the cylinders more normally worked by expanding steam. Pittsburgh locomotive manufacturer H.K. Porter produced many of the so-called fireless locomotives of the latter category (see photos on these pages) that were used in mines in British Columbia.

Right, top and *right, centre.*
These are ore trains on the electric tramway of the Nickel Plate Mine at Hedley, in the Similkameen Valley. Getting ore from the mine high on the mountainside down to the valley floor was a problem solved by the use of two systems. This electric tramway ran across the top of the mountain, with an elevation change of 180 metres; the loaded ore cars were pulled down but the empties pushed up. The elevation change was dealt with using a centrally located switchback, and the photo *right, top* shows two trains (one empty, one full) passing on the switchback. The electric tramway connected with a wired gravity tramway (photo, *right*) that was very steep, dropping 1,100 metres down to the valley floor and itself separated into two sections at a central station where the ore cars were redirected to a different cable. The cables simultaneously pulled the empties back up as the loaded cars went down. A cable and a roller to carry it can be seen in the foreground. The railway was built when the mine opened in 1902, although these photos were taken in the 1930s. The mine closed in 1955, though opened again as an open-pit mine between 1987 and 1996.

Left.
A horse-drawn ore train at the entrance to Mine No. 2 of the Nicola Valley Coal & Coke Company in Merritt in 1907. The photograph was taken by a photographer with the BC Bureau of Mines.

Above, top.
The Sullivan Mine at Kimberley was at one time the largest producer of lead and zinc in the world. The mine had an extensive system of underground electric railways and used an overhead wire, like streetcars. Here a train loaded with ore poses for a photograph at the mine portal in 1937.

Right, top, above, and right, centre top.
H.K. Porter fireless compressed-air locomotives were a favourite of underground miners for their relative safety. The pistons that drive the wheels use compressed air, stored in the large tank, instead of steam. *Right, top* is a 1910 compressed-air locomotive from the Elk River Colliery, on display at Fort Steele. *Above* is a 1911 one from Canmore Mine in Alberta, on display at Sandon, and *right, centre top* is one built in 1908 and later converted to gas operation, on display at Chilliwack Heritage Park.

Right, centre bottom.
A compressed-air locomotive at the Granby mine in Phoenix about 1914.

Right.
Main-line locomotives were used to transport coal to ports. Here Esquimalt & Nanaimo engine No. 10 is ready to depart the Extension coal mines with a trainload of coal for Ladysmith, sometime in the early 1900s.

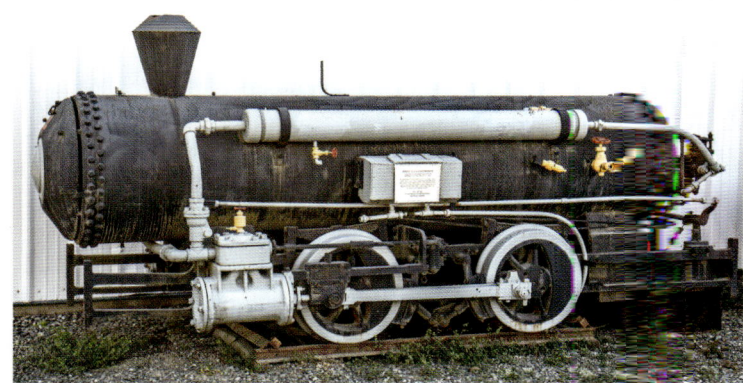

LOGGING AND MINING RAILWAYS   33

British Columbia's Railway

Above.
One of British Columbia Railway's 1983 electric locomotives built for the Tumbler Ridge line. It is preserved at the Prince George Railway and Forestry Museum.

Below.
The first official PGE train into Prince George, 1 November 1952. Two PGE diesels are preceded by a steam locomotive, CNR No. 7539, as a rather unnecessary pilot hiding the welcome board on the front of the first diesel. A large crowd has turned out for the occasion.

In 1922 the British Columbia government gave up on the idea of completing its railway—for it had been government-owned since 1918—into Prince George, despite the fact that the railbed had reached a point only 30 km away, albeit with a missing bridge over the Cottonwood River, just north of Quesnel (see page 108).

After the Second World War, BC governments were in an expansionist mood. Premier John Hart had initiated the Hart Highway project, building the road from Prince George to Dawson Creek, completed in 1952 and finally connecting Peace River residents with the rest of the province without having to drive through Alberta. (He also built a highway from Princeton to Hope, opened in 1949, ending the necessity of shipping cars by rail over that gap.)

Hart's successor, Byron "Boss" Johnson, decided to complete the Pacific Great Eastern to Prince George. The province had received several proposals after the war from Americans interested in taking over the railway and extending it to Alaska, but, mainly for nationalistic reasons, had turned them down.

Much of the railbed from Quesnel to Prince George was already in place, but the bridge over the Cottonwood River—which the province had decided was too expensive in 1922—had to be built. In 1952 it was completed, and on 12 September of that year the first PGE train rolled into Prince George. It was a work train and it arrived to no great fanfare, but on 1 November the first "official" train, loaded with dignitaries, arrived in the city. The rules stated that non–Canadian National trains had to be piloted by a CNR locomotive to cross the Fraser bridge, so, despite the PGE's pioneering uses of diesels for freight (the first had been delivered in 1948), the official train had a steam engine up front (photo, *left, bottom*).

The line at this point still ran north from Squamish, at the head of Howe Sound, but the decision had been made to extend it to its originally intended destination, North Vancouver, to finally rid the PGE of its laborious transshipment to tug-pulled barges at Squamish. The line down the eastern side of Howe Sound was to prove much more challenging, carved out of the mountainside as it had to be. Once at Horseshoe Bay, though, the original railbed of the line abandoned in 1928 could be utilized, much to the chagrin and

Right, top.
On 1 November 1952 the first official train ever the extension to Prince George crosses a bridge at Ahbau Creek, just north of Quesnel. The headboard reads, "Hello! Prince George We're Here."

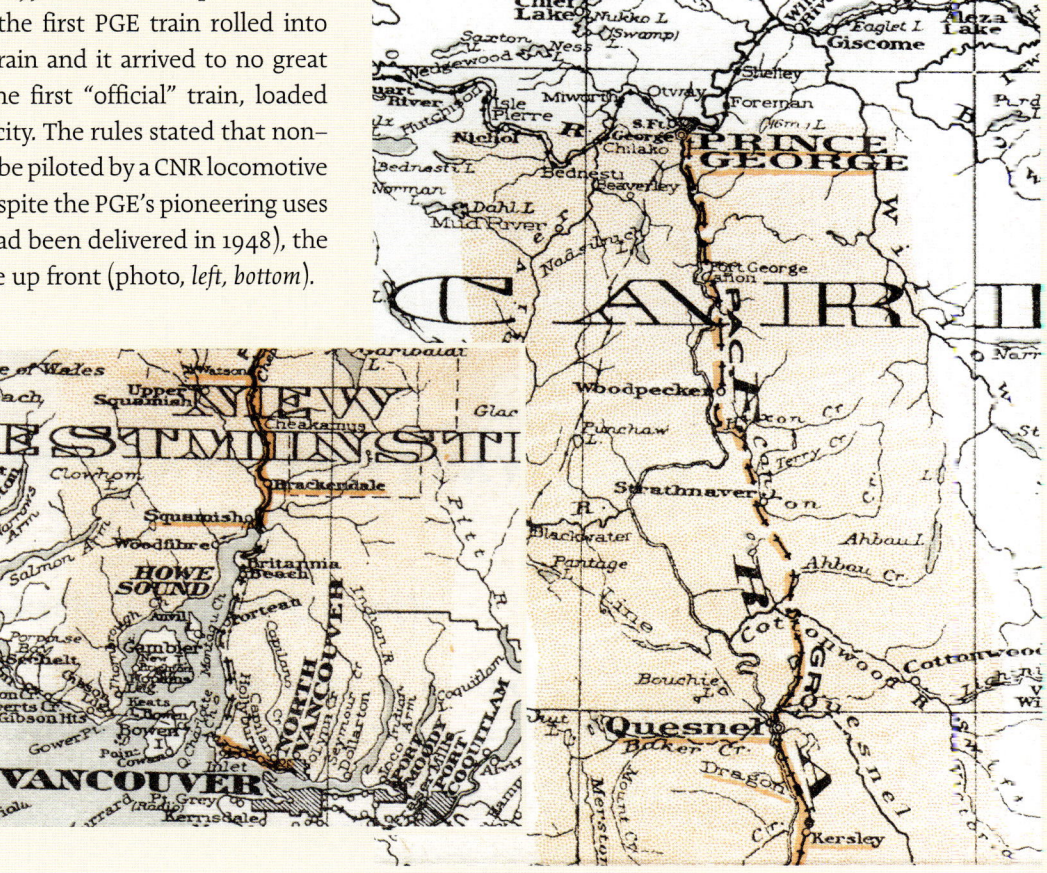

Right.
Two parts of a 1922 map show the gaps in the Pacific Great Eastern line from North Vancouver to Prince George. Existing trackage is shown in orange; the West Vancouver tracks would be torn up in 1928 and only the railbed left in place. The gaps remained until 1952 for the northern gap and 1954 for the southern.

public outcry of many West Vancouver residents, who, thinking the line would never be used again, had incorporated the railway's right-of-way into their own gardens. However, the PGE had never formally abandoned the line, but had simply let it fall into disuse.

The line down Howe Sound required the use of over 900 tonnes of dynamite and the boring of four tunnels. Track had previously been laid between Squamish and Britannia Beach to access the Anaconda copper mine at the latter location. On 10 June 1956 three trains laden with dignitaries and press travelled north to a point near Porteau Cove for a last-spike ceremony. The line was officially opened on 27 August that year, with three official trains travelling—eventually—through to Prince George, after a 17-hour delay caused by a rockslide in Howe Sound.

British Columbia's longest-serving premier, W.A.C. Bennett, came to power in 1952. He believed in railways as a tool for developing the province and promoted northern extensions of the PGE for this purpose. He had approved the Howe Sound line to link to Vancouver and other main-line railways in 1954, and the same bill authorized borrowing to finance lines to Dawson Creek and Fort St. John. The line was to link with the Alaska Highway, diverting mineral shipments to rail. In addition it was hoped the railway would carry Peace River grain and Pine Pass coal.

Federal subsidies were limited to only the first 80 km north of Prince George because Ottawa considered the Peace

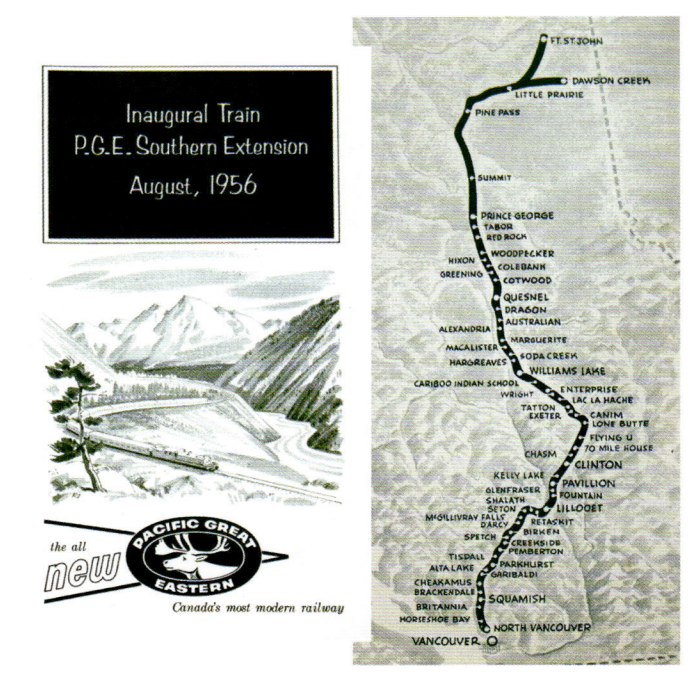

Above.
This was the cover of the menu given to passengers in the official inaugural trains from North Vancouver to Prince George on 27 August 1956. Note how the railway bills itself as "Canada's most modern railway," touting its early adoption of diesels for freight trains. (Continuing that tradition, the railway was also the first in North America to use microwave telecommunications for train dispatching, beginning in 1957.) Passengers dined on delicacies such as "North Shore Chicken Salad," "New Potatoes a la Pemberton," and "Okanagan Apple Pie." Inside was this rather premature map showing the extension of the railway beyond *Prince George* to *Dawson Creek* and *Ft. St. John*, not completed until 1958.

Left.
In 1956, new track is laid in North Vancouver at the southernmost point of the new southern extension, right where it would join the existing track. The Lions Gate Bridge can be seen in the background.

Below.
Despite its own gaps, the PGE performed a valuable service where no roads existed by ferrying vehicles on flatbed cars, just as the CPR did over the Selkirks and the Kettle Valley Railway did from Hope to Princeton (see page 101). Here Hall-Scott gas car No. 102 (originally used on the North Shore subdivision; see photo, *page 104*) ferries three cars along the shore of Seton Lake from Shalalth, near Seton Portage, headed for Lillooet, a service begun in 1933. There were ramps at either end to load and unload vehicles easily. A similar service, but just for passengers, remains in place today (see page 170).

Above.
One of the three inaugural trains to Fort St. John crosses a bridge and curved trestle across the Peace River near Taylor on 3 October 1958. The year before, the Alaska Highway road bridge here had collapsed and the nearly complete railway structure was fitted with guard rails and planked so that it could temporarily be used by road traffic as well as trains, an arrangement that began in October 1957 and continued until January 1960. The trestle shown here burned down in October 1979 and was replaced by fill and a shorter trestle to the bridge. The inaugural trains were made up of a motley collection of passenger cars—one had a Budd railcar tacked on as an extra coach—and carried passengers from the world of railways and finance. The president of the Chicago, Milwaukee, St. Paul & Pacific Railroad brought his own luxury railcar as did several other American railroad men.

River region to be adequately served by the Northern Alberta Railway; Bennett, of course, wanted a British Columbia line, not an Alberta one, and so went ahead anyway.

The line to Chetwynd was completed in 1958, and later that year two branches, one to Dawson Creek and the other to Fort St. John, an event of course celebrated with an official train (photo, *above*), for Premier Bennett was a master showman. In fact, there were again three trains. They left from North Vancouver and arrived in Dawson Creek on 2 October before proceeding to Fort St. John the next day.

A favourable economic climate for resource development in the 1960s led to the construction of a 37 km spur line from the main line north of Prince George to Mackenzie, where a large pulp mill and sawmill were being planned. The line opened in August 1966.

In 1963 a decision had been made to extend the PGE from Prince George northwest to Fort St. James, one of the very first settlements in what is now British Columbia, to facilitate development of new timber resources. This line was completed in 1968.

Reaching the Yukon had been a government goal for some time. In the late 1950s, a private enterprise proposal was briefly entertained, when Swedish industrialist Axel Wenner-Gren proposed a rail line called the Pacific Northern Railway. It was to run from Summit Lake, 50 km north of Prince George, to the Yukon border, and operate in co-operation with the PGE for onward shipment south.

In 1965 Bennett announced that the railway would be extended from Fort St. James to Takla Landing, and from there continue to Stewart, on the coast. It was later revealed that the ultimate intention had been to then build from Stewart to Whitehorse, in the Yukon, following a not dissimilar route to that of the White Pass & Yukon Railway.

BRITISH COLUMBIA'S RAILWAY 137

The Northern Alberta Railway

The Northern Alberta Railway (NAR), which figured in the deliberations of the PGE's moves into the northern part of British Columbia, reached Pouce Coupe and Dawson Creek in 1931. The company was a collection of four regional lines in northern Alberta—one of which was the Edmonton, Dunvegan & British Columbia Railway (ED&BC), a name that betrays the original intentions of its owners. The line was cheaply built, sometimes with no ballast, and like the PGE earned a nickname: Exceedingly Dangerous & Badly Constructed.

The railways had been built to serve the rich agricultural region of the Peace River but did not produce enough traffic to become viable. They were taken over by the Alberta government in 1920 and management of the ED&BC was handed over to Canadian Pacific, in return for a cash payment. By 1927 the lines had become viable and were jointly purchased by CPR and CNR and renamed the Northern Alberta Railway. It was the ex-ED&BC line that was extended to Dawson Creek in 1931.

During the Second World War the NAR line to Dawson Creek was busy ferrying men and equipment for the building of the Alaska Highway. The railway was exclusively acquired by CN in 1981. In 1958, with the completion of the PGE to Dawson Creek, the two railways had been joined.

Track between Hythe, Alberta, and Dawson Creek (correctly the Grande Prairie Subdivision between Hythe and Iracard, just east of Dawson Creek) was not used after 1998, but as a condition of purchasing BC Rail in 2004 CN agreed (in a November 2003 "Investment Partnership" agreement with BCR, and as a service commitment to the federal Competition Bureau) to reopen it. It seems that CN made repairs to the track but did not begin running trains. This section is no longer used, though the track remains in place (as of 2018) and the line has not been officially closed. Perhaps because of the controversies surrounding the sale (see page 145), CN now refuses to discuss the history of this line or say whether or not it may be reopened, the provincial Ministry of Transportation defers to the federal Competition Bureau, and the latter seems to think the agreement to reopen the line has been honoured, which clearly it has not.

Above, top. NAR No. 73 (ex-ED&BC 73), a 2-8-0 Consolidation built in 1927, now preserved at the Alberta Railway Museum in Edmonton.

Above. A 1931 system map of the Northern Alberta Railway two years after its inception. On the extreme left is the only track in British Columbia, the line completed in January 1931 into *Dawson Creek*; the stations of *Tupper*, *Gundy* and *Pouce Coupe* are also in BC.

In 1969, federal government interest in a railway to develop the Yukon led to a consultant's report (the Hedlin-Menzies report) outlining five possible routes. The easiest route seemed to be a northward extension of the Takla Landing line, which was completed that year, and the PGE then decided to build this line as far as Dease Lake. Why this decision was made is unclear, but it may have been to forestall possible expansion north from Terrace or Hazelton by the federal government–controlled Canadian National Railways. And it would give the provincial government some bargaining power and ensure the province shared in any future economic development in the North. For a short while it seemed that railway competition was alive again in British Columbia!

Work had begun the previous year on a 380 km extension from Fort St. John to Fort Nelson, in the northern corner of the province. This line was designed to link with the Mackenzie Delta via the Liard River and thus divert trade from the Far North away from Alberta into British Columbia, forestalling any possible expansion of the Northern Alberta Railway in the process. The line was completed in September 1971 and celebrated with the requisite inaugural train, delayed when it derailed near Williams Lake. Arriving at Fort Nelson, Premier Bennett gave a typical speech, in which, as author Martin Robin put it, "the old creed was summoned about thresholds, forward leaps, a greater British Columbia, and neighbourliness with the people of the Yukon and Northwest Territories."

The Dease Lake extension, on which construction had begun in 1970, however, was not to be. But it took a long time for the project to be cancelled. In 1972 Bennett was ousted at the polls by Dave Barrett and the NDP. Contractors found out that the railway's engineering estimates were far too optimistic. Volumes of fill, the amount of rock blasting, and the amount of material required to construct the railbed were much greater than had been stated on the contract tenders. Despite this, Barrett's government decided to continue. The lure of railway building to open up the wilderness had affected him too.

Ironically, perhaps, it was W.A.C. Bennett's son, William R. (Bill) Bennett, who finally cancelled the Dease extension. Elected in 1975, the new government ordered a review of the project, a royal commission, in fact, to sort out what had become a financial quagmire. Construction ceased on 5 April 1977. The commission's report in 1978 found that neither the Dease Lake extension nor the Fort Nelson line were economically viable and should not have been built.

The Dease Lake line at this point had 254 km of track already laid and included a substantial steel bridge over the Stikine River. Only 63 km of grading remained, but it was cancelled nevertheless. Trains continued to run as far north as Driftwood, just beyond the north end of Takla Lake, to service forestry companies, but then they were asked to move, to log mountain pine beetle–infested areas, and the line's trade vanished. Fort St. James became the northern end of the line. In 1991 the line was reopened as far as about 100 km north of the north end of Takla Lake (Bulkley House) to service forest companies.

Pacific Great Eastern freight cars found their way all over North America, and W.A.C. Bennett thought it a poor advertisement for the railway and the province, so on 1 April 1972 the railway's name was changed to the British Columbia Railway (BCR). It took years, of course, for all the locomotives and freight cars to be repainted, and in 1984 the name was changed again, reflecting the advertising trend of the times, to BC Rail.

Right.
This map, from a Pacific Great Eastern 1971 advertising publication called *Patterns of Growth*, shows the various northern extensions mentioned in the text. The red line north of Fort St. James is the Dease Lake extension, still under construction at that date.

Below.
A PGE poster from about 1960 shows the 1958 completed extensions to *Dawson Creek* and *Fort St. John* and the southern 1956 one to (North) *Vancouver*, with a tug-and-barge service still in place to *Seattle*. The poster shows off the railway's new diesels and Budd railcars (RDCs).

Left.
A PGE wood caboose built in 1913 displayed at the Prince George Railway and Forestry Museum.

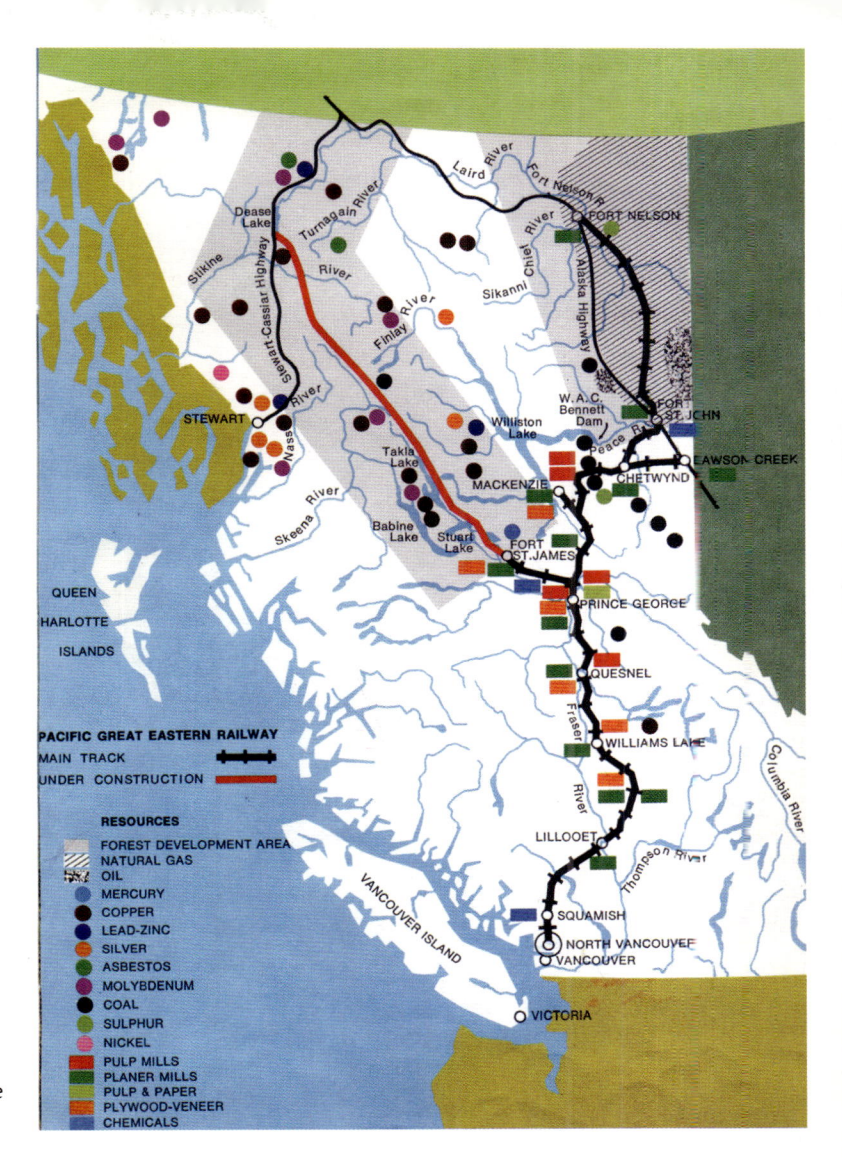

Above. The cover of a 1974 passenger train schedule shows two of the railway's Budd rail diesel cars (RDCs), self-propelled diesel multiple units (DMUs).

BRITISH COLUMBIA'S RAILWAY 139

These pages: Some scenes on the PGE/BCR in the 1970s and 1980s taken by railway photographer Dave Wilkie.

Above.
There was a significant presence of CN motive power and stock on the PGE and BCR, no doubt caused by the linkage at Prince George to that railway. Here an extra headed by three CN diesels, a BCR diesel and a coach, curves around the mountainside of Howe Sound near Brunswick Beach. The train consisted of 86 freight cars, many of which were the orange and yellow Canadian government grain hopper cars. The photo was taken on 23 February 1980. Speeders preceded all trains between North Vancouver and Garibaldi (and between Kelly Lake and D'Arcy) to guard against the train hitting a rockfall. The author lived near Horseshoe Bay for many years and remembers well the steel-on-steel whine of the speeders announcing the imminent arrival of a train.

Right, top.
A BCR switcher, still in PGE colours, with a train of logs at Squamish station on 22 April 1973.

Right, bottom.
A CN diesel, No. 9046, stands at Lillooet station on 23 May 1971 with a PGE Budd RDC set beside it. The leading car, BC33, is now preserved (see photo, *page 205*).

BRITISH COLUMBIA'S RAILWAY   141

On 20 February 1972 a long freight derailed on a tight curve above Fisherman's Cove in West Vancouver, with some of the freight cars plunging onto the road below. Luckily no one was killed, likely because it was early in the morning, though two houses were struck. But there was much public outcry. As a result of this accident BCR decided that the curve was too tight and proceeded to build a new 1,392-metre tunnel through the mountainside, emerging above Horseshoe Bay. The tunnel was completed in August 1973, and the old railbed was turned into a footpath.

In the 1970s and 1980s there was a considerable demand from China and Japan for coal (see page 156). The Tumbler Ridge branch line, completed in November 1983, was built to allow the transportation of coal from the Quintette and Bull Moose mines to a new coal terminal on Ridley Island, Prince Rupert, where it could be shipped to Japan. The decision to make it an electrified line was made because of the long tunnels required. The Table Tunnel was 9 km long and the Wolverine Tunnel 6 km long, a total of 15 km on a 130 km line. A high voltage, 50 kV, was used so that only a single substation was required. It was the only such line in Canada, and one of only four in the world. The line cost $455 million, of which $25 million was the cost of electrification.

Above.
1962 Budd rail diesel car (RDC) BC-21 in BC Rail blue, now on display at the West Coast Railway Heritage Park in Squamish (see page 202). Another RDC, BC-14, can just be seen behind it.

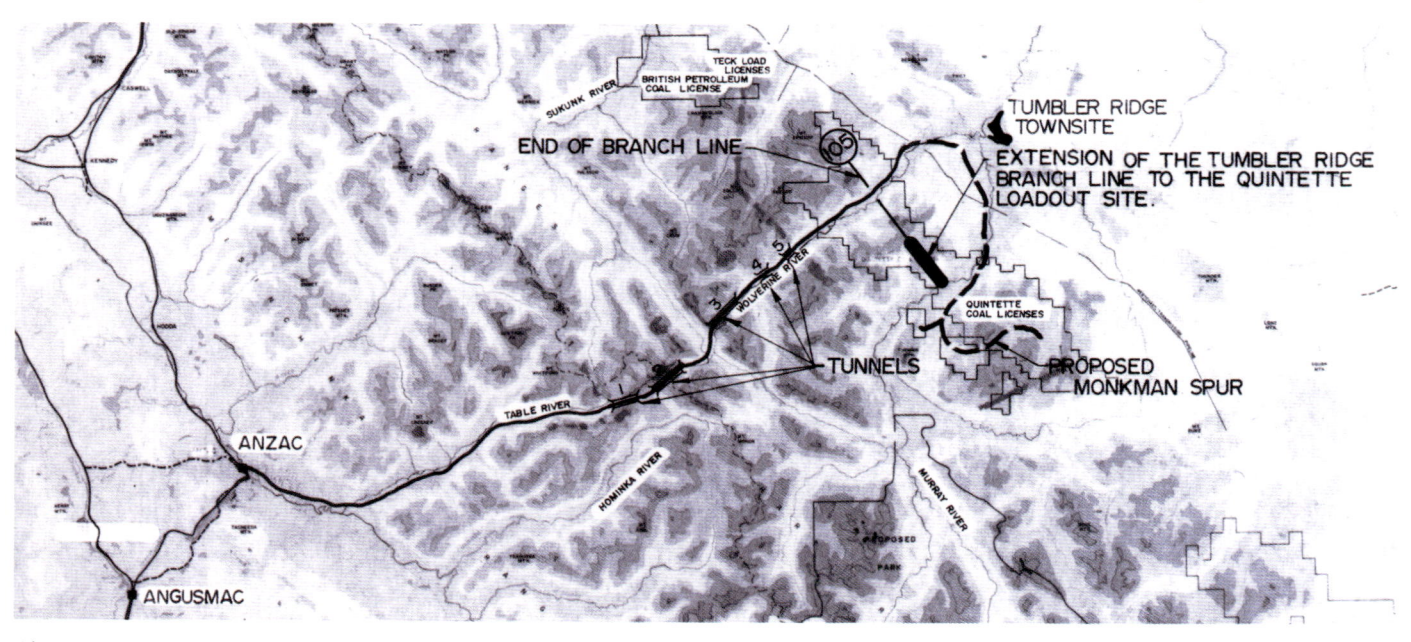

Above.
This blueprint map comes from a 1984 report prepared by BCR for the American Railway Engineering Association. The electrified Tumbler Ridge branch leaves the main line at Wakely, just south of *Anzac,* and crosses the mountains (the *Hart Ranges,* a northern extension of the Rocky Mountains) via the valleys of the *Table River* and the *Wolverine River,* with the *tunnels* as marked, to the *Quintette Coal Licenses.* At 1,163 metres elevation, the Tumbler Ridge branch was—and still is—the lowest rail crossing of the Rocky Mountains in North America.

Above. Four BCR GF6C electric locomotives head a long coal train in this photo, taken soon after the Tumbler Ridge line began operation.

Below. On 12 August 1986 railfan Tim Repp took this photograph of a coal train with a CN locomotive at its head stopped at Table, on the Tumbler Ridge branch (and shown on the map *overleaf*). Alongside are a pair of BCR electric locomotives, by this time used as helpers on the steepest grades of the line.

Seven electric locomotives built by GM Electro-Motive Division (EMD) worked the branch. Sets of four locomotives pulled 100-car trains loaded with 100 tonnes of coal as far as Tacheeda, on the main line, where regular CN locomotives took over. Before long, it was found that it was not necessary to use only electric locomotives through the long tunnels, and trains with mixed traction were often used.

Financial issues at BC Rail (as the British Columbia Railway had been renamed in 1984) plus a reduction of coal volumes—the Quintette Mine closed in August 2000—led to the removal of the electric locomotives a month later, and the closure of the extension beyond Teck (the dashed line extension shown on the map at *left*). The rest of the branch was then worked only by

BRITISH COLUMBIA'S RAILWAY   143

diesels. Then the Bullmoose Mine closed in April 2003 and service was withdrawn from the remainder of the branch. Only one electric locomotive was preserved; No. 6001 is on display at the Prince George Railway and Forestry Museum (photo, *page 134*).

With a revival of coal's fortunes and the reopening of mines, the line was also reopened in 2010 (using diesels) but closed once more in 2014 when the mines again closed. The mines reopened yet again in 2017, and rail service was resumed in September that year, after the expenditure of $23 million to refurbish the track.

Passenger train service on the BCR, which had been maintained using Budd rail diesel cars (RDCs), was ended in October 2002 to considerable outcry from tourist operators along the line. Service between D'Arcy and Lillooet is now maintained using purpose-built railcars (see page 170).

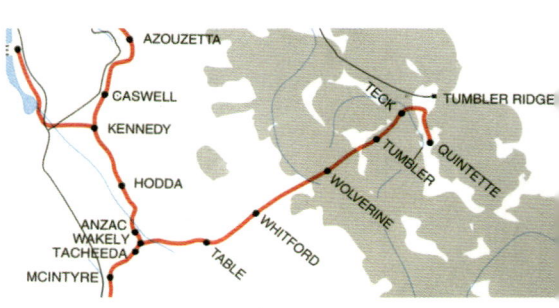

Above.
The driving cab of a BCR electric locomotive, No. 6001, now on display at the Prince George Railway and Forestry Museum. To the casual observer it looks as much like a small office as a locomotive cab. This unusual 180-degree view was taken with a circular fisheye lens.

Right.
The Tumbler Subdivision on a BCR system map from about 1990. There were two silo-like coal load-outs, one at *Teck* and one at *Quintette*.

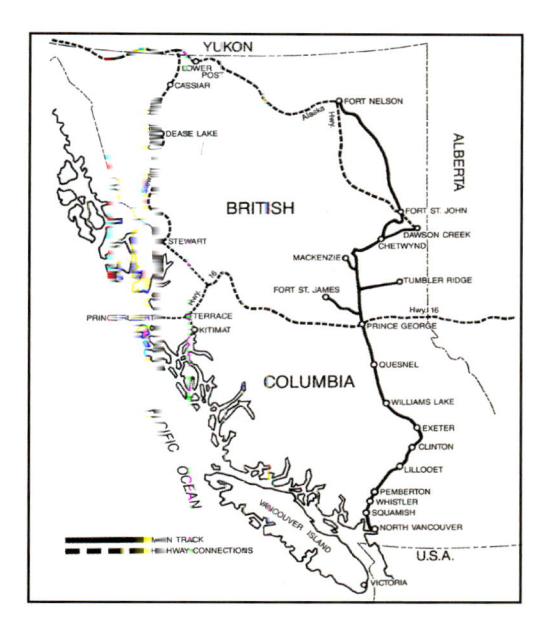

In May 2003 the BC government announced that BCR would be sold, and in November that year the government accepted a bid from Canadian National for $1 billion. All the assets of the railway would be sold, but the rail right-of-way would be leased. It was later revealed that the contracts included a right of renewal that might allow the lease to be extended for almost a thousand years—effectively a sale. The negotiations were mired in controversy, with allegations of bribes to government employees, later criminal charges and other allegations of wrongdoing. CN took over BCR on 15 July 2004, except for the Roberts Bank line (see page 158).

Above.
The BC Rail system in 1990. The main line runs from North Vancouver to Prince George, with extensions or branches to Fort St. James, Tumbler Ridge, Mackenzie, Dawson Creek, Fort St. John and Fort Nelson—a substantial network for northern resource extraction. The BCR line to Roberts Bank is not shown on this map.

Below.
Fading memories. An ex-BCR locomotive, still not repainted at the tail end of a BNSF train in Delta in September 2017.

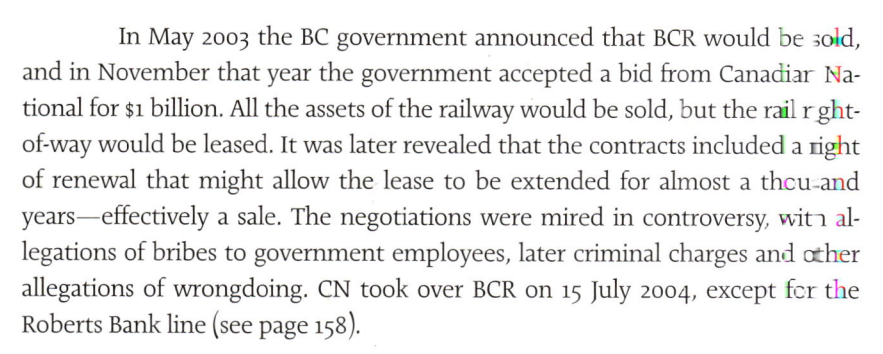

Above. A locomotive still in BCR livery is seen in the middle of a five-locomotive set on the CN main line at Ashcroft in June 2011, eight years after the railway's takeover.

Below. An impressive set of four 2013–15 GE-built CN diesels simmer in the yard at Squamish on a sunny day in May 2017.

BRITISH COLUMBIA'S RAILWAY 145

The Evolving Modern Railway

After the Second World War, British Columbia's railways, like railways continent-wide, underwent revolutionary changes. They converted themselves into heavy freight–hauling railways, embraced unit trains and containerization, and ditched passenger trains. Uneconomic lines were mercilessly closed down and new or upgraded lines created to handle the new type of traffic. In the south of the province, mileage of track declined, though in the north, as we have seen with the Pacific Great Eastern, it increased.

A comparison of the 1960 railway map of British Columbia (*overleaf*) with a modern one reveals at once the lines that have disappeared since that date. Much of the Canadian Pacific network in the south, built or acquired at great cost with

Below. This experimental "oil-electric" diesel CN No. 15820, with a lightweight engine made by British dirigible motor manufacturer Wm. Beardmore, ran the 4,726 km from Montreal to Vancouver in 67 hours in November 1925, at a time when the regular transcontinental took 87 hours. The engine was never shut down in that time. It proved the viability of such vehicles, and thirteen more were made. Two diesel road locomotives (Nos. 9000 and 9001) were built four years later, also using Beardmore engines.

Above. Oozing power, BNSF diesel-electric locomotive No. 5350 (a GE C44-9W) in its bright but well-used livery, heads a long freight train along the seafront promenade at White Rock near sunset on 16 November 2014. The locomotive was built in 2001. Such locomotives have become ubiquitous on North American freight trains.

a view to pre-empting competition from American railways, has gone. Yet some have survived, notably the Kootenay Central track south of Golden, which has been massively upgraded and is used round the clock by coal trains accessing the Elk Valley mines. The track on Vancouver Island still exists but is unused, requiring likely uneconomic upgrades if it is to be used in future.

Steam traction was soon dispensed with, as its running costs could not compete with those of the new diesel-electric locomotives. Canada was rather late in introducing them, compared with the United States, where both the Burlington Railroad and Union Pacific introduced diesel passenger trains—streamlined to boot—in 1934. And the earliest functional diesel railcar had been put into service in Europe as long ago as 1914, in Germany (a German and Swiss co-operative effort). High-speed diesel railcars were a feature of the German side of Anglo-German railway rivalry in the 1930s, with one type reaching 205 km/h, a world speed record, in 1936.

In British Columbia, CNR had used converted buses as railcars as early as 1922 (see page 92), and had run an experimental diesel train (No. 15820) across the country in 1925, but because of economic conditions had not at that time developed the idea further. In Vancouver, CNR placed its first diesel-electric switching locomotive in service twenty-one years later, in December 1946.

146   IRON ROAD WEST

The Great Northern Railway was the first to run mainline diesel passenger trains in BC, with the Vancouver to Seattle service dieselized in October 1947, connecting in Seattle with its streamlined diesel *Empire Builder* service to Chicago. In June 1950 GN introduced a three-times-daily diesel service from Vancouver to Seattle, *The International*, which was very popular, at least until the new interstate freeway between the two cities was completed a few years later.

Canadian Pacific had been studying diesels for some time, and decided to completely switch over an isolated section of its network as a guinea pig. Its Esquimalt & Nanaimo Railway made a complete switch in 1949, when both passenger services and freight became diesel hauled. The CPR was impressed with the cost savings and, after other tests, committed to change over its entire system, though it took some time. The first lines to be dieselized were those where the greatest cost saving could be expected—which was where there were the steepest grades. The first CP transcontinental passenger train into Vancouver arrived on 12 January 1950 with three General Motors demonstration units at its head, having been attached to the *Dominion* in Calgary.

The main line from Calgary to Revelstoke was converted to diesel operation by 1953. Canadian National converted later, as its grades were less severe, but diesels equated with "modern" and were needed to compete. In 1955 CPR introduced its transcontinental "luxury train," *The Canadian*—complete with state-of-the-art stainless steel dome and observation cars made by the Budd Company of Philadelphia—and CNR announced its rival *Super Continental*. Both were visually attractive streamlined trains designed to compete with the up-and-coming travel alternative—airplanes.

The Pacific Great Eastern embraced diesels early on, with the first one arriving in 1948—a 65-ton General Electric switcher No. 551 that was used on the dock at Squamish. The PGE advertised itself as "Canada's most modern railway," partly based on its use of diesels (and microwave communication).

Nowhere were diesels better suited than on a new concept developed in the late 1950s and 1960s: the unit train, first used for container traffic and then for coal. In the 1960s, "Locotrol," a radio-control system that allowed for longer trains by controlling mid-train "slaves" from the lead locomotive, was introduced. CPR was one of the earliest users. In effect, the system allowed two trains to be run joined together by precisely mimicking the speed and braking of the lead locomotive in the slave, after adjusting for timing differences. For example, the lead locomotive could be accelerating up a slope while the mid-train slave was still braking on a down-slope; the key is to keep the speed of both the same. Distributed power, as this system was termed, was not a new idea, but its automation was.

Below. Canadian National's new *Super Continental* diesel-hauled streamlined transcontinental passenger train, introduced in April 1955, is posed for this railway publicity shot on the line in the eastern Fraser Valley, with Mount Cheam in the background.

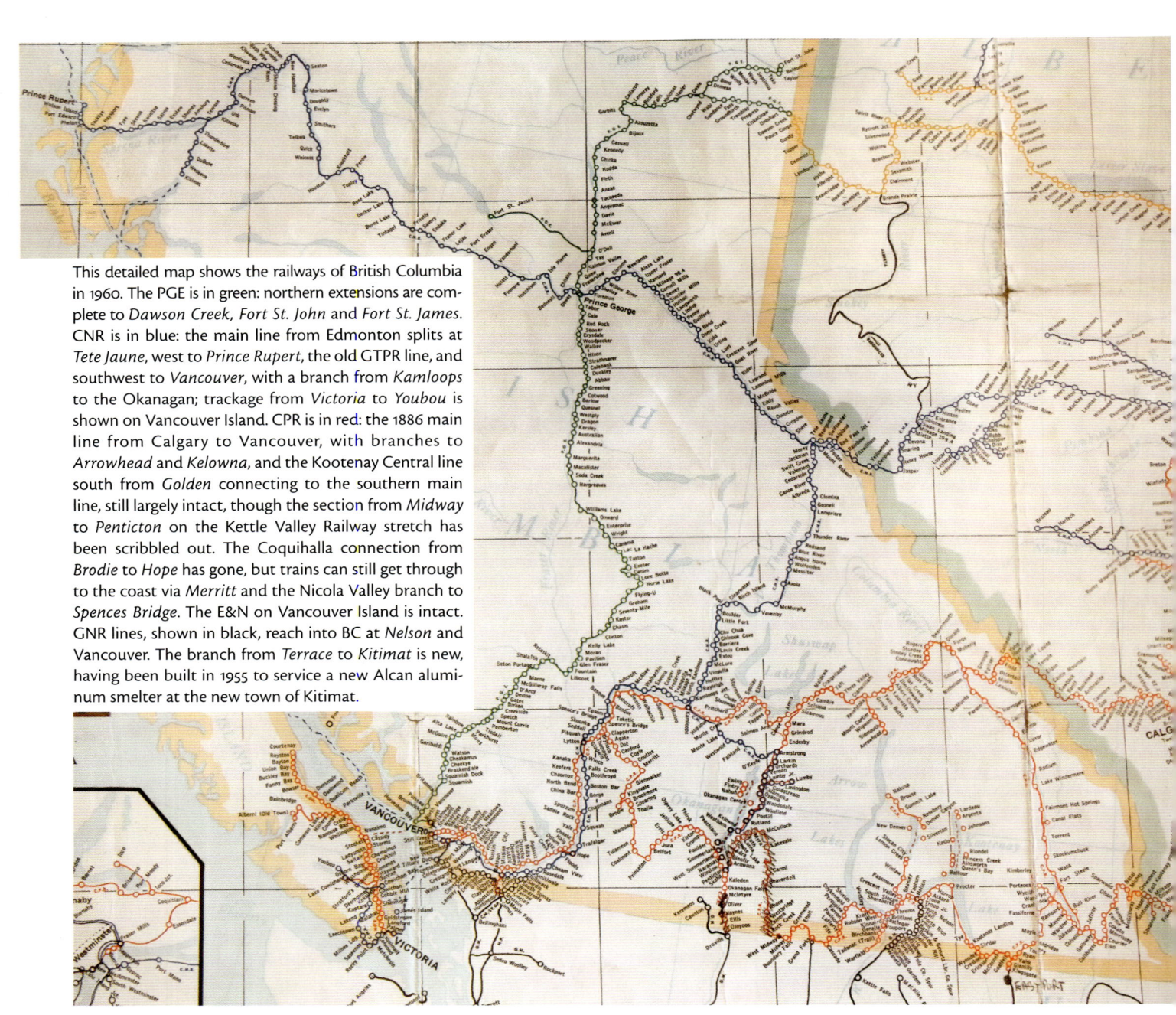

This detailed map shows the railways of British Columbia in 1960. The PGE is in green: northern extensions are complete to *Dawson Creek*, *Fort St. John* and *Fort St. James*. CNR is in blue: the main line from Edmonton splits at *Tete Jaune*, west to *Prince Rupert*, the old GTPR line, and southwest to *Vancouver*, with a branch from *Kamloops* to the Okanagan; trackage from *Victoria* to *Youbou* is shown on Vancouver Island. CPR is in red: the 1886 main line from Calgary to Vancouver, with branches to *Arrowhead* and *Kelowna*, and the Kootenay Central line south from *Golden* connecting to the southern main line, still largely intact, though the section from *Midway* to *Penticton* on the Kettle Valley Railway stretch has been scribbled out. The Coquihalla connection from *Brodie* to *Hope* has gone, but trains can still get through to the coast via *Merritt* and the Nicola Valley branch to *Spences Bridge*. The E&N on Vancouver Island is intact. GNR lines, shown in black, reach into BC at *Nelson* and Vancouver. The branch from *Terrace* to *Kitimat* is new, having been built in 1955 to service a new Alcan aluminum smelter at the new town of Kitimat.

Right.
Canadian Pacific's convoluted route across southern British Columbia was regularly used for transcontinental trains right up to the closure of the Coquihalla line (see page 99) in 1959, when the only available routing became via Merritt and the Nicola Valley branch. Southern BC passenger service ended in 1964. (For all traffic, Midway to Penticton closed in 1977 and Penticton to Spences Bridge closed in 1989.) The railway's marketing department issued a booklet for passengers in 1958 touting the scenic value of taking this route; these are two pages, on which, even at this simplified scale, the perambulations of the line are still apparent: the Jura loops, at *Carmi* and *Myra*, and the descent into the Okanagan Valley to *Penticton*. On occasion when the original main line was blocked, having an alternative route was helpful, though the passengers may not have thought so.

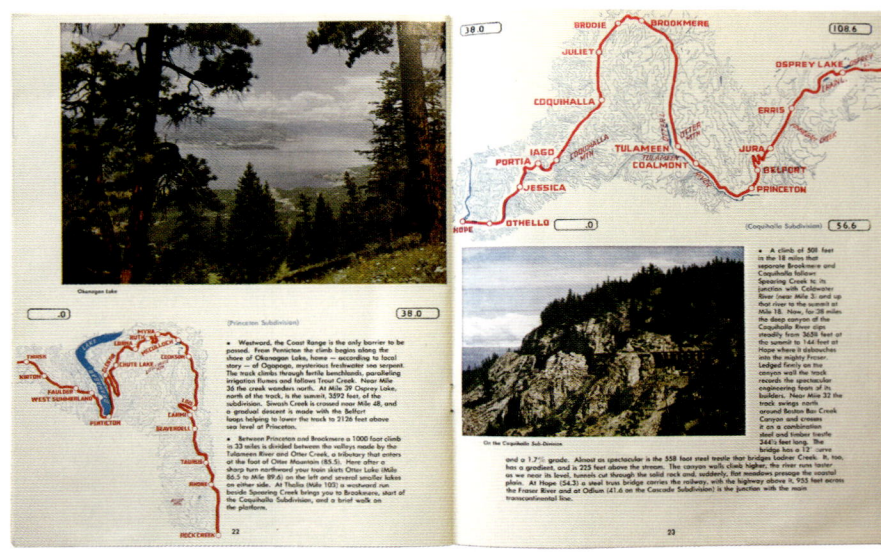

148 IRON ROAD WEST

DAILY TRANSCONTINENTAL TRAINS

WESTBOUND
THE BANFF–LAKE LOUISE WAY
Montreal-Vancouver, No. 1 & No. 7
Toronto-Vancouver, No. 3
St. Paul-Vancouver, The Soo Dominion,
The Mountaineer (July & August)

THE CROW'S NEST–COQUIHALLA CANYON WAY
Montreal-Vancouver, No. 7-11
Toronto-Vancouver, No. 3-11

EASTBOUND
THE BANFF–LAKE LOUISE WAY
Vancouver-Montreal, No. 2 & No. 8
Vancouver-Toronto, No. 4
Vancouver-St. Paul, The Soo Dominion,
The Mountaineer (July & August)

THE CROW'S NEST–COQUIHALLA CANYON WAY
Vancouver-Montreal, No. 12-8
Vancouver-Toronto, No. 12-4

Above. From the same 1958 booklet comes this listing of the transcontinental trains operated by CPR. Three trains ran each way, and four in the summer, on the main line, plus two each way on the southern line. And CNR had equivalent trains as well. Virtually all this business now goes by air.

Below.
Avid railway photographer Dave Wilkie took this photo of a rather smoky CPR diesel No. 4105 leading a freight train across the main road just north of Greenwood, on the Boundary Subdivision, on 18 July 1967. When the rail line closed, the embankment and road tunnel were removed, but part of the tunnel itself still sits beside the road, covered in graffiti.

THE EVOLVING MODERN RAILWAY

Right. A rail barge propelled by a tug, the *Iris G.*, is shown arriving at Rosebery, on Slocan Lake, with a train from Nelson via Slocan City (at the southern end of Slocan Lake) bound for Nakusp on the Upper Arrow Lake on 27 March 1985. The complete train, including the locomotive, was transferred. The locomotive is a diesel built in the mid-1950s.

Below. In a photo thought to have been taken in 1988, the *Iris G.* leaves Rosebery with two CP switchers, two cabooses, and three full log cars. Much of southern British Columbia's freight was moved using combined rail and lake service such as this, and it worked well for many years, especially before the road network was fully developed. Once it was, the rail and lake service could not compete with trucks that could travel the whole distance unimpeded. The Nakusp to Rosebery line closed and the tug-and-barge service ended on 21 December 1988, and the Slocan subdivision (from Slocan City to South Slocan) closed on 14 September 1993.

A similar, but much larger, barge service was begun in 1962 by CN to carry railcars between Prince Rupert and a connection with the Alaska Railroad at Whittier, Alaska. Called Aquatrain, the barge carries up to fifty railcars. An ocean-going tug pulls what is the largest railcar barge in the world, taking four to five days in all weathers.

Above.
A Great Northern freight train is shown at Cascade, about to enter the United States at Laurier, Washington, on 29 March 1967.

Below.
An 18-car CN transcontinental snakes its way along the steep banks of the Thompson Canyon just west of Seddall on 18 July 1971.

THE EVOLVING MODERN RAILWAY 151

Previously it had required another train crew to be operating a mid-train locomotive. Initially a separate railcar was required to carry the electronics, but such is the course of miniaturization that they are all now in a small box on the locomotive.

The idea of using containers for transporting—and in particular for transshipping—various goods in a box of uniform shape and size for ease of handling and stacking, was not in itself new; it had been used in Britain as early as 1793 on a horse-drawn coal tramway, the Little Eaton Gangway, but the large-scale application of the closed-box idea to shipping and railways dates from the 1950s.

It was a railway, in fact, that produced the first container ship. In 1955 the White Pass & Yukon Railway (WP&Y) commissioned the Vickers shipyard in Montreal to build the world's first purpose-built container ship, the *Clifford J. Rogers*. It was launched on 16 May 1955 and the following year went into service between the southern end of the WP&Y at Skagway, Alaska, and Vancouver. The ship could carry 168 containers (initially termed "caissons"), a far cry from the enormous container ships of today. At the same time the railway developed a system for attaching containers to flat railcars, making up the world's first container train. And in 1956 the railway also converted to diesel, so the train, thoroughly modern, was pulled by diesels. For some years the company was operating a completely integrated ship-train-truck containerized transportation system—another world first—from Vancouver to northern British Columbia and the Yukon. The company's next container ship was christened the *Frank H. Brown* to honour the White Pass president who conceived the integrated container, or intermodal, system.

With the increase in trade with China and other Asian countries, the volume of traffic arriving at West Coast ports for shipment by train to the East also increased. In 1977 the double-

Above.
A long container train hauled by a pair of diesel locomotives passes Bennett in northwestern British Columbia sometime in the 1960s.

Below, left.
A CP train of double-stacked containers at Savona, on Kamloops Lake. This the place Andrew Onderdonk's first contract—for building the CPR line east from Yale—ended (see page 15).

Right.
A doubled-stacked container train seen from above. The view is just east of Lytton.

152   IRON ROAD WEST

Above. The classic viewpoint for trains in British Columbia is in the Thompson Canyon, with the river in the background. A unit coal train is returning east with empty coal cars, and the incredible length of the train is apparent; the mid-train unit is only just visible below the blue truck on the highway. The photo was taken on 3 June 2012. The locomotive is a General Electric ES44AC, built in 2005.

stacked container train was introduced by Southern Pacific. These trains use well cars to lower the height of a pair of stacked containers. The efficiencies were obvious and soon most long-haul North American railways were using them, though they did first require some attention paid to the line's loading gauge—the clearances required could be an issue in tunnels and under bridges, and considerable investments had to be made to accommodate the extra height required.

Many container trains consist only of containers and are thus considered unit trains. The unit train idea was developed following large grain orders from Russia and China in 1965, and was aided by a 1967 National Transportation Act that permitted multiple-car freight rates. With the railways losing business to trucks, they turned to one type of transportation with which trucks would never complete—high-volume single-commodity shipping. The system was ideal for coal. Long coal trains never really stop: they are filled at the mine by an overhead conveyor system and sprayed with a dust-holding liquid, and are then on their way. When they reach the port they are unloaded using a rotary dumper without being uncoupled.

Similar procedures are used for two other bulk commodities—grain and potash. The colourful grain cars with "Canada" or "Alberta" or "Saskatchewan" emblazoned across their sides are common. They were introduced in 1980–81 by the federal government in conjunction with the Canadian Wheat Board and the two provincial governments and are nicknamed "Trudeau hoppers" after then prime minister Pierre Trudeau, whose government came up with the idea to facilitate international grain sales. Some 14,400 of the cylindrical hopper cars were ordered; an agreement with CP and CN in 2007 allowed for their refurbishment and the extension of their working life to fifty years. Over 8,000 of these cars still exist.

The Western Grain Transportation Act of 1983 improved the economics of shipping grain, and another National Transportation Act, in 1987, effectively abolished the Crow Rate (see page 64) that had plagued the railways for so long by keeping shipping rates artificially low.

But it was coal that ensured unit trains would become a feature of British Columbia railroading. In 1968 the Kaiser Coal

Left. A grain unit train, with "Canada" bottom-unloading hopper cars, passes Fort Langley in January 2017.

THE EVOLVING MODERN RAILWAY 153

These two pages:
Vancouver Island scenes from the 1970s.

Above.
In the warm glow of the early morning of 26 July 1978, the Esquimalt & Nanaimo Railway's Dayliner leaves the Victoria roundhouse to begin its day's work—running to Courtenay and back. This was the first day that two of the CP-liveried Budd rail diesel cars (RDCs) had worked together. The skyline of downtown Victoria can be seen in the distance. Via Rail would take over the route the following year. Service ceased in March 2011 because of deteriorating track.

Right, bottom.
CN's line to Cowichan Lake, completed in 1928, was intended to service the forest industry. Originally intended to reach Port Alberni and beyond, it was completed to Kissinger, at the head of Cowichan Lake, in 1928 (see page 92). The 1912 map (*right, centre*) shows its route and intended extension (in blue). After 1931, track ran only to Youbou. Service was withdrawn in 1979. This is the Kinsol Trestle, near the northwest tip of Shawnigan Lake. The trestle was completed in 1920, when it became the largest wooden trestle in the British Empire and one of the highest in the world. Here the last train to cross the trestle is shown, on 20 June 1979. The trestle has been preserved, reopening in 2011 as part of the Trans Canada Trail.

Far right.
There was not much traffic to be found on the subdivision on 18 October 1972 when railfan Dave Wilkie took this image of CN No. 991 and a lone caboose on a trestle 1 km north of Milne's Landing, near Sooke.

THE EVOLVING MODERN RAILWAY

Company gained a contract with seven Japanese steel companies for the purchase of 40 million tonnes of metallurgical coal from an open-pit coal mine the company was planning to develop near Sparwood, in the Crowsnest Pass. Delivery was to be made over fifteen years and required the upgrading of the old Kootenay Central line (see page 66) and the building of a new bulk terminal at Roberts Bank, in Delta, with a new 37 km rail line to connect to it.

The Great Northern competed for this business but lost out. It obtained a charter for a subsidiary, the Kootenay & Elk Railway, to build a rail line from Sparwood to the international boundary, where an American railway would take over. This was disallowed by the federal government (which had jurisdiction because the line proposed to cross the international boundary) and a proposal to get around this difficulty by creating a minuscule gap between the rail lines exactly at the boundary—thus creating two "disconnected railways"—was shot down in the courts.

Canadian Pacific did have to share the Roberts Bank port, however, and the rail line to it. The provincial government built the line in 1969–70, initially through the BC Hydro Railway and then through a new agency, the British Columbia Harbours Board Railway. (The line was transferred to BC Rail in 1984.) CP constructed the line under contract. Running rights were given to CP but later also to Burlington Northern (the merged Great Northern after 1971) and CN (see map, *overleaf*).

For coal, both CP and CN purchased special hopper cars with swivel couplings, which allowed the cars to be rotated while still coupled to the train, vastly speeding up unloading. The resultant long and heavy trains could not be hauled by a single locomotive, or set of locomotives, at the front, because the strain on the couplings would have been too great, and thus distributed power, using mid-train slave locomotives, became essential. CN did not use them at first because its grades were less severe. Also installed was a control called a Pacesetter, which allowed diesels to maintain a constant slow speed of 0.8 to 1.2 km per hour pulling trains through the loaders at the mines, while loading proceeded continuously.

Roberts Bank Superport, opened in 1970, at first had only the coal port, Westshore Terminals. It is now the busiest single coal export terminal in North America, shipping about 30 million tonnes of coal a year, all of which arrives in coal unit trains. Of this, about 35 per cent is thermal (sub-bituminous, low-sulphur) coal from the United States, transported by the Burlington Northern Santa Fe Railway (BNSF; created by further mergers in 1996), and the remainder is metallurgical or coking coal principally from the Crowsnest Pass area in southeastern British Columbia, but also from Alberta. Approximately 760 BNSF trains per year and 1,170 CP and CN trains per year carry about 13,350 tonnes of coal in 126-car trains (BNSF) or 16,100 tonnes in 152-car trains (CP/CN) to Roberts Bank. Here the cars are emptied by rotary dumpers (see pages 160–61 and 162). The coal is stored in massive piles for up to two weeks before being shipped, moved by massive crane-like 2,200-tonne mobile structures called stacker reclaimers.

Roberts Bank was expanded in 1983–84, and in 1997 a second terminal was opened, Deltaport, to handle containers. A third terminal opened in 2009, and a major additional container port is currently planned, called the Roberts Bank Terminal 2 Project.

Some 65 per cent of the containers handled arrive by rail. Deltaport is jointly owned by CP and CN but operated by Global Container Terminals Canada (GCT); in 2010 rail traffic handling was contracted to Toronto Terminals Railway (TTR), also jointly owned by CP and CN. TTR is responsible for taking trains from their drop-off point on the causeway to both the coal and container terminals and back again. TTR was originally created in 1906—and was jointly owned by CP and the Grand Trunk Railway—to assume responsibility for marshalling trains at a new union passenger station in Toronto, hence the name.

Both railways also service the container terminals in Vancouver's inner harbour, Vanterm and Centerm. Beginning in British Columbia's centennial year (hence "Centerm"), finger piers were converted to large cargo-handling areas for containers. Again, CP, CN and BNSF service these terminals.

CN's first bulk terminal port was in North Vancouver. In the late 1960s, CN decided that better access to the developing port facilities on the North Shore of Vancouver Harbour was required. A railway connecting the PGE at the foot of Lonsdale Avenue in North Vancouver across the first Second Narrows Bridge, the combined rail and road bridge (see photo, *page 115*) to the southern shore of Vancouver Harbour, had been built by the Vancouver Harbour Commissioners in 1926 and named the VHC Terminal Railway (photo, *page 235*). After 1936 the line was known as the National Harbours Board Railway, but in 1953 it was acquired by CNR. The Second Narrows Bridge, originally a combined road and rail bridge, was replaced (for the road) by the current Second Narrows Bridge (since 1994 named the Ironworkers Memorial Second Narrows Crossing). The old bridge was converted to rail-only operation and sold to CN for $1.

Still the only access CN had to its U-shaped harbour line was via its spur to the waterfront (from just east of the passenger station to the foot of Campbell Avenue), which made for difficult train movements—hence when bulk terminals were planned on the North Shore, a decision was made to improve access.

In 1969 a new Second Narrows Rail Bridge, built by CN, was opened. This fed directly into a long tunnel at its southern end, also opened in 1969. This was the Thornton Tunnel, named

Above.
A CP coal unit train returning east with empties approaches Colebrook, on the Roberts Bank line. The rail in the foreground is the ex–Great Northern now-BNSF line to Seattle. Much of the Roberts Bank line was built on the railbed of the defunct Victoria Terminal Railway (see page 51). A new long passing siding was opened at this location in 2008 to aid traffic management on the line, a section where the BNSF and Roberts Bank lines merge for over a kilometre.

Below.
A Canadian National locomotive—rather in need of a wash—and a train of double-stacked containers at Deltaport in October 2017. Coal cars can be seen in the background. Train lengths have increased over time, using distributed power, to about 1.5 km by the 1990s and to 3.5 km today. CN sometimes assembles even longer trains, up to 4.25 km long. The locomotive was built in 1980 and still carries the CN North America logo, retired in 1995.

THE EVOLVING MODERN RAILWAY 157

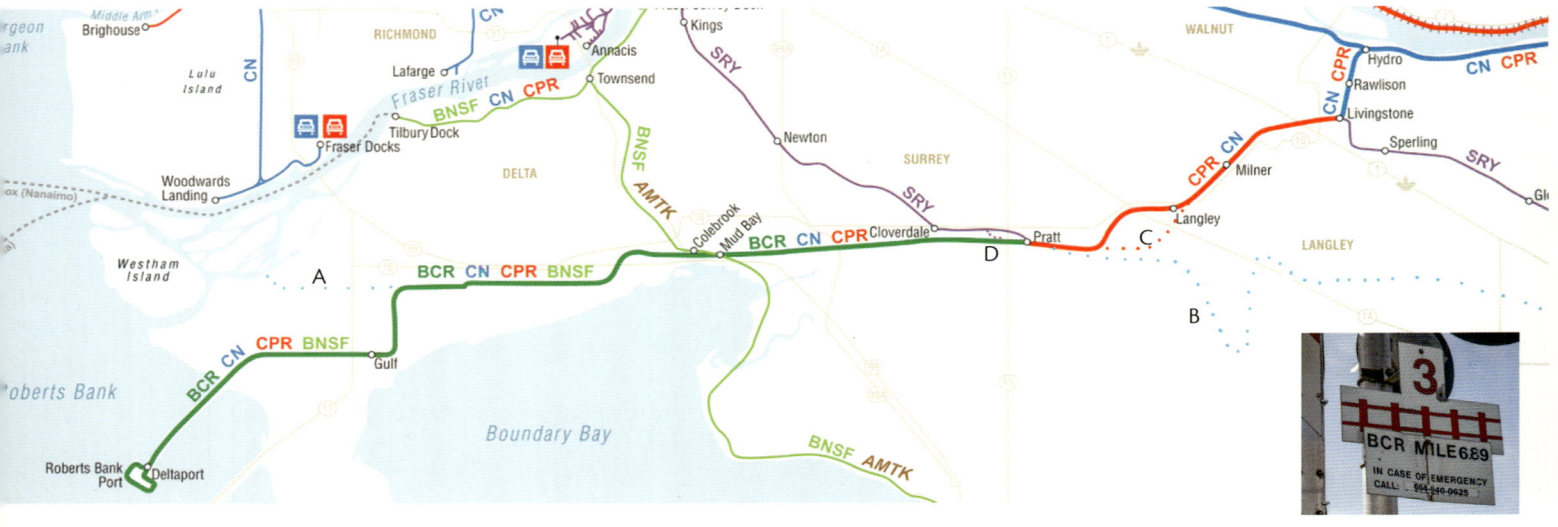

Above.
The Roberts Bank line, built in 1969–70, shown on a 2004 Railway Association of Canada map. The first train ran over this line on 30 April 1970. The BCR line (dark green) links with CP-owned track (red) at *Pratt* (the 184 St. crossing) and CN-owned track (blue) at *Livingstone* (at 232 St.), which then connects to the CN main line at *Hydro* (240 St.). This line in turn connects at Matsqui (photo, *right*) via the Mission Bridge to the CP line on the north side of the Fraser and CP track on the west side of the Fraser Canyon for eastbound traffic; CN track continues on the south side of the river (and east side of the Fraser Canyon) for westbound trains. The BNSF line (light green) leaves the BCR line at *Mud Bay* (actually Colebrook; see photo, *previous page*) for trains to the US. The purple line marked *SRY* is the Southern Railway of BC line, the old BC Hydro Railway, and before that, BC Electric Railway (BCER) interurban line to Chilliwack. The part of the line marked in red was sold to CP by BC Hydro when it divested itself of railways in 1988 to prevent any possible future monopolization of access to the port. SRY and CN were given running rights over the CP track, as they had before when it belonged to BC Hydro. The province still has passenger rights over the SRY track. The BCR line utilized part of the route of the 1903 Great Northern-owned Victoria Terminal Railway & Ferry Company (after 1908 the VV&E) line to Port Guichon, near Ladner, and the part of its original path not used by the BCR is marked with blue dots and labelled *A* (see page 50). The blue dotted line marked *B* is the 1907–08 VV&E line to Abbotsford from Cloverdale at what is now Highway 15 (see map on *page 56*); just the part not reused by BCR is shown. At *C* is the original route of the BCER/BCH line through the City of Langley via Michaud Crescent; it was rerouted north of the city to avoid the built-up area in 1970 when the BCR line was constructed, a diversion since rendered next to useless by urban growth. A short diversion of the original BCER/BCH/SRY line under an overpass built in 1976 at Cloverdale is shown by the purple dotted line at *D*. An ongoing program of grade separation has in recent years led to a number of other overpasses being built; the Cloverdale one was doubled up in 2008.

Inset, a sign at Colebrook shows the BCR ownership. The map also shows a joint line from *Townsend*, on the BNSF line south of the *Fraser River* to the Tilbury Industrial Park (*Tilbury Dock*), built in 1961.

Left.
Its image reflected in a puddle, Canadian Pacific diesel electric locomotive idles at Roberts Bank Superport awaiting its next duty. Other locomotives and a double-stacked container train can be seen in the distance. The locomotive, No. 5017, is a 2013 EMD SD30C-ECO specially rebuilt for CP with specific crashworthiness performance (hence the "C" in the model number) and emission standards.

Above.
The building of the Roberts Bank line meant that the railway companies had to co-operate to get their trains to and from the superport. This was achieved by an interchange of tracks at Matsqui, just south of the Mission rail bridge. Here a CP train is taking the spur, laid in 1969–70, onto the CP branch from Mission south to Huntingdon and onto the bridge and back to CP track on the north side of the Fraser. The CN track, on the south side of the river, is in the foreground. A similar spur was built on the other side in January 1976 to allow CN trains to access the CP track following the destruction of the main span of the New Westminster Bridge by a loose barge in December 1975. CP and CN agreed to one-way working (called a directional running agreement) east of Matsqui and in the Fraser Canyon beginning 1 January 2000, largely to avoid having to build long passing sidings in the canyon to accommodate longer trains. Now the Matsqui interchange is used to allow CN trains to access the west track going east and north and CP trains to get back to CP track going south and west. Note the modern continuously welded rail, first used in Canada by CNR in 1954.

Below.
CN and CP lease some locomotives to augment their stock of motive power with more flexibility (and some tax advantages). One of the companies leasing locomotives is CIT Group, and this CEFX 1035 is one of those, at Deltaport in October 2017. Another, CEFX 1029, can be seen behind the lead CP locomotive in the view *above*.

THE EVOLVING MODERN RAILWAY 159

Westshore Terminals at Roberts Bank on 17 January 2018. The photo was taken from the shed containing dual rotary dumpers on each of two tracks. One BNSF train is well into the dumping process while another approaches the dumper entrance. The rotary dumpers are shown *overleaf*. Automatic indexers, or positioners (the pale yellow machinery beside the tracks), are located on both the inbound and outbound sides of the dumpers. They lock on to the special rotary couplings between cars and advance the train two cars at a time to align with the dumpers. Laser sensors on top of the shed entrances locate the gaps between the cars to maintain accurate positioning. TTR engineers bring the trains to the point where the indexers lock on and pick them up again on the other side; the entire coal-dumping process is done automatically, with the locomotives in neutral. Underground conveyors take the coal from the bottom of the dumper pits to the stockpile seen at left. Note the leased locomotive, CREX No. 1208, in the consist behind BNSF No. 5751. One of the huge stacker reclaimers can be seen on the other side of the coal stockpile.

THE EVOLVING MODERN RAILWAY 161

Above.
One of the dual rotary dumpers at Westshore Terminals. *Left*, the last car to go through the dumper followed by a CP locomotive. *Right*, the rotary dumper in action on a BNSF train, rotating an entire coal car, emptying its contents into a pit 5 storeys below, from where the coal is taken up by a conveyor and transported up to the adjacent storage area, where it will remain no longer than two weeks before being shipped.

A fully loaded CP coal unit train enters the east portal of the Mount Macdonald Tunnel.

after Henry Thornton, the president of CNR from 1922 to 1932. The tunnel followed a broadly curved path under Burnaby before emerging just west of Willingdon Avenue. The 3.4 km tunnel needed a ventilation shaft in the middle, but above was a residential area of single-family houses, whose residents were not likely to appreciate the intrusion of a ventilation shaft. The problem was solved by disguising the shaft as a regular house, looking much the same as those around it. The only clues are the fact that it takes up the space of three houses and is surrounded by a neat iron fence with no obvious entrance.

The new tunnel and bridge gave CN the access it required to the North Shore, where it could service Neptune Terminals (see page 178), opened in 1970 to ship bulk coal, potash and agricultural fertilizers.

Another coal-shipping terminal, at Fraser-Surrey Docks, was approved in 2017. Here coal will be unloaded from BNSF trains into barges, which will then be towed to Texada Island, where the coal will be transshipped to ocean-going ships. The facility was approved to handle 4 million tonnes per year.

The coming of the long and heavy unit train—which became longer and heavier over time as the railways stretched the limits of what could be economically handled to maximize profits—meant that upgrades to track and other infrastructure were needed. For example, CP's track south of Golden—the old Kootenay Central line—was strengthened using crushed rock from the Sullivan Mine in Kimberley to widen the railbed, which then allowed for heavier loadings.

CP carried out a number of projects to reduce its westbound grades and provide double track. At Notch Hill, just south of Blind Bay on Shuswap Lake, a new 18 km westbound track was built that included a 2 km loop. This reduced the ruling grade from 1.8 to 1 per cent. The project was completed in 1979. The same year a 1.7 per cent grade immediately west of Revelstoke was reduced with the completion of another 7.2 km of track. And at the Continental Divide, a 1.8 per cent grade from Lake Louise to Stephen was reduced with the building of 8.9 km of westbound track in 1981.

The most important upgrade in the latter part of the twentieth century, however, was CP's Rogers Pass Project, which began in 1984 and cost the railway $500 million. The decision to proceed was likely triggered by the 1983 Western Grain Transportation Act, which effectively ended the Crow Rate and thus made it more economical for railways to ship grain from the Prairies to the West Coast.

The project reduced grades and increased capacity. Another tunnel was built, the 14.7 km Mount Macdonald Tunnel, under Rogers Pass, essentially doubling up on the 1916 Connaught Tunnel (see page 43) so that traffic could use each tunnel one way, the Macdonald westbound and the Connaught eastbound. The new westbound routing required another, shorter tunnel, the Shaughnessy Tunnel, some 1.8 km long; it was an achievement in its own right but was overshadowed by its longer brother only 800 metres away.

The project was completed in 1988, and included the 1,230-metre John Fox Viaduct, used instead of normal cut and fill to avoid destabilizing a 40-degree mountain slope.

Above. An aerial view of the Second Narrows taken in 2011 shows the rail bridge (with a train) beside the road bridge. The track disappears into the Thornton Tunnel just below the red electricity pylon.

The 34 km total length of the project contained 17 km of tunnels and six bridges totalling 1.7 km.

Because of its length, the Mount Macdonald Tunnel has a specially designed ventilation system. It has a mid-tunnel ventilation shaft and an automatic door that allows exhaust fumes to be removed from the eastern part of the tunnel while the train is in the western half, thus clearing the tunnel of fumes from a train before the next one arrives. The system can handle one train every thirty minutes.

Interestingly, the tunnel bore is 5.2 metres wide and 7.87 metres high to allow for overhead wires if the line were to be electrified in future. The tunnel is currently the longest rail tunnel in North America. It is 91 metres lower than the Connaught Tunnel, and significantly reduces the grade for westbound trains, which is typically the direction in which they are most heavily loaded.

CN also reduced grades whenever it could, though the need was less urgent than for CP as its grades were much gentler to start with. In the Tête Jaune Cache area in 1979 CN laid a 15 km cutoff track for trains coming south in the Upper Fraser Valley (the old Grand Trunk Pacific route) by diverting them onto the track coming north from Kamloops and Valemount (the Canadian Northern Pacific route), increasing the distance travelled by 30 km, with a resultant much-reduced grade. This principally affected container unit trains coming from Prince Rupert.

In 2004, Canadian National, which had been privatized in 1995, took over the British Columbia Railway, by then called BC Rail. In a controversial move leading to later court cases, the provincial government sold the assets of BCR to CN but retained ownership of the right-of-way, leasing that to CN for ninety-nine years, though, it was later revealed, there were multiple options to renew. Effectively, CN bought BCR. The only part not turned over was the Roberts Bank line, which the government had transferred from the BC Harbours Board to BCR in 1984.

One item that has changed the way railways operate but that is not evident to the casual observer is the use of Centralized Traffic Control (CTC). Instead of signals and switches being operated locally, originally within sight most of the time, a system was devised in the 1920s to allow this to be done remotely. It used the concept of Automatic Block Signalling (ABS), which ensured only one train could enter a section of track—a block—at a time. The operator would have a lighted board showing where trains were on a schematic track layout plan and could remotely set switches and change signals. The system replaced the way it was done at first, with timetables and train orders, and provided better safety as well as being far more efficient.

In the 1960s CTC systems were computerized, allowing for more complex systems and wider coverage. CN introduced the first North American coast-to-coast CTC in November 1965. Computer simulation, pioneered by CN, allowed different methods of train operation to be tested to determine the most efficient operating procedures. Computers, very expensive at the time, could also be used to optimize freight car utilization. Because of the investment required, larger companies had an edge. Today, of course, computers rule almost every aspect of railway operation, honing efficiency to its maximum and maximizing capacity, and CTC is used extensively on the busiest lines. Whether using CTC or not, control is often quite remote: whereas CP used to be dispatched from Victoria, Vancouver, Revelstoke, Penticton and Nelson, it is now dispatched only from Calgary. The BC lines of CN are controlled from Edmonton, and those of BNSF from Fort Worth, Texas. The Lower Mainland's Southern Railway of British Columbia (SRY) is dispatched, along with other short lines, by a contracted company, RailTerm, from Rutland, Vermont.

Above. A BNSF set of three locomotives eases through the White Rock seafront at dusk in May 2014. There is what seems a perennial debate about whether the Semiahmoo Peninsula line, opened by the Great Northern in 1909 (see page 54) should be moved inland, but the railway is legally entitled to this right-of-way and is unlikely to want to spend money moving it without advantage to itself.

Below. This is the original CTC for the Roberts Bank line, controlling the route from Roberts Bank (at left), to CN's Rawlison Subdivision, where the CN main line is joined (at right). Compare the depiction of the route with that on the map of the Roberts Bank line on *page 158*. The BC Hydro (ex-BCER) line is joined for a short distance; this is the section between Pratt and Livingstone on the map. Note that distances are not to scale.

Right. A duo of bright red CP diesels on switching duties on the Vancouver waterfront in September 2017. Lead locomotive 3029 was built in 1983.

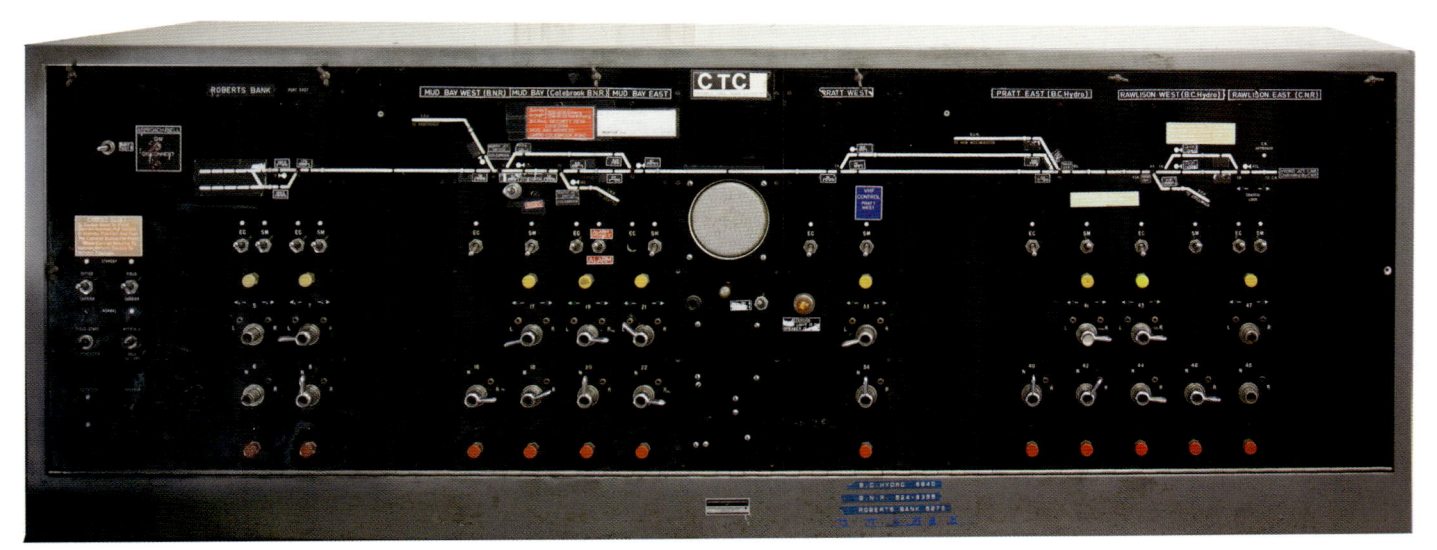

THE EVOLVING MODERN RAILWAY 165

In 1955 both CNR and CPR had introduced "luxury" transcontinental passenger trains (see page 147). They were successful for a while, but a decade later both railways were losing passengers to planes and cars.

Trans-Canada Airlines (which in 1965 became Air Canada) introduced the Vickers Viscount turboprop airliner late in 1954 and made it quicker and more comfortable to fly across the country. Planes were already becoming the way to go for thousands of travellers when in 1960 the airline introduced the first jets, the notable Douglas DC-8s. It is interesting to remember that at this time Trans-Canada Airlines was a part of Canadian National Railways, and this continued until 1978, when Air Canada was separated from CN and became a separate Crown corporation. (Air Canada was privatized in 1989.)

In addition to the rise of airlines, the Trans-Canada Highway was completed in 1962 (except for Newfoundland) and the railways also had to compete with the private car.

In May 1964, in what was really a last-ditch effort to salvage the transcontinental business, CN introduced a train called *The Panorama,* with six glass-topped passenger cars purchased from the Chicago, Milwaukee, St. Paul & Pacific Railroad (the Milwaukee Road). Built in 1952, these cars had been used on that railway's famous streamlined *Hiawatha*. These so-called "Super Domes" were 26 metres long and had glass domes 22 metres long. They were put into service between Vancouver and Montreal.

But a journey of several days could not compete for the business traveller, who could now fly in a jet from Vancouver to Toronto in five hours. The story was the same all over North America. Passenger train service between Vancouver and Seattle was ended by Burlington Northern (successor railway to the Great Northern, incorporating also the Northern Pacific, the Spokane, Portland & Seattle, and Chicago, Burlington & Quincy) in April 1971, killed not by planes but by the car and Interstate 5. That year, the new American government–subsidized Amtrak was created, and the Vancouver to Seattle train was reinstated as the *Pacific International* in July 1972. This was Amtrak's first international service.

The international train did not attract many passengers and was discontinued in September 1981. This situation continued until 1995, when the state of Washington leased new equipment for the run. Using innovative tilting articulated trainsets from the Spanish company Talgo, the Vancouver to Seattle service resumed, and after using three different names, in 1998 Amtrak arrived at the *Cascades* name used today. The original one-train-each-way service was augmented with a second train, which runs through to Portland, in 2010.

In Canada, in 1977 the federal government created Via Rail Canada, initially part of CN. On 1 April 1978 Via took over CN's passenger trains, and on 29 October that year Via also assumed responsibility for CP's passenger services. The last Canadian Pacific passenger train left the waterfront station in Vancouver on 27 October 1978—ninety-two years after the first one had arrived.

In Vancouver Via decided to use the CN station, which had more room for servicing trains and for customer parking, rather than the CP station on the waterfront. The CP station would within a few years take on another role as a transportation hub for the West Coast Express, SkyTrain's Waterfront station and the SeaBus. Budget cuts in late 1989 led to Via's decision to axe the *Super Continental* in January 1990, leaving only *The Canadian* as a transcontinental service; this train was routed via Jasper and the CN route into Vancouver, and only ran three times a week.

One other long-distance passenger train service survives in British Columbia: Via's service on the old Grand Trunk Pacific line between Jasper and Prince Rupert. The train originates in Edmonton. Clearly aimed at tourists, the train overnights in Prince George.

Above.
On a rainy 12 June 2012 an Amtrak *Cascades* train rolls through White Rock on its way to Seattle. Visitors marvel that the train runs right along the beach.

Right.
With the Downtown Vancouver skyline in the background, Amtrak *Cascades* train 517 has just left the Pacific Central Station and is seen in the Grandview Cut alongside Vancouver's SkyTrain, part of the Millennium Line that ends just round the corner at VCC-Clark station. For several months in the fall of 2017, *Cascades* temporarily used older "Superliner" equipment, shown here, which, unlike the Talgo trainsets, has no Wi-Fi or business-class seating. The train is, unusually, not equipped with a cab car for control in the other direction.

Above.
A CN "Super Dome" car, refurbished after purchase from the Milwaukee Road. The photo is from CN publicity material.

THE EVOLVING MODERN RAILWAY   167

Above. The morning Amtrak *Cascades* passes through a snowy White Rock on 25 February 2014 pulled by No. 465, built in 1998. This is the Talgo trainset, complete with matching livery on the locomotive. The power car arches upward to transition between the coaches and the higher locomotive.

Left and *below.* Amtrak *Cascades* on the Mud Bay trestle in August 2009. The wooden trestle was replaced with a concrete structure in 2016. The photos are of the front and back of the same train. No. 464 is pushing the train; No. 90278 is a cab car, or driving trailer, for train control only. The configuration allows easy reversal. This is also the Talgo trainset, with its sweeping ends.

Above.
A Via train sits at the station in Prince Rupert in July 1996 waiting for its next trip east to Prince George and Jasper. Note the ex-CP dome car.

Below.
The locomotives from the transcontinental *Canadian* train are serviced at Via Rail facility in Vancouver. *Right* are two *Canadian* coaches in the adjacent works for parts repair or replacement. The separate wheelsets nearby give the scene a strange appearance.

THE EVOLVING MODERN RAILWAY 169

Canada's Tiniest Train

Apart from the Vancouver commuter West Coast Express (see page 174), there is one rail passenger service still operating entirely within British Columbia. This is the diminutive Kaoham Shuttle, which runs between Lillooet and D'Arcy, at the south end of Anderson Lake, via Seton Portage, a total distance of 54 km.

The Pacific Great Eastern had a long tradition of using railcars to transport passengers. It used early gas cars to operate its isolated southern subdivision between 1914 and 1928 (see page 104). Between 1933 and 1961, the PGE operated a passenger and car-ferrying service between Lillooet and Shalalth, near Seton Portage (see page 136). From 1948 to 1961 the service used an ex-CNR gas car. Budd diesel railcars (RDCs) were used for the PGE's North Vancouver–Lillooet and North Vancouver–Prince George passenger service from the 1950s to 2002, when passenger service ended.

Children living in communities in the vicinity of Lillooet had for many years travelled on the Pacific Great Eastern—and the British Columbia Railway—to get to school, for the roads, if existing at all, were circuitous and mountainous. For many years the service consisted of a locomotive and a single coach (an ex–Gulf, Mobile & Ohio Railroad passenger coach named *Budd Wiser* by the students after a naming contest).

When the railway ended passenger service in 2002, BC Rail built a tiny two-car diesel passenger set for the express purpose of transporting schoolchildren. When Canadian National acquired BC Rail in 2004 it took over this responsibility as part of the 2003 sale agreement (see page 138). The diesel multiple units (DMUs) were painted in CN colours and the service continues, a partnership between the railway and the Seton Lake Indian Band, whose community it serves.

The train makes daily trips from Seton Portage, between Seton Lake and Anderson Lake (and the site of BC's very first railway in 1863; see page 12) and Lillooet, with service south to D'Arcy when booked in advance. The public can take the trip but regular travellers using the train for their daily lives are given priority. The latter's ticket price varies depending on how many passengers there are. The train carries a maximum passenger load of thirty.

Above. The Kaoham Shuttle has left the shores of Seton Lake and heads past a talus slope on the banks of the Lillooet River, heading for Lillooet.

Left. The tiny train on the shore of Seton Lake. All the photos on these pages were taken on 25 August 2017.

Above.
The Kaoham Shuttle at Lillooet. The train runs past the station on the main track, then reverses onto the station track.

Left.
The Kaoham Shuttle arrives at Lillooet. The freight cars on the track beside the train give an idea of its size.

Luxury Rail Tourism

British Columbia is home to what has become the largest privately owned luxury tourist train company in the world—with its train services marketed as the Rocky Mountaineer.

In 1990 the federal government decided to trim Via Rail's services and allow privatization of much of its daylight tourist service through the Rockies. A private company, Mountain Vistas Railtour Services (later that year renamed the Great Canadian Railtour Company), created the Rocky Mountaineer concept and was awarded the rights to operate the routes and purchase Via's equipment. The daylight-only luxury tourist train—Canada's answer to European river cruises—soon became very popular. In 1995 the company launched a premium "Goldleaf Service" using two-level custom-built dome coaches with dining areas on the bottom level and open-air observation decks at one end. Two routes were operated, one on the CP line through the Rockies and one on the CN line to Jasper.

In 1996 the Rocky Mountaineer set a record for the longest passenger train, with 37 coaches, and in 1999 it increased this record to 41 coaches; both trains were hauled by a set of three locomotives and had two power cars. In 2006 Rocky Mountaineer added two more routes, one to Whistler and one continuing on to Prince George and Jasper, and in 2013 a coastal route from Seattle was added using the BNSF line.

In 2010 Rocky Mountaineer operated an exclusive train on behalf of the Province of Alberta during the Winter Olympics of that year. A number of railcars were repainted for this event. One train set yet another record by carrying 1,323 passengers.

The Rocky Mountaineer has been awarded the title of "World's Leading Travel Experience by Train" multiple times, beating out other strong contenders such as the Venice Simplon-Orient-Express and the Deccan Odyssey in India.

One other luxury train operates in British Columbia. This is the Royal Canadian Pacific, owned by CP. It is one train, with 1950s vintage diesels and renovated 1920s business cars, all fitted out with period furniture and luxury heritage fittings. It only operates on a charter basis. It was the "Canada 150" train in 2017, used as a backdrop for centennial celebrations starting at Port Moody and progressing across the country (see page 212).

Above.
The Rocky Mountaineer on the railway bridge over the Thompson River in Kamloops, which it uses to access Kamloops (heritage) station.

Right and *below.*
A double-decker coach painted for the Province of Alberta in 2010, with the lead locomotives of that train in their blue and white livery of that time. The train is passing through Revelstoke (the "Farwell" subdivision sign can been seen. Arthur Farwell founded the settlement that became Revelstoke).

Above. Rocky Mountaineer on CN track in the Thompson Canyon on 1 June 2012. Note the yellow second locomotive, NREX 2906, leased from National Railway Equipment. The power car is immediately behind it.

Rocky Mountaineer at White Rock, on the BNSF route from Seattle to Vancouver, on 10 May 2014, a year after service on this route began.

Commuter Rail

Left.
West Coast Express EMD F59PHI No. 903 is parked for the day with its train at the Waterfront station in Vancouver. This photo was taken in 2005.

There is but one commuter railway in British Columbia, the West Coast Express (WCE). The service is owned by TransLink, the same government body that runs the transit systems of the province, and was begun in November 1995 after negotiation with Canadian Pacific, over whose lines it runs. Since 2014 the West Coast Express rail operations have been run under contract by Bombardier, the manufacturer of the 44 double-decker passenger cars the railway uses. Drivers and crew work for Bombardier. The operation covers a distance of 69 km, from Vancouver's Waterfront station—the old Canadian Pacific station—to Mission. Trains take 73 minutes to cover the distance, including six intermediate stops, which at Moody Centre (in Port Moody) and Coquitlam Central connect with SkyTrain. Trains run only at peak time in each direction (and Monday to Friday only, excluding holidays) and thus sit waiting most of the day. This is a result of the use of CP tracks, which are required by that railway most of the time and constrain the more efficient use of the WCE trains. The tracks are leased from CP (the lease terms are considered secret), and service is sometimes disrupted by freight trains. Other disruptions occur from time to time. The last train into Vancouver on the morning of 17 October 2017 was unable to stop at Coquitlam Central Station because of a bear on the platform! The commuter service is augmented by buses after all trains have departed.

Right.
West Coast Express trains parked at Waterfront station in September 2017, waiting for the evening return journey to Mission. No. 903, one of the first five locomotives delivered when the service began in 1995, is nearest the camera on the left, while No. 906, a different type, is nearest on the right. No. 906 was purchased in 2006 for use as a backup, and was in use this day because No. 904 was being serviced by Via Rail at its Vancouver Maintenance Centre.

Later that day No. 906 departs with its train on the 4.20 p.m. to Mission.

Above.
West Coast Express train with Nos. 904 (nearest camera), 902 and 906 at Waterfront station in August 2016.

Above.
West Coast Express locomotives are not reversed on arrival at Mission. For the westbound journey the trains are pushed by the locomotive and the trains controlled from a driving cab at the other end of the train. Two such driving cabs, 103 and 107, are shown here at the layover yard adjacent to the CP main line at Mission in December 2017. So called push-pull trains have been used for more than a hundred years in Europe and are still used on many high-speed trains. Amtrak Cascades often uses push-pull trains (see *page 168*). A complicated manual connection system was necessary when steam locomotives were used.

Right.
West Coast Express No. 902, one of the original five locomotives, departs with the 3:50 p.m. train to Mission, the first return of the day.

THE EVOLVING MODERN RAILWAY 175

Above. The front of an Expo Line Bombardier Mark III SkyTrain set in September 2017.

Vancouver's SkyTrain

After the City of Vancouver finally rejected the idea of building freeways into downtown, planning turned to the alternative—rapid transit. Studies and reports done in the early 1970s showed a demand for lines to Richmond, Surrey, Coquitlam and the North Shore. The latter resulted in the SeaBus, which began service in 1977, but the others had to wait until the next decade. Plans for a line to Richmond initially assumed that the Arbutus Rail Corridor would be used, the route of the CPR line to Steveston at the beginning of the century. Westside residents killed that idea. The first line was built from the downtown Waterfront station, the old CPR station, where it connected with the SeaBus, to New Westminster, pushed forward by the hosting of Expo 86. It used then newly developed linear induction technology (which used a sort of "unrolled" electric motor, with its stator and rotor producing a linear force along its length instead of torque), so new that a demonstration line about 1 km long was built first along Terminal Avenue before the technology was accepted. The one station included in this demonstration line became Main Street station.

The line opened in January 1986, in time for Expo 86, and was named after that event. An elevated line was built to avoid problems at road crossings and the greater costs of tunnelling. Because of its elevated line, it was named SkyTrain. In 1990 a SkyTrain-only cable-stayed bridge across the Fraser, called the SkyBridge, the longest transit-only suspension bridge in the world, was completed, and service was extended to Scott Road in Surrey in March 1990. A further extension to King George Highway (now Boulevard) near Surrey Memorial Hospital was opened in 1994. That was the line to Surrey.

In January 2002 the Millennium Line was opened, running from Commercial Drive and Broadway east to Lougheed Town Centre before turning south to join the Expo Line at Columbia station in New Westminster. A short extension west of Commercial-Broadway station to VCC-Clark opened in January 2006. The Millennium Line was not extended to Coquitlam as originally intended because of cost considerations at the time. That extension had to wait until December 2016, when the Evergreen Extension (at first called the Evergreen Line) was opened. This extension had seemed likely to be a form of surface streetcar for a number of years, to save money, but was finally built as an integral extension of the SkyTrain system. That was the Coquitlam line.

Above. An original two-car set and a newer two-car set are running together in this photo of the Expo Line on its elevated guideway above Boundary Road in January 2005.

Above. A long Expo Line train crosses the 1990 SkyBridge going south into Surrey in February 2017, with snow on the mountains in the distance. Also in this view are the 1937 Pattullo (road) Bridge (orange) and the 1904 New Westminster (rail) Bridge (at bottom), with a train crossing.

Right.
A Canada Line train crosses the purpose-built bridge across the Middle Arm of the Fraser River, south of Cambie Street, in June 2012.

Right, bottom.
A Canada Line train from Richmond-Brighouse station approaching Bridgeport station on a grand curve in the elevated guideway in June 2012.

The line to the south was built when it was because of another upcoming major event, Vancouver's hosting of the 2010 Winter Olympics. Bowing to public pressure from Vancouver residents, the whole of the line within the city was underground—not really a SkyTrain at all! However, at the Fraser River the line emerges straight onto another purpose-built bridge before splitting into two, a line to the airport and a line to Richmond Centre. Known when under construction as the RAV line (Richmond-Airport-Vancouver), it was given the name Canada Line, reflecting a considerable amount of federal government funding ahead of the Olympics. The line opened on 17 August 2009. That was the line to Richmond.

The Expo and Millennium line trains use an innovative system for motive power: linear induction motors, made by Bombardier. It was a controversial system when it was first introduced because of its relatively untried nature, whereas the Canada Line trains have conventional electric motors. The latter's 20 two-car sets were made by Hyundai Rotem, a South Korean company. The result is that although the 19.2 km Canada Line meets the Expo Line at Waterfront station, through trains are not possible, and the Canada Line operates independently of the others.

SkyTrain now has almost 80 km of track and 53 stations, making it the longest rapid transit system in Canada, and is the longest fully automated driverless system in the world. The full grade separation allows the system to maintain a good on-time record.

Above, top.
The Evergreen Extension of the Millennium Line opened in December 2016. An information board informed travellers of the changes beforehand. The part of the Millennium Line from Lougheed Town Centre station to Columbia is now designated part of the Expo Line, while the Millennium Line continues through to Coquitlam.

Above.
A 2001–02 Bombardier Mark II train leaves Lougheed Town Centre station on the Millennium Line's Evergreen Extension soon after the new line opened.

THE EVOLVING MODERN RAILWAY   177

Short Line & Industrial Railways

The principal short line in the province is the Southern Railway of British Columbia (SRY), branded as Rail Link, which connects many terminals to main-line transshipment points using the old British Columbia Electric Railway line from New Westminster to Chilliwack. It was owned and operated by BCER's successor, BC Hydro, between 1961 and 1988, when it was sold to the Itel Group and renamed SRY. The railway was in turn sold to the Washington Group in 1994, and then to URS, an engineering services company (itself now a subsidiary of Aecom, another multinational engineering company), in 2007.

This line is connected to a myriad of very short branches, particularly on Annacis Island, where, for example, automobile-carrying freight cars are loaded to begin their journey back east. Wharves and warehouses on both sides of the Fraser are serviced by SRY, as are customers in the Fraser Valley such as suppliers of agricultural bulk goods like feed and fertilizers. SRY has almost 200 km of track.

There are still about 32 privately owned locomotives in BC running on their owners' tracks to move heavy freight around within their premises or to assist with loading and unloading.

Neptune Terminals in North Vancouver, serviced by CN, uses three hybrid locomotives to move potash cars around. They work like a hybrid vehicle and use 25 per cent less fuel than regular locomotives. For moving coal railcars, the terminal uses an electric indexer, which is an automatic electric railcar positioner, similar to that at Roberts Bank (see page 160) to unload coal at the right place.

Some BCH/SRY and a few BC industrial railways are shown on these pages. They are a vital link between the customer and the main-line railways for both imports and exports.

Above.
No. 805, one of Neptune Terminals' brightly coloured hybrid diesels, with attached slug (a locomotive with an engine but no driving cab) No. 805A.

Below. Automobile-carrying freight cars sit in New Westminster awaiting assembly for main-line transport. A SkyTrain on the Expo Line passes in the background. Annacis Island has a major automobile import unloading dock served by SRY.

Below. A long freight train headed by three diesel switch–type locomotives on the BC Hydro (ex-BCER) line in 1968.

Left, inset.
A BC Hydro electric locomotive still uses the overhead wires with its trolley poles in this 1967 photo. The locomotive is under the old Georgia Viaduct.

Left.
Bulk agricultural products supplier Parrish & Heimbecker has a yard on the same spur as that of the Fraser Valley Heritage Railway, so when the railway needed to work a restored but not yet powered Car No. 1304 *Connaught* for ceremonies and rides in September 2017, the company lent a hand with its small but powerful diesel 5601 built in 2013 (see page 192).

Right.
Now at the Kettle Valley Steam Railway in Summerland, this Alco diesel, built in 1956, used to work at Neptune Terminals in North Vancouver. It was originally a Southern Pacific engine and also worked at a bulk terminal in Portland, Oregon.

Above.
Forestry company MacMillan Bloedel No. 1 worked not in the forests but in the lumber yard at Port Alberni. It is now preserved at the Alberni Pacific Heritage Railway.

Below.
The locomotives haven't changed much besides their colour from the 1968 BC Hydro ones shown at *left*. These are a pair of Southern Railway of British Columbia's RailLink locomotives, built in 1975 for BC Hydro, idling at Huntingdon in April 2017.

THE EVOLVING MODERN RAILWAY   179

A Legacy Preserved

Some of British Columbia's past railways and trains have been saved from the scrapper's torch for later generations to enjoy, though it must be said that other countries, in Europe in particular, have been much more fastidious in preserving their railway history, with the result that they have much more in much better condition.

Statistics are difficult, and depend on exactly what you count, but it is interesting to compare British Columbia with Britain, the birthplace of the railway and chock full, it seems sometimes, of enthusiasts. Britain has something in the region of 435 preserved steam locomotives, principally "main-line" engines, not including industrial or miniature ones), which translates into about 1 per 150,000 of its population. British Columbia has about 48 steam locomotives, of which fully 40 are logging engines. Counting only main-line locomotives, this gives 1 per 580,000 people, but if logging locomotives are included—and why not, considering this was one of the province's major industries—that gives 1 per 96,000 people, a far higher per-capita rate than Britain. And there are about 15 steam locomotives that worked in BC that are now preserved somewhere else. The conclusion, perhaps surprisingly, is that BC did quite well on the preservation front.

Much of what has been preserved was the result of enthusiast activity; governments, until relatively recently, have not seemed to care much about railways or history, despite the fact that railways were the catalyst for economic growth and settlement in many cases. British Columbia—indeed, Canada—would likely not exist in its current form had it not been for railways.

The problem is that all historical objects go through a phase where they are merely "old" and "out of date," before they get to the stage when most people can see they are worthy of saving. Thus it falls to those with a bit more vision to look ahead and save objects for that time instead of discarding them.

There are two regularly running "main-line" steam-operated railways in the province—that is, lines using locomotives that used to run on inter-regional lines of chartered railways. One is the Kamloops Heritage Railway, which uses No. 2141, a 1912 ex-CNR steam locomotive originally built for the Canadian Northern Railway; it is owned by the City of Kamloops. Although very much a main-line locomotive, it finished its working days on CNR tracks on Vancouver Island, hauling logs from Lake Cowichan to Victoria before being retired in 1958. Purchased by Kamloops

Left, top; above, top; and *above.*
The Kamloops Heritage Railway, with No. 2141 about to leave the 1927 station in Kamloops (*left, top*), arriving at the station with a spectacular show of steam (*above, top*), and crossing the railway bridge over the Thompson River in Kamloops (*above*).

A LEGACY PRESERVED 181

Kamloops Heritage Railway, CNR No. 2141, built for the Canadian Northern Railway in 1912.

Above.
The Kamloops Heritage Railway's No. 2141, resplendent in the failing light of a hot August day, waits to take its passengers for a ride. Clearly a lot of loving care has been bestowed on this immaculately turned-out locomotive.

in 1961—for $2,000—it sat on display in a park for thirty-three years before being restored to working condition and carrying passengers again in 2002. No. 2141, runs on CN tracks to and from the original CNR Kamloops railway station, itself a heritage structure built in 1927.

The other "main-line" railway is the Kettle Valley Steam Railway (KVSR), a 9 km section of the original Kettle Valley Railway built in 1913 at Summerland. It uses an ex-CPR locomotive, No. 3716, built in 1912 as No. 3916, and rebuilt in 1929, when it was renumbered as 3716. After retirement, it was first given to the City of Port Coquitlam, home of CP's extensive marshalling yards, in 1966. It was restored in 1975 by CP at its Drake Street yards in Vancouver and pulled a provincial museum train that toured the province in 1977. It was a back-up locomotive to the Royal Hudson when that locomotive was running daily tourist trips between North Vancouver and Squamish beginning in 1974, but these ended in 2001. KVSR acquired the locomotive on a long-term lease from BC Rail in 2003 and, after some restoration work, it began running again in 2005. The popular train backs onto the Trout Creek Bridge at the eastern end of its journey.

Perhaps the most popular "main-line" locomotive of all, the Royal Hudson, no longer operates a regular schedule, but is still occasionally run for special events (see overleaf).

There are three more operating steam railways in the province, all using ex-logging engines: the Fort Steele Railway, the Alberni Pacific Railway and the Cowichan Valley Railway.

The Fort Steele Railway is located, of course, at Fort Steele, just east of Cranbrook, and runs on an approximately 3 km route that connects two large loops, one at each end, for a 20-minute journey. The railway uses a beautifully restored 1923 ex–MacMillan Bloedel locomotive, built by the Montreal Locomotive Works. The railway also has a 1936 ex–Canadian Forest Products Lima Shay but it is currently not operable. The railway was also the home of the British tank locomotive *Dunrobin*, built in 1895 for the Duke of Sutherland for his private line. It was purchased with a 1909 coach by the provincial government in 1967 for Fort Steele. It attended the Steam Expo at Expo 86 (see photo, *page 212*). In 2013 it returned to Britain, purchased by the Beamish Museum in Durham County.

The Alberni Pacific Railway runs from the 1912 CPR harbourside station at Port Alberni to the McLean Mill National Historic Site, a distance of 9.6 km. Its steam locomotive, No. 7, built by American locomotive manufacturer Baldwin in 1929, worked for the MacMillan Bloedel–owned Alberni Pacific Lumber Company. Although it worked as a logging locomotive, it is of conventional type. The railway also has a 1912 Lima Shay that is being restored, and a small diesel switcher, No. 11.

Above.
The Kettle Valley Steam Railway's 2-8-0 CPR No. 3716 at the western end of the line, the Prairie Valley station, on 24 August 2017.

Right.
The train on the Trout Creek trestle and bridge (see page 98).

Below. With No. 3716 ready for the return journey, tourists pose to have their photos taken with the engine by friendly volunteer staff.

Below, right. Following the train was this rather more modern form of transportation, complete with flanged extra wheels. "The hardest thing is to take your hands off the wheel," laughed the driver. He was charged with ensuring that No. 3716 left no fires in its wake. The engine's tender had been rigged to discharge water along the length of the track to suppress fires; 2017 was one of the worst seasons in BC history for forest fires.

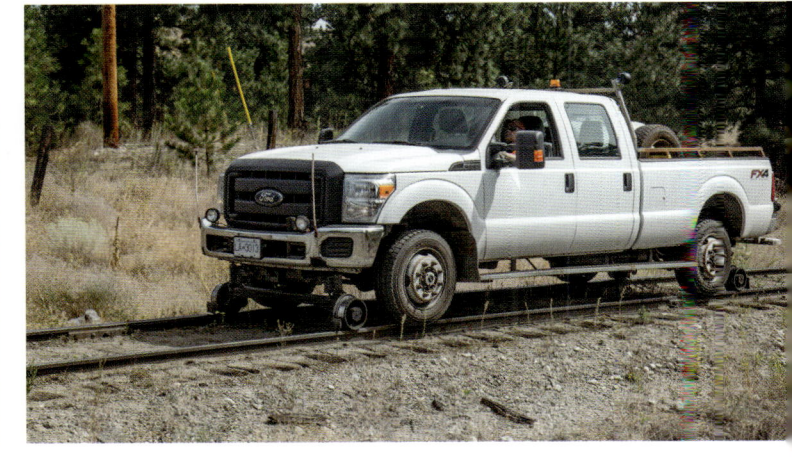

A LEGACY PRESERVED   185

British Columbia's Own

The steam locomotive known to almost all British Columbians is the Royal Hudson. With its "British Columbia" plate prominently displayed on its buffer bar, it is virtually a symbol of the province, despite having been built in Montreal. No. 2860 was the first of the Hudson class built after King George VI gave it the royal designation following No. 2850's single-engine journey across Canada with the king in 1939. The 4-6-4 semi-streamlined design was intended to yield a combination of speed and power for Canadian Pacific's transcontinental passenger trains.

In 1955, No. 2860 was rescued from the scrap line in Winnipeg. Selected by the Museum of Science and Technology in Ottawa, it was instead purchased by the Vancouver Railway Museum Association with the intention of making it the centrepiece of a new railway museum. But those plans did not come together, and the locomotive sat in the CPR's Drake Street roundhouse until 1973, when it was purchased by the British Columbia government—largely because the new premier, Dave Barrett, was a railfan—to be restored to operating condition and used as a tourist attraction on the BC Railway line to Squamish. Donations from the public and provincial and federal governments helped to restore the locomotive. Some old coaches were found and purchased from CP, and some of CP's coach workers were persuaded to restore them. Engine and coaches were painted in old CPR colours of black and dark red. On 20 June 1974 the Royal Hudson train ran to Squamish from North Vancouver for the first time and the train went into regular tourist service, carrying sixty thousand passengers a year.

In the late 1970s the Royal Hudson travelled all over North America promoting British Columbia tourism and made charter trips for special occasions. In 1999 it was taken out of service for extensive repairs, and various delays meant that it did not return to steam until 2006. By that time BC Rail had been sold to CN and that railway, like CP, seems not to like steam on its tracks, probably because it is seen as a potential source of delays. Perhaps they should look at the British experience, where restored steam locomotives—and even a new-build one—are allowed on main lines after passing reliability tests. From then on the Royal Hudson ran only on special occasions, like the run to White Rock and the Peace Arch, on the US–Canada boundary, in February 2010, as part of a special BC–Washington ceremony for the 2010 Winter Olympics beginning a few days later in Vancouver and Whistler. No. 2860's certification expired in January 2016 and the cost of necessary work to regain certification is estimated at over $1 million. In the meantime the locomotive sits in the museum at the West Coast Railway Association in Squamish as a static display (see photo, *page 203*).

Left. The Royal Hudson, with its train and a BNSF diesel for required backup, approaches the international boundary as the sun sets on 8 February 2010. *Above*, the train sits at White Rock earlier the same day, and *right*, seen through the Peace Arch early the following morning.
Above, top left. No. 2860 in steam at the WCRA yard at Squamish on 19 August 2009.
Above, top right. Royal Hudson and its train on a charter to White Rock in 1997.

A LEGACY PRESERVED

THIS LOCOMOTIVE BUILT IN CANADA IN 1923
WAS THE LAST IN LOGGING SERVICE IN B.C. IT WORKED
AT PORT RENFREW, CHEMAINUS AND LADYSMITH UNTIL
1960 WHEN IT WAS DONATED TO THE PROVINCE BY
MacMILLAN BLOEDEL CO. LTD. BOILERMAKER HERB HAWKINS
WAS BROUGHT OUT OF RETIREMENT AND IN HIS EIGHTIETH
YEAR REBUILT THE ORIGINAL BOILER BY HAND. THIS
LOCOMOTIVE IS THEREFORE DEDICATED TO ALL PIONEER
OLD-TIME MECHANICS, SUCH AS HERB, WHO MAINTAINED
STEAM EQUIPMENT DURING THE ERA OF STEAM.
ACCEPTED ON BEHALF OF THE PROVINCE AT NANAIMO, B.C.
BY THE HON. JACK RADFORD.   AUGUST 27, 1979

This page.
The Fort Steele Railway. Locomotive 2-6-2 No. 1077 glistens in the sun while waiting for its next load of passengers. The plaque (*inset, above*) is affixed to the side of the locomotive cab. The three-coach train has a motley selection of passenger cars, including, at the end, a rather incongruous 1954 British Railways coach that was acquired for use with *Dunrobin* but not returned to Britain with that engine; only a 4-wheel 1909 coach originally acquired with *Dunrobin* was returned.

This page. The Alberni Pacific Railway.
Above. On 10 August 2017, the date of this photo, extreme fire hazard meant the railway was unable to run its normal service locomotive, No. 7, a 1929 Baldwin-built engine, shown in operation in June 2013, *below*. The posted notice (*inset, above right*) says it all. Instead, diesel switcher MacMillan Bloedel No. 11 was enlisted to pull the regular train. But to make up for this, the railway's No. 2, a 1912 Lima Shay in the process of being further restored, was backed into a siding at the station for all to admire.

Below. The Alberni Pacific "Two-Spot" Shay being shunted into position. This locomotive, donated to the City of Port Alberni in 1954, took part in the 1985 Steam Expo at Expo 86 when first restored to working order. The use of steam locomotives for logging in the Alberni Valley ended in 1953.

Sorry
Until further notice we'll be running the No. 11 diesel electric locomotive.

A LEGACY PRESERVED   189

The Cowichan Valley Railway is the name given to a narrow-gauge railway loop within a museum called the BC Forest Discovery Centre in Duncan. Trains are operated on weekends during the summer by No. 25, a 1910 steam locomotive built by the Pennsylvania Vulcan Foundry Locomotive Works, and during the week by a 1940s gas logging locomotive called the *Green Hornet*, or a speeder.

The steam locomotive No. 25 has moved through a number of jobs during its career. It was used to construct the Canadian Northern Pacific railway line in the Fraser Canyon, and later transported fill for North Vancouver harbour facilities. It was purchased in 1955 by Gerry Wellburn, founder of the museum, and was run on his "Glenora Western Railway," a track layout on his land at Deerholme, south of Duncan. Wellburn collected forestry locomotives and other equipment to save them from oblivion, bringing them to the present site when the BC Forest Discovery Centre was opened in 1966. The centre currently has five steam locomotives on display, including a 1915 Climax logging engine (see photo, page 127), and several others are stored.

Two pages.
The BC Forest Discovery Centre in Duncan.
Left, top. No. 3, an ex–Mayo Lumber 1924 Lima Shay, with No. 9, an ex–Hillcrest Lumber Climax, together with another No. 9, a diesel.
Left, bottom, and *below.* An ex–Bloedel, Stewart & Welch 1911 Lima Shay that sits outside the museum, complete with a single load of logs. Constant exposure to all weathers has left this locomotive looking a little sad.
Above. A side view of No. 3, the 1924 Shay, displays the one-sided engine and the system for traction transfer to the wheels.
Left. The 1940s gas engine *Green Hornet*, pulling a train.
See also page 125 for an explanation of the different types of logging locomotive.

A LEGACY PRESERVED 191

Preserved Electric

In many ways the interurban electric railcars have fared better in terms of being preserved for future generations than have steam locomotives. And while only four city streetcars have been preserved, seven interurban cars have been saved (see list).

Nelson Electric Tramway has two of the streetcars, including one that originally ran in that city. One is leased to a downtown Vancouver restaurant (but at least it is preserved!), and one is in long-term storage.

Of the seven interurban cars, four are now at the Fraser Valley Heritage Railway (FVHR) at Cloverdale, which has cars on static display and also running on a 7.4 km part of the original British Columbia Electric Railway (BCER) Chilliwack line between Cloverdale and Sullivan, at 64 Avenue and 152 Street, Surrey. (A short section of this line just west of Cloverdale was relocated in 1976 to avoid it crossing Highway 15, instead going under a new road overpass.) The line is used by the Southern Railway of British Columbia (SRY) for freight trains, and the FVHR is thus restricted to running only on weekends. The railway has to use small generator trailers to power cars, as the overhead wire has been removed and might interfere with freight operations on the line if reinstalled. Service began in June 2013.

Left, top, and above.
Car Nos. 1225 and 1304 sit in the car barn at the FVHR two days before 1304's official return to the rails. The photo *above* was taken from inside 1225.

Left, bottom.
The official inauguration of restored No. 1304 at a ceremony attended by the lieutenant-governor, mayors, MPs, and MLAs, on a very rainy 9 September 2017. Still without its motor, 1304 is pushed by neighbour Parrish & Heimbecker's diesel switcher.

Right.
Restored BCER streetcar No. 1223 on static display in its new car barn at Burnaby Village Museum.

Preserved BC Streetcars and Interurbans

Streetcars

No. 23	Built 1906, operated in Nelson, located at the Nelson Electric Tramway.
No. 53	Built 1904, operated in Vancouver, on permanent static display inside The Old Spaghetti Factory in Gastown, Vancouver.
No. 153	Built 1908, operated in North Vancouver, owned by the City of North Vancouver, and currently in storage under Fen Burdett Stadium.
No. 400	Built 1922, operated in Victoria, located at the Nelson Electric Tramway.

Interurban Cars

No. 1207	Built 1905, operated on the Marpole–Steveston line, relocated from the Downtown Historic Railway in Vancouver to FVHR in January 2016.
No. 1220	Built 1913, operated on the Marpole–Steveston line, restored 2016–18 to static display in the Steveston Interurban Tram Building.
No. 1223	Built 1913, operated on the Burnaby Lake line, on static display at the Burnaby Village Museum.
No. 1225	Built 1913, operated on the Marpole–Steveston and Burnaby Lake lines, currently in operation at FVHR.
No. 1231	Built 1913, operated on the Marpole–Steveston and Burnaby Lake lines, relocated from the Downtown Historic Railway in Vancouver to FVHR in November 2017.
No. 1235	Built 1913, operated on the Marpole–Steveston line, located at the Canada Science and Technology Museum, Ottawa.
No. 1304	Built 1911, operated on the Fraser Valley–Chilliwack line, located at FVHR. Restored September 2017 (except motor).

Railways such as the Fraser Valley Heritage Railway collect a few specialist rail vehicles, some simply to preserve them and some to maintain track. Here we have (*above, left*) an ex-SkyTrain track inspection vehicle; (*above, right*) a Trakmobile, for track maintenance; and (*left*) a speeder, similar to those used on logging railways or by the PGE/BCR to precede trains.

Left. From 1998 to 2011 restored interurban cars Nos. 1207 and 1231 ran on weekends and holidays on a dedicated line along the south shore of False Creek as part of the City of Vancouver's Downtown Historic Railway. Alas, the project did not continue and the cars went into storage for many years before being acquired by the Fraser Valley Heritage Railway in January 2016 and November 2017, respectively. The cars were photographed here running on the False Creek line in September 2004.

Below. Car No. 1231 being squeezed under the Cambie Street Bridge—on the wrong side of the road—as it is transferred from the south side of False Creek, where it was stored, to the Fraser Valley Heritage Railway in Cloverdale in the early hours of 9 November 2017. The move, planned for months and requiring permits from all the jurisdictions it passed through, used a special rail-fitted low-bed truck and had an escort of four pilot cars and, within the city limits, four police vehicles as well.

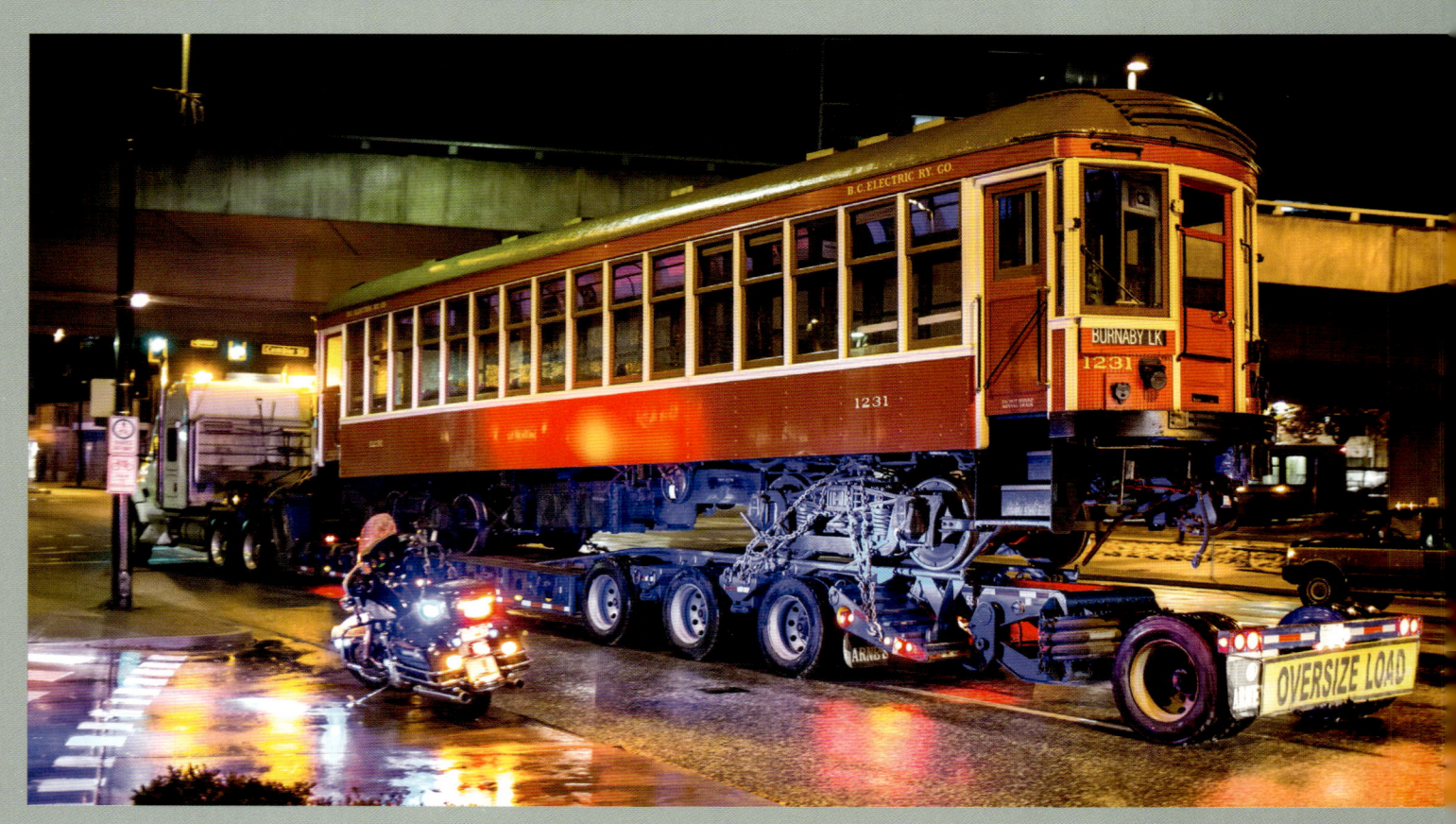

Above. Nelson's 1906 streetcar No. 23 was rescued from use as a chicken coop, but has now been carefully restored and runs every day during the summer months. Here it surmounts a rise in the track on its route along the lakefront. Nelson's streetcars are unique in British Columbia in using trolley poles to gather power from overhead lines, exactly as they did originally. After first seeing service in Cleveland, Ohio, No. 23 ran in Nelson from 1924 to 1949.

Below. The only preserved streetcar that ran in the City of Vancouver, No. 53, today sits in a restaurant in Gastown—The Old Spaghetti Factory. It was converted into a BCER salt car when it left passenger service, and in 1955 was presented to the PNE, where it was put on display.

A LEGACY PRESERVED

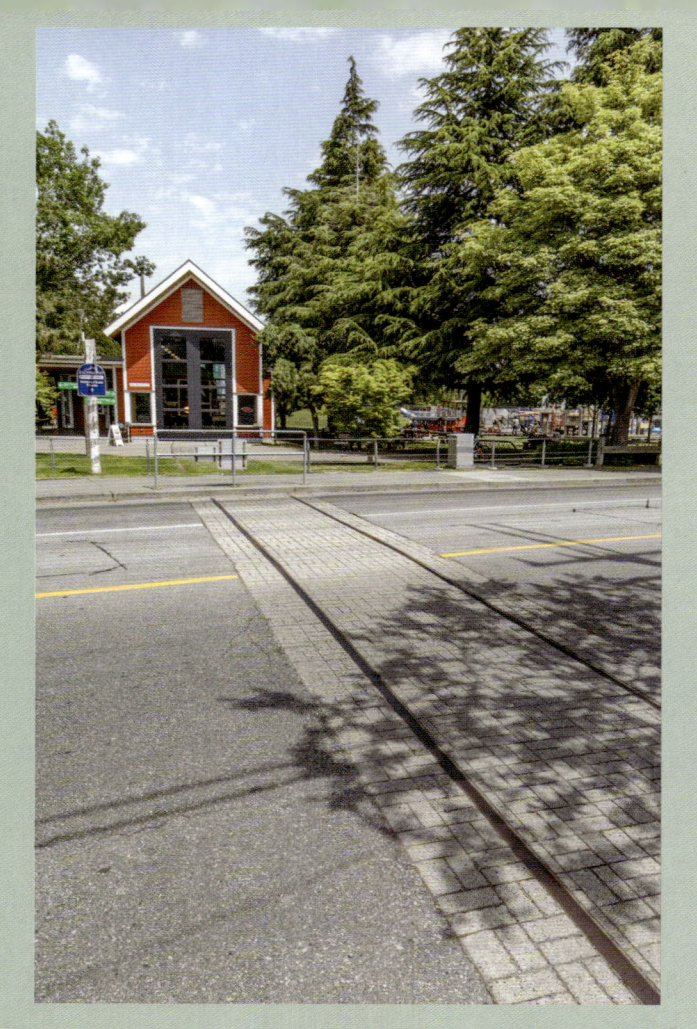

Above, left. All that remains of the Steveston interurban line is this section of rail that crosses Moncton Street in Steveston. The Steveston Interurban Tram Building is in the background. Inside it is Interurban Car No. 1220, shown *above, right,* in its recently restored and now gleaming livery.

Left. Interurban car No. 1231 in the Downtown Historical Railway barn, on the south side of False Creek on 8 November 2017. That night it was moved to the Fraser Valley Heritage Railway in Cloverdale (see photo, *page 194*).

Left.
This is Nelson streetcar No. 400, built in 1921, which ran in Victoria from 1922 to 1948. It spent twenty years as a lumber company bunkhouse before being restored by the Provincial Museum in Victoria, where it was then displayed. It was later displayed at a transportation museum in Cloverdale, which closed in 1992. No. 400 then went to Nelson, where it was further restored. It is now in running condition and is expected to be in service in 2019.

Above and *right.*
For two months before and during the 2010 Winter Olympic Games in Vancouver, the city had a modern streetcar. This was a demonstration, an effort by its manufacturer, Bombardier, to interest the city in such a system. Two Bombardier "Flexity" streetcars were loaned to Vancouver by the Brussels Transport Company in Belgium. Some 1.8 km of the line along the south shore of False Creek from near the Olympic Village was upgraded and temporary overhead wires strung. Passengers rode for free on what was named the "Olympic Line." Some 500,000 people rode the line during its two-month run, but neither the city nor the province were interested, it seems, quoting potential costs of $90 million to make the service permanent. Quite why so many other cities worldwide manage to afford this or similar and much more extensive streetcar systems, when Vancouver cannot, remains a mystery. By 2016 similar light-rail lines were planned to connect with SkyTrain in Surrey, but here largely because light rail would be cheaper than extending the SkyTrain system.

A LEGACY PRESERVED

Above. Steam locomotive No. 69 runs along the relatively gentle gradients of the track immediately outside Skagway. No. 69 was purchased new by WP&YR in 1908 and is one of the three still in service.

The White Pass & Yukon Route (WP&YR) closed down in 1982 as a freight railway but in 1988 began a revival as a tourist railway, using both steam and diesel locomotives to haul trains from Skagway, Alaska, where cruise ships dock, up to White Pass (on the US–Canada boundary line) or farther. The line is now open to Carcross, 172 km from Skagway, though most tourist trains run only to Fraser, just over the border into British Columbia, a distance of 44 km from Skagway.. The railway is a narrow-gauge (3 feet/0.9144 metre) line. The WP&YR was purchased by cruise ship operator Carnival in 2018.

Quite a few WP&YR steam locomotives have survived. Three are still in service, and there are three on static display in Dawson, one in Carcross, one in Whitehorse, and three in Skagway; none are in British Columbia, since there are no population centres in the region. At least two are preserved elsewhere in the United States. The locomotive at Carcross is none other than *Duchess*, the little locomotive that used to pull the Taku Tram (see page 71) and before that worked in the coal mines of Nanaimo (see page 13). It is the earliest surviving locomotive to have once operated in British Columbia.

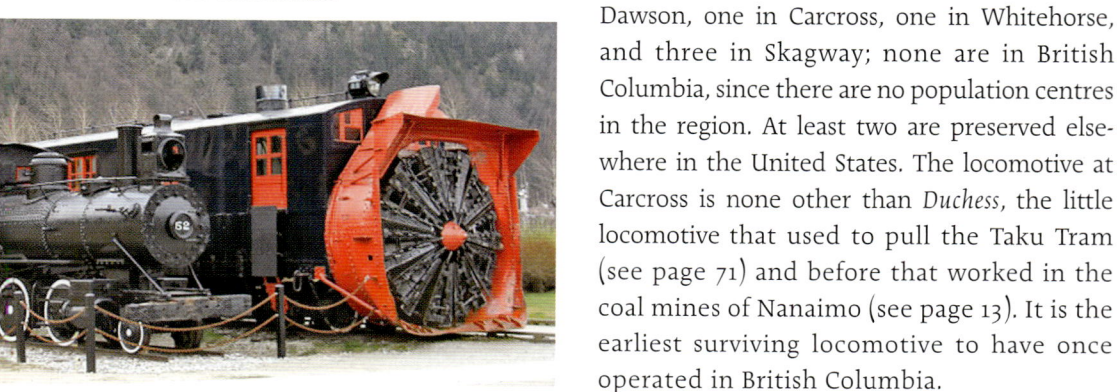

198 IRON ROAD WEST

Left, centre.
Steam locomotive No. 73 was purchased new by the WP&YR in 1947 and is one of the three used to haul tourist trains.

Left, bottom.
WP&YR No. 52 is on static display in Skagway, alongside a massive rotary snowplow and a caboose. The locomotive was built in 1881 for the Utah & Northern Railway and purchased by the WP&YR in 1898.

Above, top.
Diesel-hauled trains like this pair, laden with tourists from cruise ships, are now the rule on the WP&YR. The distinctive colours date from the period from 1969 to 1978, and were then restored in the early 1990s. These diesels, built by General Electric in 1956, were used to haul ore from the Faro lead-zinc mine, which opened in 1969. The line had to be upgraded in places. A bridge that carried the railway over a deep ravine called Dead Horse Gulch was unable to take the heavy trains and was replaced by a new bridge and tunnel that year. But a road was opened in 1978. When the mine closed in 1982, the railway closed. Note the narrow-gauge tracks.

Above.
The diminutive 1878 *Duchess* that once worked on Vancouver Island and then in northern British Columbia is on static display at Carcross, Yukon.

There are several significant railway museums in the province, displaying locomotives, coaches, freight cars and operating items from British Columbia's railway past.

One is the Revelstoke Railway Museum. This is a very suitable location for such a museum, for Revelstoke was the scene of much Canadian Pacific activity because of the steep grades just to the east. Revelstoke was for many years the place where heavy-duty engines were replaced with lighter, faster ones going west, and vice versa going east. The museum has a Mikado P-2k class 2-8-2, widely considered the workhorse of main-line railways just before the end of the steam era. It was built in Montreal in 1948 and retired only six years later. It has been on display at the museum since 1993. It is an oil-burning locomotive. Revelstoke was the first CPR location to have oil burners, which yielded an increment of greater power compared with coal-fired locomotives. While the museum is housed in a splendid bright and new-looking building, it has built wooden structures around the locomotive, making it difficult to view all of it at once, which is important for such a massive and powerful engine. The arrangement does, however, give the visitor the opportunity to view the locomotive from unusual angles, such as from above it (see photo, *overleaf*).

Also at the Revelstoke museum is a diesel, SD 5500, an SD40 model that was the second generation of diesels that replaced the steam locomotives on the main line, both as principal locomotives and pushers for the steepest grades. The museum also has a business passenger coach built in 1929 and rebuilt in 1941, and a collection of freight rolling stock and maintenance equipment that includes a caboose, a wooden and a steel boxcar, a flat car, a coal car, a tanker and two snowplows.

A LEGACY PRESERVED

These two pages.
The Revelstoke Railway Museum. Mikado CPR No. 5468, built in September 1948 for CPR's Shuswap subdivision. It is 27 metres in length and weighs 321 tonnes loaded with 18,000 litres of oil and 45,000 litres of water. The photos show how it has been displayed in the museum, with, unusually, views from above.
Far right, bottom is the locomotive's cab, with quite a complex set of controls.

Below. A caboose painted in CP Rail colours with the "multimark" symbol developed in the late 1960s. Cabooses, replaced by electronic radio end-of-train devices—sense and braking units (SBUs) or flashing rear-end devices (FREDs)—in the 1980s, are likely the most preserved type of railway rolling stock. Useful sometimes for other purposes as well as display, there are at least seventy or so preserved in British Columbia.

A LEGACY PRESERVED 201

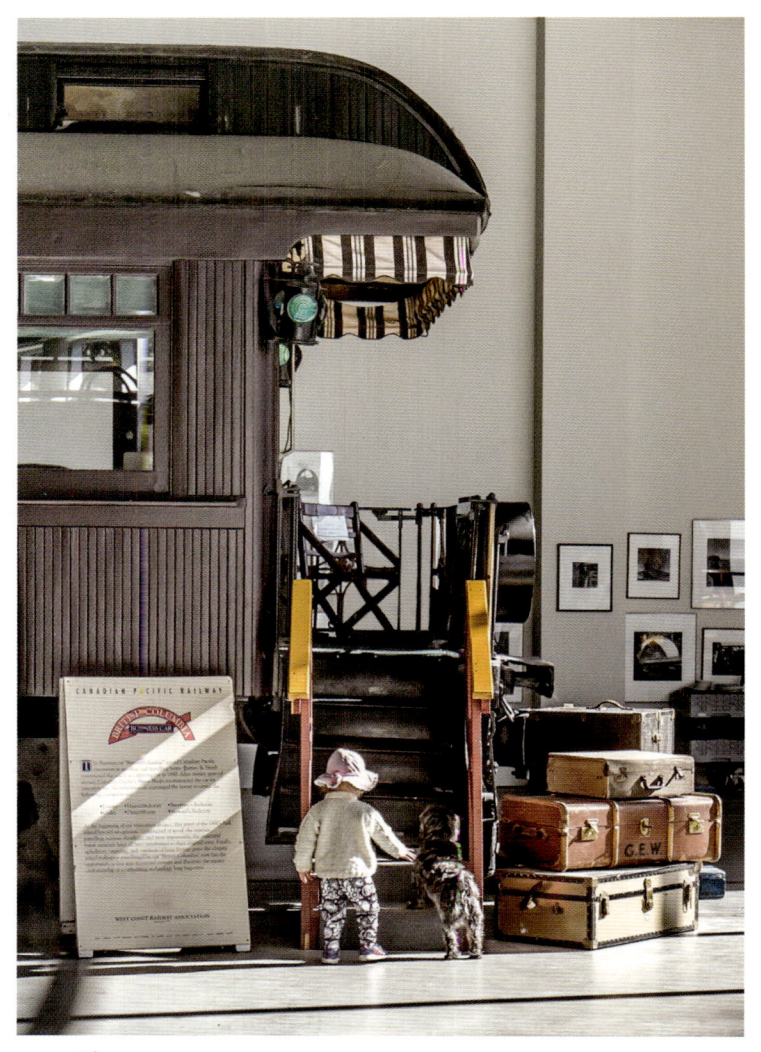

Another museum with a significant quantity of locomotives and rolling stock is the West Coast Railway Heritage Park in Squamish, most well known as the home of the Royal Hudson. The site is the home of the West Coast Railway Association (WCRA). Once on Pacific Great Eastern territory, the rails here were taken over by Canadian National in 2004. The Royal Hudson is housed in a splendid new CN Roundhouse and Convention Centre along with Pacific Great Eastern No. 2, a CPR 1890 business car, rebuilt in 1912, and other rolling stock that is rotated from display outside. The WCRA also looks after CPR Engine No. 374 at the Yaletown roundhouse in Vancouver (see page 216).

The coaches once used for the Royal Hudson train when it was running excursions between North Vancouver and Squamish are here, used for several "special trains," such as "A Day Out with Thomas" and the "Polar Express" fundraising events.

A number of diesel locomotives are also here, together with a motley collection of rolling stock in various states of repair and restoration, though, of course, the aim is to eventually restore everything. Diesels include main-line passenger ones from the 1960s as well as a PGE Budd rail diesel car (RDC) and two in BCR colours. Other diesels are freight and switcher locomotives, including the first one acquired by the PGE.

Taking pride of place among the rolling stock is a beautifully restored CPR 1895 business car, rebuilt in 1912. The coaches used for the Royal Hudson train in its excursion years are here too. Another interesting piece that would have been part of passenger trains is a CPR baggage and mail car. A PGE express car performed a similar function on that railway. Freight cars of many types abound, not to mention two cabooses, one of which is of a BCR "extended vision" design. Then there are maintenance and construction cars, such as a Jordan Spreader to groom track ballast, a rail crane, a wedge snowplow, and a shovel operator's bunk car. And several speeders; the PGE and BCR preceded every train with one to ensure that nothing had blocked the track.

Above.
A young visitor boards the 1895 CPR business car *British Columbia* at the West Coast Railway Heritage Park. The car, built for a business tycoon's luxury travel, was rebuilt in 1912, with a lounge, galley, master bedroom and dining room, plus secretary's and steward's bedrooms. It was restored by the WCRA from a very poor state of repair.

Below.
Displayed in the CN roundhouse, this is an "extended vision" BCR caboose, so called because the cupola projects beyond the side of the caboose body.

Right, top.
The West Coast Railway Association's prime exhibit, CPR No. 2860, the Royal Hudson, sits in the CN Roundhouse and Convention Centre, which is sometimes used for weddings and other celebrations so visitors may drink tea sitting right next to this powerful locomotive.

Right, bottom.
Pacific Great Eastern No. 2, a 0-6-2 Prairie-type saddle tank, built by the Baldwin Locomotive Works in Philadelphia in 1910 for the Howe Sound, Pemberton Valley & Northern Railway, which became the PGE (see page 102). It was used as a logging locomotive with the Comox Logging & Railway Company on Vancouver Island between 1920 and 1963 before being donated to the Town of Squamish and displayed in a park. It was acquired by the WCRA in 1993.

A LEGACY PRESERVED 203

Left, and *far right, bottom.*
Canadian Pacific streamlined 1952 diesel No. 4069 at the head of a passenger train in the centre of the West Coast Railway Heritage Park. It is painted in the colours the CPR used from the early 1950s to 1968–69. Mount Garibaldi forms a scenic backdrop.

Right, top.
On 3 October 2017 streamlined 1957 CNR FP9A diesel No. 6520, in primer black, sits in the railway heritage park with another scenic mountain backdrop. It had been painted black for a movie shoot the week before. In the background is PGE Express car No. 722, built in 1943 as a US troop sleeper, purchased by the PGE after the war and converted to a baggage car.

Right, centre left.
Budd RDC-3 BC-33 in PGE colours. This was a rail diesel car for 48 passengers plus post office and baggage sections. Some 398 of these versatile stainless-steel diesel multiple units, in several configurations, were built between 1949 and 1962. BC-33 is shown in service on *pages 139* and *141*.

Right, centre right.
CPR diesel switcher No. 6503, built at the Montreal Locomotive Works in 1951.

Right.
A visitor to the West Coast Railway Heritage Park in May 2017. While not exactly a historical legacy, it is a legacy of a different sort. Thomas the Tank Engine™ has become enormously popular with children in many parts of the world, not just in Britain, where the character originated with the stories of Rev. W. Awdry in 1945. Now Thomas travels the world, visiting museums and railways on Day Out with Thomas™ events. Here the (present) author's granddaughters and son pose for a photo with Thomas, at the head of an improbably long train.

Below.
PGE No. 2 in front of the CN Roundhouse and Conference Centre, under construction in August 2009. The perhaps surprising length of the locomotive with its tender is apparent from this view.

A LEGACY PRESERVED   205

Photos on these two pages:
The Prince George Railway and Forestry Museum in 2011.

Above. A rather weather-beaten General Motors–built CNR No. 9169, an F7 A class diesel built in 1951. It is unfortunate that it has to be stored outdoors.

Left.
Penny station, a "Type E" Grand Trunk Pacific station, was built in 1914 at Lindrup, 130 km east of Prince George, and moved to Penny, 10 km east of Lindrup, in 1947. Lindrup never developed enough to need a station, while Penny had a population of several thousand. The stationmaster and his family lived in the building. Note the signal on the roof. The whole building was moved to the Prince George Railway and Forestry Museum in 1988 and the interior restored to its original look. Here three speeders are lined up outside.

Right, top left.
This small diesel, No. 248, was built in 1948 and worked at Louisiana Pacific, a lumber company near Prince George.

Right, centre left.
A Jordan Spreader. These machines were quite common in the early and mid-twentieth century. They were used to grade and smooth the ballast alongside the tracks, and sometimes also to clear snow. This particular spreader was built in 1919 by the Jordan Company of Chicago for the Grand Trunk Pacific Railway and was used by Canadian National until 1984.

Above. A BC Rail Wickham double-ended track inspection vehicle. Such vehicles were used by CP and CN as well as BC Rail.

Below. A front view of the BC Rail electric locomotive No. 6001 (see also photos on *pages 134* and *144*).

In central British Columbia, the Prince George Railway and Forestry Museum has a diverse collection of railwayana, including the steam locomotive No. 1520, built in 1906 for the Canadian Northern Railway, which became part of Canadian National (see *overleaf* and *page 88*). The museum also has the only surviving British Columbia Railway electric locomotive (*right*), which hauled coal trains on the Tumbler subdivision (see page 142), and a CNR streamlined diesel No. 9169, (*left, top*).

Above.
A massive CNR wedge snowplow dating from 1950.

A LEGACY PRESERVED   207

Above.
Steam locomotive No. 1520, built in 1906 for the Canadian Northern Railway, at the Prince George Railway and Forestry Museum.

Right.
Some 20 km west of Revelstoke is Three Valley Gap Heritage Ghost Town. It houses a veritable medley of railway equipment, the majority of which, however, originated outside of British Columbia. Inside what is billed as the largest roundhouse in North America—but a new-build structure—is this ex-Canadian government business car dating from 1967. Normally it was used for the governor general, but its claim to fame is that it is the car from which Prime Minister Pierre Elliott Trudeau made his (in)famous middle-finger gesture, now popularly known as the Trudeau Salute, to protestors at Salmon Arm in 1982. It is now displayed with a life-size cardboard cutout of Trudeau on the rear balcony.

Above. CPR 2-8-0 V4A class heavyweight yard switcher No. 6947 on a roadside track at Sandon, in the Kootenays, with some old freight cars, in 2010.

At Sandon, once the scene of battles between the CPR and the James Hill–backed Kaslo & Slocan Railway—and now a ghost town after being hit by a catastrophic flood in 1956—an attempt to create a private museum has led to the saving of a 1908-built CPR locomotive, originally CPR No. 1737, renumbered as No. 6947 after a 1929 rebuild. It was brought to Sandon in 1998 and sits at the roadside along with several freight cars for a train. The incipient museum also has a collection of a number of Vancouver trolley buses sitting nearby, and a compressed-air mining locomotive (see photo, *page 133*).

In Cranbrook is the extensive Canadian Museum of Rail Travel, designated a National Historic Site in 2011. The museum concentrates on a collection of passenger cars from several eras, and as its brand name Trains DeLuxe suggests, concentrates on

Above. CPR No. 4090, built in 1953, at the Canadian Museum of Rail Travel in Cranbrook.

Below. A mining locomotive from the Britannia Beach Mining Museum on Howe Sound. The mine did not need to use a compressed-air engine because its copper ore was not potentially explosive.

Above.
A rail-borne mine mucking machine and locomotive rolled into one, together with several ore cars, sit on static display outside the Hedley Mine.

A LEGACY PRESERVED

luxury trains, with business cars, royal cars and the 1929 *Trans-Canada Limited*. The latter was a CPR transcontinental created exclusively for first-class sleeping-car passengers.

At the other end of the luxury scale, perhaps, were the utilitarian narrow-gauge mining railways that hauled ore under and above ground, from mine to transshipment point, often a main-line railway or ship. Two exist today as tourist attractions: at the Britannia Mine on Howe Sound and the Sullivan Mine in Kimberley. There are also many static displays of mining equipment on rails scattered around the province, like the one from the mine at Hedley, in the Similkameen Valley, shown on the previous page.

And naturally enough for British Columbia, there are a number of statically displayed logging locomotives, including ones at Qualicum Beach, Chemainus, Ladysmith and Cowichan Lake. Some are very accessible, others fenced in.

Then there are special events that bring out historic locomotives and even whole trains for a brief view. Of note was the 7 November 1985 celebration of the century since the driving of the last spike on the CPR at Craigellachie, which brought out the Royal Hudson and crowds to this relatively isolated spot. The monument (photo, *page 34*) remains.

Above.
MacMillan Bloedel No. 1044 was one of the last steam logging locomotives to work in the province, being retired in 1969. It is a 2-6-2T (tank) engine, also known as a Prairie type. It was built in 1924 by H.K. Porter, an American locomotive manufacturer that survives today, manufacturing industrial equipment. Here it is on display in Gerry Smith Park in Chemainus in 2017, with only a low fence around it, though the cab has been fitted with bars.

Right (all photos).
Much more protected is this MacMillan Bloedel locomotive No. 1066 at Qualicum Beach. Displayed with its original Bloedel, Stewart & Welch owner's name and number, 4, it was built by the Baldwin Locomotive Works in 1925. It is a heavy 2-8-2T used on the main line. The engine is surrounded by a high wire fence, making photographs—or even a clear view—difficult. The author photographed the main image here (*top*) using a camera on a monopod held above his head. As No. 1066, the locomotive worked at Chemainus with No. 1044 until the operation closed in 1969. It was in storage for some time, then displayed in Squamish, and in 1986 moved to its current location at Qualicum. The photo at *far right* gives some idea of the view from ground level!

Still there, but lost?
There are at least seven steam locomotives known to still exist in British Columbia—underwater. All are the result of accidents. There are sunken engines in Armstrong Lake, Beaver Cove, Anderson Lake, Seton Lake, the Elk River at Fernie, Kamloops Lake and Slocan Lake. Perhaps surprisingly, five are main-line locomotives, while only two are logging engines.

A LEGACY PRESERVED

Above.
One of the locomotives that took part in the Expo 86 "Grand Parade of Steam" was (what was then) the province's own steam locomotive, *Dunrobin*. This engine was always a bit out of place in British Columbia, having been built for a Scottish aristocrat, the Duke of Sutherland, in 1895 for his private line that connected his castle with the Caledonian Railway main line, over which he had negotiated running rights in return for a substantial investment. The BC government purchased *Dunrobin* in 1965 for $15,000, with a 1909 4-wheel saloon coach, for exhibit and occasional running at Fort Steele Heritage Village. The locomotive and coach were returned to Britain in 2011 and are now at the Beamish Museum in County Durham.

In 1986, in conjunction with Expo 86, there was Steam Expo, featuring a "grand parade of steam" along CP's waterfront line featuring original and replica locomotives from across the world and across the years. Locomotives included famous engines such as a replica of Robert Stephenson's 1829 *Rocket*, South Carolina's replica 1830 *Best Friend of Charleston*, and the original Camden & Amboy Rail Road's 1833 *John Bull*. The Royal Hudson (see page 187) and Alberni Pacific No. 2 (page 189) also took part.

A train celebrating British Columbia's 150 years from its 1858 creation as a British colony appeared in Langley for an afternoon on 30 June 2008 as part of a provincial tour; headed by CPR No. 2816, the train also included the CP streamlined diesel No. 1401.

The latter locomotive appeared again heading a train that was used as a backdrop for ceremonies to commemorate Canada 150 in 2017, starting, appropriately enough, at Port Moody, before setting off on a similar tour across Canada. By then the locomotive formed part of the Royal Canadian Pacific luxury charter train, inaugurated in 2000, the only remaining passenger service of CP.

Left, above, top and *above*.
British Columbia 150 was celebrated in 2008 partly by a train that toured the province. It was headed by CPR No. 2816, a 4-5-4 H1b Hudson type locomotive built in 1930. It is named *Empress*, though does not bear a nameplate. It is the only non-streamlined Hudson to have been preserved. Restored in 2001, it is still owned by Canadian Pacific but is kept in Calgary. Also part of the train was CPR FP9A diesel 1401 shown in the photo *above, top*. It was built in 1958. Painted in the grey, maroon and yellow livery of the period from the early 1950s to 1968–69, it is now part of CP's Royal Canadian Pacific train, and showed up as a backdrop to ceremonies for Canada 150 in 2017 (*above*).

Passenger coaches, and, in particular, cabooses, are found on static display througout the province—a coach at Port Moody, and cabooses at Coquitam, Kaslo and Midway, for example. And original railway stations survive in goodly numbers, perhaps because they were relatively easy to adapt to other useful purposes. Examples include Port Moody's 1908 station, White Rock's 1911 station and Qualicum Beach's 1914 station, all are now museums. One, Port Alberni's 1912 station, still performs its original function as a railway station, in that case for the tourist-oriented Alberni Pacific Railway (see page 189).

A LEGACY PRESERVED 213

A new residential and retail development on the north side of Victoria's Inner Harbour is to include the 1913 E&N roundhouse (*above, top*), with a 1957 CP boxcar; and this 1959 CP boxcar, surrounded by high-rises (*above*).

Above. CPR 1930 Hudson No. 2816 at Langley in 2008.

Right, bottom centre. Qualicum Beach's 1914 E&N station.

Right, bottom. A CPR caboose on the waterfront of Kootenay Lake at Kaslo, with SS *Moyie* in the background.

Below. Midway station, built in 1900, with a 1920 CP wooden caboose.

Far right, bottom. In January 2017 a CN container train passes Fort Langley station, with its 1947 CNR passenger coach on display.

Above, and inset right.
Canadian Pacific diesels No. 7009, built in 1958, and No. 4104, built in 1954, worked in Alberta, but are the same as many of the company's locomotives that operated in British Columbia. They have been restored to period livery and placed outside the restored 1900 lakefront railway station in Nelson, seen in the background. At the date of this photo in July 2018, No. 4104 had a tarpaulin partially covering it.

A LEGACY PRESERVED   215

Above and *right*.
British Columbia's oldest surviving main-line locomotive, CPR No. 374, sits outside the Yaletown Roundhouse in Vancouver in May 2017. It is hauled out a couple of times a year. This time it was for the Victoria Day weekend. At *right*, the original 1911 roundhouse turntable can also be seen.

We end close to where we started, with some of the first locomotives to run in British Columbia. The now iconic CPR Engine No. 374, which pulled the first transcontinental train into the city of Vancouver on 23 May 1887, has been restored and sits in grand style in an extension built onto the Yaletown Roundhouse, part of the old CPR servicing yards on False Creek. This after many years of slowly deteriorating on a plinth in a park in Kitsilano after being donated to the city by the CPR in 1945. In 1983, with Expo 86 on the horizon, it was restored by volunteers in time to be displayed on the roundhouse turntable for that event. Even then its future was uncertain, but in 1998 successful fundraising efforts resulted in the new display building, and it has resided there ever since, being hauled out with a winch and chain a couple of times a year.

The oldest preserved steam locomotive to run in the province, *Duchess*, is now on display at Carcross, Yukon. After its work hauling coal from the coal mines of Nanaimo to the docks, beginning in 1878, it was sold in 1900 to haul the White Pass & Yukon's Taku Tram and went north, never to return (see page 71).

Another early Nanaimo coal mine locomotive, Dunsmuir & Diggle No. 19 *Victoria*, was preserved when it retired in 1952 and sits today in a shelter in Piper Park in Nanaimo. The shelter protects it but makes it hard to view; many pass by without even knowing it is there.

And the ex–Andrew Onderdonk, ex-CPR little No. 2 *Emory*—or *Old Curly*, as it was nicknamed—which helped to build the Canadian Pacific Railway in British Columbia, sits in a forlorn shelter at the Burnaby Village Museum, open to view, but only with difficulty, as the space is so cramped. If any historic locomotive deserves a better home, it is this one, so significant it is to our heritage. But at least it is preserved; it was the much more usual fate of most of British Columbia's locomotives to be broken up for scrap.

Above.
Surely vying with CPR No. 374 as the locomotive most significant to British Columbia's history is the Andrew Onderdonk CPR construction engine No. 2 *Emory*, better known by its nickname of *Old Curly*, or often just *Curly*. It was probably built in 1877 or 1878, but perhaps earlier, and brought to BC by Onderdonk after both had worked on construction of the San Francisco seawall. The engine went on to work in the forests of South Surrey, hauling trains of logs to transshipment first into a logging ditch and then on the New Westminster & Southern north to Port Kells, or taking its train there itself. The open-side shelter it sits in at the Burnaby Village Museum is better than no protection at all but hardly saves it from wind-blown rain and snow in winter. While the perhaps more glamorous interurban BCER car No. 1223 sits nearby in a new well-lit enclosed building (see page 193), poor *Emory* sits out in the cold, on the very edge of the museum's grounds, missed by many visitors and difficult to view in any case. The photo here required a very wide-angle lens to get the whole locomotive in the frame. One can only hope better care will be taken of this historically important engine in future.

Left, top.
The shelter that houses No. 19 *Victoria* in Piper Park, Nanaimo, basks in early-morning sunshine. Although attractive and functional, the shelter makes it very difficult to view the locomotive inside.

Left.
No. 19 *Victoria* in its shelter. See also the photo on *page 12*.

Right, top.
Vancouver's Arbutus Greenway at 33rd Avenue in October 2017. The railway crossing signals are still in place but the track has been removed and replaced with a paved walk- and bike-way.

Above.
This is a type of railway that still exists and is used—a boat railway, the easiest way to transfer a boat to the water, carried on a small flanged-wheeled truck. This one is at Steveston.

Below.
A tug pulling a long set of logs passes under the old BCER railway bridge at Marpole. The trestle and bridge carried the tracks over the North Arm of the Fraser to Richmond on their way to Steveston. Today the rails are still there, as is the bridge, but the rails end on the other side of the river and the bridge is fenced off and permanently open to river traffic. But the rails peter out farther north; the Arbutus route, which it connects with in Vancouver, was sold to the City of Vancouver in 2016 for $55 million—for use as a trail. Was it a rapid transit opportunity missed?

Right, top.
There are scenes like this in all corners of the province. This is an old logging railway bridge across Skidegate Lake, on Moresby Island, Haida Gwaii. The path of the track (*far right, bottom*) is still quite clear more than sixty years after the railway closed. The 8.9 km railway, which had some grades as steep as 6 per cent and often required piles to stabilize swampy ground, was that of A.P. Allison, and was built in 1936–37. The line took logs to Cumshewa Inlet, where they were shipped to Powell River. Some six locomotives worked on this line at one time. The company was taken over by the federal government and renamed Aero Forest Products during the Second World War, as the spruce it cut was critical to the war effort. The railway returned to private hands in 1945 and continued operation until 1955.

Right, bottom.
The track of the Esquimalt & Nanaimo Railway, once owned by CP and later by Rail America, is now (in theory) operated by Southern Railway of Vancouver Island (SVI), a sister company of the Southern Railway of British Columbia (see page 178). A connection to the mainland at Annacis Island is provided by another associated company, Seaspan. The track and railbed is now owned by the Island Corridor Foundation, a non-profit governmental body set up to determine if it is feasible to reopen the line. As can be seen from this photograph taken at Qualicum Beach, the track is in a poor state of repair with partly rotted ties in many places, and needs a complete overhaul. Whether the economics of the railway will allow this and whether the line makes any sense in the modern era remains to be seen. In the meantime, the railway sits in limbo.

A LEGACY PRESERVED   219

Appendix 1: List of British Columbia Railway Incorporations

Railways can often be found marked and named on old maps and other documents bearing names that have long passed into history. They may have only been proposals, never built, or they may have been railways that later passed into the hands of competitors. The names (and terminology and spelling) typically are derived directly from the legislation itself.

This is a list of over 300 railway incorporations (charters) in British Columbia with approved routing from the legislation, plus capsule legal histories. Much, but not all, of this information is derived from *A Statutory History of the Steam and Electric Railways of Canada 1836–1937* (Canada: Department of Transport, 1938).

This list also includes bridge, tunnel or ferry company incorporations where rail traffic might be carried, plus street railways and mining tramways. It typically does not include mining, forest company railways, or others where the entire line was built on land owned or leased by the builder; these did not require legislation because they did not need the power of eminent domain (the power to acquire land for their route from owners who might not want to sell).

Alberta and British Columbia Railway Company
1908 incorporated to build from point on BC border on US boundary at the Kootenay River Crossing to Elko, thence to Cowley, AB, and on to Calgary.

Ashcroft and Cariboo Railway Company
1896 incorporated to build from Ashcroft or Kamloops to Barkerville, thence to Port Simpson, etc.
Company dissolved by Defunct Railway Companies Act, 1926–27.

Ashcroft Barkerville and Fort George Railway Company
1906 incorporated to build from Ashcroft via Bonaparte River, Lac La Hache and Quesnelle River, to Fort George, with branch to Barkerville, etc.
1908 time extension.
Company dissolved by Defunct Railway Companies Act, 1926–27.

Atlin Railway Company
1914 incorporated to build from Atlin to point on US boundary at Taku River intersection, etc.
1916 time extension.

Atlin Short Line Railway and Navigation Company
1899 incorporated to build from Taku Arm, Cassiar District, along valley of Atlintoo River, on north side of river, to near where the Atlintoo River leaves Atlin Lake, etc.
Company dissolved by Defunct Railway Companies Act, 1926–27.

Atlin Southern Railway Company
1899 incorporated to build from Log Cabin, on the White Pass to Taku Arm of Taglish Lake, from entrance of Atlintoo River into Taglish Lake and from Atlin City to Telegraph Creek; with branches, etc.
Company dissolved by Defunct Railway Companies Act, 1926–27.

Barkerville, Ashcroft and Kamloops Railway Company
1897 incorporated to build from Ashcroft or Kamloops to Barkerville, with branches, etc.
Company dissolved by Defunct Railway Companies Act, 1926–27.

Bella Coola and Fraser Lake Railway Company
1906 incorporated to build from mouth of Bella Coola River to a point 30 miles from its mouth; thence to Fraser Lake, to Fort George, to mouth of Telkwa River; with branches to Blackwater River and the Chilcotin Districts, etc.
Company dissolved by Defunct Railway Companies Act, 1926–27.

Bentinck Arm and Quesnel Railway Company
1907 incorporated to build from junction of Rau Shuswap and South Fork of Fraser River, thence up Rau Shuswap River to headwaters of Swamp River, to Keithley Creek, to Coquette Pass, to outlet of Quesnel Lake, to Quesnel Fork, to Quesnel, to Blackwater, to Kusya Lake, to Salmon River Forks, to Bella Coola, etc.
Company dissolved by Defunct Railway Companies Act, 1926–27.

Big Bend Transportation Company
1899 incorporated to build and operate tramways in conjunction with its steamship service on the Columbia River, etc.

Boundary, Kamloops and Cariboo Central Railway Company
1904 incorporated to build from Midway to Okanagan Lake and Grand Prairie (BC); thence to Kamloops, via North Thompson River to a point on the Nechaco River, to Hazelton, to the Stikine River, to Teslin Lake, and to junction of Hootalinqua River and Yukon River, etc.
1906 to build from Grand Forks to Franklin Camp, Fire Valley and Grand Prairie; time extension.

British Columbia and Alaska Railway Company
1910 incorporated to build from Lytton, via Lillooet, to Fort George, thence via Stuart River, Stuart Lake, Tacla River, Middle River and Fort Connelly, to North Tacla Lake, to Telegraph Creek, to Teslin Lake; also line to Vancouver, with branches, etc.
Company dissolved by Defunct Railway Companies Act, 1926–27.

British Columbia and Central Canada Railway Company
1911 incorporated to build from mouth of Nass River to source of Omineca River, to Peace River, to Peace River Landing, to Hudson Bay.

British Columbia and Dawson Railway Company
1911 incorporated to build from Lytton to Fort George, the mouth of the Stuart River, thence via Fort Connelly to summit between Skeena and Stikine Rivers, to Telegraph Creek, to Dawson City; also from Ashcroft to Fraser River at the Big Creek; also from Lillooet to Vancouver, etc.
1912 line from Fort George to Telegraph Creek, to Peace River Landing; time extension.

British Columbia and Manitoba Railway Company
1904 incorporated as Crawford Bay and St. Mary's Railway Company to build from Crawford Bay on Kootenay Lake easterly via Crawford Creek and St. Mary's River to Fort Steele, etc.
1906 extension of line to Lethbridge, AB; extensions farther east 1907.
1909 name change to British Columbia and Manitoba Railway Company.

British Columbia and White River Railway Company
1911 incorporated to build from US boundary at Bear Creek to the Alsek, thence via Shakwak Valley to Lake Kluane, the White River, and to boundary between Alaska and Yukon Territory.

British Columbia Central Railway Company
1906 incorporated to build from Osoyoos to Enderby and Kamloops; to Quesnel and Fort George; also from Enderby to Sicamous, from Kamloops to Quilchena and Princeton and to US boundary, etc.
1911 incorporated to build from Lillooet to Fort George, etc.
Company dissolved by Defunct Railway Companies Act, 1926–27.

British Columbia Electric Power and Gas Company /
British Columbia Electric Railway Company
1897 incorporated in UK to take over operations of Consolidated Railway and Light Company.
1900 City of Vancouver not to compete.
1907 agreement with Canadian Pacific Railway re: trackage and control of Vancouver and Lulu Island Railway.
1910 agreement with City of Victoria re: competition, and right of city to acquire railway property.

British Columbia Northern and Alaska Railway Company
1906 incorporated to build from Vancouver, via Lillooet, Fraser Valley, Tacla Lake, Stikine River and Teslin Lake, to northern boundary of province; with branches, etc.
Company dissolved by Defunct Railway Companies Act, 1926–27.

British Columbia Northern and Mackenzie Valley Railway Company
1903 incorporated to build from Nasoga Gulf via Naas and Skeena Rivers to Dease Lake, then via Dease River to northern boundary of BC. Also from Dease Lake to Telegraph Creek or Glenora, and to eastern boundary of BC and to Atlin City, etc.
1906 time extension.
Company dissolved by Defunct Railway Companies Act, 1926–27.

British Columbia Southern Railway Company
1888 incorporated as the Crow's Nest and Kootenay Lake Railway Company to build from junction of Summit Creek and Michel Creek, via Elk River to upper Kootenay River, thence via Cranbrook, Moyie Pass and Goat River to junction of Goat River and Lower Kootenay River, etc.
1888 land grant for right-of-way and terminals for Crow's Nest and Kootenay Lake Railway Company.
1890 land grant.
1891 name changed to British Columbia Southern Railway Company; line to Fort Sheppard; line from Fort Sheppard to Nelson; to Hope and New Westminster; to Tobacco Plains, etc.
1893 subsidy–land.
1893 line from Cranbrook to Pilot Bay or to Lardo River, etc.
1896 time extensions.
1897 works declared to be for the general advantage of Canada; extension of line eastwards; power to lease to Canadian Pacific Railway.
1898 lease to Canadian Pacific Railway confirmed, eastern boundary of BC to Nelson.
1901 lease of western section to Canadian Pacific Railway confirmed.
1912 repurchase of portion of land grant by provincial government.

British Columbia Yukon Railway Company
1897 subsidy lands for line of railway from head of Lynn Canal to northern boundary of BC.
1897 incorporated to build from head of Lynn Canal to northern boundary of BC.
1898 organization of White Pass and Yukon Railway Company to acquire capital stock of British Yukon Railway Company, British Columbia Yukon Railway Company, and of an American company, Pacific and Arctic Railway and Navigation Company (see White Pass and Yukon Railway).

British Yukon Railway Company
1897 incorporated to build from head of Lynn Canal, via White Pass to Selkirk, Yukon;
1897 subsidy–lands; (see White Pass and Yukon Railway).

Burrard Inlet and Fraser Valley Railway Company
1891 incorporated to build from a point on Burrard Inlet southeasterly to a point on the US boundary between Semiahmoo Bay and Township 22 NWD; with branch to Chilliwhack municipality.
1893 aid for a bridge over Fraser River at New Westminster.
1893 time extension.
Company dissolved by Defunct Railway Companies Act, 1926–27.

Burrard Inlet and Westminster Valley Railway Company
1891 incorporated to build from US boundary in Township 16, NWD to a point on north side of Fraser River, with branch to Fraser River; ferry and bridge over Fraser River.

Burrard Inlet Railway and Ferry Company
1891 incorporated to build a railway or tramway from point on north shore of Burrard Inlet to English Bay or Howe Sound; with branches; operation of ferry boats, etc.
1895 time extension; employment of Chinese or Japanese, etc.
Company dissolved by Defunct Railway Companies Act, 1926–27.

Burrard Inlet Tunnel and Bridge Company
1892 incorporated to build a tunnel under First Narrows and a bridge over Second Narrows.
Again incorporated, 1910.
1912 subsidy for railway lines Eburne to Seymour Creek, from Seymour Creek to Horseshoe Bay and from Pender Street, Vancouver, to North Vancouver.
1913 subsidy for bridge at Second Narrows.
The (first) Second Narrows Bridge opened 1925. Stock in Burrard Inlet Tunnel and Bridge Company was owned by the City of North Vancouver, District of North Vancouver, District of West Vancouver, and City of Vancouver. The bridge was damaged by a barge in 1930 and put out of commission. The company went bankrupt in 1932 and the bridge was repaired by the Vancouver Harbour Commission in 1934.

Burrard, Westminster Boundary Railway and Navigation Company
1907 incorporated to build from Vancouver to New Westminster, to Fraser River Bridge and to Port Moody; to proposed Vancouver, Westminster and Yukon Railway bridge at Second Narrows; to a point of commencement in Vancouver; from Second Narrows to Howe Sound; from New Westminster to a point between Semiahmoo Bay and Sumas; from False Creek to Point Grey and New Westminster; and from Port Moody to Stave River, etc.
1909: line to Tête Jaune Cache.
1909 company may sell to or lease to or amalgamate with Vancouver, Westminster and Yukon Railway Company.

Canadian Northern Pacific Railway Company
1910 incorporated to build from eastern boundary of BC to New Westminster, Vancouver, and to English Bluff (Tsawwassen); from Victoria to Barkley Sound, and branches; incl. power to purchase other lines (Mackenzie and Mann built the Canadian Northern across Canada principally by buying existing lines).
1912 lines to east coast of Vancouver Island; and from Kamloops to Vernon and Lumby; Vernon to Kelowna; Vernon to Okanagan Lake.
1912 subsidy–Yellowhead Pass to Vancouver and mouth of Fraser River.
1913 agreement with City of Vancouver re: transfer to railway by city of lands received from the provincial government.
1917 trackage rights with Vancouver, Victoria and Eastern Railway and Navigation Company from New Westminster to Vancouver, and Hope to Sumas Landing.

Canadian Pacific Railway Company
1880 provincial grant of lands to Dominion Government in aid of CPR construction on mainland.
1881 incorporation of CPR.
1882 CPR may build through Rocky Mountains by other route than Yellowhead Pass.
1882 proclamation for preservation of peace along line of CPR in BC.
1883 provincial grant of lands to Dominion Government in lieu of alienated lands in Railway Belt).
1886 Dominion Government turns over portions of track built under government contracts to the CPR (i.e., in BC, the track from Savona's Ferry at the western end of Kamloops Lake to Port Moody, built by contractor Onderdonk).
1890 lease of Columbia and Kootenay Railway and Navigation Company works to CPR for 999 years.
1891 lease of Shuswap and Okanagan Railway Company properties etc. to CPR for 25 years.
1892 subsidy–Revelstoke to Arrow Lake.
1897 British Columbia Southern Railway Company may lease to CPR.
1898 confirms lease of eastern section of British Columbia Southern Railway Company line to CPR with option to purchase.
1898 confirms lease of the line of the British Columbia Southern Railway Company from eastern boundary of BC to Nelson to CPR in perpetuity.
1901 confirms lease of the western section of the line of the British Columbia Southern Railway Company to CPR in perpetuity.
1903 lease of the Vancouver and Lulu Island Railway for 999 years.
1904 time extension for line New Westminster to Vancouver.
1905 agreement with the Esquimalt and Nanaimo Railway Company.
1907 agreement with the British Columbia Electric Company re: service and transfer Vancouver and Lulu Island Railway to said company.
1913 Kettle Valley Railway Company may lease to CPR.
1913 approves lease of Kettle Valley Railway Company properties to CPR for 999 years from 1 July 1913.
1914 mineral rights adjacent to CPR tunnel under construction near Rogers Pass (Connaught Tunnel, completed 1916; originally named Selkirk Tunnel).
1919 agreement re: purchase of bonds of Nakusp and Slocan Railway Company and operation of that railway by CPR.

Canadian Western Central Railway
1889 Yellowhead Pass to Bute Inlet.

Canadian-Yukon Railway
Following gold rush of 1898 to the Klondike.
1898 provision of (federal) funds to cover survey from point on existing railway into the Yukon.
1899 Dominion Government entered into contract with Mackenzie and Mann for construction of a line from the Stikine River to Teslin Lake, but approval from the Senate was not forthcoming; in 1902 $250,000 was paid to them in compensation for work done.

Canadian Yukon Railway Company
1898 incorporated to build from Douglas Channel or some other point capable of being made into a sea port, to a point on southern end of Teslin Lake; with tramways and branch lines, etc.
Company dissolved by Defunct Railway Companies Act, 1926–27.

Cariboo, Barkerville and Willow River Railway Company
1910 incorporated to build from Eagle Lake via watershed of Willow River to Barkerville; with branches, etc.
Company dissolved by Defunct Railway Companies Act, 1926–27.

Cariboo Railway Company
1890 incorporated as Ashcroft and Cariboo Railway Company to build from Ashcroft to Barkerville, etc. Also land grant.
1894 name changed to Cariboo Railway Company.
1894 Dominion incorporation of Cariboo Railway Company to build from Ashcroft to

Barkerville with extension to Fraser River; power to acquire Cariboo Railway Company of British Columbia; agreement with Canadian Pacific Railway Company, etc.
Company dissolved by Defunct Railway Companies Act, 1926–27.

Cassiar Central Railway Company
1897 incorporated to build from a point on the Stikine River to a point on or near Dease Lake; with extensions and branches, etc. Also lease of minerals and lands as aid to construction.
Company dissolved by Defunct Railway Companies Act, 1926–27.

Chilliwhack Railway Company
1891 incorporated to build from a point on the Mission branch of the Canadian Pacific Railway to a point in the Municipality of Chilliwhack, etc.
1894 subsidy: Abbotsford to Chilliwhack.
Company dissolved by Defunct Railway Companies Act, 1926–27.

Coast-Kootenay Railway Company
1901 incorporated to build from Vancouver via New Westminster to Chilliwhack, thence to a point between junction of Chilliwhack and Fraser Rivers and Yale, to a point between Penticton and US boundary, thence via the Kettle River and Town of Midway to Grand Forks, etc.
1902 aid for construction of railway from Vancouver to Midway.
1902 re: employment of aliens.
Company dissolved by Defunct Railway Companies Act, 1926–27.

Coast Yukon Railway Company
1903 incorporated to build from Kitimat Inlet to Atlin Lake, thence to Yukon River and to Alaskan boundary, via Dawson. etc.
1903–4 incorporation of Coast-Yukon Railway Company to build from Hazelton to Atlin Lake, thence to 60th parallel, etc.
1926–27 declares Coast Yukon Railway dissolved (Coast-Yukon not mentioned).

Columbia and Carbonate Mountain Railway Company
1890 incorporated to build from a point on the Columbia River, 17 miles up the river, southwesterly to head waters of Middle Fork of Spillimacheen River, etc.
Company dissolved by Defunct Railway Companies Act, 1926–27.

Columbia and Kootenay Railway and Navigation Company
1889 subsidy–land, from outlet of Kootenay Lake to junction of Kootenay and Columbia Rivers
1889 incorporated to build from outlet of Kootenay Lake, through Selkirk Mountains, to junction of Columbia and Kootenay Rivers; vessels, etc. (52 Vic., Cap 35)
1890 subsidy–lands
1890 incorporated to build from outlet of Kootenay Lake, through Selkirk Mountains, to junction of Columbia and Kootenay Rivers; vessels, etc. (52 Vic., Cap 62)
1890 (Dominion) subsidy–from outlet Kootenay Lake to junction Columbia and Kootenay Rivers.
1890 (Aug 20) lease of Columbia and Kootenay Railway and Navigation Company works to the Canadian Pacific Railway for 999 years approved.
1891 Acquisition of bonds of Columbia and Kootenay Railway and Navigation Company by CPR.
1892 subsidy–from Revelstoke to Arrow Lake
1893 extension of line to Revelstoke; branch lines, etc.
1897 line described; time extended; extension of line to Queen's Bay; to Kootenay Lake and Lower Arrows Lake , etc.

Columbia and Kootenay Railway and Transportation Company
1883 incorporated to build, in conjunction with a line of steamships, from outlet of Kootenay Lake, through Selkirk Mountains, to junction of Columbia and Kootenay Rivers, etc.
Company dissolved by Defunct Railway Companies Act, 1926–27.

Columbia and Western Railway Company
1896 subsidy–land.
1896 incorporated to build from mouth of Trail Creek to Rossland; from mouth of Trail Creek easterly or southeasterly for 20 miles; from Rossland to Christina Lake; from Christina Lake to Midway; from Midway to Penticton; branches to mines; power to acquire Trail Creek Tramways, etc.
1898 time extension for lands
1898, Aug 3 (Dominion) approves lease, in perpetuity, of Columbia and Western Company undertaking, etc, to the Canadian Pacific Railway.
1906 (BC) land grant "in full of aid votes."
1912 (BC) repurchase of Gov. of BC of portion of land grant.

Columbia River Bridge Company
1897 incorporated to build a bridge for railway, pedestrian, and vehicular traffic over the Columbia River near Robson.

Comox and Cape Scott Railway Company
1900 (Dominion) incorporated to build from a point in Wellington District, Vancouver Island, to a point in Comox District; thence northerly through Sayward and Rupert Districts to Cape Scott, etc.; agreement with Canadian Pacific Railway Company, and Esquimalt and Nanaimo Railway Company.
1901 (BC) incorporated to build from a point in Wellington District, Vancouver Island, to a point in Comox District; thence northerly through Sayward and Rupert Districts to Cape Scott, etc.
Company dissolved by Defunct Railway Companies Act, 1926–27.

Consolidated Railway Company
1894 incorporation of Consolidated Railway and Light Company. To acquire property, etc., of Vancouver Electric Railway and Light Company and other tramway and light companies in New Westminster District, etc.
1896 name changed to Consolidated Railway Company; acquisition of Westminster and Vancouver Tramway Company, the Vancouver Electric Railway and Light Company, and North Vancouver Electric Company confirmed.
See also British Columbia Electric Railway Company.

Cowichan, Alberni and Fort Rupert Railway Company
1903–4 incorporated to build from Mill Bay or Cowichan Bay via Cowichan River to Cowichan Lake, thence to mouth of Sarita River or Barclay Sound; and from a point on this line to Alberni, via Coleman Creek and Alberni Canal, to Fort Rupert; with branch to Quatsino Sound, etc.
1906 time extension; line to Victoria or Esquimalt Harbour
Company dissolved by Defunct Railway Companies Act, 1926–27.

Cowichan Valley Railway Company
1898 incorporated to build from mouth of Cowichan River to head of Cowichan Lake, thence via Franklin River to a point on the Alberni Canal; with branch to outlet of Nitinat Lake, etc.

Crawford Bay Railway Company
1901 incorporated to build from Crawford Bay via Crawford Creek and St. Mary's River to Kootenay River opposite Fort Steele; with branch lines, etc.
Company dissolved by Defunct Railway Companies Act, 1926–27.

Crow's Nest and Northern Railway Company
1908 incorporated to build from Crow's Nest Pass on Canadian Pacific Railway line via west side of north fork of Michel Creek, to junction of two north branches of Michel Creek, thence by both branches to points on the divide between waters of north fork of Michel Creek and waters of Grave Creek; with branches, etc.
Company dissolved by Defunct Railway Companies Act, 1926–27.

Crow's Nest Pass Electric Light and Power Company
1900 incorporated to build tramways in town of Fernie and in District of Kootenay, etc.

Crow's Nest Southern Railway Company
1901 incorporated to build from Michel, via Michel Creek, southwards to a point near the US boundary; also from Michel Creek northerly, along Elk River Valley, to a point on the eastern boundary of BC; also from a point on this line, near south fork of Elk River, via Kootenay Pass to a point on the eastern boundary of BC, with branches. etc. (was built from Newgate (Gateway) to Michel by GNR from Rexford, Montana. Line between Fernie and Michel abandoned 1925).
1902 repeals section re: employment of aliens.
1936 abandonment approved (Dominion) Newgate to Fernie.

Delta, New Westminster and Eastern Railway Company
1894 incorporated to build from a point on the Gulf (Strait) of Georgia in Delta municipality to New Westminster, with a branch to Abbotsford.
Company dissolved by Defunct Railway Companies Act, 1926–27.

Delta Railway Company
1887 incorporated to build from Ladner's Landing to Popcum, etc.
Company dissolved by Defunct Railway Companies Act, 1926–27.

Dolly Varden Mines Railway
1917 authority for Dolly Varden Mines Company to build from Wolf group of mineral claims via Kitzault River to public highway; thence to Alice Arm.
1935 cites abandonment of railway; vests right-of-way in Crown; provides for removal of rails.

Eastern British Columbia Railway Company
1908 incorporated to build from south fork of Michel Creek at "The Loop" up the creek to mouth of East Fork, thence up the East Fork to a point on Lot 6999, Group 1, Kootenay District.

East Kootenay Logging Railway Company
1907 incorporated to build from a point on the Crow's Nest Branch of the Canadian Pacific at Lot 5808, group 1, to Rock Creek, etc.

East Kootenay Railway Company
1898 incorporated to build from Cranbrook to headwaters of St. Mary's River, from a point on this line to the mines at Horse Thief Creek and No. 2 Creek, and from Bull River Mines to a point on the Crow's Nest Railway, etc.
Company dissolved by Defunct Railway Companies Act, 1926–27.

Edmonton, Dunvegan and British Columbia Railway Company
1907 incorporated to build from Edmonton to Dunvegan and thence via Peace River Valley westerly to Parsnip River Valley to Town of Fort George, etc.
1929 sale to Canadian National Railway and Canadian Pacific Railway jointly.
1929 incorporation of Northern Alberta Railways Company to hold and operate properties of Edmonton, Dunvegan and British Columbia Railway.

Esquimalt and Nanaimo Railway Company
1875 grant of lands to the Dominion government to aid in construction of railway between Esquimalt Harbour and Nanaimo, etc.
1882 repealed 1875 grant.
1883 refers to agreement with Dominion Government re: E&N; grants portions of lands intended for Vancouver Land and Railway Company to Dominion Government for purposes of Esquimalt to Nanaimo railway; authorizes incorporation of persons, designated by Governor in Council, as Esquimalt and Nanaimo Railway Company to build railway of same gauge as Canadian Pacific Railway from Esquimalt Harbour to Nanaimo; with power to extend to Comox and to Victoria, etc.
1884 new agreement with Dominion Government; further re: incorporation of Esquimalt and Nanaimo Railway Company, lands, etc.
1884 (Dominion) agreement with province of BC re: Esquimalt and Nanaimo Railway; lands; cash subsidy, etc.
1886 (Dominion) accepts curves in line.
1888 (Dominion) ferry service between Beecher Bay and point on Strait of Juan de Fuca in US.
1888 land grant for Beecher Bay branch/ authority to build railway.
1906 time extension—from Comox to Campbell River, Duncan's to Alberni; Englishman's River to Alberni Canal, and Comox to Alberni Canal.
1912 approves lease of Esquimalt and Nanaimo Railway Company property to Canadian Pacific Railway for 99 years, from July 1912.
1916 land grant in Songhees Indian reserve.

Fernie and Elk River Railway Company
1921 incorporated to build from Sparwood via Elk River Valley, to Kananaskis Pass, with branches, etc.
Company dissolved by Defunct Railway Companies Act, 1926–27.

First Narrows Bridge Company
1926–27 power to erect a bridge for pedestrian, vehicular and other traffic over the First Narrows of Burrard Inlet from Prospect Point to Capilano Indian Reserve, etc.
1931 tolls for street and other railways; power to build other bridge at Second Narrows, subject to agreement with Burrard Inlet Tunnel and Bridge Company.

Fording Valley Railway Company
1905–1906 (BC/Dominion) incorporated to build from junction of Elk River and Michel Creek to a point north of Fording River, thence to Fording River Valley, thence along Fording River to north of Henrietta Creek, thence along Henrietta Creek to Alberta Boundary.
Company dissolved by Defunct Railway Companies Act, 1926–27.

Fraser River Bridge Company
1926–27 power to erect a bridge for pedestrian, vehicular and other traffic over the Fraser River from Ladner to Lulu Island.
1931 bridge to be from Port Mann; railway traffic to be provided for, etc.
1934 power to erect a bridge at or near New Westminster.
1935 agreement with provincial government re: construction of Fraser River (New Westminster) Bridge.

Fraser River Railway Company
1883 incorporated to build from 49th parallel between Semiahmoo Bay and Township 22, NWD, to a point on the Canadian Pacific Railway between Township 27 and the CPR western terminus, and thence to New Westminster, etc.

1883 (Dominion) disallows incorporation.
Company dissolved by Defunct Railway Companies Act, 1926–27.

Fraser Valley Terminal Railway Company
1915 (Dominion) incorporated to build terminals and shops, etc. for railways in municipalities of Richmond and New Westminster, etc.

Goat River Water Power and Light Company
1909 incorporated to build tramways within radius of 10 miles from Goat River Canyon, Kootenay District, etc.

Graham Island Railway Company
1909 incorporated to build from Lena Island, Skidegate Inlet, Queen Charlotte Islands, to Camp Robertson, thence to Camp Wilson, to Shields Island, Rennell Sound, with branch to Masset Inlet.
1910 extends time; line to Naden Harbour or Virago Sound.
Company dissolved by Defunct Railway Companies Act, 1926–27.

Grand Trunk Pacific Railway Company
1903 incorporated to build from Moncton, New Brunswick, via Peace River Pass or Pine River Pass to Port Simpson, Bute Inlet or some other port on the Pacific coast plus branch to Dawson, Yukon.
1908 sale of portion of Metlakatla Indian Reserve to GTPR (Grand Trunk Pacific Town and Development Company).
1909 agreement with Provincial Government re: survey of Prince Rupert townsite.
1910 rights of GTPR in Hays Creek, Prince Rupert and right-of-way for pipeline in Prince Rupert.
1912 time extension for Prairie and Mountain sections.
1912 agreement with Provincial Government and with Foley, Welch and Stewart re: incorporation of Pacific Great Eastern Railway Company to build line authorized for GTPR to Vancouver, etc.
1918 provincial payment towards cost of steel railway bridge over Fraser River at Fort George.
(In 1919 the GTPR notified the Dominion government that owing to low revenues it could not continue operation.)
1919 Minister of Railways and Canals appointed receiver.
1919 adds Grand Trunk Pacific Elevator Company to properties in bankruptcy proceedings.
1920 GTPR operation and management placed under board of Canadian Northern Railway Company (Canadian National Railways).
1923 amalgamation with Canadian National Railways.

Greater Vancouver Tunnel Company Ltd.
1931 power granted to construct a tunnel for passenger and traffic under First Narrows of Burrard Inlet from Coal Harbour to a point on the North Shore.

Greenwood-Phoenix Tramway Company
1911 incorporated to build a tramway in the vicinity of Greenwood and of Phoenix for freight purposes.

Grouse Mountain Scenic Incline Railway Company
1911 incorporated to build from Lot 594, Group 1, New Westminster District, to Lot 1526, Group 1, NWD.

Hardy Bay and Quatsino Sound Railway Company
1909 incorporated to build from Hardy Bay (Port Hardy) to Coal Harbour, Quatsino Sound, with branch lines, etc.
Company dissolved by Defunct Railway Companies Act, 1926–27.

Harrison Hot Springs Tramway Company
1888 incorporated to build a tramway from Harrison Hot Springs and Agassiz, and from Agassiz to the Fraser River.
Company dissolved by Defunct Railway Companies Act, 1926–27.

Howe Sound and Northern Railway Company /
Howe Sound, Pemberton Valley and Northern Railway Company
1907 incorporation of Howe Sound, Pemberton Valley and Northern Railway Company to build from mouth of Squamish River at Howe Sound via Squamish River valley to Cheakamus River, thence to Anderson Lake; with branches, etc.
1910 name changed to Howe Sound and Northern Railway Company; increase of Capital stock.
Line was purchased by Pacific Great Eastern Railway Company.

Hudson Bay Pacific Railway Company
1908 incorporated to build from Port Simpson or Work Channel up Work Channel to Skeena River, thence to Hazelton, thence to Bulkley River, to Suskewa River, to Babine

APPENDIX 223

Lake, to Stuart Lake, etc., to eastern boundary of province; with branch lines, etc.
Company dissolved by Defunct Railway Companies Act, 1926–27.

Hudson Bay Pacific Railway Company
1911 incorporated to build from Winnipeg to Fort St. John, thence via Nass River to Port Simpson; from Fort St. John to Edmonton; running rights to other companies across Rocky Mountains, etc.
1913 time extension.

Imperial Pacific Railway Company
1901 incorporated to build from Victoria, northeasterly, by way of Tete Jaune Cache or Yellow Head Pass or Pine River or Peace River Passes, to a point near eastern boundary of province; and a line near northern boundary of province; and to a convenient harbour on the sea coast, etc.
(Perhaps the most general of all the charters!)
Company dissolved by Defunct Railway Companies Act, 1926–27.

Island Valley Railway Company
1910 incorporated to build from Skidegate Inlet, Graham Island, to Masset Inlet near mouth of the Yakown River, etc.
Company dissolved by Defunct Railway Companies Act, 1926–27.

Kamloops and Atlin Railway Company
1899 incorporated to build from outlet of Kamloops Lake to mouth of Quesnelle River, from mouth of Quesnelle River to Hazelton, from Hazelton to a point on Dease River to Atlin Lake; with branches, etc.
1900 incorporated to build from outlet of Kamloops Lake to junction of Quesnelle River with Fraser River, with branches, etc.
1901 incorporated to build from a point between Ashcroft and outlet of Kamloops Lake to junction of Quesnelle River with Fraser River, with branches, etc.
1901 incorporated (Dominion) to build from a point between Ashcroft and outlet of Kamloops Lake to junction of Quesnelle River with Fraser River, with branches, etc.
1902 repeals section dealing with employment of aliens.
Company dissolved by Defunct Railway Companies Act, 1926–27.

Kamloops and Yellowhead Pass Railway Company
1906 incorporated to build from Kamloops, via North Thompson, Canoe River and McLellan's Creek to Tete Jaune Cache; with branches, etc.
Company dissolved by Defunct Railway Companies Act, 1926–27.

Kaslo and Lardo-Duncan Railway Company
1897 incorporated to build from Kaslo by Kootenay Lake to Lardo, thence to Upper Kootenay Lake, thence to headwaters of Duncan River; with branch to Trout Lake and Arrow or Lardeau Lakes, etc.
1897 incorporated (Dominion) to build from Kaslo to Lardo, etc; agreements with Kaslo and Slocan Railway Company or Canadian Pacific Railway Company.
1900 subsidy–from Duncan Lake towards Lardo or Arrow Lake etc.
Company dissolved by Defunct Railway Companies Act, 1926–27.

Kaslo and Slocan Railway Company
1892 subsidy–land from Kaslo to Slocan Lake.
1892 incorporated to build from Town of Kaslo to Fish and Bear Lakes, thence to mines near Carpenter and Sandon Creeks; with branches to Montezuma Camp Mines and Jardine's Camp, etc.
1894 application to a narrow-gauge line if so built.
1895 any tramways not to interfere with K&S but may act as feeders.
1921 (Dominion) approves lease of Kaslo and Slocan Railway properties to Canadian Pacific Railway for 99 years from 1 January 1920.

Kaslo and Slocan Tramway Company
1893 incorporated to build a tramway and street railway in and from Kaslo up the valley of Kaslo Creek to Bear Lake.
Company dissolved by Defunct Railway Companies Act, 1926–27.

Kettle Valley Railway Company
1901 incorporation of Kettle River Valley Railway Company to build from US boundary at Cascade City, via Kettle River to US boundary at Carson City; with branch from Grand Forks, up the north fork of the Kettle River for 50 miles, and from Grand Forks, via Greenwood, to US boundary at Midway, etc.
1904 lines to Fire Valley, Vernon, Quilchena, Franklin Camp, and Killarney; running rights over Nicola, Kamloops and Similkameen Coal and Railway Company lines.
1904 running rights over Nicola, Kamloops and Similkameen Coal and Railway Company lines.
1909 line from Penticton to Nicola.
1910 line to Fraser River.
1910 agreement with Provincial Government re: construction etc. Midway and Vernon Railway Company line; acquirement.
1911 (Dominion) name changed to Kettle Valley Railway Company Line to Osoyoos Lake; line to Allison or Princeton; line to Steamboat Mountain Mining Camp.
1912 subsidy–Penticton to US boundary, and for bridge over Fraser River.
1912 line, Vernon to Penticton; time extension.
1912 subsidy–line to Hope and for bridge over Fraser River.
1913 subsidy–Merritt to Penticton; Penticton to Midway; line to Hope.
1913 lines Summers Creek to Copper Mountain and Voigt Mining Camps; Vernon to Penticton; to Otter Summit, and from Tulameen up the Tulameen River for 50 miles; companies may lease to Canadian Pacific Railway.
1913 approves lease of Kettle Valley Railway Company properties to Canadian Pacific Railway Company for 999 years from 1 July 1913.
1914 line Otter Summit to Aspen Grove mineral district; joint section with Vancouver, Victoria and Eastern Railway and Navigation Company.
1916 agreement with Vancouver, Victoria and Eastern Railway and Navigation Company re: trackage, etc.
1920 time extension; line from Coalmont to Granite Creek coal areas.
1920 agreement with Provincial Government re: construction of line from Coalmont to coal areas, etc.
1920 agreement with Provincial Government re: extension of line from Penticton wharf to Dog Lake (Skaha Lake).
1931 line from Skaha Lake to Okanagan Falls.

Kootenay and Arrowhead Railway Company
1901 incorporated (Dominion) to build from Lardo to Duncan, thence to Arrowhead, with branches; company may lease to Canadian Pacific Railway Company.
1903 approves lease of Kootenay and Arrowhead Railway properties, etc., to Canadian Pacific Railway for 999 years from 1 August 1901.
(Line was Lardeau to Gerrard.)

Kootenay and Athabasca Railway Company
1886 incorporated (Dominion) to build from head of Kootenay Lake via shore of Trout Lake and Trout Creek to Canadian Pacific Railway line at west crossing of Columbia River; thence along Columbia River to Gold River, thence to source of Gold River; with power to extend line to Boat Encampment and through Athabasca Pass and Canoe Pass.
1887 land grant from Dominion Land Reservation to north end Kootenay Lake.
1887 incorporated to build from at or near Revelstoke to head of Kootenay Lake.
1889 repeals 1887 incorporation.
Company dissolved by Defunct Railway Companies Act, 1926–27.

Kootenay and North West Railway Company
1898 incorporated to build from Golden to Canal Flat, thence to Cranbrook; from Golden northerly, via Columbia River, Canoe River, and Parsnip River and Fort McLeod to 56th parallel; thence to valley of Liard River, thence to northern boundary of province or to Teslin Lake; with branches, etc.
Company dissolved by Defunct Railway Companies Act, 1926–27.

Kootenay, Cariboo and Pacific Railway Company
1903 incorporated to build from Golden, via Columbia River and Canoe River to Tete Jaune Cache; thence via Fraser River to Giscome Portage, thence to Port Simpson, or to Bute Inlet; with branch to Barkerville, etc.
1903 (Dominion) incorporated to build from Golden, via Columbia River and Canoe River to Tete Jaune Cache; and to Barkerville and Fort George, etc.
Company dissolved by Defunct Railway Companies Act, 1926–27.

Kootenay Central Railway Company
1901 subsidy.
1901 incorporated to build from Fort Steele to Elko and the US boundary and from Fort Steele to Windermere and to Golden, etc.
1901 (Dominion) incorporated to build from Fort Steele to Elko and the US boundary and from Fort Steele to Windermere and to Golden, etc.; company may sell or lease to Canadian Pacific Railway Company.
1910 approves lease of Kootenay Central Railway Company property to Canadian Pacific Railway Co. for 999 years from 1 January 1911.
1912 line Gateway to Galloway.

Kootenay Development and Tramways Company
1903 incorporated to build a tramway from head of Kootenay Lake to headwaters of Duncan River, from Kaslo to headwaters of south fork of Kaslo Creek, and from Crawford Bay to headwaters of Crawford Creek; with branches, etc.
Company dissolved by Defunct Railway Companies Act, 1926–27.

Kootenay Lake Shore and Lardo Railway Company
1893 incorporated to build from US boundary at the Kootenay River up the river to Kootenay Lake, thence along the west shore of the northern end of the lake, with

branches to headwaters of Lardeau and Duncan Rivers, etc.
Company dissolved by Defunct Railway Companies Act, 1926–27.

Kootenay Power Company
1892 power to construct tramways from Nelson and within a 25-mile radius of Nelson, etc.

Kootenay Railway and Navigation Company
1888 subsidy and incorporated to build from outlet of Kootenay Lake through Selkirk Mountains to junction of Columbia and Kootenay Rivers; steamships, etc.
Company dissolved by Defunct Railway Companies Act, 1926–27.

Ladner Bridge Company
1926–27 power to erect a bridge for passenger and traffic purposes over the Fraser River from Ladner to Lulu Island.
1931 bridge to be from Deas Island; re: tolls.
1933 approval of plans by Governor General in Council.
1934 agreement with provincial government re: construction of bridge from Deas Island.
1935 tolls; extension of company franchise to tunnel or ferry rights.

Lake Bennett Railway Company
1901 incorporated to build from headwaters of Dyea River to Lake Bennett and thence to 60th parallel.
Company dissolved by Defunct Railway Companies Act, 1926–27.

Lardeau and Kootenay Railway Company
1893 incorporated to build from Lardeau City via Lardeau Pass to a point on the Northwest Shore of Kootenay Lake; with power to extend to Nelson and build branch to Fish Creek.
Company dissolved by Defunct Railway Companies Act, 1926–27.

Lardeau Railway Company
1897 incorporated to build from Galena or Thumb Bay on Upper Arrow Lake to forks of Lardeau River, with branches to Trout Lake, Fish Creek, and up the north and south branches of the Lardeau River.
Company dissolved by Defunct Railway Companies Act, 1926–27.

Lions Gate Bridge Company
1926–27 power to erect bridge at First Narrows of Burrard Inlet from Prospect Point to Capilano Indian Reserve.

Liverpool and Canoe Pass Railway Company
1891 incorporated to build from Liverpool, on the Fraser River, via Fraser River delta to Canoe Pass; and branch to Ladner's Landing.
Company dissolved by Defunct Railway Companies Act, 1926–27.

Menzies Bay Railway Company
1910 incorporated to build from Menzies Bay, Vancouver Island, to junction of Salmon River and Memekay River; and from Menzies Bay to Quinsan River at Lot 81, near 50th parallel, etc.
Company dissolved by Defunct Railway Companies Act, 1926–27.

Morrissey, Fernie and Michel Railway Company
1903 incorporated to build from Fernie to mouth of Morrissey Creek, thence to Lodgepole Creek, to Flathead River about 25 miles from US boundary; to US boundary; also from Fernie to a point 28 miles from mouth of Michel Creek; with branches, etc.
(This railway was owned by the Crow's Nest Pass Coal Company, a subsidiary of Great Northern Railway.)

Mountain Tramway and Electric Company
1898 incorporated to build from points on the Nakusp and Slocan Railway to mines in McGuigan Camp and Whitewater Basin; and from points on the Columbia and Kootenay Railway Crow's Nest line, etc., to mines, etc.
Company dissolved by Defunct Railway Companies Act, 1926–27.

Naas and Skeena Rivers Railway Company
1911 incorporated to build from Portland Inlet to headwaters of Skeena River.
Company dissolved by Defunct Railway Companies Act, 1926–27.

Nakusp and Slocan Railway Company
1893 incorporated (Dominion) to build from Nakusp to the forks of Carpenter Creek; vessels; agreements with Canadian Pacific Railway Company for leasing etc.
1893 incorporated to build from Nakusp to the forks of Carpenter Creek.
1894 agreement with Canadian Pacific Railway Company and with Commissioner of Works for BC re: operation of railway; guarantee of bonds, etc.
1894 subsidy–Nakusp to the forks of Carpenter Creek.
1895 any tramways not to interfere but may act as feeders.
1898 (Dominion) line from Three Forks to Whitewater Creek; telegraph and telephone lines, docks, etc.
1919 agreement of Provincial Government with Canadian Pacific Railway Company re purchase of bonds of N&S and further operation of railway by CPR.
1921 (Dominion) approves lease of Nakusp and Slocan Railway to CPR for 99 years from 1 July 1920.

Nanaimo-Alberni Railway Company
1897 incorporated to build from Alberni to Nanaimo.
Company dissolved by Defunct Railway Companies Act, 1926–27.

Nanaimo Electric Tramway Company
1891 incorporated to build a street railway in Nanaimo and adjacent areas.
Company dissolved by Defunct Railway Companies Act, 1926–27.

Nelson and Arrow Lake Railway Company
1893 incorporated to build from Nelson to Slocan River, thence along Slocan River to Slocan Lake to New Denver; thence by Nakusp Pass to Upper Arrow Lake; with branches to headwaters of Carpenter and Four-Mile Creek.
Company dissolved by Defunct Railway Companies Act, 1926–27.

Nelson and Fort Sheppard Railway Company
1891 incorporated to build from outlet of Kootenay Lake, at Nelson, to Fort Sheppard, via valley of Cottonwood, Smith Creek and the Salmon River, etc.
1892 subsidy–land, from Nelson to Fort Sheppard.
1896 (Dominion) telegraph and telephone lines; construction upon highways, etc.
1918 defines land granted railway company.
(Sold to Great Northern Railway 1943.)

Nelson Street Railway Company
1910 confirms Nelson City bylaw re: agreement for street railway service.

New Westminster and Port Moody Railway Company
1882 incorporated to build from New Westminster to Port Moody or other point on Burrard Inlet.
Company dissolved by Defunct Railway Companies Act, 1926–27.

New Westminster and Vancouver Short Line Railway Company
1889 incorporated to build from point on the north side of Fraser River between Pitt River and Lot 172, to Vancouver.
1896 new incorporation.
Company dissolved by Defunct Railway Companies Act, 1926–27.

New Westminster Southern Railway Company
1883 incorporated to build from 49th parallel between Semiahmoo Bay and Township 16, NW District, to New Westminster and to point on Burrard Inlet.
1883 disallowed incorporation.
1887 incorporated to build from a point between Semiahmoo Bay and Township 16, NWD, to point on Fraser River opposite New Westminster.
1889 re: point of terminus in New Westminster, etc.
1905 authority for New Westminster Southern Railway Company to lease or sell to Vancouver Victoria and Eastern Railway and Navigation Company (owned by the Great Northern Railway). (The line between Brownsville and Port Kells was sold to the Canadian Northern Pacific Railway in 1916; the remainder of the NWS lines were sold to VV&E in 1924.)
Company dissolved by Defunct Railway Companies Act, 1926–27.

Nicola, Kamloops and Similkameen Coal and Railway Company
1891 incorporated to build from western end of Nicola Lake to Princeton; thence to Osoyoos Lake; and from Nicola to South Thompson River and to Kamloops, etc.
1903 extension line to Spence's Bridge.
1903 (Dominion) subsidy–Spence's Bridge to Nicola Lake.
1904 (Dominion) running rights for Kettle River Valley Railway Company over lines of Nicola, Kamloops and Similkameen Coal and Railway Company.
(This line was built from Spence's Bridge to Nicola. On 16 November 1905 it was leased to the Canadian Pacific Railway for 999 years.)

Nicola Valley Railway Company
1891 incorporated to build from Spence's Bridge, on Canadian Pacific Railway via Nicola River to a point on the western end of Nicola Lake; and branch to junction of Voght River and Coldwater River.
1892 (Dominion) subsidy Spence's Bridge to Nicola Lake + 28 miles additional 1894.

APPENDIX

Northern Pacific and British Columbia Railway Company
1915 incorporated to enter with the American railway, Northern Pacific Railway Company, into agreements with Vancouver, Victoria and Eastern Railway and Navigation Company re: leasing and running rights; vessels; wharves; lands, etc.

Northern Vancouver Island Railway Company
1910 incorporated to build from Hardy Bay or Port McNeill to Coal Harbour on Quatsino Sound, etc.
1911 incorporated to build from Hardy Bay or Port McNeill to Coal Harbour or to Rupert Arm, Quatsino Sound, with branches, etc.
Company dissolved by Defunct Railway Companies Act, 1926–27.

North Star and Arrow Lake Railway Company
1898 incorporated to build from Cranbrook to North Star Mine and to Kootenay Lake, and from a point on this line to Upper Arrow Lake, etc.
1899 line from Fort Steele to Golden, etc.
Company dissolved by Defunct Railway Companies Act, 1926–27.

Okanagan and Kootenay Railway Company
1890 land grant.
1890 incorporated to build from Sproat's Landing, (i.e., Robson) via Lower Arrow Lake, Fire Valley and Cherry Creek to Vernon, etc.
Company dissolved by Defunct Railway Companies Act, 1926–27.

Pacific and Hudson Bay Railway Company
1911 incorporated to build from Kimsquit at head of Dean Channel to Fort Fraser, thence to Fort James and Fort McLeod, thence to Coal Brook, Dunvegan and Peace River Landing, then Fort McMurray and Churchill or Port Nelson on Hudson Bay.

Pacific and Peace River Railway Company (1)
1883 incorporated to build from Port Simpson to some point on the Peace River east of Fort Dunvegan (Alberta); with tramways, vessels, etc.

Pacific and Peace River Railway Company (2)
1898 incorporation of Kitimaat Railway Company to build from Kitimaat Inlet, Douglas Channel, to Kitseless Canyon on Skeena River, thence to Germansen Creek, Omineca, and from Skeena River to Telegraph Creek, etc.
1899 line from Kitimaat Inlet to Copper River, thence to Telegraph Trail, thence to south end of Babine Lake, thence to Germansen Creek at junction with Omineca River; name changed to Pacific and Peace River Railway Company.
Company dissolved by Defunct Railway Companies Act, 1926–27.

Pacific Coast Coal Mines Ltd.
1909 Pacific and Peace River Railway Company (1).
1883 incorporation confirmed; power to build and acquire tramways in districts of Cranberry and Cedar, etc.

Pacific Great Eastern Railway Company
1912 agreements of provincial government with Foley, Welch and Stewart and of the Grand Trunk Pacific Railway Company with Foley, Welch and Stewart re: incorporation of Pacific Great Eastern Railway Company, etc.
1912 incorporated to build from Vancouver to Lillooet and to Grand Trunk Pacific Railway line at Fort George; with branches, etc.
1913 amendments to route.
1914 additional provincial guarantee of securities for railway company line from Fort George to Dominion Peace River Block authorized.
1916 provincial government may advance $6 million to PGE.
1918 agreement of Provincial Government with Foley, Welch and Stewart et al., re: acquirement of capital stock of PGE by the Provincial Government.
1919 vesting of powers of Pacific Great Eastern Development Company in PGE Railway.
1925 land grant–Vancouver to Prince George and Prince George to Pouce Coupe.
1929 discontinuance of railway service or establishment of reduced service on North Shore District line (North Vancouver to Whytecliff, West Vancouver).

Pacific Northern and Eastern Railway Company
1903 incorporated to build from Hazelton to Teslin or Atlin Lake; from Hazelton, via Skeena, Babine, Driftwood, Omineca and Finlay Rivers to Peace River Pass or Pine River Pass, thence to eastern boundary of province, etc.
Company dissolved by Defunct Railway Companies Act, 1926–27.

Pacific Northern and Omineca Railway Company
1900 incorporated to build from Kitimaat Inlet to Hazelton, with branches, etc.
1902 branch line from Hazelton to junction of Bulkley River and Telkwa River.
1902 (Dominion) incorporated to build from Kitimaat Inlet to Hazelton, thence to Teslin or Atlin lake; with branch from Hazelton, via Peace River Pass, to Edmonton.
1908 subsidy Kitimaat to Telkwa River.
1909 branch line from junction of Skeena River and Copper River to junction of Bulkley River and Telkwa River.
Company dissolved by Defunct Railway Companies Act, 1926–27.

Pacific, Peace River and Athabasca Railway Company
1914 incorporated to build from mouth of Naas River to Skeena River to Bear River and Bear Lake; thence to North Takla Lake; to Fort McMurray and to Prince Albert.
1915 new lines: Kitimaat Arm to Aiyansh, Blackwater River to Bear River.

Pacific Railway Company
1910 incorporated to build from US boundary at Salmon River, following Salmon River to its source; with branches, etc.
Company dissolved by Defunct Railway Companies Act, 1926–27.

Peace and Naas River Railway Company
1911 incorporated to build from Nasoga Gulf, up the Naas River to Kitwancool River, thence towards Babine River, thence to junction of Babine and Neel-kit-Kwa River, thence to National River, to Pine River, thence by Pine River Pass to eastern boundary of province; with branches, etc.
Company dissolved by Defunct Railway Companies Act, 1926–27.

Penticton Railway Company
1910 incorporated to build from Penticton to vicinity of Osoyoos Lake, etc.
Company dissolved by Defunct Railway Companies Act, 1926–27.

Pine Creek Flume Company
1899 incorporated to build and operate tramways for passengers and freight, etc.

Pine Pass Railway Company
1910 (Dominion) incorporated to build from Edmonton to junction of McLeod and Athabasca Rivers, thence to Grand Prairie, thence to Pouce Coupe, thence via Pine River Pass to Fort George.

Portland and Stickine Railway Company
1898 incorporated to build from Observatory Inlet, or Portland Canal, to Telegraph Creek, with branches, etc.
Company dissolved by Defunct Railway Companies Act, 1926–27.

Portland Canal Railway Company
1907 incorporated to build from head of Portland Canal up the Bear River Valley for 30 miles, with power to build branches up Glacier Creek, Bitter Creek and American Creek.
Company dissolved by Defunct Railway Companies Act, 1926–27.

Port Moody, Indian River and Northern Railway Company
1910 incorporated to build from Port Moody to a point on Burrard Inlet, thence westerly to point on eastern shore of North Arm of Burrard Inlet (Indian Arm); thence to mouth of Mesliloet or Indian River, etc.
Company dissolved by Defunct Railway Companies Act, 1926–27.

Prince Rupert and Port Simpson Railway Company
1909 incorporated to build from Prince Rupert to Port Simpson, with branches, etc.
Company dissolved by Defunct Railway Companies Act, 1926–27.

Quatsino Railway Company
1903 incorporated to build from Hardy Bay or Fort Rupert to a point on the West Arm or Rupert Arm of Quatsino Sound; with branches, wharves, etc.
Company dissolved by Defunct Railway Companies Act, 1926–27.

Queen Charlotte Islands Railway Company
1901 incorporated to build from a point on Rennell Sound, Graham Island, to Skidegate Harbour; and from a point on this line to Masset Inlet.
1902 repeals section re: employment of aliens.
1905 incorporated (2) to build from a point on Rennell Sound, Graham Island, to Skidegate Harbour; and from a point on this line to Masset Inlet.
Company dissolved by Defunct Railway Companies Act, 1926–27.

Red Mountain Railway Company
1893 incorporated to build from Sheep Creek at US boundary to Red Mountain and Trail Creek Mines (Rossland), etc.
(This line belonged to the Great Northern Railway; the line, from Patterson to Rossland, was abandoned in 1921.)

Revelstoke and Cassiar Railway Company
1898 incorporated to build from Revelstoke via Columbia River and Canoe River to Tête Jaune Cache, thence to 56th parallel; thence to Dease Lake or Teslin Lake, etc.
Company dissolved by Defunct Railway Companies Act, 1926–27.

Rock Bay and Salmon River Railway Company
1900 incorporated to build from Johnstone Strait to Upper Campbell Lake; and from Johnstone Strait to north end of Bear Lake; with branches; tramways, etc.
Company dissolved by Defunct Railway Companies Act, 1926–27.

St. Mary's and Cherry Creek Railway Company
1906 incorporated to build from near Bayard, along east side of Luke Creek to Lot 341; thence to point on Cherry Creek near Lot 710; with branch from Lot 341 to point on Cherry Creek, west of Lot 339, etc.

St. Mary's Valley Railway Company
1906 incorporated to build from Marysville to St Mary's Lake, thence to western end of the lake, thence to Crawford Bay on Kootenay Lake.
Company dissolved by Defunct Railway Companies Act, 1926–27.

Shuswap and Okanagan Railway Company
1886 incorporated to build from Sickamoose Narrows (Sicamous) up the left bank of the Shuswap River, to a point on the north end of Okanagan Lake, etc.
1887 subsidy cash for Sickamoose Narrows to Okanagan Lake/repealed 1890.
1890 Provincial guarantee of bonds.
1891 (Dominion) agreement with Canadian Pacific Railway Company re: lease and operation of S&O; extension of line to Osoyoos Lake.
1915 (Dominion) approves lease of S&O properties to CPR for 999 years from 1 July 1915.

Similkameen and Keremeos Railway Company
1901 incorporated to build from Penticton via Shingle Creek to Fish Lake Pass, thence by Keremeos Canyon to Keremeos Valley, thence to Keremeos, thence southerly to Similkameen Valley, to US boundary at Similkameen River Crossing, branches, etc.
1904 revives charter; extends time.

Skeena River and Eastern Railway Company
1898 incorporated to build from point on Skeena River to eastern boundary of province, with branches, etc.
Company dissolved by Defunct Railway Companies Act, 1926–27.

Skeena River Railway, Colonization and Exploration Company
1898 incorporated to build from Skeena River to Yellowhead Pass and from head of Skeena River to its mouth; steamships, etc.
Company dissolved by Defunct Railway Companies Act, 1926–27.

South East Kootenay Railway Company
1898 incorporated to build from Fort Steele to point at least 5 miles from US boundary; with branches, etc.
1906 incorporated to build from US boundary at the Flathead River to McGillivray on Crow's Nest section of Canadian Pacific Railway; with branches, etc.
Company dissolved by Defunct Railway Companies Act, 1926–27.

Southern Central Pacific Railway Company
1903 (Dominion) incorporated to build from Vancouver via Kootenay Pass to point on Old Man River (Alberta) thence to point on Hudson Bay at least 100 miles north of Churchill (Manitoba); vessels, ferries, etc.

Southern Okanagan Railway Company
1906 incorporated to build from Penticton to point on US boundary.
Company dissolved by Defunct Railway Companies Act, 1926–27.

South Kootenay Railway Company
1899 incorporated to build from Fort Steele to point where Kootenay River crosses US boundary; with branches, etc.
Company dissolved by Defunct Railway Companies Act, 1926–27.

Stave Valley Railway Company
1905 incorporated to build from Vancouver to a point between Ruskin and mouth of the Pitt River, and to mouth of Upper Stave River and to Lillooet Lake, etc.
Company dissolved by Defunct Railway Companies Act, 1926–27.

Stickeen and Teslin Railway, Navigation and Colonization Company
1897 land grants and tax exemption.
1897 incorporated to build from Glenora to southern end of Teslin Lake.
1899 land grant repealed.
Company dissolved by Defunct Railway Companies Act, 1926–27.

Toad Mountain and Nelson Tramway Company
1891 incorporated to build a tramway from Silver King Mine, Toad Mountain, to Nelson, etc.
Company dissolved by Defunct Railway Companies Act, 1926–27.

Trail Creek and Columbia Railway Company
1895 incorporated to build from Trail Creek Mines (Rossland) to a point on the Columbia River north of mouth of Trail Creek (Trail) with power to extend line to junction of Kootenay River and Columbia River.
1897 line from Trail Creek Mines to point on Kettle River north of US boundary.

Tsimpsean Light and Power Company
1907 incorporated to build tramways within radius of 75 miles from mouth of K-tada River. etc.

Upper Columbia Navigation and Tramway Company
1891 incorporated to build from Golden to a steamboat landing on Columbia River from west shore of Mud Lake to north end of Upper Columbia Lake; and from head of navigation on Upper Columbia Lake to the Kootenay River, etc.
1892 subsidy–land.
1901 grant of land and cash in lieu of 1892 grant.
Company dissolved by Defunct Railway Companies Act, 1926–27.

Upper Columbia Railway Company
1887 incorporated to build from Golden to head of Upper Columbia Lake; with power to extend to Cranbrook, etc.

Vancouver and Coast-Kootenay Railway Company
1902 incorporated to build from Vancouver to New Westminster, to Chilliwhack, to Midway; and from point on this line south of Fraser River to mouth of Fraser River, with suitable ferry to Vancouver Island to connect with the City of Victoria; provincial subsidy; company may not amalgamate with Canadian Pacific Railway Company.

Vancouver and Grand Forks Railway Company
1901 incorporated to build from Vancouver to New Westminster, to Chilliwhack, to Hope, to headwaters of Coldwater River, to west fork of Otter River, to junction of Otter River and Tulameen River, to Princeton, to Keremeos, etc., with branches, etc.
1902 repeals section re: employment of aliens.
Company dissolved by Defunct Railway Companies Act, 1926–27.

Vancouver and Lulu Island Electrical Railway and Improvement Company
1891 incorporated to build from Vancouver to North Arm of Fraser River, thence across Sea Island and Lulu Island, thence to some point on the south side of Lulu Island, with steam ferry to Ladner's Landing, etc.
Company dissolved by Defunct Railway Companies Act, 1926–27.

Vancouver and Lulu Island Railway Company
1891 incorporated to build from Vancouver to North Arm of Fraser River, thence across North Arm to Lulu Island, thence across Lulu Island to South Arm of Fraser River, thence, by ferry to Ladner's Landing; motive power to be either steam, electricity, or horses, etc.
1900 revives and continues Acts, extends time.
1901 company may sell or lease to Canadian Pacific Railway.
1903 (Dominion) approves lease of V&LI to Canadian Pacific Railway Company for 99 years from 1 August 1901.
1907 agreements with British Columbia Electric Railway (BCER) and the CPR re: track and service.
(Line became BC Electric interurban line to Steveston.)

Vancouver and Nicola Valley Railway Company
1908 incorporated to build from Nicola Lake, via Nicola Valley to junction of Nicola and Coldwater Rivers, thence by Coldwater River to Coquihalla River, thence to Hope, thence to New Westminster, thence to Vancouver; with branches, tramways, etc.
Company dissolved by Defunct Railway Companies Act, 1926–27.

Vancouver and Northern Railway Company
1909 incorporated to build from Vancouver, via Seymour Creek Valley, to watershed north of Loch Lomond, thence to north arm of Burrard Inlet (Indian Arm); and a branch line via Furry Creek Valley to Howe Sound; with power to extend line, etc.
Company dissolved by Defunct Railway Companies Act, 1926–27.

Vancouver and Westminster Railway Company
1900 incorporated to build from Vancouver to some point on the Westminster branch of Canadian Pacific Railway at or near New Westminster, with branches, etc.
Company dissolved by Defunct Railway Companies Act, 1926–27.

Vancouver Coal Mining and Land Company
1881 authority for the company to build railway along the Esplanade in Nanaimo.
Company dissolved by Defunct Railway Companies Act, 1926–27.

Vancouver Electric Railway and Light Company
1886 incorporation of Vancouver Street Railways Company to build street railways in Vancouver and adjacent areas.
1889 incorporation (2) of Vancouver Street Railways Company to build street railways in Vancouver and adjacent areas.
Amalgamation of Vancouver Street Railways Company, the Vancouver Electric Illuminating Company and the Vancouver Electric Railway and Light Company under name of latter.
1894 incorporation of Consolidated Railway and Light Company to acquire properties, etc., of Vancouver Electric Railway and Light Company.
1896 acquisition of Vancouver Electric Railway and Light Company by Consolidated Railway Company confirmed.

Vancouver, Fraser Valley and Southern Railway Company
1906 incorporated to build from Vancouver to New Westminster, thence to US boundary near Douglas; also from New Westminster Bridge up the Fraser Valley to Chilliwhack; also from point on Fraser River, westerly to Ladner's Landing, etc.
1909 company may sell or lease to or amalgamate with Vancouver Power Company and British Columbia Electric Railway Company.
(BCER built its interurban line to Chilliwack using this charter.)

Vancouver Island and Eastern Railway Company
1908 subsidy–Campbell River towards Fort George.
1908 incorporated to build from Victoria to Seymour Narrows on Vancouver Island; with ferry to Bute Inlet or Frederick Inlet on mainland; and a line from Bute Inlet or Frederick Inlet, via Yellowhead Pass, to Edmonton.
1910 branch line to Quatsino Sound.

Vancouver Land and Railway Company
1882 incorporated to build from Esquimalt Harbour to Seymour Narrows, etc.; company may extend line to Victoria.
1883 grant of portion of lands set out in 45 Vic. Cap 15 to Dominion Government for Esquimalt and Nanaimo Railway.
1884 Dominion–same as 1883 BC.
Company dissolved by Defunct Railway Companies Act, 1926–27.

Vancouver-Nanaimo Railway Transfer Company
1897 incorporated to operate a ferry for railway cars from point on Burrard Inlet or Fraser River to connect with Esquimalt and Nanaimo Railway at Nanaimo.
Company dissolved by Defunct Railway Companies Act, 1926–27.

Vancouver, Northern, Peace River and Alaska Railway and Navigation Company
1891 incorporated to build from Vancouver, via Seymour Creek, Pemberton Meadows and Chilcotin Pass to Fort George, thence to Stickeen River; with branches to Giscome Portage, Fort St. John, Barkerville and Forks of Quesnelle River, etc.
Company dissolved by Defunct Railway Companies Act, 1926–27.

Vancouver, Victoria and Eastern Railway and Navigation Company
1897 incorporated to build from Vancouver to New Westminster, thence across the Fraser River and easterly through Hope Mountains to Rossland; with branch to Kamloops and branch to point on coast between US boundary and Fraser River, etc.
1905 declares VV&E entirely subject to Dominion Government authority; lines defined; agreements with US railways; agreements with certain railway companies
1905 Victoria Terminal Railway and Ferry Company and New Westminster Southern Railway Company may sell or lease to VV&E.
1908 (Dominion) approves sale of Victoria Terminal Railway and Ferry Company properties to VV&E.
1908 (Dominion) sale of Vancouver, Westminster and Yukon Railway to VV&E.
1911 + 1912 rights of railway company to lands held in Vancouver secured.
1913 correction of description of False Creek lands conveyed to railway company by City of Vancouver.
1914 joint section with Kettle Valley Railway Company.
1915 incorporated Northern Pacific and British Columbia Railway Company.
1916 agreement with Kettle Valley Railway Company re: trackage.
1917 trackage rights for Canadian Northern Pacific Railway Company from New Westminster to Vancouver and from Hope to Sumas Landing.
1918 agreement with Northern Pacific Railway Company re: joint section.
1932–33 agreement with Northern Pacific Railway Company re: abandonment of line from Sumas to Colebrook and joint use of other section.
(This company was owned by the Great Northern Railway.)

Vancouver, Westminster and Yukon Railway Company
1901 incorporated to build from Vancouver to New Westminster; also from Vancouver to Squamish valley; thence to Lillooet, Quesnel, Hazelton, Teslin Lake, Dawson City; with branches, etc.
1906 branch lines; running rights to other companies.
1908 subsidy Vancouver to Fort George.
1908 approves sale of portions of railway project to VV&E.
1909 time extension for branch lines; agreement with Burrard, Westminster Boundary Railway and Navigation Company.
1910 time extension for main line.
(The Pacific Great Eastern line followed this route north.)

Vancouver, Westminster, Northern and Yukon Railway Company
1899 incorporation of Vancouver, Northern and Yukon Railway Company to build from Vancouver via Seymour Creek; via Seymour Creek to Squamish Valley, thence to Lillooet, to Quesnelle, to Hazelton, to northern boundary of province; with branches to Fort St. John, Howe Sound, etc., docks, lands, etc.
1900 line to New Westminster; name changed to Vancouver, Westminster, Northern and Yukon Railway Company.
Company dissolved by Defunct Railway Companies Act, 1926–27.

Velvet (Rossland) Mine Railway Company
1902 incorporated to build from Rossland to Velvet Mines, thence to point on US boundary, etc.

Vernon and Okanagan Railway Company
1891 incorporated to build from Vernon to a point on Osoyoos Lake.
Company dissolved by Defunct Railway Companies Act, 1926–27.

Victoria and Barkley Sound Railway Company
1909 incorporated to build from Victoria, via Otter Point and San Juan, to point on Barkley Sound near Sarita River; with branch lines, etc.
1909 incorporated (Dominion) to build from Victoria, via Otter Point and San Juan, to point on Barkley Sound near Sarita River; steam ferry; branch line to Beecher Bay.
Company dissolved by Defunct Railway Companies Act, 1926–27.

Victoria and Esquimalt Railway Company
1873 incorporated to build from Victoria to Esquimalt Harbour; contingent upon choice of Pacific Terminus for Canada Pacific Railway.
1876 repeal proviso of contingency upon location of Canada Pacific Railway; authorizes construction; not to conflict with Canada Pacific Railway, etc.

Victoria and North American Railway Company
1891 incorporated to build from Victoria to Beecher Bay.
1891 (Dominion) authority to operate ferry from Beecher Bay to point in US on Strait of Juan de Fuca.
Company dissolved by Defunct Railway Companies Act, 1926–27.

Victoria and Saanich Railway Company
1886 subsidy for line Victoria to North Saanich.
1886 incorporated to build from Victoria to Shoal Harbour in North Saanich
Company dissolved by Defunct Railway Companies Act, 1926–27.

Victoria and Seymour Narrows Railway Company
1902 aid for construction of line between Wellington and Seymour Narrows.
1902 incorporated to build from Victoria, via Nanaimo, and Alberni Townsite to point on Seymour Narrows or Elk Bay.
Company dissolved by Defunct Railway Companies Act, 1926–27.

Victoria and Sidney Railway Company
1892 incorporated to build from Victoria to townsite of Sidney in North Saanich District.
(Built and operated until 1919, when company went into receivership and line was abandoned. Was owned by Great Northern Railway.)

Victoria Electric Railway and Lighting Company
1889 incorporation of National Electric Tramway and Lighting Company to build tramway in and from Victoria to Esquimalt, Craigflower Bridge, the Gorge, the Royal Oak, Cadboro and Oak Bays, etc.
1890 authority for extensions and connections.

1894 name changed to Victoria Electric Railway and Lighting Company; power to sell, lease or amalgamate, etc.
(Victoria Electric Railway and Lighting Company property was sold to Consolidated Railway Company on 11 April 1896 under foreclosure.)

Victoria, Saanich and New Westminster Railway Company
1889 incorporated to build from Victoria to Swartz Bay; with branch from Victoria to Esquimalt also from Point Roberts to Ladner's Landing and New Westminster; branches to Vancouver, Canoe Pass, Garry Point, etc., elevators, etc.
1921 re-incorporation.

Victoria Terminal Railway and Ferry Company
1901 incorporated to build along certain streets in Victoria to connect the Victoria and Sidney Railway with the Esquimalt and Nanaimo Railway, etc.
1902 repeals section re: employment of aliens.
1905 authority to sell or lease its car ferry service and its railway line to Vancouver, Victoria and Eastern Railway and Navigation Company (VV&E).
1906 line from Mud Bay to point on US boundary at Blaine to connect with the Seattle and Montana Railway; sale or lease of this line.
1908 approves sale of Victoria Terminal Railway and Ferry Company properties to VV&E.

Victoria Tramway Company
1883 incorporated to build street railways on the streets of Victoria and upon the Esquimalt Road.

Victoria, Vancouver and Westminster Railway Company
1894 incorporated to build from Point Garry, on Fraser River, via Richmond, South Vancouver and Burnaby to New Westminster; with branch to Vancouver, etc.
Company dissolved by Defunct Railway Companies Act, 1926–27.

Westminster and Vancouver Tramway Company
1890 incorporated to build a tramway between New Westminster and Vancouver, etc.
1891 amalgamation of Westminster Street Railway Company with Westminster and Vancouver Tramway Company under latter name.
1894 land grant.
1896 acquirement by Consolidated Railway Company confirmed.

Westminster Street Railway Company
1890 incorporated to build street railway upon streets of New Westminster and adjacent areas, etc.
1891 amalgamation of Westminster Street Railway Company with Westminster and Vancouver Tramway Company under latter name.

White Pass and Yukon Railway Company
1898 (Great Britain): organization of White Pass and Yukon Railway Company to acquire capital stock of British Yukon Railway Company, the British Columbia Yukon Railway Company, and of an American company, the Pacific and Arctic Railway and Navigation Company.
(This railway acquired steamships of the Canadian Development Company and these were turned over to the British Yukon Navigation Co., incorporated in BC. They operated from Whitehorse north to Dawson City.)

Yale-Northern Railway Company
1901 incorporated to build from Grand Forks to mouth of East Fork of Kettle River, thence to Summit Creek, thence to headwaters and to mouth of Eagle Creek, etc.
1902 repeals section re: employment of aliens.
Company dissolved by Defunct Railway Companies Act, 1926–27.

Appendix 2: Whyte Wheel Notation System for Steam Locomotives

Wheels	Common Name	Diagram Front Back
0-4-0	Switcher	OO
2-6-0	Mogul	oOOO
2-6-2	Prairie	oOOOo
2-8-0	Consolidation	oOOOO
2-8-2	Mikado	oOOOOo
2-8-4	Berkshire	oOOOOoo
2-10-0	Decapod	oOOOOO
2-10-2	Santa Fe	oOOOOOo
2-10-4	Selkirk	oOOOOOoo
4-4-0	Standard	ooOO
4-4-2	Atlantic	ooOOo
4-6-2	Pacific	ooOOOo
4-6-0	Ten Wheeler	ooOOO
4-6-4	Hudson	ooOOOoo
4-8-2	Mountain	ooOOOOo
4-8-4	Confederation/Northern	ooOOOOoo

The first number is the number of leading carrying wheels, the second number the coupled driving wheels, and the third the trailing carrying wheels.

Sources

All photographs and illustrations not otherwise credited are taken by, or in the collection of, the author.

Page positions are indicated as follows: t=top, b=bottom, l=left, r=right, c=centre

Abbreviations:
BCA   British Columbia Archives
CVA   City of Vancouver Archives
CPRA Canadian Pacific Railway Archives (now at Exporail, Delson, Quebec)
LAC   Library and Archives Canada
LC   Library of Congress
NMC   Library and Archives Canada, National Map Collection
PMA   Penticton Museum and Archives
UBC RBSC University of British Columbia Rare Books and Special Collections
VPL   Vancouver Public Library
WCRA West Coast Railway Association

Page

13b	Hudson's Bay Company Archives G1/142
15	VPL
18b	CVA AM54 S4 Can N94
19b	CVA AM54 S4 Can N96
20b	NMC 13190
21t	NMC 16809
22t	NMC 142653
23	Revelstoke Railway Museum
24tc	LC
24bl	CPRA 30759-6
26	CVA
29b	CVA AM54 S4 Can P2
30t	CVA AM54 S4 371 2820
30b	UBC RBSC G3514 V3 1886 S6
33	CVA
34	Revelstoke Railway Museum
35	VPL
36lc	Land Title and Survey Authority 150488
36b	UBC RBSC G3514.V3 1886.S6
37t	LAC C24465
37rc	D.R. Harris, 1905. VPL 912.71135 H35n 1905 Copy 2
38t	Kelowna Museum and Archives 3076
39c	LAC AC901 P3 No. 0459
39b	SS Sicamous Museum, Penticton
42	UBC RBSC Imperial Menu, Chung Collection
43t	CVA 586-503, photo Don Coleman
43cl	CPRA A15510
44–45	Dave Wilkie, WCRA
46bl	CVA Map 158
47	From Lindsay Thacker, Barrie Sanford Collection
48cl	Jim Foulkes Collection
48rt, rc, rb	City of Surrey (COSMOS map)
50tl	Delta Museum and Archives 2003-045
50tr	Delta Museum and Archives 1971-1-1062
51tr	City of Surrey Archives 203.04
51b	CVA 102-17
52	D.R. Harris, 1905. VPL 912.71135 H35n 1905 Copy 2
53b	CVA 1913 Goad Atlas
54t	City of Surrey Archives 205.30
55b	UBC RBSC Leitch and Taylor 1913
56tl	City of Abbotsford + City of Chilliwack
56cr	Land Title and Survey Authority 1914
56b	Township of Langley
58	Nelson Museum
59t	UBC RBSC G3511 K65 H2 1893 P4
59b	Nelson Museum
61b	UBC RBSC G3511 K65 H2 1893 P4
63tl, tr	Rossland Museum
63b	Land Titles and Survey Authority 9T12 Old Maps
64t, b	Rossland Museum
65t	Land Titles and Survey Authority 7T3
65b	UBC RBSC G3511 G4 1914 C3
66t, bl	Charles Mackinnon Campbell via Charles Campbell
67t	Charles Mackinnon Campbell via Charles Campbell
69 (map)	Land Title and Survey Authority 38T9 Old Maps
71rcb	LC
73	VPL 21860
73bl	CVA 7-79
74tl	Fraser Valley Heritage Railway
74b	UBC RBSC SPAM 287
75tl	Henry Ewert Collection
75tr	Fraser Valley Heritage Railway
75b	City of Surrey Archives 91.012
76t	BC Hydro A0927
77b	BC Transit Authority
80	NMC 48975
81t	LAC 123743
84–85b	PMA
85t	LAC PA-123743
86b	*BC Saturday Sunset*, 14 Dec 1912; BC Legislative Library
87t	*BC Saturday Sunset*, 3 May 1913; BC Legislative Library
87b	CVA AM1535 CVA 99-1261
89b	VPL
90bl	NMC 5974
90br	*BC Saturday Sunset*, 30 Mar 1912; BC Legislative Library
93cr	UBC RBSC 624-9A, Vancouver Map & Blueprint, 1914
92-93b	CVA Pan N87 W.J. Moore, 10 March 1917
95b	PMA
96cl, bl	SS Sicamous Museum
97t	PMA
97br	Google Maps
98t	PMA
101cr	Princeton Museum
101br	Nicola Valley Museum & Archives
102bl	LAC s1100 [1905-1912]
102br	LAC
105t (map)	UBC RBSC G3511 P3 1915 P3
105t, cl, cr, bl	CVA 99-743, 99-741, 99-743
106tl	UBC RBSC G3511 1914 C3
106tr	North Vancouver Archives 2442
106b	North Vancouver Archives 6901
107	BCA Bordertown Collection H-05715
108cr	UBC RBSC G3511 P3 1915 P3
108b	CVA 99-1487
109 (photos, top to bottom)	CVA 99-1314, 374-185, 660-130
109 (maps)	UBC RBSC G3511 P3 1915 P3

112t	*Railway Wonders of the World*, 8 March 1935
112b	Otto Perry, Denver Public Library OP-20606
113t	VPL
113c	Leonard Frank
113b	Otto Perry, Denver Public Library OP-20499
114tl	CVA
114b	CVA
115	VPL
116	BCA Bordertown Collection F-06061 1933
118t	CVA
118b	CVA AM1545 S3 CVA 586
119b	BCA Bordertown Collection F-05717
120t	Revelstoke Museum (greyscale photo) + Revelstoke Railway Museum (colour photo), composite
120b	BCA Bordertown Collection H-02894
123t	CVA
123c	Nelson Museum
124t, b	CVA
126t	CVA
128-129t	CVA W.J. Moore panorama
128bl	VPL
129c	Elwood White, Robert Turner Collection
131t	Drew Jacksich
132t, c	Hedley Museum
133tl	Kimberley Museum
133cbr	Charles Mackinnon Campbell
134b	Prince George Railway and Forestry Museum
135t	BC Rail Collection, WCRA Archives
136t	UBC RBSC SPAM 16644
136bl	BC Rail Collection, WCRA Archives
136br	LAC Amicus 10365384
137	BCA Bordertown Collection F-09359
139t	From: *Patterns of Growth*, PGE, 1971
139bl	WCRA
140-41 (3 photos)	Dave Wilkie, WCRA
142b	From: *Construction of the Tumbler Ridge Branch Line in Northeastern British Columbia*, British Columbia Railway Engineering Dept, 1984. UBC Library TF27.B75 C65 1984
143t	Prince George Railway and Forestry Museum
143b	T.O. Repp/railpictures.net
146b	LAC R231-2886-E
147	LAC, CN Corporate Archives
148t	Revelstoke Railway Museum
149b	Dave Wilkie, WCRA
150t	Bill Hooper/railpictures.net
150b	Dave Wilkie, WCRA
151t, b	Dave Wilkie, WCRA
154t, b	Dave Wilkie, WCRA
154c	VPL
155	Dave Wilkie, WCRA
158t	Railway Association of Canada (1996 map)
162	From *The Line*, CPR Public Relations, 1998. CPRA/ExpoRail
178t	Neptune Terminals
189bl	Drew Jacksich
198t	Shutterstock
198c	nivèk Woods
199t	Shutterstock

Above.
Illuminated by the last rays of the winter sun, a BNSF unit coal train passes the White Rock on that city's waterfront on 4 January 2014. Mount Baker forms a scenic backdrop.

Above.
On 8 November 2017 interurban car No. 1231 may have looked as though it was in service here on the south False Creek line in Vancouver, but in fact is being slowly pushed to a rendezvous with a low-bed rail transporter that will take it to the Fraser Valley Heritage Railway in Cloverdale that night (see photo, *page 192*).

Further Reading

Auditor General of British Columbia. *Switching Tracks: A Review of the BC Rail Investment Partnership.* Victoria: Office of the Auditor General, 2007
Bradley, R. Ken. *Historic Railways of the Powell River Area.* Victoria: British Columbia Railway Historical Association, 1982.
Brown, Ron. *Rails Over the Mountains: Exploring the Railway Heritage of Canada's Western Mountains.* Toronto: Dundurn, 2016.
Cohen, Stan. *The White Pass and Yukon Route: A Pictorial History.* Missoula, Montana: Pictorial Histories Publishing Company, 1997.
Conn, Heather, and Henry Ewert. *Vancouver's Glory Years: Public Transit 1890–1915.* North Vancouver: Whitecap Books, 2003.
Cruise, David, and Alison Griffiths. *Lords of the Line.* Markham, Ontario: Viking/Penguin, 1988.
Daniels, Rudolph. *Trains Across the Continent: North American Railroad History.* Bloomington, Indiana: Indiana University Press, 2000.
Ewert, Henry. *The Story of the B.C. Electric Railway Company.* North Vancouver: Whitecap Books, 1986.
Fleming, R B. *The Railway King of Canada: Sir William Mackenzie 1849–1923.* Vancouver: UBC Press, 1991.
Garden, J.F. *British Columbia Railway.* Revelstoke: Footprint Publishing, 1995.
Green, Mervyn T. "Mike." *Industrial Locomotives: A Catalogue of Industrial Locomotives and Short Lines of British Columbia and Yukon Territory.* Vancouver: Pacific Coast Division, Canadian Railroad Historical Association, 1992.
Harris, Lorraine. *British Columbia's Own Railroad.* Surrey: Hancock House, 1982.
Hayes, Derek. *Historical Atlas of Vancouver and the Lower Fraser Valley.* Vancouver: Douglas & McIntyre, 2005.
———. *Historical Atlas of the North American Railroad.* Berkeley: University of California Press, 2010.
———. *British Columbia: A New Historical Atlas.* Vancouver: Douglas & McIntyre, 2012.
Hind, Patrick O. *The Pacific Great Eastern Railway Company: A Short History of the North Shore Subdivision 1914–1928.* North Vancouver: North Vancouver Museum and Archives Commission, 1999.
Kelly, Brian and Daniel Francis. *Transit in British Columbia: The First Hundred Years.* Madeira Park: Harbour Publishing, 1990.
Kozma, Leslie S. 'The Truth About 7 April 1914." *CN Lines,* Vol. 17, No. 1, Issue 62, June 2013.
Lamb, W. Kaye. *History of the Canadian Pacific Railway.* New York: Macmillan, 1977.
Lavallée, Omer. *Van Horne's Road: The Building of the Canadian Pacific Railway.* Markham, Ontario: Fitzhenry & Whiteside/Fifth House, 2nd ed., 2007.
Leighton, Frank. *Plans, Ports and Politics: 50 Years Helping Build British Columbia and the World.* (Bloomington, Indiana): Trafford Publishing (e-book), 2017.
Leonard, Frank. *A Thousand Blunders: The Grand Trunk Pacific Railway and Northern British Columbia.* Vancouver: UBC Press, 1996.
Lewis, Donald C. *Rail Canada Volume 3: Diesel Paint Schemes of the CPR.* Winfield: LPD Publishing, 1978 and 1998.
Love, J.A. *Canadian National in the West* (volume 3). Calgary: B.R.M.N.A., nd.
McCombs, Arnold M., and Wilfrid W. Chittenden. *The Fraser Valley Challenge: An Illustrated Account of Logging and Sawmilling in the Fraser Valley.* Harrison Hot Springs: Treeline Publishing, 1990.
Mackay, Donald. *The Asian Dream: The Pacific Rim and Canada's National Railway.* Vancouver: Douglas & McIntyre, 1986.
———. *The People's Railway: A History of Canadian National.* Vancouver: Douglas & McIntyre, 1992.
MacLachlan, Donald F. *The Esquimalt & Nanaimo Railway: The Dunsmuir Years.* Victoria: British Columbia Railway Historical Association, 1986.
Minter, Roy. *The White Pass: Gateway to the Klondike.* Toronto: McClelland and Stewart, 1987.
Neuberger, Richard L. "Pacific Great Eastern." *Railroad Magazine,* Vol. 47, No. 4, January 1949, pp. 10–31.
Pole, Graeme. *The Spiral Tunnels and the Big Hill: A Canadian Railway Adventure.* Canmore, AB: Altitude Publishing, 1995.
———. *Gravity, Steam and Steel: An Illustrated History of Rogers Pass on the Canadian Pacific Railway.* (Markham, ON): Fifth House, 2009
———. *Rails Across the Rockies: Surveying and Constructing the Great Railways of the West.* Hazelton: Mountain Vision Publishing (e-book), 2014
Rees-Thomas, David M. *Timber Down the Capilano: A History of the Capilano Timber Company and Railroad Logging on Vancouver's North Shore.* Victoria: British Columbia Railway Historical Association, 1979.
Roberts, Earl, and David Stremes (eds.). *Canadian Trackside Guide.* Ottawa: The Bytown Railway Society, 2018 and previous years.
Robin, Martin. *The Rush for Spoils: The Company Province 1871–1933.* Toronto: McClelland and Stewart, 1972.
———. *Pillars of Profit: The Company Province 1934–1972.* Toronto: McClelland and Stewart, 1973.
Sanford, Barrie. *The Pictorial History of Railroading in British Columbia.* Vancouver: Whitecap Books, 1981.
———. *McCulloch's Wonder: The Story of the Kettle Valley Railway.* 2nd ed. North Vancouver: Whitecap Books, 2002
———. *Steel Rails & Iron Men: A Pictorial History of the Kettle Valley Railway.* North Vancouver: Whitecap Books, 2003.
———. *Royal Metal: The People, Times and Trains of New Westminster Bridge.* Vancouver: National Railway Historical Society, British Columbia Chapter, 2004.
———. *Railway by the Bay: 100 Years of Trains at White Rock, Crescent Beach and Ocean Park 1909–2009.* Vancouver: National Railway Historical Society, British Columbia Chapter, 2009.
Stevens, G.R. *Canadian National Railways.* 2 vols. Toronto: Clarke Irwin, 1960.
Turner, Robert D. *West of the Great Divide: An Illustrated History of the Canadian Pacific Railway in British Columbia 1880–1986.* Victoria: Sono Nis Press, 1987.
———. *Logging by Rail: The British Columbia Story.* Victoria: Sono Nis Press, 1990.
———. *Vancouver Island Railroads.* Winlaw: Sono Nis Press, 1997.
Turner, Robert D., and J.S. David Wilkie. *Steam Along the Boundary: Canadian Pacific, Great Northern and the Great Boundary Copper Boom.* Winlaw: Sono Nis Press, 2007.
Veazey, Phyllis. "John Hendry and the Vancouver, Westminster and Yukon Railway." *BC Studies,* No. 59, Autumn 1983, pp. 44–63.
Wedley, John R. "A Development Tool: W.A.C. Bennett and the PGE Railway." *BC Studies,* No. 117, Spring 1998, pp. 29–50.
Wilson, Ralph, and Don Thomas. *The Line: Calgary, Alberta to Vancouver, British Columbia.* Calgary: Canadian Pacific Railway Communications and Public Affairs, 1998.

Index

Page numbers in **bold** indicate illustrations.

Abernethy-Lougheed Logging Company, **128**
Alaska Railroad, 150
Alberni Pacific (Heritage) Railway, 9, **125**, **131**, **179**, **184**, **189**, 213
Alberta Railway Museum, **138**
Alta Lake, **108**
Amtrak, 8, **166–68**, **175**, **239**
Anderson, Alexander Caulfield, 12
Annacis Island, **178**
A.P. Allison Logging, **218**
Aquatrain, **150**
Arbutus Greenway, **218**
armoured train, **121**
Ashcroft, **145**
Atlantic Express, **28**
Atlin Short Line & Navigation Company, 71
Atlin Southern Railway, **68**
Automatic Block Signalling (ABS), **164**
Awdry, Rev. W., **204**
baggage cars, 74, **202**, **204**; No. 722 (PGE), **33**
barges, 33, 81, 115, 139; Aquatrain, **150**
Barrett, Dave, 138, 187
Basque, **93**
BC Forestry Discovery Centre, **5**, **123**, 190, **191**
BC Hydro Railway (BCH), 8, 74, 156, **178**
BC Mountaineering Club, **109**
BC Rail, 8, 139, 143, 163; system map, **145**. *See also* British Columbia Railway (BCR)
Beamish Museum (UK), 184
Beardmore, William & Co., **146**
Bellingham Bay & British Columbia Railway, 37
Bennett, Nelson, 46
Bennett, W.A.C., 136–39
Bennett, William R. (Bill), 138
Best Friend of Charleston, 212
Big Hill, 20, **24–26**, 42
Bloedel, Stewart & Welch Railway (BS&W), **50**
boat railway, **218**
Bombardier, 174, **197**
Borden, Robert, 93
bridges: Ahbau Creek (PGE), **135**; Bridge 10 near Altamont (PGE), **107**; Canada Line, Vancouver, **177**; Canyon Creek, **101**; Connaught (Cambie), **76**; Cottonwood River (PGE), 108, **135**; False Creek (bascule), **93**; Fraser River at Hope, **97**, **100**; Fraser River at Prince George, **82–83**, **84**, **109**; Georgia Viaduct, **178**; John Fox Viaduct, 163; Kokish River (Englewood Railway), **131**; Lions Gate Bridge, **136**; Marpole (BCER), **218**; New Westminster Bridge, **51**, **52**, 74, **92**, **117**, **159**; North Shore Subdivision (PGE), **105**; Peace River near Taylor, **137**; Pender Street, **55**; Quebec, **85**; Second Narrows Bridge, **53**, **115**, 156, **163**; Similkameen River (VV&E), **99**; Skidegate Lake, Moresby Island, **218**; SkyBridge, Vancouver, **176**; Spences Bridge across Nicola River, 94, **96**, **99**; steel, **70**; Stikine River (PGE), **138**; Stoney Creek, **27**; Sumas River, **56**; Thompson River in Kamloops, **181**; Trout Creek Canyon (KVR; KVSR), **98**, **184**, **185**; Tulameen River (Bridge of Dreams) (KVR), **99**
Britannia Beach Mining Museum, **209**
British Columbia 150, **213**
British Columbia Central Railway, 102
British Columbia Electric Railway (BCER), **7**, 8, 37, 52, **55–56**, 72, **73–76**, **192**
British Columbia Harbours Board Railway, 156
British Columbia Mills and Trading Company, 123
British Columbia Railway (BCR), 8, 51, **139–40**. *See also* BC Rail
British Columbia Southern Railway, 62, 64, **65**
British Electric Traction Company, 72

British Great Eastern Railway, 102
Burlington Northern & Santa Fe Railway (BNSF), 8, **145**, 156, **157**, **160**
Burlington Northern Railway, 8, 156, 166
Burlington Railroad, 146
Burnaby Central Railway, 9
Burnaby Village Museum, **17**, **124**, **193**, 216, **217**
business cars, **172**, **202**, 210
cab car (driving trailer), 4, **166**, **168**, **175**, 239
cabooses, **139**, **150**, **200**, **202**, 213, **214**
Campbell, Charles McKinnon, 66–67
Canada Line, **177**
"Canada 150" train, **172**, 212, **213**
The Canadian, 8, **147**, 166, **169**
Canadian Forest Products (Canfor), 130
Canadian Museum of Rail Travel, **209**
Canadian National Railways/Canadien National (CNR/CN): acquires GTPR, **88**; armoured trains, **121**; barge service, **150**; brief history, 8; container trains, 156; *Continental Limited*, **116**; daily transcontinental trains in 1958, **149**; diesels used by PGE and BCR, **140**; Fraser Canyon, **7**; grade reduction projects, 163; Hotel Vancouver, **115**; interchanges shared with CP, **159**; land grant at False Creek, **93**; main line, **145**; oil-electric diesels, 146; partnership with BCR, **138**; routes in 1912, 1931, **154**; routes in 1960, **148**; silk trains, 113; "Super Dome" cars, **166**, **169**; "The Triangle Tour," 118; transcontinental passenger train, **147**, **151**, 166; Vancouver station, **111**. *See also* Via Rail
Canadian Northeastern Railway, 93
Canadian Northern Pacific Railway (CNPR), 8, 54, **55**, 90, **92**; last spike, **93**
Canadian Northern Railway (CNoR), 8, **17**, 54, **57**, 85, **88–89**, 91, **101**; Vancouver station, 93
Canadian Pacific Railway (CPR): acquires NAR, **138**; automobile "special train," **35**; barge service, **150**; brief history, 8; competition with GNR, 7; container trains, 156; daily transcontinental trains in 1958, **149**; Dunsmuir Tunnel, **114**; financing for construction, 15–16; first scheduled passenger train, **29**, **31**; first to reach Vancouver, **30**; Fraser Canyon construction, 90; Fraser Valley branches, **36**; freight trains, **44–45**; Hudson locomotives, 116; interchanges shared with CN, **159**; land grants and monopoly, 46, 52, 59, 62, **64–65**, 72, 96; Last Spike monument, **34**, 210; main line in Vancouver, **115**; map 1905, **53**; map 1911, **55**; map 1960, 146; map of main line into Vancouver, **31**; poster-timetable, **29**; promotion, **86**; Rogers Pass Project, 163; route in 1882, **21**; routes in 1960, **148**; route to the coast, 94; royal train 1901, **33**; Selkirk locomotives, **112**; silk trains, 113; transcontinental, 58; transcontinental passenger train, **147**, 166; work train, **43**; Yahk tie operation, **126**, 128
Canadian Western Central Railway, 89
Canadian Yukon Railway Company, 89
Cascade, **151**
Cascades, 9, **166**, **168**
Centerm, 156
Centralized Traffic Control (CTC), **164**
Charger, Siemens, **239**
Chemainus, 210
Chicago, Milwaukee, St. Paul & Pacific Railroad (the Milwaukee Road), **137**, 166
Chilliwack Heritage Park, **133**
Chinese labourers, 29, 40
CIT Group, **159**
Clanwilliam Lake, **119**
Clement, Lewis, 40
Clifford J. Rogers, 152
CN Roundhouse and Convention Centre, **202**
Colebrook, **157**
Columbia & Kootenay Railway, 58, **59**, 62, **65**
Columbia & Western Railway, 62, **63–65**, 94
Colvalli, **66**
commuter trains, **174–75**
Comox Logging & Railway Company, **103**, 128, **129**, 130
Connaught (Cambie) Bridge, **76**
Connaught, Duke of, **74**
Connaught Tunnel, **43**, 115, 163

234   IRON ROAD WEST

container trains, **152**, 153, 156, **157**
Continental Limited (CNR), 116
Corbin, Daniel C., 58, **59**, 62
Cottonwood Railway, 9
Cottonwood River bridge (PGE), 108, 135
Courtenay, 154
Cowichan Valley Railway, 9, 184, 190
Craigellachie, 20, **22**, **34**, 210
Cranbrook, 209
Crocker, Charles, 40
Crow Rate (Crow's Nest Pass Agreement), 64, 114, 153, 163
Crow's Nest & Kootenay Lake Railway, 64, **65**
Dayliner (E&N/CP), **152**
Defunct Railway Companies Dissolution Act, 86
Delta, 145
Deltaport, 155, **157**
derailments, 7, 27, 59, **66**, 138, 142
diamond crossings, 52, **76**, 96
diesel multiple units (DMUs), **139**, **170**, **204**
directional running agreements, **159**
Dominion, 111, 119, 147
Downtown Historical Railway, **194**, **196**
Dozer, Carl, 12–13
driving trailers (cab cars), 4, **144**, 166, 168, **175**, **178**, 239
dumpers, **160**, 162
Dunsmuir, James, **41**, 89
Dunsmuir, Robert, 13, 40–41
Dunsmuir Tunnel, 37, **114**
Eagle Pass, 19
Edmonton, Dunvegan & British Columbia Railway (ED&BC), **138**
Eholt, 67
Empire Builder, 147
Englewood Railway, 130, **131**

Esquimalt & Nanaimo Railway (E&N), 8, 13, 15, 40–41, **119**, 147 213;
   Dayliner, 154; routes in 1960, **148**
Euclataw, 13
Expo 86, 176, 184, **189**, **212**, 216
Expo Line, **176–78**
Fairhaven & Southern Railway, 46
False Creek, **53**, **55**, **93**, **114**, **118**
False Creek (bascule) Bridge, **93**
Farwell, Arthur, **172**
ferries, **16**, 19–20, 46, 50, 89, 92, **106**, 158
Field, **113**
Field Hill. *See* Big Hill
Finmoore, 83
Fleming, Sandford, 14–15, **22**, 78, **80**, 89–90
Fliegender Hamburger (Flying Hamburger), 111, 146
Foley, Welch & Stewart, 80, 90, 102
forest fires, 27, 30, 61, 125–28, **185**
Fort George, **83**, **85**–**87**
Fort George Railway, 9
Fort Langley, 153, **214**
Fort Salmon, **86**
Fort Steele Heritage Village, **212**
Fort Steele Railway, 9, 184, **188**
Frank H. Brown, 152
Fraser Canyon, 7
Fraser River rail bridge (Prince George), 82–83, **84**, **109**
Fraser Valley Heritage Railway (FVHR), **7**, **9**, **72**, **74**, **76**, **179**, **192**, **194**
FRED (flashing rear end device), 200
freight cars, 9, **31**, **38**, **77**, **121**, 139, **140**, 164, **171**, **178**, 202, 209
George VI, **111**, 115–16, 187
Gilman, L.C., 99
"Glenora Western Railway," 190
Glidden, Charles J., **35**

Above.
Vancouver Harbour Commissioners Terminal Railway No. 202 rests on the Vancouver waterfront in the early 1930s. The VHCTR was opened in 1926 and utilized the Second Narrows Bridge, opened for road traffic the year before, to connect the north and south sides of Vancouver Harbour. The railway became the National Harbours Board Railway in 1936 and was acquired by CNR in 1953.

Global Container Terminals Canada (GCT), 156
GM Electro-Motive Division (EMD), 143
Gore, T.S., **29**
grades, 20–21, 41, 43, **47**, **53–54**, **66**, **78**, 96, **97**, 98, **113**, **116–17**, 123, 130, **143**, 163, 199, 218. *See also* Big Hill; Grandview Cut
Grand Forks Railway, 9
"Grand Parade of Steam," 212
Grand Trunk Pacific Railway (GTPR), 8, **15**, **78–81**, **84–86**, 88, 90, 93, **101**, **102**, **109**, 166; first passenger train from Prince Rupert, **82**; last spike, **83**
Grand Trunk Pacific Steamship Company, **81**
Grand Trunk Railway (GTR), 78, 156
Grandview Cut, **53**, **55**, **116–18**, 166
The Great Canadian Railtour Company, 8, **173**
Great Northern Railway (GN), 7, **47**, **50**, **53**, **55**, 58, **64–65**, **94**, **96–97**, 99–100, **101**, **111**, 147, 156, **164**; freight trains, **118**, **151**; routes in 1960, **148**; Vancouver "Union" station, **93**
Great Trail, **97**. *See also* Trans Canada Trail
Green Point Logging, **128**
Hammond, George, **83**
Hart, John, 135
Hays, Charles Melville, 78, 85
Hedley, **96**
Hedley Mine, **209**
Heinze, F. Augustus, 62
Hendry, John, 46, 51–52, **55**, **102**
heritage railways. *See* Alberni Pacific (Heritage) Railway; Chilliwack Heritage Park; Fort Steele Railway; Fraser Valley Heritage Railway (FVHR); Kamloops Heritage Railway; Kettle Valley Steam (Heritage) Railway (KVSR); Nelson Electric Tramway Society; West Coast Railway Heritage Park
Hiawatha, 111, 166
Hill, James J., 7, 46, 50–51, **56**, 58, 94, 96, 99
Hill, Louis, 94, 99–100
Hillcrest Lumber, **129**
Hope, **101**
Hope Bridge (Fraser River), 97, 100
hopper cars, 140, **153**, 156
Howe Sound & Northern Railway (HS&N), 102
Howe Sound, Pemberton Valley & Northern Railway (HSPV&N), 102, **103**, **106**
Hudson, G.H.E., **38**
Huntington, Collis, 40
Illecillewaet Valley, **28**
inclines, 111, **128**, 130
Indian reserves, 80, **83**
industrial railways, **178**
The International Limited (GNR), **111**, 147
interurban electric railcars, **192–93**; No. 1207 (BCER; FVHR), **72**, **194**; No. 1220 (Steveston Interurban Tram), **196**; No. 1225 (FVHR), **75**, **195**, **240**; No. 1223 (BCER; Burnaby Village Museum), **193**, **217**; No. 1231 (Downtown Historical Railway; FVHR), **75**, **196**; No. 1304 (Connaught car) (BCER; FVHR), 7, **74**, **76**, **179**, **193**; No. 1402 (BCER), **75**; No. 1700 (BCER), **75**. *See also* streetcars
Iris G. (tugboat), **150**
John Bull, 212
John Fox Viaduct, 163
Johnson, Byron "Boss," 135
jitneys, **73**
Kaiser Coal Company, 153
Kamloops Heritage Railway, **1**, **6**, 9, **91**, **181**, **183**
Kaoham Shuttle, **13**, **170–71**
Kaslo & Slocan Railway, 7, 58, **60–62**
Kells, Henry, **47**
Kelowna Pacific Railway, 92
Keremeos, **96**
Kettle Falls International Railway, 8–9
Kettle River Valley Railway (KRVR), 96
Kettle Valley Railway (KVR), 9, 42, 62, **65**, **94**, **96–97**, **98–99**, 100, **101**
Kettle Valley Steam (Heritage) Railway (KVSR), **10–11**, **95**, **98**, **179**, **184–85**
Kilgard Brick Company, **56**
Kootenay & Elk Railway, 156

Kootenay Central Railway, **66**, 146, 156
Lambert, A.G., **123**
Langley, 89
Laurier, Wilfrid, 78
light rail lines, **197**
Lillooet, **140**, **171**
Liverpool & Canoe Pass Railway, 51
locomotives: 4-4-0 (GNR; logging), **126**; Alco diesel, **179**; assisting with braking, **33**; CEFX 1035 and 1029 (leased from CIT Group), **159**; 6400 class (CNR), 116; Climax logging, **5**, **125**, **127**, **190**; compressed-air, **133**, **209**; Consolidation 2-8-0, **28**; CREX No. 1208, **160**; diesel, 74; diesel (BNSF), **187**; diesel (CN), **145**; diesel (CPR), **150**, **152**; diesel (PGE), **134**; diesel General Electric (WP&YR), **199**; diesel SD 5500 SD40 (Revelstoke Railway Museum), **199**; diesel switch-type (BCH), **178**; *The Duchess* (WP&YR), **71**, **198**, **199**, **216**; electric (BCR), **134**; electric freight with octagonal cab (BCER), **76**; Engine No. 2 (E&N), **40–41**; Engine No. 10 (E&N), **41**; Engine No. 132, **28**; Engine No. 371, 29; Engine No. 374 (CPR; WCRA), **14**, **30–31**, **114**, **202**, **216**; ex-BCR, **145**; 1935 ex-Canadian Forest Products (Fort Steel Railway), **184**; 1923 ex-MacMillan Bloedel (Fort Steele Railway), **184**; first in Penticton, **97**; first in Prince Rupert (GTPR), **81**; General Electric ES44AC (CPR), **153**; Heisler logging, 125, **130**; Lima Shay, **126**, **129**, 184; logging, 123–130, 190–91, 210; mid-train slave, 156; mining, 66, **67**, 68, 71, **132–33**, **209**, 210; No. 1 (MacMillan Bloedel), **179**; No. 1 (V&S), later No. 5 (BS&W), **50**; No. 1 (WP&YR), **68**; No. 3 (PGE) (steam, yard engine), 104, **106–7**; No. 10 (E&NR), **133**; No. 103 (GTPR), **82**; No. 112 (GTPR), **78**; No. 202 (VHCTR), **235**; No. 212 (GN), **47**; No. 314 (2-8-0 Consolidation) (CPR), **26**; No. 465 (Amtrak), **168**; No. 479 (CPR), **119**; No. 614, **85**; No. 991 (CPR), **154**; No. 1047 (CNoR), **89**; No. 1077 2-6-2 (MacMillan Bloedel; Fort Steele Railway), **188**; No. 1085 (BNSF), **164**; No. 1140 (CPR), **87**; No. 1405 (Amtrak, Siemens Charger), **4**; No. 1426 (CNR class H-10 4-6-0, armoured), **121**; No. 1520 (CNR) (formerly No. 1223 CNoR), **88**, **207**; No. 1603 (M4a 2-8-0 pusher, CPR), **34**; No. 2405 (GTPR), **84**; No. 2423 (CNR N class), **117**; No. 2701 (CPR 4-6-2 G4 Pacific), **119**; No. 2753 (CNR N class), **118**; No. 3029 (CP diesel), **164**; No. 3460 (CPR), **77**; No. 3716 2-8-0 (formerly 3916) (construction CPR; KVSR), **10–11**, **95**, **184–85**; No. 4090 (CPR), **209**; No. 4104 (CPR diesel), **215**; No. 4105 (CPR diesel), **149**; No. 5083 (CNR J class Pacific), **113**; No. 5117 (CNR J class 4-6-2 Pacific), **116**; No. 5326 (CN), **157**; No. 5434 (CN), **143**; No. 5466 (CPR 2-8-2 Mikado), **120**; No. 5751 (BNSF), **160**; No. 5809 (Santa Fe 2-10-2 CP), **113**; No. 5902 (Selkirk CPR), **112**; No. 5903 (CPR 2-10-4 Selkirk T1a), **112**; No. 5920 (CPR Selkirk T1b class 2-10-4), **120**; No. 6044 (CNR U class Mountain type 4-8-2), **120**; No. 7009 (CPR diesel), **215**; No. 7340 (CPR), **38**; No. 7539 (CNR steam), **134**; No. 9000 (CNR diesel electric, armoured), **121**; No. 9046 (CNR diesel), **140**; No. 7 1929 Baldwin (Alberni Pacific Railway), 184, **189**; No. 9 Climax logging, **123**; No. 9 Climax logging (Hillcrest Lumber; Cowichan Valley Railway), **191**; No. 10 Climax logging (Hillcrest Lumber), **129**; No. 99 Climax logging (Abernethy-Lougheed Logging), **128**; No. 9 *Columbia* (construction, CPR), **19**; No. 73 2-8-0 Consolidation (NAR, ex-ED&BC 73), **138**; No. 2141 2-8-0 Consolidation class (CNoR; CNR; Kamloops Heritage Railway), **1**, **6**, **91**, **181**, **183–84**; No. 9 diesel (Cowichan Valley Railway), **191**; No. 248 diesel (Louisiana Pacific Lumber; Prince George Railway and Forestry Museum), **206**; No. 4069 1952 diesel (CPR), **204**; No. 6505 diesel (CN), **147**; No. 5350 diesel-electric, GE C44-9W (BNSF), **146**; No. 5017 diesel-electric EMD SD30C-ECO (CP), **158**; No. 11 diesel switcher (MacMillan Bloedel; Alberni Pacific Railway), 184, **189**; No. 5601 diesel switcher (Parrish & Heimbecker), **179**, **193**; No. 6503 diesel switcher (CPR), **204**; No. 6001 electric (BC Rail), **134**, **144**, **207**; No. 2 *Emory* or Old Curly (CPR construction; logging; Burnaby Village Museum), **17**, **19**, **123**, **124**, **216**, **217**; No. 9169 (formerly No. 1737) F7 A class diesel (CNR; Prince George Railway and Forestry Museum), **206–7**; No. 1401 FP9A diesel (CPR), 212, **213**; No. 6520 1957 FP9A diesel (CNR), **204**; No. 6007 GF6C electric (BCR), **143**;

236   IRON ROAD WEST

No. 2816 4-5-4 H1b Hudson *Empress* (CPR), **212**–13; No. 7 *Kamloops* (construction, CPR), **18**; No. 1 1911 Lima Shay (Bloedel, Stewart & Welch; Cowichan Valley Railway), **191**; No. 2 Lima Shay (Alberni Pacific Railway, logging), **125**; No. 3 1924 Lima Shay (Mayo Lumber; Cowichan Valley Railway), **191**; No. 5468 Mikado P-2k class 2-8-2 oil-burner (CPR; Revelstoke Railway Museum), **120**, 199, **201**; No. 15820 oil-electric (CN), **146**; No. 2860 4-6-4 Royal Hudson (CPR), **111**, 116, **117**, 184, **187**, **202**, 212; No. 4 *Savona* (construction, CPR), **20**; No. 5903 2-10-4 Selkirk T1a (CPR), **3**; No. 2 steam, 0-6-2 "Prairie"-type saddle tank (PGE; WCRA), **103**, 104, **105**–6, 204; No. 2 steam, saddle tank (PGE; WCRA), **202**; No. 25 1910 steam (CNPR; Cowichan Valley Railway), **190**; No. 52 steam (WP&YR), **68**, **199**; No. 69 steam (WP&YR), **198**; No. 73 steam (WP&YR), **199**; No. 111 steam (Canadian Forest Products), **130**; No. 1044 steam logging 2-6-2 "Prairie"-type tank (MacMillan Bloedel), **210**; No. 551 switcher (PGE), **147**; No. 1066 2-8-2T (MacMillan Bloedel), **210**; No. 2 "Two Spot" 1912 Lima Shay (Alberni Pacific Railway), **189**, 212; No. 6947 2-8-0 V4A class yard heavyweight switcher (CPR), **209**; Nos. 902, 903, 904 and 906 EMD F59PHI (WCE), **174**–75; Nos. 151 and 152 (Rail Link), **179**; Nos. 5504 and 5550, **45**; Nos. 6401 and 6410 (Via Rail), **169**; Nos. 8012 and 8019 (Rocky Mountaineer), **173**; Nos. 805 and 805A hybrid diesel (Neptune Terminals), **178**; Nos. 199 and 202 class 33, later B-20, 4-4-0, (New Westminster Southern), **46**; Nos. 9000 and 9001 diesel road (CN), **146**; Nos. 302 and 304 EMD SW 1200 diesel (Englewood Railway), **131**; NREX 2906, **173**; 1940s gas *Green Hornet* (Cowichan Valley Railway), **191**; Shay, **67**; steam, **75**; switcher (BCR), **140**; switcher (CPR), **4**; tank *Dunrobin* (Expo 86; Beamish Museum, UK), 184, **188**, **212**; unidentified 4-4-0, **32**; Wellington No. 19 *Victoria* (Dunsmuir, Diggle & Co.), **12**, 216, **218**; *Yale* (first construction, CPR), **17**

"Locotrol," 147

logging railways, 122–31

loops, 21, 42, **45**, 97, 98–99, **148**, 163, 190

Macdonald, John A., **15**, 40

Mackenzie, Alexander, 15

Mackenzie, William, 88–93

Mallard, 111

Mann, Donald, 88–93

Matsqui interchange, **159**

McBride, Richard, **75**, **86**, 89–90, 93, 97, 102

McCulloch, Andrew, 42, 96, **97**, 99–100

Merritt, **101**

Midway, **214**

milk trains, 77

Millennium Line, **166**, **176**–77

mining railways, 132–33

Moberly, Walter, 14

Moore, W.J., **128**

Mount Garibaldi, **204**

Mount Mackenzie, **120**

Mount Macdonald Tunnel, **162**, 163

Mount Robson, **120**

museums. *See* Alberta Railway Museum; BC Forestry Discovery Centre; Beamish Museum (UK); Britannia Beach Mining Museum; Burnaby Village Museum; Canadian Museum of Rail Travel; Port Moody station; Prince George Railway and Forestry Museum; Qualicum Beach station; Revelstoke Railway Museum; *Sicamous* (sternwheel steamer); Transit Museum Society (Brussels); Vancouver Railway Museum Association; West Coast Railway Heritage Park; White Rock

Nakusp & Slocan Railway, **61**–62

Nanaimo, **119**

Nanaimo, **13**

narrow-gauge railways, 8, 13, 59, 125, 190, 198, **199**, 210

National Electric Tramway & Lighting Company, 72

National Harbours Board Railway, 156, **235**

National Railway Equipment, **173**

National Transcontinental Railway, 78, 85

National Transportation Acts (1967, 1987), 153

Nelson & Fort Sheppard Railway, 9, 58, **59**, 62

Nelson Electric Tramway Company, 72, **192**

Nelson Electric Tramway Society, 9

Above.
A southbound train in the Thompson Canyon near Goldpan Provincial Park. This was originally the Canadian Northern rail line and shows the immense engineering difficulties that railway faced having to build on the west side of the river. The CP (northbound) line is in the foreground.

Above.
Pacific Great Eastern No. 2 on display at the West Coast Railway Heritage Park in Squamish.

Nelson station, 215
Neptune Terminals, 163, **178**
Newport, **106**
New Westminster, **36**
New Westminster Bridge, **51, 52,** 74, **92,** 117, 159
New Westminster Southern Railway (NWS), **46–49,** 51, 90, 94, 123, **124**
Nicola, Kamloops & Similkameen Coal & Railway Company, 94
Nicola Valley Coal & Coke Company, **132**
Nimpkish Timber Company, 131
North American Railways (NAR), 8
Northern Alberta Railway (NAR), 137, **138**
Northern Pacific Railway, 37
North Vancouver, **136**
Oliver, John, 101–2
"Olympic Line," **197**
Onderdonk, Andrew, 16–17, **18,** 19–21, 90, **124, 216, 217**
Othello Tunnels (Quintette Tunnels), 99–**100**
Pacesetter, 156
Pacific, **84**
Pacific Central Station, 92
Pacific Great Eastern Railway (PGE), 8, **13, 85, 102–9, 134–37, 138–40,** 147, 170; first official train into Prince George, **134–36**; last spike ceremony, 136; routes in 1960, **148**
Pacific International, 166
Pacific Northern Railway, 137
The Panorama, 166
Parrish & Heimbecker, **179**
passenger trains: BCR schedule 1974, **139**; BCR service ended 2002, **144**; CN transcontinental 1971, **151**; CPR 1886, **29**; CPR 1940, **119, 147**; first to arrive in Vancouver 1887, **31**; GNR 1909, **94, 96**; GNR 1916, 100; inaugural GTP train 1911, **82**; in museums, 202, 209, 212–13; power for steep grades, 111, **113**; Red Mountain Railway, **63**–64; speed on Big Hill, 24; tourist, **172**; transcontinental, 166, **187**; Via Rail, 8
Payne's Bluff (K&S), **60**
Peace Arch, **187**
Peace River bridge (near Taylor), **137**
Penny, **206**
Penticton, **97,** 99
Phoenix (mine), **66–67**
Pioneer, 12–**13**
Pioneer tracklaying machine, **79**

Port Alberni, 86
Port Coquitlam, 36
Port Guichon, **50–51**
Portland Canal Short Line Railway, 93
Port Mann, **90, 92,** 118
Port Moody station, 213
P.P. & J. Railway (Push, Pull & Jerk), **123**
Prairie Valley, **185**
Prince George, **83, 84, 109, 136, 140**
Prince George Railway and Forestry Museum, **88, 139, 144, 206–8**
Prince Rupert, **79,** 80, **81,** 169
Princeton, **97, 98, 101**
push-pull trains, **166, 168, 175**
Qualicum Beach station, **210,** 213, **214**
Quiney, James, 73
Quintette Tunnels (Othello Tunnels), 99–**100**
railcars: Budd, **137**; Budd diesel (RDC), **170,** 202; Budd diesel (RDCs, DMUs), **139, 154**; Budd RDC-3 car BC33, **139–41, 204**; Budd RDC two-car, **142**; No. 101 (PGE) (gas-electric), 104; No. 102 (PGE) (gas-electric), 104, **136**; No. 103 (PGE) (gas-electric), **104–5**
Rail Link, **178**
rail trails, **218**
Railway Association of Canada, **158**
Rainbow Lodge, **108**
Red Mountain Railway, 62, **63–64**
Redpass Junction, **120**
Repp, Tim, **143**
Revelstoke, **120, 172**
Revelstoke Railway Museum, **32, 120,** 199, **200–201**
Roberts Bank line, **157–59,** 163, **164**
Roberts Bank Superport, **152,** 156, **160**
Roberts Bank Terminal 2 Project, 156
Robin, Martin, 138
Rocket, 212
Rocky Mountaineer, **6,** 8, **172–73**
Rogers, Jeremiah, 123
Rogers, Major Albert Bowman, 20, **21–22**
Rogers Pass, **22, 28**
Rogers Pass Project, 163
Ross, James, 20–21
roundhouses, 31, **55, 84, 114, 154, 187, 202, 208, 216**

Royal Canadian Pacific, 8, **213**
Royal City Planing Mills, **126**
Royal Hudson, **111, 117,** 184, **187, 202,** 210, 212
St. Paul, Minnesota & Manitoba Railway, 46
St. Paul & Pacific Railway, 46
Sandon, 5?, 61, **62,** 209
Schwitzer, John E., 42, **43**
SeaBus, 1?6, 176
Seattle, Lake Shore & Eastern Railway, 37
Second Narrows Bridge, **53, 115,** 156, **163**
Semiahmoo Peninsula line, **164**
Seton Lake, 170
Shaughnessy, Thomas, 96, 100
Shaughnessy Tunnel, 163
Shawnigan Lake, **154**
Shuswap & Okanagan Railway, 38–39
Sicamous (sternwheel steamer), **39**
Siemens Charger, **239**
Similkameen River Bridge (VV&E), 99
SkyBridge Vancouver, **176**
SkyTrain, ?, ?3, 74, **114, 166, 176–78, 194, 197**
sleeper cars, **204**
Slocan Lake, **150**
Smith, Donald, 22
Smithe, William, 30
Smithers, Alfred, 85
snowplows, **32, 68,** 100, **207**
snowsheds **27–28,** 100
Southern Pacific Railroad, 153
Southern Railway of British Columbia (SRY), 8, 74, **178, 192, 218**
Southern Railway of Vancouver Island (SVI), 8
speeders, **81, 140, 194,** 202, **206**
Spiral Tunnels, **42–45,** 96–97
Spokane Falls & Northern Railway, **59,** 62
spreaders, 206
Squamish, **103, 106, 109, 140, 145**
standard-gauge railways, **6,** 62, 68, 112, 125
Stanford, Leland, 40
steamboats, 71, **109**; *Aberdeen*, 38; *Clifford Sifton*, **70**; *Gleaner*, **70**; *Okanagan*, **39**; *Sicamous*, **39**; SS *Prince George*, **81**; *Victoria* (ferry), **50**
steam railways, 110–21, 123, **179,** 181, 184, 187
Stephen, George, 16, **22**
Steveston Interurban Tram Building, **196**
Stikine River Bridge (PGE), 138
Stoney Creek Bridge, **27**
streetcars, 72–73, **106**; Bombardier "Flexity," **197**; destroyed in 1950, **77**; No. 23 (Nelson), **195**; No. 53 (BCER; Old Spaghetti Factory), **72, 195**; No. 400 (Nelson), **196**. *See also* interurban electric railcars
Sullivan, John G., 108
Sullivan Mine, **133**
Summerland, **98, 179**
Super Continental, **147,** 166
switchbacks, 62, **63, 70,** 128, **132**
Table Tunnel, 142
Taku Tram 7?, 198
Talgo trainsets, **166, 168**
Tate, D'Arcy, 102
terminals, 47, **50,** 51, 53, **57,** 104, **115,** 156, **157, 160, 162,** 235
Terrace, 121
Theodosia, Powell Lake & Eastern Railway, **129**
Thomas the Tank Engine™, **204**
Thompson Canyon, **151, 153,** 173
Thornton, Henry, 162
Thornton Tunnel, 156, 162, **163**
Three Valley Gap Heritage Ghost Town, **208**
Toronto Terminals Railway (TTR), 156
track inspection vehicles, **194, 207**
Trail Creek Tramway, 62, **63**
Trakmobile, **194**
tramways, ?, 62, **63, 71,** 72, **132, 192, 196,** 198
Trans-Canada Airlines, 166

Trans-Canada Highway, 166
Trans-Canada Limited, 210
Trans-Canada Railway, 78
Trans Canada Trail, **154**. *See also* Great Trail
Transit Museum Society (Brussels), **196**
TransLink, **174**
trestles: Canyon Creek, **101**; Canyon of the Cheakamus River, **109**; at E&N mile 6, **41**; False Creek, 52; Goldstream, **40**; Kinsol Trestle, **154**; Lake Mountain Road, **56**; Little Sheep Crossing, **63**; Marpole (BCER), **218**; Milne's Landing near Sooke, **154**; Mountain Creek, **23**; Mud Bay, **168**; near Fruitvale, **59**; Peace River near Taylor, **137**; Sumas Lake, **57**; Trout Creek Canyon (KVR; KVSR), **185**
Trudeau, Pierre, 153
Trudeau Salute, 208
Trueman, R.H., **61**
Tulameen River Bridge (Bridge of Dreams) (KVR), **99**
Tumbler Ridge line (BCR), **142–44**
tunnels: Connaught Tunnel, **43,** 115, 163; Dunsmuir Tunnel, **37, 114,** 114;

Below.
In steam locomotive days it was common for trains to start lineside fires. The second eastbound CPR train from Port Moody in 1886 was partly consumed by a forest fire (see page 30). These days, lineside fires are much less common, but they do happen. Here, in July 2018, just north of Spences Bridge, a southbound coal train passes the site of a fire started by a train two days earlier. The red colour is fire retardant.

Hope Mountains, 96, 99; Mount MacDonald, **162**; Mount Royal in Montreal, 92; near Horseshoe Bay, 142; north of Greenwood on Boundary Subdivision, **149**; Othello Tunnels (Quintette Tunnels), 99–100; Shaughnessy Tunnel, 163; Spiral Tunnels, **42–45**, 96–97; Table Tunnel, 142; Thornton Tunnel, 156, 162, **163**; Wolverine Tunnel, 142
turntables, **114, 208, 216**
underwater locomotives, 210
Union Pacific Railway, **79**, 146
unit trains, 66, **153**, 156, **157, 162**, 163
Utah & Northern Railway, **68**
Vancouver: 1886 map, **31**; skyline, **166**; SkyTrain, **176**; streetcars, **72**; Waterfront station, **174–75**
Prince George bridge, across Fraser River, 82–83, **84, 109**
Vancouver & Lulu Island Railway, 36
Vancouver, Fraser Valley & Southern Railway, 74
Vancouver, Victoria & Eastern Railway (VV&E), **37**, 47, 53–54, **55–57**, 65, 91, 94, **96**, 98–99, **101**
Vancouver, Westminster & Yukon Railway (VW&Y), **51**, 52, **53**, 102
Vancouver Electric Railway & Light Company, 72
Vancouver Harbour Commissioners Terminal Railway (VHCTR), 104, **115, 235**
Vancouver Island, **154–55**
Vancouver Railway Museum Association, 187
Vancouver Terminal Railway & Ferry Company, **50**, 51
Van Horne, William Cornelius, 20–21, **22**, 29–30, 58
Vanterm, 156
Vernon, Forbes, 38
VHC Terminal Railway, 156
Via Rail, 8, 166, **169**

Victoria & Sidney Railway (V&S), **50–51**
Victoria: first train into station, **41**; roundhouse, **154, 214**; skyline, **154**; streetcars, **72, 214**
Victoria Terminal Railway, **47**, 53, **57, 157**
Waddington, Alfred, 14
Walkem, Anthony, 15
Warren, James, 99
Wellburn, Gerry, 190
Wellington Colliery Railway, 13
Wenner-Gren, Axel, 137
West Coast Express (WCE), 8, **170, 174–75**
West Coast Railway Association (WCRA), 9, 187, 202
West Coast Railway Heritage Park, **103**, 202, **203–5, 238**
Western Forest Products, 130
Western Grain Transportation Act (1983), 153, 163
Westminster & Vancouver Tramway Company, 72
Westshore Terminals, **160, 162**
Whistler, **108**
White, Elwood, **130**
White Pass & Yukon Railway (WP&YR), 8, **68, 70**, 71, 152, **198–99**
White Rock, 54, 117, 146, 164, 166, 168, 187; museum, **214**; station, 213, **214**
Whytecliff, 104
Wilkie, Dave, **140, 149, 154**
Winter Olympics (2010), **177, 197**
Wolverine Tunnel, 142
wye, **108**
Yahk, **126**
Yaletown Roundhouse, **216**

Above.
The train doesn't stop here anymore... Commemorating the once frequent passenger service at White Rock's waterfront station, this bronze statue, called "The Passenger," was placed in 2015 and now waits patiently for the next train that never comes. Only freights pass him by, but perhaps one day soon the passenger train will again stop at White Rock.